THE
NUCLEAR
<u>READER</u>

STRATEGY, WEAPONS, WAR

Second Edition

THE
NUCLEAR
READER

STRATEGY, WEAPONS, WAR

Second Edition

Edited by

Charles W. Kegley, Jr.
University of South Carolina

Eugene R. Wittkopf
Louisiana State University

St. Martin's Press
New York

Editor: Larry Swanson
Project Editors: Peter Jonathan Marcus, Bruce S. Glassman
Production Supervisor: Stacey Donohue
Graphics: G & H Soho
Cover Design: Ben Santora
Cover Art: Ben Santora

For information, write:
St. Martin's Press, Inc.
175 Fifth Avenue
New York, NY 10010

ISBN: 0-312-00498-2

ACKNOWLEDGMENTS

Part I: Strategy

"Nuclear Temptations: Doctrinal Issues in the Strategic Debate," by Theodore Draper. Abridged from Theodore Draper, "Nuclear Temptations," *The New York Review of Books*, Vol. 30, Nos. 21 and 22 (January 19, 1984), pp. 42–48. Reprinted with permission of the author from *The New York Review of Books*. Copyright © 1984 Nyrev, Inc.

"Nuclear Strategy: What It Is and Is Not," by William C. Martel and Paul L. Savage. From William C. Martel and Paul L. Savage, *Strategic Nuclear War: What the Superpowers Target and Why* (Contributions in Military Studies, No. 43, Greenwood Press, Westport, CT, 1986), pp. 172–86. Copyright © 1986 by William C. Martel and Paul L. Savage. Reprinted with permission of the authors and publisher.

"MAD versus NUTS: Can Doctrine or Weaponry Remedy the Mutual Hostage Relationship of the Superpowers?" by Spurgeon M. Keeny, Jr. and Wolfgang K. H. Panofsky. Reprinted by permission of *Foreign Affairs*, Winter 1981/82. Copyright 1981 by the Council on Foreign Relations, Inc.

"Nuclear Strategy and the Challenge of Peace: The Moral Evaluation of Deterrence in Light of Policy Developments, 1983–1988," by the National Conference of Catholic Bishops. Abridged from *A Report on "The Challenge of Peace" and Policy Developments 1983–1988* from the NCCB ad hoc Committee on the Moral Evaluation of Deterrence Policy © 1988 United States Catholic Conference, Washington, DC.

"Global Security Without Nuclear Deterrence: The Necessity for Alternatives," by Robert Johansen. From *Alternatives* 12 (October 1987), published by Butterworths, Guildford, UK. Reprinted by permission of the author and publisher.

Acknowledgments and copyrights are continued at the back of the book on pages 357–358, which constitute an extension of the copyright page.

PREFACE

Public opinion polls and the agendas of political parties and interest groups in the United States and elsewhere in the Western world have shown repeatedly that issues relating to nuclear weapons and war are a dominant public concern. That concern is rooted in a seemingly intractable predicament: on the one hand, nuclear weapons threaten the destruction of human civilization as we know it; on the other, they are the very instruments relied on to avert the threatened disaster. Under such conditions, a number of issues have understandably captivated public attention and become the focal point of policy debates throughout the world. These include (1) the maintenance of stable deterrence on which world peace seems to rest so precariously, (2) the utility of nuclear weapons as instruments of foreign policy, (3) the means of limiting their quantity and quality and perhaps abolishing them altogether, and (4) the horrors that might befall humanity should nuclear deterrence fail.

The second edition of *The Nuclear Reader: Strategy, Weapons, War* is designed to expose the range of opinion and prescription regarding these urgent matters. The perspective is primarily that of the United States, and the focus is primarily the competition between the two nuclear giants, the United States and the Soviet Union. Nonetheless, within these confines, the range of opinion is wide and the viewpoints are compelling. Our purpose in compiling the essays in this book is to illuminate these opinions and viewpoints, while simultaneously drawing attention to the complexities of the issues inherent in the nuclear predicament and taking account of recent developments in strategic doctrine, weapons innovation, and arms control that are fated to influence the prospects for global stability in the twilight of the twentieth century and the dawn of the next. The urgency of keeping the nuclear genie in its bottle requires such knowledge and understanding.

Many people provided advice and assistance when we first developed this collection and as we revised it. In addition to those acknowledged in the first edition, we wish to thank Peter Auyeung, Virginia Anselman, Mary Joyce Burns, P. Edward Haley, Steve W. Hook, Bert E. Swanson, and Kurt D. Will for their contributions to this edition. We also wish to thank Larry Swanson of St. Martin's Press for his continued support of our work and Peter Jonathan Marcus and Bruce S. Glassman, project editors, who contributed to bringing the book to completion.

CHARLES W. KEGLEY, JR.
EUGENE R. WITTKOPF

For Suzanne
C.W.K.

For Barbara, Debra, and Jonathan
E.R.W.

CONTENTS

Part II   Weapons   *129*

Part III   War   *245*

STRATEGY, WEAPONS, AND WAR IN THE NUCLEAR AGE

Charles W. Kegley, Jr., and
Eugene R. Wittkopf

The invention of nuclear weapons and their continuing proliferation have imposed on humankind a series of momentous—some would say intractable—challenges and policy problems. It is not an exaggeration to assert that by building extensive nuclear arsenals, humankind has devised the potential to extinguish itself as a species.

The awareness of these threats has expanded dramatically in recent years, stimulated in no small part by the attention given to the "nuclear predicament" by scientists, policymakers, politicians, academics, and the mass media. More so than at any time since the aftermath of Hiroshima and the depths of the cold war, the prevention of nuclear war has returned to the top of the global agenda. Indeed, public concern about the causes and consequences of a nuclear war is likely to disappear only if deterrence fails, with a nuclear holocaust perhaps bringing human history to a tragic end. Herein lies the nuclear predicament, one defined by knowledge, hope, and fear: "Atomic fire has become an inescapable part of the human heritage. Wisely controlled, it will remain unused in war and can prevent the reoccurrence of large-scale conventional conflict. Unwisely attended, it will break forth at some unpredictable time and consume much of humanity."[1]

To facilitate an understanding of the issues that underlie this predicament, *The Nuclear Reader* seeks to elucidate the major positions advanced by informed debaters. It is organized around three generic concepts central to discussions of nuclear politics: namely, *strategy*, *weapons*, and *war*.

The first concept (Part I) looks at the various *strategies* that have been constructed either to fight or to prevent a nuclear war. The articles focus on major politico-military doctrines, such as deterrence, mutual assured destruction, and nuclear utilization, and on the major issues that separate debaters on doctrinal problems and strategic policies. These selections offer background information on the historical evolution of strategic theory on which the current global peace precariously rests, as well as proposals to minimize risks by means of nuclear superiority, the maintenance of mutual deterrence, or ballistic missile defense. The essays make clear that positions on these strategic issues are often incompatible with one another, and they were purposely chosen to highlight these theoretical controversies.

The second organizing concept, *weapons* (Part II), offers information and opinion regarding appropriate ways to control current nuclear arsenals or

1

those that might be contemplated so as to ensure that weapons serve their intended political purposes. As in Part I, the essays seek to expose the range of ideas and opinion about how best to harness the threat that nuclear weapons pose.

The third and final organizing concept, *war* (Part III), completes the coverage by confronting the possible causes and the consequences of nuclear war. The essays in this part consider how a nuclear war might begin, what it might be like, how it might be conducted, and what its consequences could be.

These three conceptual categories—strategy, weapons, and war—are overlapping and interconnected, perhaps synergistically. A new development or initiative in one area may generate changes in another. For instance, technological changes in weapons' precision have required subsequent changes in strategy. Conversely, new departures in doctrine often rationalize the creation of new weapons systems. Similarly, changes in war-fighting capabilities (may) have modified the probability of war and mobilized efforts to revise doctrine to curtail the probability of a nuclear strike. Thus, change in any one dimension of the nuclear situation may be expected to exert pressure for changes in the other two. This synergy is illustrated by the claim that nuclear weapons led to the concept of deterrence, which led to the nuclear arms race, which generated pressures for both arms control initiatives and new strategic doctrines. Having come full circle, the interactive process continues, feeding on itself as it moves from one dimension to the next.

Despite *The Nuclear Reader*'s three-part organizing scheme, it encourages its readers to decide for themselves how these dimensions of the nuclear problem affect one another. For it is an empirical question if and how developments in one sector influence developments in another. As Spurgeon M. Keeny, Jr., and Wolfgang K. H. Panofsky observe in our third selection in Part I, "It is not at all clear in the real world of war planning whether declaratory doctrine has generated requirements or whether the availability of weapons for targeting has created doctrine." The direction of causation among the three dimensions (and the influences acting on them) thus requires critical examination.

THE DISUTILITY OF FORCE AND STRUCTURAL TERRORISM

In order to understand current nuclear strategies, weapons, and war, it is necessary also to understand current international politics and to speculate about the impact of nuclear weapons on both national and international security.

In an international system that since its inception in the seventeenth century has given states the sovereign right to use military force to settle disputes, war has been recurrent; understandably, therefore, national preparation for war by acquiring arms has been a nearly universal preoccupation.[2] Indeed, an anarchical international political system provides little incentive for states to reduce their armaments. The strategy underlying most countries' national security policies could be summed up by the time-honored dictum, "If you want peace, prepare for war."

But with the destruction of Hiroshima in 1945, this pattern was altered, perhaps permanently and irrevocably. In 1981 Pope John Paul II noted: "In the past, it was possible to destroy a village, a town, a region, even a country. Now it is the whole planet that has come under threat."

In *The Absolute Weapon*, Bernard Brodie offered in 1946 a now classic definition of the changes caused by atomic weapons in strategy in world affairs.[3] Recognizing that with the creation of weapons of mass annihilation "mankind had brought upon itself a deadly peril," Brodie anticipated that it was only a matter of time before these weapons would be possessed by more than one country. And when that time came, he argued, the purposes of American strategy would have to be revised:

> The first and most vital step in any American security program for the age of atomic bombs [should be] to take measures to guarantee to ourselves in case of attack the possibility of retaliation in kind. [We no longer need be] concerned about who will *win* the next war in which atomic bombs are used. Thus far the chief purpose of our military establishment has been to win wars. From now on its chief purpose must be to avert them. It can have almost no other useful purpose.[4]

Since Brodie's prophecy and prescription, the destructiveness of the weapons of war has grown enormously. Carl Sagan, the Pulitzer Prize–winning astronomer, describes today's nuclear arsenals:

> There are some 50,000 nuclear weapons in the world, most of them far more powerful than the weapons which utterly devastated Hiroshima in 1945. In fact, the energy equivalent of all the nuclear weapons in the world is enough to annihilate one million cities. There are only 2,300 cities on the planet with populations of more than 100,000 people. Every major city on the planet could be destroyed and there would be 15,000 strategic weapons left over in the arsenals of the United States and the Soviet Union. A single U.S. nuclear submarine could destroy 160 Soviet cities, and of course vice versa. [These instruments of destruction are] genies of death awaiting the rubbing of the lamp.[5]

Under these conditions, in which expanding nuclear arsenals may have made the use of these weapons suicidal, Brodie's prognosis seems to have been borne out, and thus the "game" of international politics played by the most heavily armed has shifted from waging war to deterring it. Paralyzed by their own power, the superpowers, the United States and the Soviet Union, have for over four decades managed their relationships without recourse to war. War *has* been deterred (even if those without nuclear weapons have warred among themselves and with the great powers since World War II). A *pax atomica* has arisen, as Winston Churchill reasoned it might when he envisioned the emergence of an age of superpower peace based on mutual deterrence.[6]

The bases of this precarious but prolonged superpower peace, sustained now for nearly a half-century, are multiple.[7] The simple formulas that "the curse is the cure" and "the menace is the miracle" fail to take into account other contributing factors. But whatever the sources of nuclear peace, it is clear that the environment for the conduct of diplomacy—and the prospects for humankind's future—have been radically transformed by these weapons. A new system has been created. It was Churchill, again, who showed that he understood this when he introduced into the vocabulary the idea of peace resting on "a balance of terror."

Let us extend this metaphor. Can the nuclear age be appropriately characterized as one predicated on *terror*?

To be sure, the destructiveness of nuclear weapons makes for truly terrifying "nuclear nightmares."[8] No one can contemplate the peril in which the entire globe has been placed by the existence of these weapons and the potential for their use without experiencing a true sense of terror. As Churchill warned, "The Stone Age may return on the gleaming wings of science, and what might now shower immeasurable blessings upon mankind, may even bring about its total destruction. Beware, I say; time may be short."

Carl Sagan dramatized the terror of the nuclear age thus:

> Imagine a room awash in gasoline, and there are two implacable enemies in that room. One of them has 9,000 matches; the other has 7,000 matches. Each of them is concerned who's ahead, who's stronger. Well, that's the kind of situation we are actually in. The amount of weapons that are available to the United States and the Soviet Union are so bloated, so grossly in excess of what's needed to dissuade the other, that if it weren't so tragic, it would be laughable. What is necessary is to reduce the matches and to clean up the gasoline.[9]

Sagan's metaphor suggests that the nuclear age is terrorizing because it is a situation or set of circumstances from which there is no readily available escape. And because this situation includes the relationships among nations and peoples, their fears, and their weapons technologies—relationships that color the entire fabric of international politics—it might be described as *structural terrorism*.

Consider, for example, four simple propositions concerning terrorists and terrorism of the sort that the world has witnessed numerous times in recent years:

- Terrorists threaten indiscriminate violence.

- Governments are unable to guarantee their citizens protection from such violence.

- Because there is no protection from such violence, terrorism produces fear and anxiety with which individuals cope psychologically through repression and denial.

• Terrorists rely on their ability to inflict death and destruction to win compliance with their political objectives.

With but a few changes in words, each of these propositions could be used to describe nuclear weapons or the policies of those states that possess them. No one, it seems, including those countries and peoples that might not be directly involved, would be immune from the immediate or long-term ravages of nuclear war. Indeed, the very threat of death and destruction by one nuclear adversary against another has become a key element in the preventive strategy known as deterrence. But governments cannot provide a foolproof guarantee that deterrence will succeed—which is, in fact, one of the principal elements in the current debate about nuclear weapons that prompted this book. And although some believe we must learn to live with nuclear weapons, the anxiety of life with them seems to be reduced only by sublimation—which is why and how the psychological terror of the nuclear age appears to have dissipated in the years since its inception.

Finally, just as terrorists and those governments alleged by others to engage in "state terrorism" (that is, government-sponsored terrorism directed by one country against the citizens or institutions of another) rely on threats or acts of violence to achieve their goals, so, too, the nuclear states depend on the threatened use of force and mass destruction to achieve their policy objectives. If state terrorism is condemned, why not nuclear terrorism?

Both terrorism and nuclear weapons have become dominant factors in contemporary international politics. The power of each is derived from and contingent upon the continuation of a threat system rather than its elimination. Both demand the legitimation of violence, because both are sustained by the anxiety and fear they inspire. Both are targeted principally on the populations of the most advanced industrial societies, which are the primary hostages of their threat of death and destruction. And both erode the individual and global security for which the world searches.

If the nuclear predicament can be likened to the practice of international terrorism, what makes it distinctive, in the second instance, is that the terror of the nuclear age has also become part of the international system's *structure*.[10] The structure of a social system is conventionally defined as a basic, enduring, and institutionalized organization of things and their relationships. To state that the nuclear age is an age of structural terrorism, therefore, is also to assert that the nuclear threat is an attribute of the international system, affecting many aspects of behavior and patterns of life on earth.

The emergence of this structural attribute has put human existence at risk, and it can be said to dominate, even govern, world affairs. It rules by the force of its terror. Accordingly, structural terrorism has changed the world in many ways; it has given world politics properties that set the contemporary system apart from its historical predecessors.

In addition, structural terrorism has a special importance because, unlike other structures that can be modified to improve or diminish the quality of life, it may have become so entrenched that it cannot be eradicated. There is an irony in this, for, as Norman Cousins has noted, what man has made can unmake man.[11] The insecurities that nuclear weapons produce, the costly worldwide race for arms that these fears provoke, the habits that have been created from thinking about their uses, the industries and military establishments that lobby for their further expansion, and the momentum of history and push of technology all are potent forces within a self-perpetuating, synergistically reinforcing system that encourages its own preservation . . . or destruction.

To characterize current world politics as marked by structural terrorism is to assert that the prevailing levels of armaments pose to the world its most serious threat. It is also to aver that this threat cannot be contained. For structural terrorism deprives the human species of freedom from fear. No one is safe; all, from the most impoverished to the most wealthy, are its potential victims. The material costs to human welfare of preparations for a war that dare not be waged are immeasurable; structural terrorism also diminishes the world's standard of living and compromises its ability to enhance its collective welfare to the extent otherwise possible.

Structural terrorism is a systemic condition that arises from the choices of many states, whose policies and decisions have contributed to its development. But the paradox is that most states have not benefited from the collective structure their individual actions have inadvertently created. By preparing for war in order to preserve peace, states find themselves competing in an arms race that may culminate in the very disaster that each seeks to avoid. Nuclear arms may indeed have enhanced the national security of their possessors, but they may also have decreased global security by increasing the probability of national and human obliteration.

To assume that structural terrorism is the international system's most threatening feature is not to deny that the world also suffers from other less serious, but nonetheless extremely costly, structural deficiencies.[12] But because structural terrorism risks the extinction of all humankind, it terrorizes life on a scale heretofore neither experienced nor possible. In short, structural terrorism describes a circumstance unique in human history. What is also unique, therefore, is that for the first time in world history, the choice, borrowing a perceptive phrase from Martin Luther King, Jr., has become "either nonviolence or nonexistence."

It is important to recall that what Winston Churchill first described as a balance of terror is a product of human invention; humankind was not born with it—it had to be created. It may be an invention that, with hindsight, few would prefer. But it has been invented nonetheless, and with its invention have come powerful obstacles to its removal, as we have noted. As discomforting as may be its pessimistic viewpoint, the conclusion of the Harvard Nuclear Study Group is compelling: "Humanity has no alternative but to hold [the] threat [of infinitely destructive nuclear war] at bay and to learn to live . . . in the world we know: a world of nuclear weapons, international rivalries, recurring conflicts, and at least some risk of nuclear crisis. . . . Living with nuclear weapons is our only hope."[13]

Or is it? Some would quarrel with this conclusion, and, inspired by the need to free humanity from the fear accompanying nuclear weapons, seek ways of escaping the conditions described by "structural terror." As the selections in this anthology will disclose, a variety of proposals have been advocated for this purpose. Two, in particular, stand out: arms control and strategic missile defense. The first, symbolized by the signing in 1987 of the INF (intermediate-range nuclear forces) treaty, represents one potential path to a nuclear-free world, but one in which many obstacles remain. The second, the Strategic Defense Initiative (SDI), represents an ambitious technological approach to make nuclear weapons, in the words of Ronald Reagan, "impotent and obsolete." The barriers to this objective are also multiple. Ballistic missile defense (BMD), like other technological developments in the past, may lead to a world in which insecurity and the prospects of nuclear war are increased rather than reduced. Hence, we are confronted with a perplexing, unpleasant choice: learning to live with nuclear weapons, or learning to live with the unforeseen conditions that may arise from efforts to reduce their potency. Both scenarios are fraught with uncertainties, complications, and dangers.

Because a nuclear-free world is not probable in the foreseeable future, structural terrorism appears destined to continue both to describe and to influence world conditions. The purpose of *The Nuclear Reader* is thus to illuminate this reality. The selections that follow should help the reader understand the nuclear predicament and the choices it has created, including the choice of living with nuclear weapons or seeking their abolition.

NOTES

1. Albert Carnesale et al. (The Harvard Nuclear Study Group), *Living with Nuclear Weapons* (Toronto: Bantam, 1983), p. 5. Portions of this study are reprinted in Part III of this book.

2. For documentation and summaries of trends in both military capabilities and the incidence of war over time, see Charles W. Kegley, Jr., and Eugene R. Wittkopf, *World Politics: Trend and Transformation*, 3d ed. (New York: St. Martin's Press, 1989).

3. Bernard Brodie et al., eds., *The Absolute Weapon* (New York: Harcourt Brace, 1946). Brodie updated and elaborated this statement in *War and Politics* (New York: Macmillan, 1973), especially pp. 375–432.

4. Brodie et al., p. 76.

5. Commencement address, University of South Carolina, Columbia, S.C., May 12, 1984.

6. Churchill stated this thesis in 1953 when he confessed that he occasionally had "the odd thought that the annihilating character of [nuclear] weapons may bring an utterly unforeseeable security to mankind. . . . It may be that when the advance of destructive weapons enables everyone to kill anybody else no one will want to kill anyone at all." He elaborated on this in 1955, with the speculation that "after a certain point has passed, [things may get so bad that they get better, and] . . . it may be that we shall, by a process of sublime irony, have reached a stage in this story where safety will be the sturdy child of terror, and survival the twin brother of annihilation."

7. For an analysis, see John Lewis Gaddis, "The Long Peace: Elements of Stability in the Postwar International System," *International Security* 10 (1986): 99–142.

8. See Nigel Calder, *Nuclear Nightmares: An Investigation into Possible Wars* (New York: Penguin, 1979).

9. Quoted by Anne H. Ehrlich and Paul R. Ehrlich, Newsletter, Friends of the Earth, p. 1 (no date).

10. "Structural terrorism" and its sources and consequences are explored also in Charles W. Kegley, Jr., T. Vance Sturgeon, and Eugene R. Wittkopf, "Structural Terrorism: The Systemic Sources of State-Sponsored Terrorism," in Michael Stohl and George A. Lopez, eds., *Terrible Beyond Endurance: The Foreign Policy of State Terrorism* (Westport, Conn.: Greenwood Press, 1988), pp. 13–31.

11. Public address delivered at the University of South Carolina, March 15, 1979.

12. Structural terrorism is similar to the concept of *structural violence*, which refers to those of the earth's inhabitants "harmed, maimed, or killed by poverty and unjust social, political, and economic institutions, systems, or structures." Thus structural violence is said to inflict two kinds of injury: "it either kills its victims or it harms them in various ways short of killing." Gernot Köhler and Norman Alcock, "An Empirical Table of Structural Violence," *Journal of Peace Research* 13 (1976): 343. The concept of structural violence was first developed by Johan Galtung in his article "Violence, Peace, and Peace Research," *Journal of Peace Research* 6 (1969): 167–191. See also his *The True Worlds* (New York: Macmillan, 1980) for an elaboration. For estimates of the aggregate damage to life because of structural violence and armed conflict, see Köhler and Alcock, cited above, and William Eckhardt and Gernot Köhler, "Structural Violence and Armed Violence in the Twentieth Century: Magnitudes and Trends," *International Interactions* 6 (1980): 347–375.

13. Carnesale et al., pp. 19, 255. This conclusion is not without controversy. For an assessment that challenges it and proposes approaches to eliminating the threat of nuclear extinction, see Jonathan Schell, *The Abolition* (New York: Knopf, 1984), as well as some of the thinking presented in other segments of *The Nuclear Reader*.

Part I: Strategy

To "provide for the common defense." These challenging words of the United States Constitution identify a mission that this country—and for that matter all others—must define as a national priority. To seek to protect one's nation from external threats is the *sine qua non* of every nation's definition of the national interest in an anarchical international arena.

Since the advent of the nuclear age, the ability of the United States and other countries to provide for the common defense has been considerably compromised. President John F. Kennedy was not engaging in hyperbole when he noted that nuclear weapons "have changed all the answers and all the questions," for nuclear weapons have challenged the validity of traditional approaches and previous doctrines. Because of them, world politics takes place in a threat system whose very structure terrorizes its inhabitants and diminishes the ability of its leaders to provide the national security they seek.

Prior to the nuclear age, the primary strategic task of national leaders was simply to promote their country's interests abroad and security at home. A national strategy (whether grand or improvisational, calculated or incoherent) presumed the identification of foreign policy goals, a plan for realizing them, and guidelines for dealing with external challenges.[1] Following the German theoretician Karl von Clausewitz, military force was considered to be the most important component of strategy. War was seen as the continuation of politics by other, albeit extreme, means.

Under the emergent conditions of "structural terrorism" (as described in the preceding introduction to *The Nuclear Reader*), policymakers have been forced to confront the novel questions of what to do *with* nuclear weapons and what to do *about* them. Accordingly, the nuclear age has forced a re-evaluation of conventional conceptions of national strategy. The capacity of nuclear weapons to cause unprecedented destruction has challenged the traditional view that military might is merely another instrument of foreign policy. Although, as we shall see, some continue to believe that nuclear weapons can be used to exercise influence in the same way that other instruments of policy can, many now question the usefulness and safety of force as a method of bending others to one's will.[2] As a result, opinions regarding strategy in the nuclear era have become divided and discordant. Strategic theory is now in a state of arrested ambiguity; its current condition has been

9

labeled a "morass," and the doctrine of deterrence has been described as "now in a state of confusion amounting almost to disintegration."[3]

Without agreement on a conception of strategy to replace the Clausewitz-ean formula that served the prenuclear era so well, some talk of strategy in terms of ends, and others do so in terms of tactics, procurement policies, targeting doctrines, and weapons deployment. One scholar illustrates the semantic problem by asking that employment, declaratory, acquisition, and deployment policies be distinguished.[4] Similarly, another scholar has asked that *doctrine* be emphasized and that strategic doctrine be defined as "a set of operative beliefs, values, and assertions that in a significant way guide official behavior with respect to strategic research and development (R&D), weapons choice, forces, operational plans, arms control, etc."[5] Apparently (as argued by William C. Martel and Paul L. Savage in the second reading selection), no conception of nuclear strategy enjoys consensual support. As a result, debate concerning strategic issues defies easy characterization, and comparison of viewpoints is difficult.

To cut into this conceptual thicket requires that some underbrush be removed. In order to give some order to our discussion of strategy and its boundaries, this book presumes that nuclear strategy under conditions of structural terrorism revolves around the question *"For what political purposes can nuclear weapons be used?"*

This point of departure does not, of course, take us very far. But it does suggest as a corollary another division that further defines thinking about strategic issues. On the one hand, as we shall see shortly in the readings in Part I, one school of thought contends that nuclear weapons can be used to serve the full range of options to which they might be put. These include both war-fighting and war-winning options made possible through the acquisition of preemptive, first-strike capabilities. Opposing this, on the other hand, is a school of thought that assumes that nuclear weapons can be used for only one political purpose, namely, the deterrence of an adversary's attack.

Even this dichotomy breaks down into intermediate positions. Many argue, for example, that the uses to which nuclear weapons can and should be put are situational, that is, the circumstances of the decision-making environment at any particular decision point should define the range of viable options. (This position is somewhat akin to "situation ethics," which maintains that the principles governing the propriety of conduct depend on the situation and not on immutable norms for behavior.) Others support a doctrine that sanctions the use of nuclear weapons, but only for defense. The argument here is that in order to deter attack, one's adversary must believe in one's threat to use nuclear weapons in retaliation. Still others argue that deterrence cannot be condoned morally because it implies the use of weapons that cannot discriminate enemies from innocents, although, as is sometimes acknowledged, deterrence itself requires the possession of nuclear weapons and even the threat to use them in a retaliatory strike. Opinion on strategic issues thus is distributed along an extended continuum, with the use of nuclear weapons for purposes of "compellence" and persuasion at one end and for deterrence and dissuasion at the other end.[6]

Regardless of their differences, theorists in *all* schools of strategic thought share concern for and are preoccupied with preserving peace and preventing nuclear war. Even those advocating the utility of a war-fighting strategy recognize the dangers of escalation inherent in the actual execution of such a strategy, and *all* dread and seek to guard against an enemy's pursuit of a nuclear war-fighting strategy. (In this sense, the superpowers' postures are mirror images—each sees the other's potential acquisition of a preemptive capability as a threat to stability.) From either end of the continuum, there-fore, strategies for preserving stability through deterrence have assumed cen-ter stage; all strategists regard the capability to deter as indispensable, even if some (agreeing with Edward Teller's fear, expressed in 1974, that "reliable deterrents do not exist") doubt that such a goal is achievable.

For this reason, deterrence is often regarded as a strategy in itself, rather than one element in a comprehensive strategy. A preference, however, is not a policy. To avoid confusing a passion and a program, a position and a policy, it is necessary to understand the possible meanings of deterrence; this is difficult, as deterrence, like strategy, also is a concept that invites confusion.[7] At its core, however, is a rather simple idea: Deterrence is a condition created when an aggressor's attack is prevented by threatening retaliation. Or, as Emma Rothschild put it, "Deterrence in a more or less pure form consists of the following threat: 'Do not attack me because if you do, something unacceptably horrible will happen to you.'"[8] The doctrine of nuclear deter-rence has been summarized by Jonathan Schell as embracing the beliefs

> . . . that nuclear weapons offer nations effectively unlimited force; that winning a nuclear war is impossible; that it is imperative, therefore, to stop such a war from ever beginning; that the weapons themselves play a crucial role in that effort; that an invulnerable retaliatory force is of particular importance; that there is a special danger inherent in any capacity, on either side, for destroying the nuclear forces of the other side in a first strike; and that "perceptions" and "psychology" play an essential role in convincing the adversary that any aggression by him will lead only to his annihilation, and so in maintaining the "stability" of the whole arrangement.[9]

Although the foregoing encapsulates the fundamentals of deterrence, ideas can easily become muddled in debates about which policies can best attain the desired condition of deterrence. For example, analysts disagree in their evaluation of the advantages and liabilities of military superiority as opposed to parity; launch-on-warning as opposed to launch-on-attack or "quick launch" retaliatory policies; counterforce as opposed to countervalue tar-geting; the transition from offense to defense; battlefield nuclear weapons; ballistic missile defense; civil defense; the impact of arms control agreements on stability; and the like. These and other aspects of the current debate are examined in the following selections, which also illuminate the diversity of prevailing positions.

Our first selection is an informed survey of current strategic thinking. Its author, Theodore Draper, describes what he terms *nuclear temptations*: a series of strategic proposals advocating new uses for the new generation of accurate and versatile nuclear weapons. These weapons tend to drive strategy, he argues;[10] they make available new strategic options that in turn invite their actual use. Technological developments in weapons undermine the preservation of deterrence, for the new temptations threaten to destroy the foundations on which peace has rested throughout the post–World War II era.

By framing the discussion underlying much of the debate surrounding strategic thinking, Draper provides the intellectual baggage necessary to evaluate strategic issues. In doing so, he rejects the "temptations" that have been recently recommended as a basis for defense policy in the United States (a viewpoint that when advanced provoked a strident response from others, including then Secretary of Defense Caspar Weinberger).[11] "The main enemy at present," he asserts, "is not a nuclear balance that results in mutual deterrence; it is the propaganda about the feasibility of nuclear war by way of precise and discriminating weapons allegedly capable of avoiding mass destruction." Some will find this conclusion reasonable, and others will see it as disregarding the strategic options that such weapons make possible. But regardless of one's reaction to his conclusion, one should consider his thesis and warning that "the main reason nuclear weapons have not been used thus far is precisely the belief that they cannot be launched for any useful political purpose and that mutual mass destruction can be of no conceivable benefit to either side. But now Pied Pipers of a protracted nuclear war are trying to lure us to break through the psychological barriers to nuclear war."

Ideas have consequences. To illuminate further the premises underlying discussions of nuclear strategy, William C. Martel and Paul L. Savage delineate in "Nuclear Strategy: What It Is and Is Not" the important analytic distinctions between a cluster of interrelated concepts. These concepts, unfortunately, are often used interchangeably, with muddled thinking and incoherent strategies the result. The meanings of such seemingly simple terms as "policy" and "strategy" and their relationship to such core concepts as deterrence, capability, counterforce, countervalue, and the like are introduced. Appropriately, the critical importance of nuclear targeting options— and the probable consequences that emanate from the alternatives available— is given special attention in the context of American strategic doctrine. The dangers resulting from the tensions between these targeting plans, as well as the instabilities in deterrence which may arise from the failure to take cognizance of the logical implications of these options, are exposed in a way that accounts well for many of the problems confronting the development of an integrated, comprehensive strategic plan.[12]

Moreover, Martel and Savage illuminate the incompatibilities created between doctrine and force structure in U.S. nuclear strategy, as revealed by the procurement, deployment, and basing decisions that have been considered. Their inspection affirms Draper's thesis that technological developments often drive strategy, instead of the other way around; the absence of appreciation of the doctrinal consequences of weapons systems imposes, they contend, unacceptable risks.

This proposition is explored in greater detail in the conclusion of Martel and Savage's article, which considers the thesis that the nuclear strategies and force structures of the United States and the Soviet Union have converged over time. The symmetrical shift of both superpowers to counterforce targeting and to greater emphasis on a first-strike capability, as well as the convergence of the superpowers' strategies on nuclear decapitation (destruction of command centers) and on a defense-oriented deterrence policy, heightens the dangers. Paradoxically, by adopting similar strategies for avoiding war with one another, the superpowers have increased rather than reduced their mutual vulnerability. These strategies, the authors conclude, may undermine—not strengthen—the security that each superpower seeks.

Our next selection examines the strategic and doctrinal implications of the one facet of strategic planning that Draper finds most disturbing: the pursuit of war-waging capabilities. That threat has grown exponentially in the last quarter of the twentieth century. In "MAD versus NUTS," Spurgeon M. Keeny, Jr., and Wolfgang K. H. Panofsky explore further the implications of this trend. Using the acronym NUTS to characterize various doctrines that have gained currency to justify the use of nuclear weapons in war (whose advocates can be described as "nuclear utilization theorists"), they question the belief that a nuclear utilization targeting strategy can eliminate the essentially MAD character of nuclear war under conditions of mutual assured destruction. Although they find the MAD doctrine inadequate, they find the dangers inherent in NUTS unacceptable. They thus find themselves in company with Draper, and the reasons on which they base their position illuminate the most fundamental issues dividing contemporary strategic theorists. How the MAD-versus-NUTS debate is resolved is destined profoundly to affect the prospects for future strategic stability.

Strategic doctrines can be evaluated in terms of their efficacy and practicality. They also can and must be evaluated in terms of their moral implications, for, as Jonathan Schell has urged, strategic doctrine allows humankind only two paths, one that ultimately "leads to death, the other to life."[13]

The most comprehensive investigation of the ethical problems of nuclear strategy was at the time of its publication in 1983 the celebrated pastoral letter by the National Conference of Catholic Bishops drafted under the leadership of Joseph Cardinal Bernardin. It compared strategic doctrines with the principles of Christian doctrine and found the former largely unacceptable. The plans—or what Draper might call the "temptations"—being constructed or then already officially endorsed were perceived to violate a number of principles central to the "just-war" tradition in Christian theology, especially the stipulations that the resort to violence be (1) *discriminate,* by giving noncombatants immunity; (2) *proportionate,* by limiting any collateral harm caused by war to a level commensurate with the good intended or the evil to be avoided; and (3) *reasonable* in its probability of success. As the pastoral letter then made clear, these norms prohibited acceptance of many of the strategic plans then in place or under consideration, and they challenged such prominent features of American strategic doctrine as counterpopulation (countervalue) warfare and unrestricted counterforce warfare.

When released in 1983, the moral position adopted in the pastoral letter provoked great controversy. By recommending a strategy for peace that severely limited the uses of nuclear weapons ("never!"), by restricting how the threat of their use could be expressed (only to deter an attack), but by allowing nuclear weapons to be possessed nonetheless, the bishops arrived at a "strictly conditioned" acceptance of nuclear weapons, one that came close to a "you can have them but you can't use them" position.[14] It was thus not surprising that this carefully reasoned position generated widespread commentary, both for and against it.[15]

Since the bishops' pastoral letter was issued in 1983, a number of developments in strategy and weapons systems, as well as in the global political system, have taken place. To keep abreast of these profound changes, the bishops prepared a revised statement in 1988. The emergent moral dilemmas posed by nuclear weapons and strategy are reprinted in our fourth reading selection, here entitled "Nuclear Strategy and the Challenge of Peace: The Moral Evaluation of Nuclear Deterrence in Light of Policy Developments, 1983–1988." This comprehensive assessment brings into focus a congeries of salient strategic issues, while concentrating on deterrence as a condition for the maintenance of international peace. The preservation of deterrence through policies that promote it is regarded as critical because, as the bishops' revised Report notes, "when one looks back on the evolution of the nuclear age, it is highly unlikely that anyone would have chosen to have our present situation result. . . . Yet . . . deterrence has been a significant factor in preventing the use of nuclear weapons." The position defines deterrence not as an entity "but [as] a policy involving . . . weapons systems, force posture, declaratory policy, targeting doctrine, and the relationship of these to the objectives of security policy and . . . arms control policy." In taking account of developments that have occurred, the new Report once again repeats the "absolute categorical" prohibition against the deliberate targeting of civilians, and reaffirms its strong disapproval of the first use of nuclear weapons, but it retains its approval of deterrence that may require the threat of nuclear weapons for retaliation under certain "strict conditions." The purpose of the new Report is "to build a barrier against nuclear use" by challenging those who ascribe to the view that nuclear weapons are "normal" or "controlled" instruments of military policy.[16]

By far the most important new development that the bishops' revised Report addresses is the Strategic Defense Initiative (SDI) to which the United States has given prominence as a means of defending against attacking missiles. On January 12, 1987, Secretary of Defense Caspar W. Weinberger claimed that "the SDI program signals not the abandonment of deterrence

but a desire to fortify it in a way that would actually reduce the risk of war—
. . . a nonoffensive, non-nuclear way of helping to maintain the peace." The
bishops' Report questions whether the space-based ballistic missile program
is really meant to enhance deterrence, or to replace it. Asking people to
evaluate this proposal not by its intended objectives but by its likely consequences, the bishops conclude that an anti-missile system would *not* provide
a solution to the moral problems of nuclear deterrence by making nuclear
weapons obsolete. Instead, they might make acquisition of a first-strike capability without fear of retaliation a possibility. The bishops thus question
the contention that a missile defense system is morally superior to deterrence.
Also emphasized in the statement is a strong moral endorsement of the Soviet–
American Anti-ballistic Missile Treaty of 1972, alongside the complaint that
both superpowers had since its signing deployed several new weapons systems
in violation of the spirit if not the letter of that treaty. The bishops' new
Report thus subscribes to the belief that nuclear deterrence is morally acceptable, and that the prospects for this policy to bring about the desired
result of preserving peace would be enhanced through pursuit of negotiations
for the reduction and control of both nuclear and conventional arms. The
statement endorses the morality of arms control and the "deep cuts" in strategic weapons that have been proposed as a basis for arms control talks.

In our fifth selection, "Global Security without Deterrence: The Necessity
for Alternatives," Robert Johansen addresses the debate by offering a rebuttal
to those who embrace the MAD doctrine and/or, like the bishops, advocate
a "strictly conditioned" moral acceptance of nuclear deterrence.[17]

Johansen draws his inspiration from those such as Jonathan Schell, who
warns that we recognize, in Schell's words, "what a doomsday machine really
is, and what it means to intend, in certain circumstances, to use one." Mutual
assured destruction risks destruction of the entire world, and therefore a
strategy entailing that risk cannot be justified, Johansen argues, because,
again in Schell's words, it entails the "unresolvable contradiction of 'defending' one's country by threatening to use weapons whose actual use would
bring on the annihilation of one's country and possibly of the world as
well."[18]

For Johansen, deterrence is the problem, not the solution; deterrence is not
morally acceptable under any circumstances because of the catastrophe that
would result should deterrence fail. The efforts to enhance nuclear deterrence
through the creation of new weapons have in fact undermined the prospects
for international security and stimulated, not reduced, the arms competition,
he contends. Even with the Strategic Defense Initiative, Johansen believes that
deterrence cannot provide adequate security in the long run; "the prospects
for long-term avoidance of war are too low." Deterrence, he alleges, encourages a chronic arms buildup; it obstructs negotiations to reduce U.S.-
Soviet military competition and therefore requires that peace rest on the threat
of all-out war; it also heightens the irrational psychological impulses that in
the past have led to war; and finally, and most importantly, Johansen con-

tends that "there is, in fact, no substantial evidence that the international system has become more stable with nuclear weapons than it would have been without them." As a consequence, it is mistaken to seek to preserve peace through the preservation of either the balance of power or balance of terror; in the nuclear age, as in the past, those balances can be expected to erode and war ultimately to erupt.

Johansen therefore concludes that it is necessary for governments to move beyond nuclear deterrence and to relinquish dependence on nuclear weapons. To do that, he recommends a number of initiatives. Among them is the development of real arms control, predicated on an attack of the belief that increases in arms can increase security. Second, the role of military force in international relations needs to be reconsidered, because "the risk of nuclear war cannot be substantially reduced without eliminating major conventional war as well . . . ." And finally, Johansen recommends reliance on nonmilitary solutions to the economic and poitical problems that breed war.

In "The Long-Term Future of Deterrence," Joseph S. Nye, Jr., evaluates the ideas advanced by both the Catholic bishops and Robert Johansen. In asking "Can deterrence last forever?" Nye relies on an unabashedly historical perspective for clues and lessons. Observing that deterrence *has* worked thus far, Nye stresses that we cannot be assured that it will work forever. The effects of accident, of irrationality in the making of strategic choices, and of psychic stress, misperceptions, and bureaucratic pathologies in crisis situations, he warns, all increase the probabilities that escalation and preemption might bring about a nuclear war. His assessment pays particular attention to the Strategic Defense Initiative (SDI) as one among a number of developments that are likely to interrupt the conditions under which deterrence has been practiced for nearly half a century.

The likelihood that technology will compound instead of alleviate these risks is less than assuring. But in focusing on the nature of contingency and uncertainty in estimates of the prospects for deterrence and the probable avoidance of nuclear war, Nye introduces a sophisticated and sobering level of insight into what, admittedly, is a largely unanswerable question. His analysis makes clear why debate about nuclear strategy does not permit clear, unambiguous answers, and why solutions to the nuclear dilemma are so difficult to identify.

In reviewing the debate about deterrent strategies and war-fighting options, one soon discovers that much of the discourse centers not simply on abstract considerations of the efficacy of policy programs and their ethics but also, understandably, on the impact of the superpowers' actual policies and practices. If the superpowers' strategies are to be assessed accurately, their *declared* strategic doctrines must be investigated, especially the postures of the Soviet Union and the United States toward nuclear weapons and the policy options that those weapons presumably create.

The basic outlines and assumptions underlying the nuclear strategy of the United States are open to public scrutiny. The same is not as true of the Soviet

Union. Nevertheless, both superpowers have found it prudent to pronounce publicly their doctrinal positions (but not their tactical plans or true military capabilities!), which is one reason why these strategies provoke so much debate about their wisdom and morality. Moreover, the weapons systems assembled and the targeting modes they allow or require do much to define their possible strategic uses. Some would even say that the weapons systems' capabilities determine strategy, although others contend that declared doctrine is instrumental because strategic doctrine fuels rather than follows the technological expansion of the arms race. The general strategic goals and operational plans of the two superpowers are discussed in our next two selections.

In "Soviet Nuclear Strategy and Arms Control under Gorbachev: New Thinking, New Policy," Peter Zwick weighs the available evidence and concludes that Gorbachev is serious about arms control and that he has made fundamental changes in Soviet nuclear strategy. To Zwick, Gorbachev clearly has made a difference. That difference is seen most particularly in the Soviet leader's stress on the necessity that the superpowers' rivalry be restricted to peaceful competition, and his challenge to the view of his predecessors that a nuclear war is potentially "winnable." Soviet military doctrine incorporates "war-fighting" and defensive elements in the event that deterrence should fail, but embraces mutual assured destruction (MAD) rather than seeking a substitute for it. These departures are interpreted in light of the Strategic Defense Initiative (SDI) and the recent breakthroughs in arms control negotiations.

Observing that Soviet and American policies began to converge on the goal of arms reductions at precisely the same time that they began to diverge on the issue of nuclear deterrence, Zwick explains Gorbachev's opposition to SDI on the grounds that, if created, an effective ballistic missile defense system would reduce the incentives for arms reductions; for the Soviets, the fewer the number of offensive strategic weapons that exist, the more vulnerable the remaining Soviet arsenal would be to a preemptive strike made possible by an effective American strategic defense system. Therefore, to bring about the reductions in nuclear arms to which President Reagan and General Secretary Gorbachev both pledged their support would, in Gorbachev's view, be detrimental to Soviet security interests and ultimately to world peace if American ballistic missile defenses are developed.

Soviet strategy is shaped in part by the strategies formulated by its primary adversary. U.S. nuclear strategy and its goals are described well in a comprehensive summary provided by the U.S. Office of Technology Assessment. In "U.S. Nuclear Strategy: Characteristics and Common Criticisms," the durable nature of the American strategic approach to nuclear weapons is noted.[19] To contain the Soviet Union and to deter nuclear war, as well as to terminate a nuclear war at the lowest possible level of violence and on terms most favorable to the United States if a nuclear confrontation should occur, the United States has relied on what since 1980 has been called a "countervailing strategy" of deterrence, and has sought to develop measures that would enhance crisis stability in those situations of high tension in which the threat of a nuclear exchange is likely. More recently, a shift from an offense- to a defense-based strategy has been given attention with the Strategic Defense Initiative.

Also included in the Office of Technology Assessment's interpretation of America's strategic nuclear doctrine as it has been maintained over the past two decades is a useful analysis of the criticisms that are commonly expressed about it. A typology or set of categories describing alternative positions among strategists is developed which divides strategic thought about the mil- itary utility of nuclear weapons into three schools of thought: "retaliation- only," "prevailing," and "defense dominance." The array of opinions that are associated with each of these interpretations is described, as are the pre- sumed advantages and disadvantages associated with each position.

The potential impact of ballistic missile defense on nuclear strategy has become the central issue in contemporary strategic debate. Ballistic missile defense (BMD) commands a prominent place in strategic discourse because the transition from an offense-oriented to a defense-based strategy promises to transform in problematic and profound ways the purposes to which the nuclear weapons will be put and the strategies that will be designed to govern their use. The SDI permeates virtually every dimension of the topics covered in *The Nuclear Reader*. Given its controversial and as yet uncertain status, opinions about its feasibility and consequences understandably vary widely, as shown in Table I-1. For this reason, we focus in the remainder of Part I on the attributes of this initiative and its relationship to strategic planning.

In "The Objectives of Ballistic Missile Defense," Robert M. Bowman pro- vides a penetrating evaluation of BMD as a strategic issue. He identifies four purposes to which ballistic defense might be put: (1) to replace deterrence by the threat of retaliation with a policy of assured survival based on a near- perfect defense against all types of offensive weapons, (2) to enhance deter- rence by reducing the vulnerability of retaliatory offensive forces, (3) to put into place a disarming first strike capability by providing a protective shield against a sufficient portion of an adversary's missiles, and (4) to limit, should deterrence fail, the damage that would be inflicted by reducing the number of warheads that might penetrate the United States.

Each of these objectives is assessed against the backdrop of the require- ments for their realization and the possibility that feasible technologies can be developed for their successful implementation. This assessment leads to the conclusion that "to pursue an extremely effective defensive shield while retaining offensive weapons carries an enormous danger of provoking war or causing one by accident, while yielding very little hope of providing suf- ficient protection to enable the nation to survive." For this reason, Bowman concludes, the latter two potential objectives for creating these systems should be rejected. On the other hand, the objective of replacing deterrence, while seemingly impossible, is regarded as a legitimate objective of long-range basic

Table I-1 Strategic Defense Initiative Debate: Some of the More Commonly Heard Arguments for and against President Reagan's SDI

Proponents' Case:	Opponents Argue:	Proponents Reply:	Opponents' Case:	Proponents Argue:	Opponents Reply:
1. A defensive shield will make nuclear weapons obsolete.	Because a star-wars system can't be perfect, it won't remove the threat of nuclear war entirely.	You don't need perfection. With even a limited defense, an opponent wouldn't know how many of his warheads will get through, so he'd be less likely to strike first. If he does strike first, a defense would preserve more of the U.S. retaliatory force.	1. SDI threatens to base weapons in space.	SDI offers a chance to negotiate treaties that nearly eliminate nuclear weapons.	The arms race wouldn't end: One way to counter a defense is to build more missiles. In fact you'd add *two more* races: one over defensive weapons and one over countermeasures.
2. Because SDI-type defenses would thwart the use of ICBMs, it will lead to the United States and the U.S.S.R. to reduce voluntarily their nuclear arsenals.	One way to beat a defense is to build more missiles to overwhelm it. This would lead to violations of arms treaties. So would testing and deployment of SDI-type weapons. All of this would pull the rug out from under the arms control process.	Deterrence is still shaky, despite arms control treaties. Look at how nuclear arsenals have grown since World War II.	2. SDI will undermine the ABM Treaty, which presumes that if there are no defenses the strategic balance will be more stable.	You assume a defense is deployed. SDI is a *research* problem being conducted within the limits of the ABM Treaty. Besides, the Soviets have their own star-wars program.	SDI may be research, but some of the demonstrations planned involve devices that could be seen as "components" under the ABM Treaty, hence testing them would be a violation.

Table I-1 (*continued*)

Proponents' Case:	Opponents Argue:	Proponents Reply:	Opponents' Case:	Proponents Argue:	Opponents Reply:
3. SDI-type defenses could neutralize accidental or unauthorized launches or attacks by terrorists or other third parties	There are cheaper ways to prevent accidents. Put command-destruct devices on missiles to destroy them if they're launched accidentally. As for terrorists, they're more likely to deliver a bomb in a suitcase or car trunk than on an ICBM.	Any system that can reduce the number of casualties is worth building.	3. Even if 95 percent effective—much higher than current estimates—a defense system will allow enough warheads to get through to inflict untold damage on the American society.	Without defenses, all of the warheads in a Soviet first strike could hit the United States, destroying our ability to retaliate.	We can retaliate using submarine-based missiles. Even if a defense stops some Soviet warheads, it would still let enough through to destroy the United States as a nation.
4. SDI would enhance deterrence by helping U.S. retaliatory forces survive a nuclear attack. This would discourage Soviet leaders from launching a first strike.	But SDI might give the United States confidence to strike first in a crisis. After all, it's easier for an imperfect defense to counter a ragged response than a coordinated first strike.	This is a defensive system; it is not designed to make aggression easier. Besides, when the United States had clear nuclear superiority it didn't engage in nuclear blackmail.	4. A star-wars system will be destabilizing because its orbiting weapons will be vulnerable to attack and because the Soviets could build more offensive weapons to overwhelm it.	One object of SDI is to make it so expensive for the Soviets to overwhelm it that they give up that option. And because this reduces the utility of nuclear weapons, the Soviets should be more willing to negotiate arms reductions.	Possible countermeasures are numerous. They're already being explored by the United States and the Soviets. While we put weapons into orbit, they'll put countermeasures on a new generation of ICBMs.

Table I-1 (continued)

Proponents' Case:	Opponents Argue:	Proponents Reply:	Opponents' Case:	Proponents Argue:	Opponents Reply:
5. SDI would help protect U.S. allies in Europe against nuclear attack.	Maybe so, but it then leaves Western Europe open to *conventional* attack.	Conventional war is preferable to nuclear war—especially since conventional weapons can be recalled.	5. The United States will have to convince the Soviets that relying on ballistic-missile defenses is better than relying on the doctrine of mutually assured destruction.	The Soviets have always placed a high value on defenses, even if they're marginal. SDI merely shows that the United States values defense, too.	True, the Soviets value defense: They are beefing up their air defense screen. But that doesn't mean it will be easy to talk them out of the ABM Treaty.
6. SDI takes advantage of the U.S. technological lead over the Soviets.	That doesn't mean the Soviets won't respond. Since World War II, they've matched many U.S. weapons developments.	A high-tech race works to the U.S.'s advantage: If the Soviets copy U.S. technology, the United States will be ahead of the race.	6. America's allies are concerned that SDI will speed the arms race between the United States and the U.S.S.R.	Perhaps. But the Europeans are also intrigued by the possibility that getting a share of the SDI pie will help their high-tech industries.	Given our efforts to halt the transfer of militarily sensitive technology, allied participation is likely to be quite limited.
7. Technological spinoffs from SDI will help the rest of the U.S. military and even find civilian uses.	The classified status of most SDI research will prevent quick use of spinoff technology. SDI may draw research money and manpower away from civilian work. It would be better just to spend the money for commercial R & D.	There are plenty of examples of commercial technology that came from classified military programs. Take a look at jet engines and nuclear power.	7. The cost of a star-wars system is likely to be prohibitive.	Cost estimates at this point are flaky. There is no clearly defined system on which to base them. Besides, Reagan Administration officials have said that if research shows that a cost-effective defense can't be designed, it won't be pursued.	We *do* have spending targets for the SDI research program: $26 billion by 1990. So much will have been spent by that time that the program will become self-perpetuating, even if it proves infeasible to deploy a defense.

Source: Lisa Remillard, *The Christian Science Monitor*, November 12, 1985. © 1985 TCSPS.

research, and the second, to develop BMD to enhance deterrence, is regarded as feasible if it is implemented within reasonable costs and within the constraints of the 1972 Anti-Ballistic Missile Treaty.

Regardless of the options chosen, in the final analysis, Bowman concludes, "it is absolutely essential that the objective of such a program be clearly defined." A rational strategy, the author contends, begins with a clear identification of the purposes to which any weapons system using nuclear capabilities would be put. It is disturbing that much of the debate about defensive systems has not given sufficient thought to the objectives such an initiative is designed to fulfill. Bowman would agree both with Draper and with Martel and Savage that technological innovations have driven strategy in the absence of systematic thought about the purposes to which the technological developments might constructively and safely be put.

To conclude our examination of strategic issues in Part I, Andrew C. Goldberg examines in "Offense and Defense in the Postnuclear System" the possible emergence of a "postnuclear" world. Three "futures" or potential scenarios are perceived as likely. In the first, the superpowers would avoid the "deep cuts" in the offensive systems currently being contemplated and proceed to break out of the ABM Treaty with deployment of defenses from space in the mid-1990s. The second would result if Soviet proposals to prevent construction of strategic defenses are accepted and arms control agreements emerge which sharply reduce strategic nuclear weapons and eventually eliminate the need for ballistic missile defense systems. And the third future poses a system that follows the current American approach to arms control, namely, one in which doctrine and force structures will continue to embrace offensive capabilities concomitant with a relatively vigorous pursuit of strategic defenses. This future calls forth the likelihood of a transition in which offensive ballistic missile systems decline while strategic defenses grow.

None of the "futures" presented promises assured survival or freedom from fear of nuclear weapons. The insecurities that have cast their shadow over the world since the advent of nuclear weapons are unlikely to disappear in any of these futures, and controversies about nuclear strategy are likely to remain regardless of which eventually develops.

By emphasizing how decisions regarding weapons capabilities influence strategic planning, Goldberg's essay prepares the way for the discussion of weapons in Part II of *The Nuclear Reader*. Recent developments in weapons systems require new strategies to govern their use and to prevent the destruction that they threaten. The need somehow to control those weapons so that they serve their intended political purpose—the prevention of nuclear war—thus becomes imperative.

NOTES

1. It is, of course, an empirical question whether the processes through which nations formulate foreign policies do, indeed, display the attributes that satisfy the assumptions of rational decision making. For a discussion that draws on the extensive literature on foreign policy making

to analyze the processes through which U.S. policies and strategies are formulated, see Charles W. Kegley, Jr., and Eugene R. Wittkopf, *American Foreign Policy: Pattern and Process,* 3d ed. (New York: St. Martin's Press, 1987).

2. For a discussion of the limits and uses of military might in the nuclear age, see Klaus Knorr, "On the International Uses of Military Force in the Contemporary World," *Orbis* 21 (Spring 1977): 5–27, and Robert J. Art, "To What Ends Military Power? The Future of Force," in Charles W. Kegley, Jr., and Eugene R. Wittkopf, eds., *The Global Agenda,* 2d ed. (New York: Random House, 1988), pp. 31–37.

3. The former characterization was voiced by Donald M. Snow in *The Nuclear Future* (University, Ala.: University of Alabama Press, 1983), pp. 1–34. The latter description is offered by Jonathan Schell, *The Abolition* (New York: Knopf, 1984), p. 48.

4. Milton Leitenberg, "NATO and WTO Long Range Nuclear Forces," in Karl E. Birnbaum, ed., *Arms Control in Europe* (Laxenburg: Austrian Institute for International Affairs, 1980), p. 10.

5. Fritz W. Ermarth, "Contrasts in American and Soviet Strategic Thought," *International Security* 3 (Fall 1978): 138.

6. *Compellence* is a strategy that envisions the use of nuclear weapons to exercise influence, to coerce others to act in ways they would not otherwise behave in the absence of that influence. *Deterrence,* in contrast, threatens retaliation in order to prevent an actor from contemplating an attack. This distinction is analogous to that between persuasion and dissuasion as strategic goals in international bargaining. For discussions in the context of the evolution of strategic doctrine in the United States, see Kegley and Wittkopf (1987), especially pp. 80–104; Thomas C. Schelling, *Arms and Influence* (New Haven, Conn.: Yale University Press, 1966); and J. David Singer, "Inter-Nation Influence," *American Political Science Review* 57 (June 1963): 420–430.

7. For a useful discussion, see Patrick M. Morgan, *Deterrence: A Conceptual Analysis,* 2d ed. (Beverly Hills, Calif.: Sage Publications, 1983).

8. Emma Rothschild, "The Delusions of Deterrence," *The New York Review of Books,* 14 April, 1983, p. 40.

9. Schell, p. 36.

10. The experience of one strategist addresses this proposition: Lord Zuckerman reports ("Nuclear Fantasies," *The New York Review of Books,* 14 June, 1984, p. 7) that "during the twenty years or so that I myself was professionally involved in these matters, weapons came first and rationalizations and policies followed."

11. See Draper's debate with Weinberger in *The New York Review of Books,* 18 August, 1983, and his subsequent debates with Albert Wohlstetter in "Nuclear Temptations: An Exchange," *The New York Review of Books,* 31 May, 1984, pp. 44–50, as well as in the 19 January, 1984, issue of the same journal.

12. For a recent effort to meet this perceived need, see The Commission on Integrated Long-Term Strategy, *Discriminate Deterrence* (Washington, D.C.: U.S. Government Printing Office, 1988). For a trenchant critique that argues that this report's recommendations are neither integrated nor comprehensive, and that they compound rather than correct the incoherence afflicting contemporary U.S. strategic thinking, see Paul Kennedy, "Not So Grand Strategy," *The New York Review of Books,* 12 May, 1988, pp. 5–8.

13. Jonathan Schell, *The Fate of the Earth* (New York: Knopf, 1982), p. 231.

14. Bruce Russett, "Ethical Dilemmas of Nuclear Deterrence," *International Security* 8 (Spring 1984): 36–54.

15. For representative assessment of the bishops' original statement, see Susan Moller Okin, "Taking the Bishops Seriously," *World Politics* 36 (July 1984): 527–54. One of the most visible critiques of the bishops' initial position was that voiced by the well-known strategic theorist Albert Wohlstetter, in his "Bishops, Statesmen, and Other Strategists on the Bombing of Innocents," which was printed in the first edition of *The Nuclear Reader* (New York: St. Martin's Press, 1985, pp. 58–76). In contrast to the first pastoral letter, Wohlstetter advocated a warfighting nuclear strategy, claiming that it *is* ethically acceptable to make contingency plans for war in the event that deterrence should fail and to develop the capability to wage it with nuclear weapons. In his view, technological advances had created opportunities for new departures in strategic doctrine which would make limited nuclear war practicable; deterrence based on a MAD strategy, he concluded, should be jettisoned, and in its place a counterforce strategy implemented that would allow the United States to utilize nuclear weapons to pursue political purposes. In assuming this position, Wohlstetter prescribed the very kind of strategy that Draper characterized as tempting but objectionable and that Keeny and Panofsky labeled unrealistic.

Wohlstetter called for the acquisition of military capabilities that would allow the United States to confront the Soviet Union on the battlefield, to fight, to survive, and to emerge victorious. In embracing this view, Wohlstetter approached the position of Colin S. Gray and Keith Payne, other strategists who urged [in "Victory Is Possible," *Foreign Policy* 39 (Summer 1980): 14–27] that the United States prepare to use its nuclear arsenal, and not necessarily only in response to a nuclear attack.

16. See Bruce Russett, "The Bishops, SDI, and Deterrence," *Commonweal* 115 (20 May 1988): 295–297.

17. For a representative example of this position, see Paul M. Kattenburg, "MAD is the Moral Position," pp. 77–84, in the first edition of *The Nuclear Reader*. Like the bishops, Kattenburg argued that peace depends on making a credible threat; to Kattenburg, the path to maintaining deterrence is one that ensures an adversary's awareness that the United States would answer an attack decisively and without restraint. But unlike the bishops, who see the means of nuclear weapons as unacceptably disproportionate to the ends, Kattenburg sees the viability of MAD as contingent upon decision makers' willingness to accept the use of nuclear weapons in self-defense: "the morality of the end sought in this case justifies the apparent immorality of the means," p. 83. For an argument that, like Kattenburg's, contends that there is no alternative to MAD, see Glenn C. Buchan, "The Anti-MAD Mythology," *The Bulletin of the Atomic Scientists* 37 (April 1981): 13–17.

18. Schell, *The Abolition,* p. 48.

19. Implicitly, this continuity represents a problem if, as Secretary of Defense Casper Weinberger concluded (9 October, 1985), "the world has changed so profoundly since the 1950s and 1960s when most of our strategic ideas were formulated, that many of these concepts are now obsolete."

1 NUCLEAR TEMPTATIONS: DOCTRINAL ISSUES IN THE STRATEGIC DEBATE

Theodore Draper

There are so many aspects of the nuclear war problem that anyone who talks about it, especially in a relatively short span of time, must choose a particular aspect to deal with. It is all too easy to get tangled up in terminology, technicalities, or the controversies of the moment. I am going to discuss what I consider to be the chief danger or threat of nuclear war. It is what I call "nuclear temptations," by which I mean nothing more than the temptations to use nuclear weapons. These temptations have taken various forms, some of which are still with us. But temptations in this field, as in life generally, come with inhibitions, and so one will naturally lead to the other as we go along. . . .

In the Clausewitzian sense, the grand strategy of nuclear war is . . . simple, though that does not mean that everything about it is very easy. Its strategic simplicity is what permits us—non-nuclear experts and non-military professionals—to think seriously about the problem of nuclear war. One such simple conception is that of nuclear "deterrence," and it did not need nuclear experts or military professionals to think of it. . . .

The first atomic bomb was dropped on Hiroshima on August 6, 1945. Only a month later, . . . the University of Chicago [initiated] . . . an "Atomic Energy Control Conference." . . . Two of the participants are of the greatest interest to us.

One was Professor Jacob Viner [who] . . . was, of course, no atomic expert or military professional. But he already knew one thing . . . "A single atomic bomb can reduce a city and its population to dust." From this simple enough premise, . . . Viner made a striking allusion to the strategic military implication of atomic warfare. Though the United States was then the only country to have the bomb, Viner already foresaw that the monopoly could not last and, moreover, that a stage of parity, or equal destructiveness, was bound to come about.

Here is a key sentence in a memorandum he wrote for the conference: "Retaliation in equal terms is unavoidable and in this sense the atomic bomb is a war deterrent, a peace-making force." The term "deterrent" was thus used for the first time in this connection. In his later talk, in November 1945, Viner developed the thought behind his original insight. That thought might

Note: Footnotes have been deleted. Subtitle has been added.

be summed up in this way: If one atomic power is capable of retaliating in kind against another atomic power, each is capable of deterring the other from using atomic weapons.

The second pioneer in this field was Bernard Brodie, then at Yale University. Brodie had specialized in the history of naval warfare, but he too was no nuclear expert or military professional. He also attended the Chicago conference, where he spoke directly on "Strategic Consequences of the Atomic Bomb." . . . Brodie's talk contained a mention of "possible deterrent value" in connection with the atomic bomb. The word "deterrent," therefore, had crept into Brodie's thinking at this time, but the summary of his talk on record is too cryptic to reveal fully what he may have meant.

But whereas Viner, as far as I can tell, dropped the subject after 1945, Brodie stayed with it for the rest of his life. In a book published in 1946, Brodie produced the classic formulation of the military consequence of atomic weapons. Three of his sentences have been quoted innumerable times, but I may perhaps be excused for quoting them once again, because they sum up the essence of the matter better than anything else:

> Thus far the chief purpose of our military establishment has been to win wars. From now on its chief purpose must be to avert them. It can have almost no other useful purpose.

Brodie thus hit on the main point—the strategic essence—that this weapon was capable of such mutual destruction that it could have no useful purpose except to make war between atomic or thermonuclear powers irrational and suicidal.

Previous wars had been rational to the extent that they had served some political purpose. . . . [But] what would a nuclear power intend to achieve by waging a nuclear war against another nuclear power? Win the war? But what does victory mean if the enemy has a nuclear force that can retaliate in kind? What is victory worth if the nuclear aggressor must take the risk— at the very least the risk—of mutual devastation? . . .

The question immediately raises another: Do nuclear weapons represent a qualitative rather than a quantitative change in warfare? If the answer is qualitative, as most theorists agree, there is no experience or precedent for conducting it. Armed forces learn how to use new weapons by trial and error. The function of the machine gun, for example, was misconceived at the outset. It took time and failure to learn how to use the machine gun to best advantage. But no one in his senses—to use Clausewitz's language—is going to be able to learn how best to use nuclear weapons, especially those of the greatest destructiveness, by a process of trial and error. The risk and the cost make such experimentation in real combat prohibitive.

Some such reasoning flowed from the fundamental insight first stated by Viner and Brodie. Their analysis has been refined; various distinctions have been introduced; but the central idea of deterrence is still very much with us. It was recently restated by former Secretary of Defense Robert McNamara, who was not always such a firm believer. In an article [*Foreign Affairs* (Fall 1983)] the newspapers played up as if he had said something new and original, McNamara wrote that nuclear weapons *"are totally useless—except only to deter one's opponent from using them."* Viner and Brodie had been there thirty-seven years earlier. For this they should be properly honored.

But the idea of deterrence has peculiar flaws in it. It is by its very nature not a strategy for waging war; it is rather a nonstrategy or an antistrategy. In all previous human history, weapons have been invented to be used; the more effective they were, the more they were used. But nuclear weapons are too effective to be used. This paradox is almost too much for the military mind, and its civilian counterparts, to bear.

This nuclear nonstrategy is also very expensive. It devours untold sums of the national budget, incredible quantities of rare and costly materials, prodigious amounts of human knowledge and ingenuity. And all this for something that cannot or should not be used? All this for something that is merely intended to deter someone else from using it?

Another problem with deterrence is linguistic. In ordinary usage, deterrence is treated as if it were a thing, a doer, an active agent. The question is asked, "If deterrence fails?"—as if deterrence by itself can fail or succeed. This reification of deterrence is natural enough, but it can be grossly misleading and distorting. The concept of deterrence is nothing more than a mode of analysis, a shorthand for a relationship between nuclear weapons and political decision making. The weapons do not make decisions to be used or not to be used; political leaders make the decisions. If nothing can be gained from using these weapons, the political leaders will or could be deterred from using them. If "deterrence" fails, the political leaders—or those who have elected or tolerated them—will have failed. As long as hostility and rivalry persist, weapons will be their instruments, not their causes. The real success or failure of deterrence depends on political thinking, not on unthinking objects that obey the will of men.

Deterrence, then, is not a stockpile of weapons. Just here is the source of the greatest misunderstanding of and discomfort with the whole doctrine of deterrence. Because a stable balance of nuclear weaponry is necessary for the deterrent effect, it is all too common to transfer the hatefulness of those weapons to the balance that inhibits their use. Those weapons will not disappear however much we may fear and detest them; the idea of deterrence cannot be blamed for bringing them into existence or making them continue to exist. To reject deterrence because the weapons are rejected is to give up one of the few—perhaps the only convincing rationale why the weapons cannot be used for any sane, credible purpose. It is the link with politics that is the best hope of deterring the employment of nuclear weapons.

Even here, however, there is a hitch. The same nuclear weapon that can be used for deterring can also be used for fighting. This ambiguity is inherent in nuclear weapons, and we may have to live with it as we live with many lesser ambiguities in our lives. Some people seem to think that they have to be against deterrence because they are against nuclear weapons, as if one has to approve of nuclear weapons because one may favor a policy of deterrence. The real dividing line should be between those who wish to give nuclear weapons a war-deterring and those who wish to give them a war-fighting role. The distinction cannot be determined in practice solely by whether nuclear weapons are involved; they are inevitably involved in both cases. We must draw the line by determining whether the level of nuclear weaponry far exceeds the requirements for deterrence, whether the types of weapons are far more suitable for war fighting than for war deterring, and whether the official strategic doctrine encourages or requires the use of nuclear weapons. In this case as in so many others, policymakers are far more apt to give themselves away by their actions than by their words.

In some sense, then, deterrence is psychological or, better yet, political. It depends on the political calculation of political leaders who might want to use nuclear weapons for political gain. If there could be no gain, there would be no point in their use. Nevertheless, the equation is always going to be made by human beings, not by the weapons themselves. There is something scary about the responsibility of mere human beings for such ultimate decisions. It is for this very reason that rationality is our best hope and guide in this awful predicament. By rationality, I do not mean to suggest the need for any great feat of wisdom or foresight; nothing more is needed than the rational will to survive—and the leaders of even the most aggressive and detestable regimes have that. The worst way of dealing with the problem is to build up an atmosphere of mindless terror, which almost surely leads to fatalism or abdication.

We would be in an even worse position than we are in already if we thought that deterrence worked its wonders automatically and inevitably. Nothing could be more dangerous than taking deterrence for granted. We would then be really vulnerable to accidents and misjudgments; that they *can* happen is what must make us guard against them or at least take the necessary precautions to minimize their damage. The subtlety of Bernard Brodie's mind was never better displayed than in this little-noted observation in his late, great work, *War and Politics*:

> It is the curious paradox of our time that one of the foremost factors making deterrence really work well is the lurking fear that in some massive confrontation crisis it might fail. Under these circumstances one does not tempt fate.

The temptation is to say: Since no conceivable use of nuclear weapons makes sense, let's get rid of them. We don't go on building cars or computers or anything else in order *not* to use them. Why go on building nuclear weapons in order not to use them?

The logic is impeccable; the reality is something else. In the first place, all nations having nuclear weapons would have to get rid of them altogether, simultaneously. There is no serious chance of that happening. More than that, it would be necessary to get rid of the knowledge of how to make nuclear weapons. That is not even worth dreaming about; it is out of the question. There are a great many things in life easier to get rid of than nuclear weapons—cigarettes, for example. No one expects us to get rid of cigarettes—or cigarette smokers—all at once, universally and simultaneously. Probably no one expects us to get rid of them ever.

So we have been left with the nonstrategy of deterrence. It amounts to this: We have nuclear weapons; we are going to have them; but the weapons themselves are of such a nature that we—and other nuclear powers—dare not use them.

It is not the most elegant or satisfying solution—if it can be called a solution. As long as these weapons exist, there is always the danger that they may be used. At best, deterrence belongs to the lesser-evil, or *faute-de-mieux*, variety of human conduct. No one likes to choose the lesser evil—but isn't that what we are doing most of the time in our lives? We rarely get the chance to choose between the perfect good and the ultimate evil. The problem of the lesser evil is not that it is less but just how much less it is. If a lesser evil is infinitely preferable to the greater evil, we are lucky to have it. So let us not scoff at lesser evils, even in the case of nuclear arms.

Nevertheless, the less-evil nature of nuclear deterrence makes it vulnerable to pulls from two directions. One is the utopian—simply to do away with these weapons altogether, unilaterally or universally. The utopian program is not my subject, so I do not have to discuss it. The other pull, however, is my subject—it is "nuclear temptations."

It is best to start with a brief history of these temptations.

The original temptation came in with the defense strategy of NATO. The temptation arose from the problem of finding a means of defending Western Europe against what was conceived to be an overwhelming Soviet advantage in conventional, or non-nuclear, forces. NATO adopted a military policy of using atomic weapons to deter or to defeat a conventional attack.

That is still official NATO doctrine. General Bernard Rogers, the [former] Supreme Allied Commander in Europe, declared that the alliance, if attacked conventionally, would have to resort to nuclear weapons "fairly quickly," unless its conventional strength were considerably increased, which seems to be unlikely. I do not wish to linger on this—the original—nuclear temptation, because it is an old story. At this point I merely wish to point out that this policy was adopted when the Soviets did not have or were far behind in nuclear weapons; the same policy, however, prevails in a condition of nuclear parity, that is, the "retaliation in equal terms" that Jacob Viner predicted in 1945.

This form of deterrence also has a serious flaw. The most controversial of nuclear weapons are those than can reach the Soviet Union from the United States and the United States from the Soviet Union—the ICBMs, or intercontinental ballistic missiles. They are known as "strategic deterrents"—a misuse of the term "strategic," which, unfortunately, has by now become customary. . . .

It has long been difficult to believe in the efficacy—or, as the current jargon has it, "credibility"—of this deterrent. No president, it has been argued, would risk the devastation of the United States in defense of someone else's territory, even that of Western Europe. The first obligation of an American president is to the safety of the United States, whatever other obligations there may be. The argument goes that the use of the strategic deterrent against the Soviet Union would lead to the use of the Soviets' strategic deterrent against the United States, with the result of mutual devastation. So [Lawrence Freedman], one of the best students of the nuclear war problem—English, not American—has flatly stated: "The United States would be irrational to commit suicide on behalf of Western Europe. . . ." Charles de Gaulle had said more or less the same thing [more than] two decades ago. It is not a new problem, but no one has yet thought of a good answer.

So now we have at least two serious problems with traditional deterrence— it depends on a huge investment in weapons that will never be used; and it assumes the willingness of an American president to risk the devastation of the United States in behalf of other countries, albeit allies. There are other problems, no doubt, but these two are enough for our present purpose.

For at least three decades now, efforts have been made to get around such problems. It is these efforts that have brought about the most tempting inducements to use nuclear weapons.

First, there were the so-called tactical nuclear weapons, which are still with us. Tactical nuclear weapons, developed in the early 1950s, were small enough to be used on a battlefield. NATO officially decided in 1954 to use tactical nuclear weapons in defense of Europe. The Soviets then introduced tactical nuclear weapons on their side. Thus a distinction was created between "strategic" and "tactical" nuclear weapons. In effect, there were now "bad" nuclear weapons—the strategic—because they were most useful against cities and civilian populations, and there were "good" nuclear weapons, because they could be used within a much smaller area by enemy units in combat.

The development of tactical weapons brought with it another temptation— that of "limited nuclear war." A limited war would have to be "controlled," so now we had another tempting proposition—the "controlled" and "limited" nuclear war. If, in effect, the only weapons used were the smaller, less destructive ones, a nuclear exchange could be said to be "controlled" and "limited." The two terms were really interchangeable because a nuclear war would have to be controlled to be limited and limited to be controlled.

Now, in order for a nuclear war to be limited and controlled, it was necessary to fit the technology to the strategy. The new technology was supposed to produce nuclear weapons that were precise enough to be "discriminating." That was the favorite word—"discriminating." The Hiroshima type of weapon had been hopelessly imprecise and undiscriminating. It was effective only against big targets, such as cities. But the smaller, tactical weapons were now touted as precise and discriminating, so that they could avoid mass destructiveness.

For example, Henry Kissinger first attracted widespread attention in 1957 with a book called *Nuclear Weapons and Foreign Policy*. It advocated a policy of waging limited nuclear war, largely based on the new tactical weapons. Kissinger then sought "to break down the atmosphere of special horror which now surrounds the use of nuclear weapons" and "to overcome the trauma which attaches to the use of nuclear weapons." And what kind of weapons were needed to accomplish these goals? They had to be, Kissinger then thought, both "destructive" and "discriminating."

A great fuss was made about the limited-war doctrine in the late 1950s. Its nuclear version was so shaky that Kissinger—to his credit—repudiated his earlier position in another book [*The Necessity for Choice*] in 1961, only four years later. In 1957, he had come out in favor of limited nuclear war and against conventional war; in 1961, he came out against limited nuclear war and in favor of conventional war, with the use of nuclear weapons only as a last resort.

Yet the technological solution to the nuclear dilemma continued to captivate. In 1973, Fred Charles Iklé, [a former] under secretary of defense for policy, advocated "taking advantage of modern technology" by exploiting "the potential accuracy of 'smart' bombs and missiles." He wanted "assured destruction" of the enemy's "military, industrial and transportation assets" instead of "the killing of vast millions," as if one were the antithesis of the other. This strategy, Iklé admitted, was not an alternative to deterrence; it was nothing more than a change of form, not of substance. Thus the technological nostrum for conducting nuclear war in a way to avoid the destruction of cities and the massacre of civilians is hardly a new idea; it goes back at least a quarter of a century in one form or another, as if we could return to a nuclear version of the premodern art of warfare.

What was wrong with those "discriminating" and "accurate" nuclear weapons? In the first place, they were not discriminating or accurate enough. In June 1955, NATO held an exercise to find out what casualties might result in tactical nuclear warfare. In less than three days, it was found, 1.5 to 1.7 million people could expect to be killed and 3.5 million wounded if only 268 bombs fell on German soil. The rate of German casualties would be five times that suffered in World War II as a whole. In 1960, NATO maneuvers in Schleswig-Holstein showed that between 300,000 and 400,000 civilian deaths were to be expected within forty-eight hours of the initiation of tactical nuclear warfare. These figures did not take into account the effects of radiation and follow-up diseases. At that time the future German Chancellor Helmut Schmidt was moved to protest: That the concept of tactical nuclear warfare "should remain in force is inconceivable."

Something else was even more troublesome and embarrassing. Where was this limited war with tactical nuclear weapons going to be fought? The obvious answer was: in Europe and, primarily, in Germany. On second thought, the Europeans in general and Germans in particular were not enamored of this prospect. A limited nuclear war is a war limited to Europe. That circumstance has always made a limited war more attractive to Americans than to Europeans.

The problem of tactical nuclear weapons was soon compounded by that of so-called intermediate nuclear weapons. Intermediate weapons may be defined as those with a range great enough to reach the Soviet Union from Western Europe and to reach Western Europe from the Soviet Union. They are thus classified somewhere between the tactical nuclear weapons, with a range short enough to be used on a battlefield, and the strategic nuclear weapons, with an intercontinental, or Soviet-American, range. The Soviet SS-20s and the American Pershing IIs [both banned by the INF agreement examined in Part II– eds.] are typical of the intermediate weapons.

The Pershing IIs illustrate a point that I have previously tried to make about the ambiguity of nuclear weapons. One reason the European members of NATO originally wanted Pershing IIs was that they were supposed to "couple" European and American nuclear weaponry. It was reasoned that a threat to the Pershing IIs would be regarded in the United States as great enough to bring into play the "strategic," or intercontinental, weapons in the United States. But then doubts arose. It was also charged that the Pershing IIs could just as well "decouple," or dissociate, the nuclear defense of Europe from that of the United States. An alarm was raised that an American president was more likely to accept Soviet retaliation against weapons in Europe than against those in the United States.

Which is right? It seems to me that either one may be right—or wrong. The weapons themselves will not couple or decouple; they can be used for either purpose. The decision will be made politically in circumstances we cannot now foresee. Ambiguity and uncertainty hover over almost every aspect of the nuclear question. Anyone who can believe that the United States would passively permit the domination or destruction of Western Europe could be convinced of the decoupling theory: those who find it hard to imagine that the United States would not regard such an attack on Western Europe as a mortal threat to itself will lean over to the coupling side. The irony is, however, that the decision [would not have been made] because there [were] a few hundred more intermediate-range weapons in Europe; the same decision would be made without them, because the United States is coupled with Western Europe by interest, culture, and geopolitical imperatives, not by any particular weaponry.

In any case, temptations soon came in new guises. Four terms characterize the variations on the old theme—options, escalation, flexible response, and counterforce.

The idea of "options" was brought forward to get rid of the nightmare of all-out nuclear war. It held that the president had to have something between all or nothing to defend against a Soviet attack. The concept of "options" seemingly left everything wide open, from any kind of conventional war to any kind of nuclear war or a combination of both.

The temptation to use nuclear weapons, if necessary, was therefore inherent in the concept of "options." But when might it be necessary? It was hoped that a war could be waged, at least at the outset, at the lowest level of violence, in a conventional manner. But the losing side, it was also realized, was bound to try to overcome some disadvantage by a process of escalation, that is, by bringing new forces or weapons into play.

Thus "options" and "escalation" were intimately related: the process of escalation was bound to result in the optional use of nuclear weapons. Abstractly, one could envisage the process of escalation going from conventional warfare to the use of tactical nuclear weapons, then to intermediate nuclear weapons, and finally to strategic nuclear weapons.

But "options" and "escalation" were really parts or aspects of a more basic doctrine—that of "flexible response." It was officially adopted by NATO, in 1967, at the urging of the United States and after much resistance by the Europeans. The Europeans had always preferred to put their trust in the American strategic nuclear umbrella to deter the Soviets from any kind of war, conventional as well as nuclear. Flexible response, or, as it was also called, graduated deterrence, implied that a war could be fought conventionally or with lesser nuclear weapons in Europe before the United States might be called on to use its strategic nuclear weapons, that is, the very weapons that risked American self-destruction. Nevertheless, flexible response remains official NATO doctrine to this day.

Flexible response has one irresistible attraction. It can be all things to all countries and all people. It does not, in principle, promise to use nuclear weapons; it does not promise not to use them. It is an accordion-like policy; you can stretch it out or pull it in as much as you like.

The reality about flexible response is something else. It has one fatal military defect: it does not tell what kind of war to prepare for. It tells military planners to prepare for any kind of war, which is exactly the same as telling them that they cannot prepare for any particular war. Choices always have to be made, and choices cannot be made if the response is so flexible that it must cover all possible eventualities.

In fact, a choice has been made. That choice has boiled down to one between a conventional war and a nuclear war. In 1982, General Rogers explained: "If flexible response is to be credible, it must be supported by an adequate military capability for each leg of the NATO triad of forces—strategic nuclear, theater nuclear and conventional." In order to keep the nuclear threshold in Europe as high as possible, he advocated an adequate conventional deterrent, which would require an average annual real increase in defense spending of about 4 percent for the six years between 1983 and 1988. The NATO members had previously agreed on an annual 3 percent increase, which had not been met. [The target increase in fact was not met. Even if it had been, there was] much skepticism that it would really be enough, because the putative enemy need only increase his conventional forces to match.

More recently, General Rogers [*Foreign Affairs* (Summer 1982)] has told a rather more somber story: "The record shows that nations in the Alliance have never fully met their commitments to conventional force improvements. As a result NATO, while continuing to proclaim its faith in the declaratory policy of Flexible Response, has in fact mortgaged its defense to the nuclear response." So we are back to the nuclear temptation in the name of Flexible Response.

Of all the nuclear temptations, however, the most seductive and most menacing is still to come; it is the "counterforce" doctrine. It is different in kind from the other three I have just mentioned—options, escalation, and flexible response. These three theoretically leave open the possible use of nuclear weapons and to that extent do not foreclose the issue. The counterforce doctrine requires the use of nuclear weapons, but in a certain way.

For those not accustomed to nuclear jargon, two terms should be briefly explained. They are countervalue and counterforce. Countervalue means nuclear attacks against cities or civilian populations and industries in highly populated areas. Counterforce refers to nuclear attacks against military targets, such as the enemy's own nuclear weapons, military units, or facilities.

The counterforce doctrine first appeared, in the late 1950s and early 1960s, for two main reasons. It was argued that attacks against cities were not *militarily* productive; they killed the wrong people, namely civilians. And attacks against enemy cities were bound to bring similar attacks against our own cities, with the result that no American president was likely to adopt a countervalue, or city-oriented, strategy.

Counterforce presents a very strong temptation to use nuclear weapons, because it promises to take much of the horror out of nuclear war. No one can contemplate with equanimity a devastating attack on the entire social fabric of any country, let alone our own, but an attack on its nuclear weapons or even military establishment does not arouse quite the same repulsion. In one way or another, all present efforts to make nuclear war more feasible go back to the counterforce doctrine.

Here again, the doctrine needed a technological foundation. It was necessary to make two main assumptions. One was that military targets were physically or geographically separate and distinct from civilian targets. The other was that it was possible to develop nuclear weapons capable of distinguishing between the two. Again, as in the case of tactical weapons, the favorite terms are "precise" and "discriminating," but now they seem to be applied to all kinds of nuclear weapons, even those of greatest range and most destructive power.

The counterforce strategy was actually adopted by Secretary McNamara in 1962 during the Kennedy administration. But he then quickly backed away from it and became a convert to a form of the classical deterrence doctrine, which he called "mutual assured destruction," meaning that if both sides were assured of destruction, they would stay away from it as serving no conceivable political purpose. In effect, the goal again became how not to fight a nuclear war rather than how to fight one.

[It is instructive to note that] McNamara's choice of words invited the unfortunate acronym MAD. Critics of deterrence theory love to ridicule it as if it were a description of the doctrine. Professor Michael Howard has suggested that a better term would be "mutually assured *deterrence*," which would still have permitted the acronym MAD but made it seem less mad.

The reasons for this shift are just as valid today as they were then. In the first place, for counterforce to work, both sides have to adopt the same policy. No one, however, expects the United States and the Soviet Union to agree on how to fight a nuclear war or to guarantee their adherence to the same strategy in advance.

It was also realized that a counterforce policy was likely to cause such great civilian casualties that the line between counterforce—military—and countervalue—civilian—was purely theoretical and largely illusory. A Department of Defense study in the 1960s estimated that between 30 and 150 million Americans and a comparable number of Russians were likely to die in a nuclear war, even if efforts were made to stay away from highly populated areas. In 1981, a group of UN experts found that a minimum of five to six million immediate civilian casualties and 400,000 military casualties would result if 1,500 nuclear artillery shells and 200 nuclear bombs were used by both sides against each other's military targets. In effect, counterforce targeting was no panacea for what ailed countervalue.

Another reason for the shift away from counterforce strategy was somewhat more complicated and takes us some way into the darker recesses of nuclear war theory. It was the threat of a first strike. This threat has always hovered over nuclear war strategy, but it became particularly acute in the case of counterforce planning, which implies in the first place an attack against the enemy's nuclear forces.

The trauma of the first strike comes about in the following way: Basically, there are two ways of conceiving a possible nuclear war. One is that it will resemble a conventional, or non-nuclear, war—only more so. There will be one or more fronts; a development of hostilities with some degree of gradualness; a mixture of weaponry; in general, a protracted, more or less controlled escalation. The other conception is peculiar to nuclear war. It can be conceived as an almost immediately catastrophic exchange, with millions of casualties suffered in one, two, or three days.

Neither of these alternatives is particularly appealing—to put it mildly. The protracted nuclear war would be, at best, a protracted agony. As for the nuclear cataclysm, nothing more need be said about it. So the problem presents itself: how to get around both of these unpleasant alternatives?

The logic of the situation points to a way out—to knock out the enemy's nuclear weapons before they can be fired. If they—or most of them—could be knocked out at the very outset, the enemy would be prevented from waging a cataclysmic or protracted nuclear war. In short, a first strike is, logically, the most effective way to wage a nuclear war. That is what makes it so tempting and dangerous.

But to be successful a first strike must benefit from two preconditions: it must be thorough, and it must come as a surprise. If it is not thorough, it invites retaliation, which would begin a cycle of mutual devastation. If it does not come as a surprise, it would invite a preemptive first strike by the other side.

Of course, no nuclear nation will admit that it has ever contemplated or is even capable of contemplating a surprise attack and an unprovoked first strike. What cannot be denied is that they are inherent in the logic of the nuclear dilemma. That is why both sides fear them so much and charge the other with preparing for them.

But logic does not exhaust reality. The full reality is that a surprise attack and a first strike would be an infinitely risky business. They would have to be totally successful or they would open the aggressor to devastating retaliation and retribution. Without any experience of nuclear warfare, no one knows, and no one can know, what a surprise attack would achieve. It would have to be a go-for-broke operation. In the abstract, the first strike would seem like an attractive proposition. In the real world, it is an almost senseless gamble.

In any case, for these reasons and others, McNamara gave up the counterforce temptation after 1962. But now we are getting it again, and in a worse form than ever before.

The present phase began in 1974, during the Nixon administration. It was sponsored by then Secretary of Defense James Schlesinger. His new policy was basically no more than a variation on an already old theme—that of "options." The argument, still in vogue today, maintained that the president should not be limited to choosing between no nuclear war and all-out nuclear war. He should instead be able to engage in all forms and degrees of conventional and nuclear war. Schlesinger's National Security Study Memorandum of 1974 brought forward the option of threatening Soviet military targets.

After Schlesinger came Harold Brown, secretary of defense in the Carter administration. In 1980, President Carter issued Presidential Directive 59, which played more variations on the theme of "options." This directive has never been made public, so we are dependent on what Mr. Brown and other insiders have said about it.

According to Mr. Brown: "There is a good chance that any US-Soviet nuclear exchange would escalate out of control." Nevertheless, the United States must prepare for just such a nuclear exchange, that is, a limited nuclear exchange that would probably escalate out of control. Why? Because the United States must have a "victory-denying" response—"victory-denying" is typical of the fudging language customary in this field—to a Soviet effort to obtain victory in a limited nuclear war.

Notice: The whole idea is predicated on the assumption that the Soviets may seek some sort of nuclear superiority to obtain victory in a limited nuclear war—the same sort of war that is unlikely to stop short of an all-out exchange. After all this, Mr. Brown also tells us that "superiority is an idle goal." Yet without superiority, victory could not be obtained in a limited nuclear war and it would almost certainly escalate out of control. If Presidential Directive 59 follows Mr. Brown's exposition, it is a mishmash of contradictory premises and prescriptions.

After Brown came Caspar W. Weinberger, the [first] secretary of defense in the Reagan administration. Mr. Weinberger is another wholesale options merchant. He . . . offered the president one of the most treacherous options of all, though the idea may not have originated with him or his advisers. This option is the conduct of a protracted nuclear war in which the United States "must prevail" or out of which it must "emerge" with "terms favorable" to us. This policy was enshrined in a document entitled "Fiscal Year 1984–1988 Defense Guidance," issued in the spring of 1982, which had to be leaked in order for ordinary citizens to know about it.

Ironically, Mr. Weinberger . . . . indirectly criticized his own policy. The idea of a protracted or prolonged nuclear war is so indefensible that he tried to repudiate it in a letter sent to a number of US and foreign publications in August 1982. He also tried to repudiate the concept of a nuclear victory in a letter sent to me in July 1983. What seems to have happened is this: The policy of waging a protracted nuclear war and of prevailing in such a war has been adopted officially but disavowed publicly. The least that can be said of this two-tracked or two-faced policy is that it is a strange way of conducting serious business in a democracy.

Here is Mr. Weinberger on both sides of these issues:

For protracted nuclear war: US forces must be able to maintain "through a protracted conflict period and afterward, the capability to inflict very high levels of damage" on Soviet industry. Should a Soviet attack "nevertheless occur, United States nuclear capabilities must prevail under the condition of a prolonged war."

Against protracted nuclear war: "I am increasingly concerned with news accounts that portray this Administration as planning to wage protracted nuclear war, or seeking to acquire a nuclear 'war-fighting' capability. This is completely inaccurate. . . ."

For winning: ". . . United States nuclear capabilities must prevail. . . . earliest termination of hostilities on terms favorable to the United States"; . . . "to achieve political objectives and secure early war termination on terms favorable to the United States and its allies." "You show me a Secretary of Defense who's planning not to prevail and I'll show you a Secretary of Defense who ought to be impeached."

Against winning: ". . . we do not believe there could be any winners in a nuclear war"; ". . . [it is] our belief that there could be no winners in a nuclear war."

Finally, a still greater temptation has recently been put forward by influential nuclear war theorists. Like most temptations, nuclear or otherwise, there is nothing new or original about it; it merely pushes the temptation further than anyone has dared to do in the past. These tempters advocate the development of nuclear weapons that could attack targets so "precisely and discriminately" that they could safely be used against the enemy's weapons "without mass destruction." Their nuclear war would be something like a Ping-Pong game in which each side would "precisely and discriminately" drop its nuclear warheads on the other side's weapons. Since this scheme holds out the prospect of avoiding mass destruction, it is more tempting than the prospect of repeating the heavy civilian casualties and widespread destruction of the two conventional world wars in this century.

As I have tried to show, we have been through all this before. Targeting the enemy's weapons or military facilities may reduce civilian casualties at the outset, but these will still be so high—somewhere in the millions—that it is irresponsible and heartless to play around with the likelihood of avoiding mass destruction. The Soviets, at least, have clustered many of their nuclear weapons and installations in proximity to their cities, especially Moscow. There would be no way of adequately testing our precise and discriminating weapons, even if—someday—we should have them. There is no reason to believe that both sides would agree to use precise and discriminating weapons only, especially if one side should be put at a disadvantage in the development of such weapons. There is no reason to believe that either side would trust the other, even if they both agreed to use such weapons only. If those precise and discriminating weapons did not knock out all or most of the other side's nuclear weapons at once, retaliation could only take the form of a more indiscriminate counterattack. For one thing, the same type of weapon would no longer be available to both sides; for another, one side's precise and discriminating weapons would already have been shot off, thus no longer offering a useful target to the other.

Thus the technological cure is a form of the disease. It is actually a prescription for a potential first strike, the most dangerous of all nuclear temptations. It is interesting to note than an analysis was made in 1968 to determine the relative number of casualties in the event of a Soviet or an American first strike. The paradoxical result was a finding that there would be more American casualties in the case of an American first strike than in the case of a Soviet first strike. The paradox arose because it was figured that the side striking first would go after military targets, whereas the retaliating side would mainly hit cities. All of which suggests that this is not a subject for weak nerves or soft heads. . . .

But "what if deterrence fails?" This question is often asked, with an air of triumph, as if the possible failure of deterrence were a reason for rejecting it. Such an attitude is comparable to that of rejecting a life-support system in a hospital because it may fail or be inadequate to keep a mortally ill patient alive. Yet the possibility of failure does confront us with the fearful problem of what to do if some sort of nuclear war should break out. Toward the end of his life, Bernard Brodie gave [in 1978] the answer that the main goal should be "to terminate it as quickly as possible and with the least amount of damage possible—on both sides." That was the attitude of one who had thought that almost anything was better for mankind than total nuclear war. I have also been driven ineluctably to this conclusion, without, however, pretending to know how it will be possible to terminate a nuclear war with the least possible damage. Yet Brodie's view is infinitely preferable to [that of Colin S. Gray, *International Security* (Summer 1979)], which calls for a "Nuclear Strategy: The Case for a Theory of Victory" or of another [Robert Jastrow, in *Commentary* (March 1983)] which claims that the Soviet Union has found a theory of victory by way of nuclear "superiority."

To my mind, the obvious answer to the question "What if deterrence fails?" is that we do not know what will happen. We have no experience with the failure of nuclear deterrence, and without experience we have little or nothing to go by. Wars have been notoriously unpredictable, and nuclear wars must surely be the most unpredictable of all. We do not know how, where, by whom, or to what extent deterrence would fail. It would seem to be the most ordinary prudence and elementary common sense to make sure that we are not responsible for its failure, that we do whatever we must to limit the damage to ourselves and our allies, and to induce the other side to terminate the conflict as quickly as possible in its own interest. But all this is so far in the realm of the contingent and unpredictable that no one can be sure what such a war would be like or how the antagonists and the world at large could even survive it in recognizable condition. This very uncertainty is an element of deterrence. If it is any comfort, we know more about how to deter a nuclear war, judging from almost half a century of some sort of deterrence, than we know how to fight one.

I am, therefore, a believer in the lesser evil of nuclear deterrence. I believe in it because it is by far the lesser evil, not because it is good. The main enemy at present is not a nuclear balance that results in mutual deterrence; it is the propaganda about the feasibility of nuclear war by way of precise and discriminating weapons allegedly capable of avoiding mass destruction. The main reason nuclear weapons have not been used thus far is precisely the belief that they cannot be launched for any useful political purpose and that mutual mass destruction can be of no conceivable benefit to either side. But now the Pied Pipers of a protracted nuclear war and of precise and discriminating nuclear weapons are trying to lure us to break through the psychological and political barriers to nuclear war.

Lord Henry Wotton told Dorian Gray that the only way to get rid of a temptation is to yield to it. Clearly that would not do in this case. The only way for us to get rid of this temptation is to know it for what it is and to reject it precisely and discriminatingly.

"To use or not to use"—that is the "to be or not to be" of our time and for as long as we can now foresee.

2 NUCLEAR STRATEGY: WHAT IT IS AND IS NOT

William C. Martel and
Paul L. Savage

. . . As there is much to suggest that we often fail to distinguish between what is meant by policy and strategy, it is essential to differentiate between the two. In theory, a nuclear policy is that broad set of operational principles which represent how a nation will fight a nuclear war. A further distinction is in order. There is *declared* policy which symbolizes what the nation wants its adversary and its constituents to think it will do in a nuclear war. For obvious reasons, the declared policy may not reflect necessarily what the nation's policy actually is. By contrast (and exclusion), *real* policy is the plans for how the war actually will be fought. Again, it should be obvious that the real policy is a closely and jealously guarded secret of the state, usually classified as "code-word" information. For real policy to be effective, many argue that it should be kept as secret as possible, as an enemy's uncertainty about one's actual plans for war will foster a measure of security: The enemy never can know exactly what one will do or how effective such actions might be. This in encapsulated form is the traditional approach to nuclear policy. In recent years, at least since the advent of the nuclear age, a number of prominent civilian and military strategists have argued (correctly) that it is not entirely necessary to shroud nuclear policy in a cloud of absolute secrecy to deter a war. Some enemy knowledge about one's real policy, such as the intention of killing millions of civilians in retaliation for any nuclear attack, can have a healthy influence on stability and the potentially provocative and adventurous proclivities of the adversary. This, parenthetically, in abridged form is the case for assured destruction.

Thus, on a simplified level, nuclear policy, whether declared or real, signifies what one will do in a nuclear war. The much larger issue, which often is confused with policy, is nuclear strategy. Strategy is an explicit formulation of what, in this case, a nuclear war will do for the global interests of the state. This may sound paradoxical, for everyone knows (or should know) that a nuclear war can never be in the interests of any state at any time. The more manageable and practical way to express nuclear strategy is to ask how the *threat* of nuclear war can be used to further the interests of the state. . . . The paradox is that . . . the prospect of a nuclear war, or even the specter of the threat, is not an acceptable basis for nuclear policy or strategy. And

Note: Some footnotes have been deleted, and one has been renumbered to appear in appropriate order.

even for those civilian and military thinkers who can sidestep this emotional quandary, there remains an aversion to certain domains of nuclear policy or strategy on the grounds that some "theories" lead to more thinkable (i.e., plausible) scenarios of nuclear war, and thereby increase the probability of such an occurrence. When in the general populace there is such a deep and irreversible revulsion against the formulation of nuclear policy and strategy, and when in the intellectual circles there are deep fissures over the structure that nuclear policy ought to take, we have a prescription for disaster. The obvious and immediate result is that nuclear policy will not be a firm structure that is reinforced by a broad and bipartisan political consensus. An even more likely result is that nuclear policy will become (and remain) a vacillating and ephemeral structure, driven by the dictates of technology, and therefore characterized by the institutionalization of intermittent chaos, turbulence, and occasional reform.

. . . The gulf that separates not only the disparate intellectual schools of thought on nuclear policy, but also the public and establishment views on nuclear policy, could be the decisive explanation for the apparent vacillation in American nuclear policy. . . .

. . . On a contemporary scale, the issue is whether nuclear deterrence ought to be based on annihilatory retaliation or protracted war-fighting. How one views this debate will go a long way toward highlighting the ills of strategy formulation in the United States. And since we cannot deduce a policy without first knowing what the strategy is, this will serve to highlight the relationship between the two.

Fundamentally, US nuclear policy can be based either on the threat of retaliation against the population centers of the enemy, or the destruction of the military resources of the enemy. Each can contribute to stable deterrence as long as neither presents the threat of a credible first-strike capability. Yet, in terms of the debate over nuclear strategy the two positions never can be reconciled: The first sees deterrence as a function of certain civilian slaughter, while the second views deterrence as the ability to destroy nuclear forces. . . . A policy based on civilian slaughter has serious practical and ethical dilemmas associated with it and . . . a counterforce policy always appears destabilizing because it is virtually indistinguishable from a preemptive capability. . . .

The central issue, however, remains that in the midst of this systemic dispute over the aim of strategy, the United States has not the slightest hope of establishing a coherent nuclear policy, one that has the broad-based support not only of the defense establishment, but also the public, the Democratic and Republican parties, and the numerous interest groups, religious organizations, and political factions that typically display intense interest in nuclear issues. . . . Just as a coherent US foreign policy cannot emerge out of the Congress, a rational nuclear policy and all that is associated with it (weapons, organizations, and so forth) cannot flourish in such a fragmented environment. . . . More often than not, American nuclear policy is driven by technological imperatives rather than conceptual themes. And if it is clear that this reliance on technology is a well-entrenched phenomenon in the United States, the systemic problem is that it may not be as dominant in the Soviet Union, at least that it may not occur as frequently or with the same magnitude . . . . It [therefore] is essential to examine some of the dominant elements of nuclear policy as they relate to the evolution, whether progressive or regressive, of US nuclear policy.

NUCLEAR TARGETING: THE EXECUTION OF POLICY

Perhaps the most explicit form of nuclear policy is the targeting doctrine, which specifies the types of targets that are to be attacked and the effects thereof on both policy and strategy. . . . To the extent that nuclear policy is operationalized, it occurs when it is expressed as an explicit targeting doctrine. Just as it is not possible for nuclear policy to evolve out of an incoherent strategy, a coherent targeting doctrine cannot emerge *de novo* out of an ambiguous nuclear policy. In this "tree" of nuclear strategy, policy, and targeting, all of the errors will be magnified the farther one proceeds down the "branches" of the policy to the actual plans for war.

In the United States the ultimate targeting document is the SIOP (Single Integrated Operational Plan), which is a highly classified compendium of contingency plans for nuclear war. . . . On a simplified scale, the SIOP is composed of a variety of general options or "packages" for targeting in a nuclear war that encompass the spectrum of all conceivable options from counterforce to countervalue scenarios. Each targeting package, however, consists of hundreds of potential targets, that are designated to be attacked with specific weapons in the US arsenal. Perhaps the best way to conceptualize such a target plan is to picture a large matrix with thousands of cells, wherein each cell represents one discrete targeting option. If large numbers of cells are clustered into one package, one generates a set of targeting possibilities. So that the inherent flexibility of the SIOP is retained, each nuclear weapon on the launchers can be programmed to hit a variety of targets, and while a particular weapon will hit only one target, before launch the target can be selected from among a number of targets (perhaps as many as 99) stored as "target constants" in the memory of the launch center's targeting computer. Thus, the SIOP is a list of thousands of potential targets and a smaller number of target packages. In a nuclear war, the National Command Authorities (NCA) can select a particular option or package of options from the SIOP to suit the circumstances of the war.

All of this is, more or less, how it ought to be. The problem, however, arises in the types of targets that are incorporated in the American targeting plan. To understand how the confusion in policy affects targeting, let us [distinguish] between counterforce and countervalue targets. Ideally, one should select targets on the basis of their potential lethality. Counterforce sites such as silos, for instance, would be a logical choice because of the lethality of the ICBMs contained therein. Yet, in a constrained (i.e., realistic) environment of finite nuclear arsenals, the targets that are chosen must be within the targeting capabilities of the nuclear forces. In the case of the United States, the failure to shift from countervalue to counterforce capabilities translates into a SIOP that . . . appears to be dominated by urban-industrial targets. Simultaneously, however, the pressure to move in the direction of counterforce options has resulted in the illusion that much of the US ICBM force and segments of the SLBM and bomber forces are targeted against Soviet counterforce sites, despite the inherently self-disarming nature of the exercise. . . . While the countervalue option on a retaliatory level may be the most realistic option for the United States, there are signs that the arsenal is pointed in the direction of a counterforce first-strike attack in the event that a Soviet first-strike attack appears imminent. We should recall, first, that the United States consistently has disavowed a first-strike doctrine (just as have the Soviets), and second, that a counterforce first strike is an illusory option given that even under the most favorable of circumstances it would strain the American arsenal to its operational limit.

We can trace this revolution in US targeting to the tension between counterforce and countervalue options, and on a larger scale to the confusion in nuclear policy. In our view, this confusion is related to the tendency for nuclear policy to evolve in the direction of counterforce options. With considerable justification, many have opposed just this change for the simple and compelling reason that it destabilizes the nuclear balance. As true as that assertion may be, and frankly, we think that the charge . . . is correct, the concern is that there is a greater danger in a targeting policy that imagines counterforce to be a *realistic* option. In fact, such thinking pushes the United States in the direction of a first-strike doctrine that, worse yet, cannot be supported by the capabilities of the arsenal.

If we confine ourselves to the operational desiderata of the first strike, there are enormous difficulties for the United States. . . . A first-strike attack against the USSR's counterforce targets would disarm the United States without the expectation that the Soviet Union would find all of its arsenal destroyed. Looking beyond the operational to the political issues of a first strike, this trend, at least in the United States, can create immense political problems. If, as the result of the untenable assumptions about the countervalue nature of nuclear war, the United States finds itself without adequate counterforce capabilities (relative to the Soviet target complex), and the possibility of a first-strike doctrine, it is not surprising if the political consensus on nuclear policy continues to evaporate. Perhaps it is the failure to differentiate between a counterforce and a first-strike policy (for the two are quite distinct) that accounts for the turbulence in American nuclear policy.

In any event, we find that the first element of a nuclear policy is how one plans to use nuclear weapons against specific targets. In our view, the United States now finds itself in the position of possessing a dominantly countervalue posture with only limited counterforce capabilities, that is governed by an incoherent policy. However, to the extent that there are some evolutionary forces at play in policy, it appears to be in the direction of a first-strike doctrine, for reasons that are clear. First, the countervalue option is seen as incredible because it guarantees a similar response by the Soviets. Second, the existing Soviet arsenal threatens the US nuclear arsenal with nearly complete destruction in a preemptive attack. And, it is as unacceptable to lose US nuclear forces by riding out the attack as it is to depend on an essentially countervalue response. In effect, the vulnerability of American forces is as unacceptable as urban-industrial targeting. Third, the only solution to this dilemma is the adoption of a *crisis* first-strike doctrine that may be either preemptive or responsive (moments after one detects a Soviet launch). Thus, we believe that the disintegration of nuclear policy and the resultant instability in deterrence are attributable to the inability of the United States to coordinate advances in weaponry with the evolution of policy, as well as to the rapid development of Soviet counterforce capabilities. While there are different causes for this turmoil, the effect is the same.

DEPLOYMENT OF NUCLEAR WEAPONS

The second significant dimension of nuclear policy is the weapons that are deployed. More than words or innuendos, weapons provide the clearest indication of what one's policy is, and what it must be. Just as a counterforce policy makes no sense if the arsenal has predominantly countervalue capabilities, a countervalue policy makes no sense if one has the weapons to support a counterforce policy. . . . Beyond this quite obvious, although often forgotten, dictum of military policy, it remains to be seen how a nation, in this case the United States, structures its nuclear forces. Here, we will focus on . . . [two] critical elements of deployment that affect the viability and coherence of nuclear policy: the weapons, [and] how the weapons are based. . . .

Weapons

Fundamentally, a nuclear policy involves either counterforce or countervalue options, and operates on a preemptive or a retaliatory basis. In our view, the nuclear policy of the United States has shifted . . . to predominantly counterforce options (despite the paucity of true counterforce-capable weapons), and simultaneously from a retaliatory to a preemptive doctrine. In the latter case, this is the result of the vulnerability of US land-based forces and the shift to a counterforce capability that creates pressures to use the force against Soviet targets before the Soviets have the chance to do the same. We emphasize that none of this applies in day-to-day affairs, but only in a full-blown political or military crisis, wherein the use of nuclear weapons might become a realistic option. If we consider how radical this shift is, particularly in view of the political significance of the emergence of a first-strike doctrine in a polity that tacitly forswears such a policy, then it is necessary to reflect on the factors that influenced this gradual evolution. . . . [The] force of technology and the incessant influence of the Soviet Union, in conjunction with a policy that was losing political and intellectual support among specialists and non-specialists alike, were the twin vectors of strategic decay.

On a different level, the deployment of the new weapons such as MX, Trident, Midgetman, B-1, and cruise missiles, which are being or will be introduced into the American nuclear arsenal, clearly do not have the broad-based consensus that a coherent and credible policy requires. Again, despite the clear symptoms of dissent that manifest themselves within the groups that define nuclear policy, the United States is forging ahead with weapons that do not have a firmly established place in American policy or strategy. Rather than having a conceptual framework, we have deferred to our technological infrastructure for a solution to the problem of "where do we go in nuclear policy." One example is the bomber force: Aside from the perennial Air Force argument that the bomber force is the *sine qua non* of stable deterrence because it complicates Soviet first-strike calculations, the driving question really is whether it still makes sense to spend billions of dollars on the (questionable) ability of bombers to penetrate Soviet airspace. Is this still practical in the age of ballistic missiles?

An entirely different issue concerns the deployment of weapons that have a hard-target kill capability. Is it sensible to deploy a handful of MX or Midgetman ICBMs in light of the fact that the Trident SLBM will be as effective as the ICBMs in terms of hard-target kill, as well as more survivable than the ICBMs? An even more important question is the structure of American targeting policy, for only after resolving what it is that we seek to do can we properly acquire weapons. Thus, there is no acceptable answer as to whether the United States ought to deploy Trident, with or without MX, until we have settled what US nuclear policy ought to be. And if that does not happen, the United States will continue to deploy an arsenal that does not have a clear and rational foundation in nuclear policy.

Basing

The function of basing in nuclear policy is to provide the most survivable and enduring weapons possible. If this objective can be achieved, the United States thereby gains the assurance that it can follow its targeting plans without the fear of losing its forces in a preemptive attack. To date, we believe that the United States has failed completely in the selection of *ICBM, bomber, and command post* basing options that will preserve the force against most (but clearly not all) *reasonable* threats. For many, a rational basing mode is one that protects the force, or a component of the force, against all conceivable nuclear or conventional attacks. In the narrow sense of ensuring that the largest possible number of forces will survive an attack, this definition of an acceptable basing mode is as appropriate as it is logical, for basing certainly must address the survivability of the missile in the silo or the bomber at the base. But once we step beyond this rather simplistic requirement for basing, we suggest that the basing mode for strategic forces has an equal, if not larger, function in nuclear policy. We propose a more comprehensive definition of basing that includes the concept, which is hardly novel, of "national vulnerability." It is the vulnerability of the nation, in particular its people, industry, and resources, to the direct and indirect effects of a nuclear attack that should be a dominant factor in the selection of basing modes.

It certainly is important that a basing system protect nuclear forces, so that the forces may survive to threaten retaliation against the attacker. Suppose, however, that some basing modes increased the vulnerability of the urban population to damage as a function of their proximity to the base. . . . Civilian losses [can be] expected to occur as the result of post-attack radioactive fallout, near misses, and outright guidance system failures. Such losses [will be] measured in the *tens* of millions in "pure" counterforce attacks against both the United States and the Soviet Union. By far one of the larger concerns . . . [is] that these unintentional, but nonetheless real, losses might compel the victim(s) to escalate to assaults on urban targets in order to balance civilian losses, thus shifting a nuclear war from a limited exchange to unrestrained urban annihilation. All this could happen because of the decision to locate nuclear forces near or upwind of major urban centers. From the perspective of policy or strategy, basing decisions of this sort hardly could be said to exemplify foresight, rationality, or coherent strategic planning. Thus, what we must address are the elements of basing that properly constitute part of a rational and coherent nuclear policy. By definition, a nuclear policy that falls short in this most critical area must be dismissed as an abject failure and an utter negation of what a real policy is all about. . . .

SIGNS OF CONVERGENCE

In the 1960s two eminent political scientists raised the possibility that despite the severe polarization of the American and Soviet ideological systems, the systemic and plausibly acultural forces of technology, economics and bureaucracy could lead to a convergence of the two systems. More than a *rapprochement* or détente and less than outright reconciliation, Brzezinski and Huntington wondered whether the two deadly superpowers someday might find that infrastructural forces had led to a convergence.[1] Here many of their significant differences would be submerged beneath the necessities of existence in a world where technological, economic, and bureaucratic factors are more important than ideologies. . . .

. . . There are signs that the United States and the Soviet Union are converging in several critical areas of nuclear policy. This in itself is not remarkable. What is extraordinary is the degree to which the nuclear policies

3 MAD versus NUTS: CAN DOCTRINE OR WEAPONRY REMEDY THE MUTUAL HOSTAGE RELATIONSHIP OF THE SUPERPOWERS?

Spurgeon M. Keeny, Jr., and
Wolfgang K. H. Panofsky

Since World War II there has been a continuing debate on military doctrine concerning the actual utility of nuclear weapons in war. This debate, irrespective of the merits of the divergent points of view, tends to create the perception that the outcome and scale of a nuclear conflict could be controlled by the doctrine or the types of nuclear weapons employed. Is this the case?

We believe not. In reality, the unprecedented risks of nuclear conflict are largely independent of doctrine or its application. The principal danger of doctrines that are directed at limiting nuclear conflicts is that they might be believed and form the basis for action without appreciation of the physical facts and uncertainties of nuclear conflict. The failure of policymakers to understand the truly revolutionary nature of nuclear weapons as instruments of war and the staggering size of the nuclear stockpiles of the United States and the Soviet Union could have catastrophic consequences for the entire world.

Military planners and strategic thinkers for [40] years have sought ways to apply the tremendous power of nuclear weapons against target systems that might contribute to the winning of a future war. In fact, as long as the United States held a virtual nuclear monopoly, the targeting of atomic weapons was looked upon essentially as a more effective extension of the strategic bombing concepts of World War II. With the advent in the mid-1950s of a substantial Soviet nuclear capability, including multimegaton thermonuclear weapons, it was soon apparent that the populations and societies of both the United States and the Soviet Union were mutual hostages. A portion of the nuclear stockpile of either side could inflict on the other as many as 100 million fatalities and destroy it as a functioning society. Thus, although the rhetoric of declaratory strategic doctrine has changed over the years, mutual deter-

Note: Some footnotes have been deleted, and the others have been renumbered to appear in appropriate order.

rence has in fact remained the central fact of the strategic relationship of the two superpowers and of the NATO and Warsaw Pact alliances.

Most observers would agree that a major conflict between the two hostile blocs on a worldwide scale during this period may well have been prevented by the specter of catastrophic nuclear war. At the same time, few would argue that this state of mutual deterrence is a very reassuring foundation on which to build world peace. In the 1960s the perception of the basic strategic relationship of mutual deterrence came to be characterized as "Mutual Assured Destruction," which critics were quick to note had the acronym of MAD. The notion of MAD has been frequently attacked not only as militarily unacceptable but also as immoral since it holds the entire civilian populations of both countries as hostages.[1]

As an alternative to MAD, critics and strategic innovators have over the years sought to develop various war-fighting targeting doctrines that would somehow retain the use of nuclear weapons on the battlefield or even in controlled strategic war scenarios, while sparing the general civilian population from the devastating consequences of nuclear war. Other critics have found an alternative in a defense-oriented military posture designed to defend the civilian population against the consequences of nuclear war.

These concepts are clearly interrelated since such a defense-oriented strategy would also make a nuclear war-fighting doctrine more credible. But both alternatives depend on the solution of staggering technical problems. A defense-oriented military posture requires a nearly impenetrable air and missile defense over a large portion of the population. And any attempt to have a controlled war-fighting capability during a nuclear exchange places tremendous requirements not only on decisions made under incredible pressure by men in senior positions of responsibility but on the technical performance of command, control, communications and intelligence functions—called in professional circles "C^3I". . . . It is not sufficient as the basis for defense policy to assert that science will "somehow" find solutions to critical technical problems on which the policy is dependent, when technical solutions are nowhere in sight.

In considering these doctrinal issues, it should be recognized that there tends to be a very major gap between declaratory policy and actual implementation expressed as targeting doctrine. Whatever the declaratory policy might be, those responsible for the strategic forces must generate real target lists and develop procedures under which various combinations of targets could be attacked. In consequence, the perceived need to attack every listed target, even after absorbing the worst imaginable first strike from the adversary, creates procurement "requirements," even though the military or economic importance of many of the targets is small.

In fact, it is not at all clear in the real world of war planning whether declaratory doctrine has generated requirements or whether the availability of weapons for targeting has created doctrine. With an estimated 30,000 warheads at the disposal of the United States, including more than 10,000 avowed to be strategic in character, it is necessary to target redundantly all urban areas and economic targets and to cover a wide range of military targets in order to frame uses for the stockpile. And, once one tries to deal with elusive mobile and secondary military targets, one can always make a case for requirements for more weapons and for more specialized weapon designs.

These doctrinal considerations, combined with the superabundance of nuclear weapons, have led to a conceptual approach to nuclear war which can be described as Nuclear Utilization Target Selection. For convenience, and not in any spirit of trading epithets, we have chosen the acronym of NUTS to characterize the various doctrines that seek to utilize nuclear weapons against specific targets in a complex of nuclear war-fighting situations intended to be limited, as well as the management over an extended period of a general nuclear war between the superpowers.[2]

While some elements of NUTS may be involved in extending the credibility of our nuclear deterrent, this consideration in no way changes the fact that mutual assured destruction, or MAD, is inherent in the existence of large numbers of nuclear weapons in the real world. In promulgating the doctrine of "countervailing strategy" in the summer of 1980, President Carter's Secretary of Defense Harold Brown called for a buildup of nuclear war-fighting capability in order to provide greater deterrence by demonstrating the ability of the United States to respond in a credible fashion without having to escalate immediately to all-out nuclear war. He was very careful, however, to note that he thought that it was "very likely" that the use of nuclear weapons by the superpowers at any level would escalate into general nuclear war.[3] This situation is not peculiar to present force structures or technologies; and, regardless of future technical developments, it will persist as long as substantial nuclear weapon stockpiles remain.

Despite its possible contribution to the deterrence of nuclear war, the NUTS approach to military doctrine and planning can very easily become a serious danger in itself. The availability of increasing numbers of nuclear weapons in a variety of designs and delivery packages at all levels of the military establishment inevitably encourages the illusion that somehow nuclear weapons can be applied in selected circumstances without unleashing a catastrophic series of consequences. . . . [T]he recent uninformed debate on the virtue of the so-called neutron bomb as a selective device to deal with tank attacks is a depressing case in point. NUTS creates its own endless pressure for expanded nuclear stockpiles with increasing danger of accidents, accidental use, diversions to terrorists, etc. But more fundamentally, it tends to obscure the fact that the nuclear world is in fact MAD.

The NUTS approach to nuclear war-fighting will not eliminate the essential MAD character of nuclear war for two basic reasons, which are rooted in the nature of nuclear weapons and the practical limits of technology. First, the destructive power of nuclear weapons, individually and most certainly in the large numbers discussed for even specialized application, is so great that the collateral effects on persons and property would be enormous and, in scenarios which are seriously discussed, would be hard to distinguish from the onset of general nuclear war. But more fundamentally, it does not seem possible, even in the most specialized utilization of nuclear weapons, to envisage any situation where escalation to general nuclear war would probably not occur given the dynamics of the situation and the limits of the control mechanisms that could be made available to manage a limited nuclear war. In the case of a protracted general nuclear war, the control problem becomes completely unmanageable. Finally, there does not appear to be any prospect for the foreseeable future that technology will provide a secure shield behind which the citizens of the two superpowers can safely observe the course of a limited nuclear war on other people's territory. . . .

[The authors continue with a discussion of the horrendous consequences of a nuclear war, consequences that point to the conclusions that a nuclear war would be devastating and that each of the two superpowers is inescapably vulnerable to the capacity of the other to destroy it—regardless of who launches the first missile. They then critique the views of those who support the concept of a nuclear war-fighting capability, and especially those advocating the development of theater nuclear forces (TNF) and the associated doctrine that a nuclear war can remain limited. Contending, finally, that the protection of populations against large-scale attack is impossible, they are driven to the conclusion that nuclear utilization theory is indeed NUTs— that it cannot succeed without imperiling civilization as we know it—*eds.*]

. . . [We] are fated to live in a MAD world. This is inherent in the tremendous power of nuclear weapons, the size of nuclear stockpiles, the collateral damage associated with the use of nuclear weapons against military targets, the technical limitations on strategic area defense, and the uncertainties involved in efforts to control the escalation of nuclear war. There is no reason to believe that this situation will change for the foreseeable future since the problem is far too profound and the pace of technical military development far too slow to overcome the fundamental technical considerations that underlie the mutual hostage relationship of the superpowers.

What is clear above all is that the profusion of proposed NUTS approaches has not offered an escape from the MAD world, but rather constitutes a major danger in encouraging the illusion that limited or controlled nuclear war can be waged free from the grim realities of a MAD world. The principal hope at this time will not be found in seeking NUTS doctrines that ignore the MAD realities but rather in recognizing the nuclear world for what it is and seeking to make it more stable and less dangerous.

NOTES

1. See, for example, Fred Charles Iklé, "Can Nuclear Deterrence Last Out the Century?" *Foreign Affairs,* January 1973, pp. 267–85.
2. The acronym NUT for Nuclear Utilization Theory was used by Howard Margolis and Jack Ruina, "SALT II: Notes on Shadow and Substance," *Technology Review,* October 1979, pp. 31–41. We prefer Nuclear Utilization Target Selection, which relates the line of thinking more

closely to the operational problem of target selection. Readers not familiar with colloquial American usage may need to be told that "nuts" is an adjective meaning "crazy or demented." For everyday purposes it is a synonym for "mad."

3. See Harold Brown, Speech at the Naval War College, August 20, 1980, the most authoritative public statement on the significance of Presidential Directive 59, which had been approved by President Carter shortly before.

4 NUCLEAR STRATEGY AND THE CHALLENGE OF PEACE: THE MORAL EVALUATION OF DETERRENCE IN LIGHT OF POLICY DEVELOPMENTS, 1983–1988

The National Conference of Catholic Bishops

. . . The particular theme which *The Challenge of Peace* [the U.S. bishops' pastoral letter of 1983] focused upon and to which we return in this Report is the unique dangers posed by the nuclear arsenals. The uniqueness arises from the scope and degree of devastation these weapons can wreak. In the nuclear debate of the 1980s the kind of destruction which the arsenals of the superpowers can cause has been brought home to the public with new urgency and great specificity. Rather than repeat these statistics and predictions here, it is more pertinent to state the widely shared conclusion which flows from an understanding of the meaning of nuclear war; nuclear war remains a possibility, but it is increasingly seen as devoid of the rational political purpose and moral limits which have made war a justifiable activity in the past. Nuclear weapons threaten to destroy the very objectives which once provided the political and moral justification for using force. . . .

It is easier to draw this conclusion than it is to pursue its consequences. For living in the nuclear age means that we can condemn nuclear war, but we will still have to live with nuclear weapons. There are several dimensions to the nuclear dilemma: the scientific community unlocked the mystery of nuclear power—we will never return to an age when the knowledge of how to build nuclear weapons is absent; military strategists are commanded to prepare for nuclear war, but to do so in a fashion which reduces the possibilities that it will ever occur; political leaders threaten to resort to nuclear weapons if necessary, and simultaneously proclaim that their use is unthinkable; the general public fluctuates between moments of great fear of nuclear holocaust, great hope that negotiations will solve the nuclear dilemma and the normal instinct of suppressing any thought about this perplexing and frightening reality. . . .

Note: Footnotes have been deleted.

This Report is designed to continue the quest for a world rid of the nuclear danger and to continue the process of defining the political and moral direction which should guide national policy and personal choice in the nuclear age. . . .

. . . The Report is divided into three sections: (1) a review of the moral teaching of *The Challenge of Peace*; (2) an assessment of certain policy developments related to the teaching of the pastoral letter; and (3) a judgment on the moral status of deterrence in [1988].

I. THE CHALLENGE OF PEACE: A SUMMARY STATEMENT

The distinctive characteristic of *The Challenge of Peace* is that it is a religious-moral evaluation of the political, strategic and technological dimensions of the nuclear age. . . .

. . . The classical tradition of legitimating and limiting the use of force confronts the reality of the nuclear revolution. This confrontation was dramatically symbolized in John Paul II's statement at Hiroshima in 1982: "In the past it was possible to destroy a village, a town, a region, even a country. Now it is the whole planet that has come under threat." This assessment, specifying the qualitatively new destructive potential introduced by nuclear weapons, served as a premise of the more detailed analysis of the pastoral letter. . . .

. . . The policy section had three components: moral evaluation of the *use* of nuclear weapons, the strategy of *deterrence,* and then a set of policy *prescriptions.*

A. Use of Nuclear Weapons

The Challenge of Peace made three distinct judgments on the use of nuclear weapons. The judgments comprise a spectrum, moving from absolute prohibition through a prudential proscription to a presumption against use.

The absolute prohibition is the pastoral letter's categorical rejection of counter-city or counter-civilian bombing of any kind: "Under no circumstances may nuclear weapons or other instruments of mass slaughter be used for the purpose of destroying population centers or other predominantly civilian targets.". . .

A different kind of moral judgment is rendered on the initiation of nuclear war. The absolute categorical character of the first case is replaced by a complex form of reasoning blending moral principles with empirical assessments of the chances of escalation, the possibilities of limiting the effects of using nuclear weapons and the degree of risk involved in taking the world into the nuclear arena. The conclusion of this process of evaluation is the judgment that: "We do not perceive any situation in which the deliberate initiation of nuclear warfare, on however restricted a scale, can be morally justified." This "no first use" conclusion is joined with a broader theme of the pastoral: "We seek to reinforce the barrier against any use of nuclear weapons.". . .

The third case of use, retaliatory (or second) use in a "limited exchange," typically refers to the kind of nuclear war-fighting envisioned in Central Europe. Here the pastoral letter is less categorical than its opposition to civilian bombing and it is less clear than its opposition to first use. The basic argument of this section is to establish a presumption against second use by raising a series of questions about the possibility of limiting the effects of nuclear weapons. The presumption is not a prohibition; the effect of the presumption, however, is to place the burden of proof on those who assert that "limited use" is politically and morally possible. The logic of the letter is to make the burden of proof a very heavy one. Essentially, the "just-war" or "limited war" ethic asserts that one should have moral certainty that weapons to be used can be employed within the limits of the twin moral principles of discrimination and proportionality.

The questions raised about the possibilities of maintaining a "limited use" of nuclear weapons highlight the multiple pressures which make limitation very unlikely. The dynamic of technological warfare, the normal range of human error, the lack of experience with nuclear war-fighting which all powers fortunately share, all create a tone of radical skepticism in *The Challenge of Peace* about the language of limited war as applied to nuclear conflict. . . .

Nonetheless, at the conclusion of its assessment of nuclear use, *The Challenge of Peace* has neither advocated any form of use nor has it condemned every conceivable use of nuclear weapons *a priori*. There is in the letter a narrow margin where use has been considered, not condemned but hardly commended. From this narrow margin the pastoral moves to an evaluation of deterrence.

B. The Strategy of Deterrence

The Challenge of Peace based its evaluation of deterrence on the just-war ethic. . . . The letter examined theories of deterrence, the arguments about nuclear "war-fighting" as a strategy and the debate which has surrounded plans for nuclear targeting. Without repeating the full argument here we call attention to the detailed assessment of these questions found in . . . *The Challenge of Peace*.

The "dilemma of deterrence" . . . is the problem of how to sustain a credible deterrent (to prevent nuclear attack while refraining from any intent to target civilians or to violate the limits of proportionality). Anyone who has tried theoretically or practically to reconcile these objectives knows the inherent tension between them. In *The Challenge of Peace* we acknowledged the need for a deterrence strategy but also asserted that "not all forms of deterrence are morally acceptable" . . . .

The principal limit defining a justifiable deterrent is the prohibition against directly targeting or striking civilians. The pastoral letter asserts the prohibition, which we reaffirm here. . . .

The second limit placed on justifiable deterrence is the principle of proportionality. It is particularly needed to address two questions analyzed in the pastoral letter. The first is the damage done by attacks on "military or industrial" targets located near civilian centers. Second is the damage envisioned in various forms of nuclear war-fighting strategies.

The first problem is inherent in the existing deterrence strategies of both superpowers, since each targets the industrial capacity of the other. There will inevitably be continuing arguments about what constitutes a "proportionate threat" to deter or what is "proportionate damage," but we remain convinced that "there are actions which can be decisively judged to be disproportionate. A narrow adherence exclusively to the principle of noncombatant immunity as a criterion for policy is an inadequate moral posture for it ignores some evil and unacceptable consequences. Hence, we cannot be satisfied that the assertion of an intention not to strike civilians directly, or even the most honest effort to implement that intention, by itself constitutes a 'moral policy' for the use of nuclear weapons."

The second problem, war-fighting strategies, arises from the quest for a coherent connection between "deterrence and use" policies, and from the search for "discriminate deterrence.". . . The "dilemma of deterrence" is not ameliorated by notions that nuclear weapons are "normal," "controlled" instruments of military policy. The logic of the pastoral letter, reasserted here, is to build a barrier against nuclear use, and to confine the role of deterrence to "the specific objective of preventing the use of nuclear [weapons]."

The conclusion of *The Challenge of Peace* on deterrence . . . deserves repetition here: "These considerations of concrete elements of nuclear deterrence policy, made in light of John Paul II's evaluation, but applying it through our own prudential judgments, lead us to a strictly conditioned moral acceptance of nuclear deterrence. We cannot consider it adequate as a long-term basis for peace. . . .

The "strict conditions" which the pastoral imposed on deterrence involved two kinds of restraints. The first involved a "temporal" dimension; in the language of the pastoral, deterrence is not a "long-term" answer to the nuclear question. . . .

The "temporal condition" contained in *The Challenge of Peace* is an attempt to reflect and specify the meaning of the papal dictum that deterrence should be seen as part of a complex process leading to a new political relationship. In this sense the temporal condition is meant to test "the direction" of the deterrence relationship and the policies which sustain it. . . .

The second condition placed on deterrence policy by the pastoral letter is designed to test the "character" or the "component elements" of the deterrent. The test applied is rooted in moral categories, using the principles of proportionality, noncombatant immunity, last resort and the risks implied in different forms of deterrence policy. Testing the character of weapons, forms of deployment and declaratory policy in this way corresponds to the classical concerns of arms control, which stress less the numbers of weapons in the deterrence relationship than the impact certain weapons have on the stability of the nuclear balance. . . .

C. Criteria and Conditions for Policy Evaluation

These criteria and conditions should be used together as a framework for assessing several aspects of nuclear strategy.

1. CRITERIA FOR CONDITIONAL ACCEPTANCE OF DETERRENCE . . .

a. If nuclear deterrence exists only to prevent the *use* of nuclear weapons by others, then proposals to go beyond this to planning for prolonged periods of repeated nuclear strikes and counterstrikes, or "prevailing" in nuclear war, are not acceptable. They encourage notions that nuclear war can be engaged in with tolerable human and moral consequences. Rather, we must continually say "no" to the idea of nuclear war.

b. If nuclear deterrence is our goal, "sufficiency" to deter is an adequate strategy; the quest for nuclear superiority must be rejected.

c. Nuclear deterrence should be used as a step on the way toward progressive disarmament. Each proposed addition to our strategic system or change in strategic doctrine must be assessed precisely in light of whether it will render steps toward "progressive disarmament" more or less likely.

2. CONDITIONS FOR CONDITIONAL ACCEPTANCE OF DETERRENCE . . .

In light of the criteria we opposed the following proposals:

a. The addition of weapons which are likely to be vulnerable to attack, yet also possess a "prompt hard-target kill" capability that threatens to make the other side's retaliatory forces vulnerable. Such weapons may seem to be useful primarily in a first strike; we resist such weapons for this reason and we oppose Soviet deployment of such weapons which generate fear of a first strike against U.S. forces.

b. The willingness to foster strategic planning which seeks a nuclear war-fighting capability that goes beyond the limited function of deterrence outlined in this letter.

c. Proposals which have the effect of lowering the nuclear threshold and blurring the difference between nuclear and conventional weapons.

In support of the concept of "sufficiency" as an adequate deterrent, and in light of the existing size and composition of both the U.S. and Soviet strategic arsenals, we recommended:

a. Support for immediate, bilateral, verifiable agreements to halt the testing, production, and deployment of new nuclear weapons systems.

b. Support for negotiated bilateral deep cuts in the arsenals of both superpowers, particularly those weapons systems which have destabilizing characteristics.

c. Support for early and successful conclusion of negotiations of a comprehensive test ban treaty.

d. Removal by all parties of short-range nuclear weapons which multiply dangers disproportionate to their deterrent value.

e. Removal by all parties of nuclear weapons from areas where they are likely to be overrun in the early stages of war, thus forcing rapid and uncontrollable decisions on their use.

f. Strengthening of command and control over nuclear weapons to prevent inadvertent and unauthorized use. . . .

The application and refinement of these criteria and conditions to a range of policy questions is the task of the rest of this Report. . . .

II. POLICY DEVELOPMENTS: ASSESSMENT AND RECOMMENDATIONS

Three areas of nuclear policy are directly relevant to the conditions set by *The Challenge of Peace:* (1) the politics and strategy of arms control policy; (2) technological developments and the arms race; and (3) the economic impact of defense spending.

A. Arms Control Policy

Arms control is fundamentally a political process which Catholic teaching sees as a step toward disarmament. Arms control should be viewed, therefore, in light of the political relationship which has prevailed between the superpowers, and the new opportunity . . . which presents fundamental choices to the Soviet Union and the United States.

The new opportunity, even if utilized, should not be expected to dissipate or dissolve the basic realities of U.S.-Soviet relations. . . . [The] two nations are divided by history, philosophy, polity and conflicting interests. . . . Arms control can be a catalyst to an improved political relationship; and changes in the political context of superpower relations can open the road to new steps in controlling weaponry. This reciprocal relationship of politics and strategy means, in part, that a failure to move forward on the arms control front will very likely make progress in other areas of U.S.-Soviet relations more difficult.

Essentially the task of testing the new opportunity in superpower relations will require both political vision and strategic wisdom. The latter is needed to restrain the nuclear competition and to reduce its component elements. The former is required to set limits on the political competition which will be in the interests of the major powers, but will also decrease the hold of bipolar politics on others in the international community.

Turning specifically to arms control, . . . the following developments stand out:

1. THE INF TREATY. The INF Treaty, signed by Mr. Reagan and Mr. Gorbachev on December 8, 1987, represents the first bilateral arms control accomplishment since the SALT I Treaty (1972). The treaty provides for abolition of two classes of nuclear delivery systems (Intermediate-Range and Shorter-Range missiles). Although these weapons constitute a small percentage of the strategic arsenals of the superpowers, the dual significance of reconstituting the arms control process with a treaty and of achieving actual reductions in nuclear weaponry constitute steps in accord with the criteria of *The Challenge of Peace*.

The INF Treaty, in the view of its supporters and its critics, inevitably points beyond itself to other larger arms control questions. . . .

2. THE NUCLEAR AND SPACE TALKS (NST). The negotiations on strategic forces and space-based defenses are the next step beyond the INF Treaty. In line with the criteria of *The Challenge of Peace*, we support the "deep cuts" formula (1600 launchers and 6000 warheads) which is being used in these negotiations. We welcome these proposed reductions even while noting the accepted fact that the *kinds* of weapons which are constrained or reduced are the more important criterion than the *number* reduced. In the NST, there are important quantitative (number) and qualitative (kind) reductions which are being negotiated. These negotiations deserve and have our strong support.

3. EXISTING TREATIES. While NST proceed, we find it imprudent and counterproductive to erode or dismantle fragile restraints on an arms competition vigorously in progress. Hence, we support maintaining the limits established in the SALT I–ABM Treaty on defensive systems and we oppose the U.S. decision not to abide by the SALT II limits on offensive forces. Finally, we reaffirm the recommendation of the 1983 pastoral that negotiation should be vigorously pursued on a comprehensive test ban treaty.

4. NEW DEPLOYMENTS. The INF Treaty and the NST must be seen within the context of other developments in the 1980s. Even as the superpowers have carried on nuclear negotiations, they have also proceeded with nuclear modernization programs (i.e., the development of new weapons) which are the product of decisions taken in the 1970s and early 1980s. Since the 1970s, the Soviet Union has deployed four new strategic systems and several thousand warheads. The United States is carrying forward new deployments on every leg of the strategic triad (land-based missiles-ICBMs; submarine launched missiles-SLBMs; and bombers). Both the Soviet Union and the

United States, therefore, are deploying weapons which, in both number and kind, run contrary to the conditions of *The Challenge of Peace*. . . .

5. INDEPENDENT INITIATIVES. During the 1980s both the United States and the Soviet Union have taken steps which fit the category of "independent initiatives" found in *The Challenge of Peace,* but in each case the initiative was not reciprocated. The NATO alliance made decisions in 1980 and again in 1983 to withdraw a total of 2,400 battlefield nuclear weapons from the European theatre.

In August 1985 the Soviet Union announced a unilateral moratorium on nuclear testing which it extended through 1986; the Soviets have now resumed nuclear testing. . . .

This assessment of certain major trends in superpower relations does not capture all the pertinent dimensions of the arms control picture. Two major areas which will have an increasing importance in the 1990s are conventional arms control and non-proliferation policies. The legitimate concern paid to the unique qualities of the nuclear danger should not distract needed attention from the control of conventional armaments. This is a global problem, going far beyond the bounds of direct superpower relations and beyond the interaction of the NATO and Warsaw Pacts. . . .

In the East-West framework the relationship between nuclear and conventional arms control will be increasingly important. Precisely if it is possible to proceed with "deep cuts" of 30–50% in strategic arsenals, will the need to evaluate a corresponding move on the conventional front become clear. In *The Challenge of Peace* we said that our emphasis on controlling the nuclear arms race was not intended to make the world safe for conventional war. To address this concern, the future of arms control negotiations will have to pay greater attention to relating progress on the nuclear front to steps on conventional arms control. . . .

The second neglected area of the 1980s has been the problem of nuclear proliferation. Since the Non-Proliferation Treaty (NPT) came into force (1970) a framework for controlling the proliferation of nuclear weapons has existed. The non-proliferation negotiations and the non-proliferation order established by the treaty essentially constituted a compact between the major nuclear states and the non-nuclear powers. Essential to the compact was the commitment of the superpowers to restrain and reverse the "vertical" arms race in return for a pledge from non-nuclear states to refrain from "horizontal" proliferation.

In 1995 the NPT is due for renewal; it is clear that several key non-nuclear states are dissatisfied with the present regime and the role of the nuclear powers in it. This is not the only, or perhaps not even the principal threat to non-proliferation. Local and regional problems may in the final analysis be the decisive determinant in a proliferation decision. But the status of the compact on vertical and horizontal proliferation is directly under the control of the Soviet Union and the United States. The imperative to renew progress on arms control before the NPT is due for renewal is a primary consideration in the arms control picture.

Finally, the assessment of specific aspects of U.S.-Soviet policies on arms control does not adequately convey the critical character of the present moment. In *The Challenge of Peace* we noted that one of the distinguishing elements of the nuclear age is that we cannot afford one serious mistake. The consequences would be catastrophic—probably beyond our capacity to imagine. In the United States we have known the fear generated by Three Mile Island and the Soviet and European populations have experienced the reality of Chernobyl, but these events are mere shadows compared to the devastation and terror which even a "limited" nuclear exchange would produce.

The nuclear debate of the 1980s has resulted in a higher level of public sensitivity to the fragile hold we have on our common nuclear future and an increased awareness of the moral dangers of the nuclear age. Even those in the expert community who stress that deterrence is "robust" or "stable," acknowledge that we cannot simply presume that deterrence which "has worked" for forty years will surely continue "to work." The possibilities of technical accident, human miscalculation or diplomatic crisis—taken singly or together—pose permanent threats to the system which the superpowers now rely upon for "security."

These possibilities of failure exist in the very nature of nuclear deterrence. The more troubling fact is that recent trends in the character of weapons being deployed accentuate the dangers of deterrence. Large, MIRVed, very accurate missiles, often deployed as vulnerable targets, tilt the nuclear balance toward a preemptive posture on both sides. In the technical literature on the nuclear balance, analysts of quite different policy persuasions agree that present trends are not conducive to deterrence stability. From this analysis the question arises whether it is possible and useful to conceive of "going beyond deterrence.". . .

In light of this assessment, our evaluation of the last five years does not produce a single simple conclusion. The INF Treaty has been signed and some other possibilities are now on the negotiating table which, if completed, would fulfill some key criteria of the pastoral letter. But in the face of this still uncertain promise, there stands the historical fact of major additions to the strategic arsenals of both superpowers, weapons whose character and numbers decidedly increase the danger of [the occurrence of] nuclear war. . . . This pattern of policy is not adequate to the moral danger of the age, that these arsenals, by miscalculation or mistake, will escape human control and destroy in an hour what humanity has taken centuries to build and shape.

The "conditional acceptance" of deterrence found in *The Challenge of Peace* is directly tied to the pursuit of arms control and, ultimately, disarmament. The arms control successes cited in this Report should be welcomed. But the opportunities missed when arms control was shunted aside for years at a time deserve equal attention. To some degree the arms control successes of the present are compensating for lost opportunities in the past decade.

Failure to pursue arms control systematically erodes support for deterrence. In the coming decade the moral legitimacy of deterrence policy will be tested precisely by the linkage of deterrence, arms control and disarmament.

B. Technological Developments

Technology acts as a two-edged sword in the nuclear competition; some technological changes (e.g., Permissive Action Links) contribute to increasing control of nuclear weapons; other developments (e.g., MIRVing) have had a long-term destabilizing impact. Since 1983, developments in missile accuracy, anti-satellite weapons, and stealth technology have continued the bivalent influence of technology on the arms race. The dilemmas of command, control and communication systems (C^3) illustrate this well. Some improvements in C^3 are dangerous if they enhance "war-fighting" capabilities and feed the illusion of surviving an extended nuclear exchange. Other improvements would decrease reliance on strategies of launch under attack or launch on warning, and so enhance the stability of deterrence in crisis. These latter improvements are at present hardly keeping up with the expansion and evolution of weaponry; they require vigorous attention at the level of technology and at the level of superpower political understanding. . . .

But the most significant change by far in the area of technology and policy has been the proposal of President Reagan to pursue a defense against ballistic missiles. Technically described as the Strategic Defense Initiative (SDI), it originated on March 23, 1983 in a Presidential address to the nation. . . .

The proposal, described as "radical" by both then Secretary of Defense Weinberger and critics of the SDI, holds particular importance . . . for [two] reasons. First, . . . the defensive proposal now permeates the debate about nuclear policy. A recent report of the Aspen Institute Strategy Group observed: "Virtually all issues related to arms control, alliance security and Soviet-American relations are now linked to SDI in one way or another." [Second], the proponents of SDI, from the President to the Secretary of Defense to supporters in the public debate, all have made the claim that SDI constitutes a superior moral policy to that of deterrence as we have known it in the nuclear age. Individually and collectively these reasons point toward the need to address the SDI proposal. Here, we seek to outline the character of the SDI debate, using representative public positions, and then to comment on it in light of relevant moral principles.

1. SDI: WHAT IS IT?   In simple terms, SDI is a research program charged with investigating the technological possibilities of defense against ballistic missiles. But the description cannot remain simple, for even within the Reagan Administration there is a certain pluralism in describing the scope and purpose of SDI. The President's address described the goal of the program in terms of rendering nuclear weapons "impotent and obsolete." Mr. Weinberger described the meaning of the SDI proposal as a "radical rejection of

benign acquiescence in reliance upon the threat of mutual destruction." Taken at face value these descriptions depict a program designed *to transcend* a policy of deterrence based on the threat of nuclear retaliation.

Almost from the beginning of the SDI program, however, official statements have included a more modest goal, not to transcend deterrence but *to enhance* deterrence. In 1984 Mr. Weinberger spoke of three justifications for the SDI program: to hedge against a Soviet breakthrough on defensive technologies, to guard against a Soviet breakout of the ABM Treaty, and, finally, "the very real possibility that American science and technology will achieve what appears to some to be an impossible dream." The first two reasons do not transcend deterrence, the third looks to that goal.

Enhancing deterrence means using defensive systems in a mode which will complicate Soviet planning for a preemptive strike against American land-based ICBMs. The Administration case is neither a pure instance of area defense (of population) nor point defense (of missiles) but a mix of partial area and partial point defense designed to forestall Soviet confidence in resorting to a nuclear attack.

These two descriptions of the SDI (transcending and enhancing deterrence) have created a certain confusion in the public debate, since the technological challenge and strategic rationale for the two are substantially different. In spite of a less than clear policy focus, Congressional support for SDI . . . [has been forthcoming]. . . .

Both the specific proposal of the SDI—a multilayered defense designed to attack ballistic missiles in the four stages of their trajectory (boost phase, post-boost phase, mid-course flight and terminal phase)—and the strategic concept sustaining it have come under criticism. The public debate has focused on the technological feasibility of SDI and its impact on strategic stability and arms control.

2. SDI: TECHNOLOGY, STRATEGY AND ARMS CONTROL.   The nuclear debate has always had a forbiddingly technical character, but the SDI controversy has raised the technical discussion to a new plateau of complexity. Both the density of the technological data and the diversity of expert opinions make the debate about the feasibility of the system a crucial point in the policy arena. Diversity of opinion should not be taken to mean the experts are equally divided; there seem to be substantially more doubters in the scientific community than advocates of SDI.

Yet the Administration . . . continued to be optimistic in its assessment of the feasibility of SDI—at least the SDI designed *to enhance* deterrence. Paul H. Nitze spoke in March 1986 of "impressive advances" in the investigation of SDI technology. The progress is such that "the United States has good reason to believe that SDI technologies hold the promise of feasible, survivable and cost-effective defenses." Dr. George Keyworth, science adviser to President Reagan when SDI was proposed, spoke to the [bishops'] ad hoc Committee in terms which seemed to reach beyond Nitze's cautious "promise" to a tangible product. Describing the technological progress made since 1983, Keyworth said:

> That progress meant that by the time of the Geneva Summit in 1985 we could, with some confidence, picture a boost-phase defense system driven by any of several *different* technologies. . . . These numbers describe an awesome technological capability; a battery of perhaps a dozen such weapons would so overwhelm the offensive forces that countering them by proliferation would be out of the question. So if in March 1983 we were asking IF we could develop SDI, we can now ask how best to choose from those that are emerging.

The evaluations of feasibility coming from other voices in the scientific and strategic community have often been notably more cautious. Perhaps the preeminent critical contribution to the technical debate from outside the Administration has been the report commissioned by the American Physical Society (APS). The APS convened a Study Group "to evaluate the status of the science and technology of directed energy weapons" [DEW]. . . . Its detailed assessment lends weight to its cautious prediction:

> Although substantial progress has been made in many technologies of DEW over the last two decades, the Study Group finds significant gaps in the scientific and engineering understanding of many issues associated with the development of these technologies. Successful resolution of these issues is critical for the extrapolation to performance levels that would be required in an effective ballistic missile defense system. At present, there is insufficient information to decide whether the required extrapolations can or cannot be achieved. Most crucial elements required for a DEW system need improvements of several orders of magnitude. Because the elements are inter-related, the improvements must be achieved in a mutually consistent manner. We estimate that even in the best of circumstances, a decade or more of intensive research would be required to provide the technical knowledge needed for an informed decision about the potential effectiveness and survivability of directed energy weapon systems. In addition, the important issues of overall system integration and effectiveness depend critically upon information that, to our knowledge, does not yet exist.

The APS Study Group eschewed the policy issues of arms control, strategic stability and cost. Two other recent studies are more policy-oriented, joining their judgments on the feasibility of SDI to arms control concerns. The Aspen Strategy Group report argues that meeting the Administration's own criteria of survivability and cost-effectiveness would effectively rule out any deployment of space-based defenses until well into the 1990s. The Strategy Group specifies three challenges facing SDI: (1) many innovations which assist the defense also enhance offensive capabilities; (2) effective boost phase defense "seems problematic"; and (3) terminal phase defense seems unlikely using SDI's non-nuclear technology. . . . But supporters and critics of SDI join in recommending research conducted within the parameters of the ABM Treaty, and research which is not pushed by political objectives, but governed by scientific criteria.

The purpose in setting forth Administration positions and these reports is not to count or even to weigh authorities on the feasibility and arms control issues, but to illustrate how the SDI debate is being joined.

3. SDI: THE MORAL ARGUMENT. One of the characteristics of the nuclear debate of the 1980s . . . has been a growing dissatisfaction with the theory and policy of deterrence. The standard doctrine has come under critique from the left and the right of the political spectrum and both have resorted to moral as well as political-strategic arguments to stress the shortcomings of deterrence. The moral case propounded for defensive systems fits into this wider atmosphere of dissatisfaction with deterrence. Both President Reagan and former Secretary Weinberger regularly appeal to the moral motivation and moral quality of the SDI. Supporters of the SDI pick up on this theme, joining a critique of Mutual Assured Destruction [MAD] theories to an argument about the moral stability which will accompany a defense dominated nuclear relationship. . . .

The case made for the moral superiority of SDI is primarily an ethic of intention; using the just-war ethic, supporters of SDI review the nuclear age, pointing out how classical deterrence doctrine has been willing to abide or endorse threats against innocent populations. In contrast to this posture, a case is made describing the *intended objectives* of SDI: either the transition to a world where the nuclear threat has been negated or at least to a world where the principal targets shift from populations to weapons. Stated at the level of intentionality, the SDI case seeks to capture the moral high ground, undoubtedly contributing to the popularity of the program with the general public.

But the complexity and the stakes of the policy debate on SDI require that the moral argument be pressed beyond its intended objectives. The SDI debate is less a dispute about objectives or motives than it is about means and consequences. To probe the moral content of the effects of pursuing the SDI is to raise issues about its risks, costs and benefits.

Giving proper weight to the effects of pursuing SDI moves the focus of the moral argument back from the desirability of freeing the world from the *factual condition* of an assured destruction posture (an objective commended by everyone) to the *technological feasibility* of fulfilling this intention, to the potential risks for *strategic stability* of an offensive-defensive arms competition, and to the *economic costs* and *trade-offs* which pursuit of SDI will require in a deficit-ridden federal budget. These categories of feasibility, stability and cost are already prominent in the SDI debate. The point here is to assert that the moral character of SDI cannot be determined apart from these other elements precisely because consequences count in a moral assessment.

First, while the feasibility argument is primarily a scientific-technological question, there are risks associated with pursuing some technological paths: risks to the existing arms control regime; risks of introducing dimensions of uncertainty into the already delicate political-psychological fabric of deterrence; risks that defensive systems can have real or perceived offensive uses;

finally, risks that some forms of SDI would be ineffective against an adversary's first-strike, but more effective against a retaliatory second-strike, thereby eroding crisis stability. Assessing these risks—evaluating which are prudent to pursue, which are too high to tolerate—involves a moral as well as a technological judgment. Precisely because of the number and quality of scientific judgments which have warned against precipitous movement toward SDI, it is necessary to stress the need for continued technological scrutiny and moral restraint concerning a decision which might later be regretted.

The second question concerns the impact of the defensive option on strategic stability. The critics of deterrence (*The Challenge of Peace* included) detail several negative factors in the deterrence regime, but the judgments of Vatican II, Pope John Paul II and the pastoral letter also posit a role for deterrence in a world of sovereign states armed with nuclear weapons. While the need to move "beyond deterrence" is asserted by both Pope John Paul II and the U.S. bishops, there is also found in their statements the logic of the 1976 Vatican statement at the United Nations: that a move beyond deterrence should not place the world in a more dangerous condition than our present plight. Hence, moves beyond deterrence are open to scrutiny. They must be assessed in light of their impact on the basic purpose of deterrence— its role in preventing the use of nuclear weapons.

Assessment of SDI in light of its impact on strategic stability will force the moral argument onto the path of examining the contrasting views of whether the "transition" from assured destruction to common security can be carried off with acceptable risk. Supporters of the SDI argue from the moral and the strategic perspective about the opportunities it provides to transform the nuclear dilemma—to end the mutual threats which constitute the present delicate deterrence balance. These arguments stress the *goal* of the transition.

While this goal is undoubtedly attractive the more compelling moral case presently rests with those who specify the likely risks of an aggressive SDI program at this time: (1) the obstacle it poses to effective movement on arms control; (2) the possible shift toward offensive use of this defensive system; (3) the further "tilt" of the deterrence relationship toward preemptive strategies during the transition period. No one of these results is a certain consequence of pursuing SDI deployment but the collective danger they pose to the dynamic of deterrence leaves us unconvinced of the merits of proceeding toward deployment of the system. The combination of the technological and the strategic evaluations of the present status of SDI appear to us to promise serious risks and very hypothetical benefits at this time.

The feasibility and strategic stability arguments are central to the policy debate about SDI. Third, the economic argument—the escalating cost of SDI in a time of continuing budget deficits and in a decade which has seen deep cuts in programs for the poor at home and abroad—has particular moral relevance. . . . A program which fails to attract a clear consensus on technological-strategic grounds should not be allowed to command resources at a time when other human needs go unfulfilled.

In summary, our primary purpose in this section has been to dispel the notion that the moral character of SDI can be decided simply by examining it in terms of the objectives (or ends that it intends). These are not the only morally relevant factors that need to be taken into account in rendering a moral judgment about SDI. Judged within an adequate moral framework, one that takes into account the relevant moral circumstances surrounding this policy, . . . it is our prudential judgment that proposals to press deployment of SDI do not measure up to the moral criteria outlined in this Report. . . .

III. THE STATUS OF DETERRENCE: AN EVALUATION

The judgment of "strictly conditioned moral acceptance" of deterrence in 1983 was meant to convey the strategic paradox and moral problem we encountered in evaluating nuclear policy. The essential moral question, defined above, remains: can credible deterrence be reconciled with right intention, proportionality and discrimination?

In 1983, we were not persuaded to condemn deterrence, nor were we prepared to simply endorse it. Its contribution to peace is the paradoxical role it plays in restraining the use of nuclear weapons. We could not disapprove this claim, and we found some reasons to be convinced by it. At the same time, the negative dimensions of the deterrence relationship—its danger, its costs, its capacity to perpetuate divisions in international affairs—were there for all to see. Hence, the *most* we could say in support of deterrence was "conditional acceptance."

Since *The Challenge of Peace* was published, the ethical commentary on it and on the problem of nuclear deterrence has been voluminous. . . .

It is possible to sketch the broad outlines of this commentary. Some, using the principles of discrimination and proportionality, as we did, believe that emerging technology in the nuclear field (increasing accuracy and miniaturization of warheads) will provide a deterrent force which is both strategically credible and morally justifiable. When this technological faith is combined with a certain definition of the threat facing the West, it seems to provide for its supporters a coherent moral theory of deterrence. Nuclear threat and even use are a proportionate response to the political threat faced by the West, and the new technology provides a legitimate means to use if deterrence fails.

A very different analysis of the nuclear relationship finds justification of deterrence policy—even conditional acceptance—a mistaken view of what exists. In this moral assessment, deterrence policy is inherently tied to a willingness to go to counter-society warfare, bursting all the moral bonds needed to keep warfare within the moral universe. This reading of the nuclear reality finds no grounds for any acceptance of the existing strategy of deterrence.

These choices, and variants of them, were before us when we wrote *The Challenge of Peace*. Our answer to the moral dilemma of deterrence policy, then and now, is less clear-cut than either of these positions. In trying to address all the factors of the deterrence relationship—including the values served by it and those threatened by it—it has seemed to us a problem where absolute clarity in one answer often sacrifices part of the problem to be solved. Our judgment is not as confident about technology as the first view, or as convinced about the intrinsic evil of nuclear deterrence taken as a whole as the second view.

Deterrence, of course, is not an entity but a policy. It is a policy involving several component elements: weapons systems, force posture, declaratory policy, targeting doctrine, and the relationship of these to the objectives of security policy and—an aspect of it—arms control policy. As others have noted, when one looks back on the evolution of the nuclear age, it is highly unlikely that anyone would have chosen to have our present situation result. The deterrence relationship has been shaped by many forces, not all of them coherently related to each other.

Yet, any assessment of the policy of deterrence will be hard-put not to acknowledge that in a world of widespread nuclear knowledge and at least six nuclear powers, deterrence has been a significant factor in preventing the use of nuclear weapons. . . .

But this side of the nuclear equation must be balanced against the various costs of nuclear deterrence. The political cost of two powers holding the fate of the northern hemisphere (and probably much of the south too) hostage is clearly an unacceptable way to structure international relations. Even the caution of superpowers is not immune from criticism, since they have found ways to engage each other through proxy forces in other nations, often at the expense of the latter. . . .

Psychologically, the costs of living with the nuclear threat have been documented in both East and West. Economically, the diversion of resources over the long term to the nuclear competition has merited the critique and condemnation of secular and religious leadership. Finally, as we have analyzed above, the deterrence relationship is not static. The technological drive in recent years has moved the competition in directions which erode the stability of deterrence and increase the chance of nuclear use.

We remain convinced that the policy of nuclear deterrence is not a stable long-term method of keeping the peace among sovereign states. This is still the foundation of our evaluation of deterrence policy. We are also convinced that in the short-term and mid-term assessment of our future the best moral evaluation is neither to condemn deterrence outright nor to accept it as self-regulating or "normal."

More precisely, we are persuaded to renew the judgment of *The Challenge of Peace*: that nuclear deterrence merits only strictly conditioned acceptance.

In a dangerous world, a world of both widespread nuclear knowledge and extensive nuclear arsenals, we find condemning nuclear deterrence too drastic a solution and embracing it too simple a response. With Pope John Paul II we hope: "that all countries, and especially the great powers, will perceive more and more that the fear of 'assured mutual destruction,' which is at the heart of the doctrine of nuclear deterrence, cannot be a reliable basis for security and peace in the long term."

This assessment of various elements of deterrence policy is less dramatic than a single univocal judgment, but we believe it is more adequate to the complex pattern of U.S.-Soviet relations which exists today and is most appropriate for us as we call on our own country and other nations to pursue more effectively bilateral and multilateral arms control and to move decisively toward progressive disarmament. . . .

Our committee's response is not to drop "conditional acceptance," but to advocate more actively a series of measures which still very much need to be undertaken to meet the conditions of *The Challenge of Peace*. Our "conditional acceptance" is not an endorsement of a status-quo that we find inadequate and dangerous. It is a position that requires us to work for genuine and far-reaching changes in the policies that guide nuclear arsenals of the world. More particularly it requires us to continue to pursue and advocate a more secure and morally justifiable basis for peace based on the following criteria:

1. Deterrence based on the direct targeting of urban populations is morally unacceptable. We oppose it in all cases.

2. Deterrence policy implemented by weapons which combine size, accuracy and multiple warheads in a credible "first-strike" posture adds unacceptable risk to the deterrence relationship. We, therefore, oppose existing trends, and will oppose future policies, which push the deterrence posture of both superpowers in this direction.

3. The dynamic of the existing policies of both superpowers enhances the risk of the preemptive use of nuclear weapons. We advocate reversal of this process as the first goal of arms control policy.

4. The levels of strategic armaments far exceed the requirements of survivable second-strike deterrence—the only posture to which conditional acceptance can be given. We support "deep cuts" in strategic forces as the second goal of arms control policy.

5. The risks of provoking an offensive and defensive competition between the superpowers and the existing disparity of views about the nature, purpose and feasibility of space-based defense are more compelling to us than the promises made about the program. We oppose anything beyond a well defined research and development program clearly within the restraints of the ABM Treaty.

6. Our acceptance of deterrence is conditioned upon serious efforts at restraining proliferation. Existing policies of the superpowers are clearly in-

adequate on this question. We urge a renewed effort in the coming decade to halt the spread of nuclear weapons.

7. The first major nuclear arms control treaty was a partial ban on testing. Twenty-five years later the U.S. and Soviet Union, along with the other nuclear states, have failed to fulfill the promise of that first step. We call for a renewed effort, pursued with much greater purpose and conviction, to complete negotiations on a comprehensive test ban treaty. We call for ratification of both the Threshold Test Ban Treaty and the Peaceful Nuclear Explosions Treaty.

8. The competition in non-nuclear arms must also be addressed. We urge more concerted efforts to outlaw the production, possession and use of chemical and biological weapons, and to reduce conventional forces to a new balance compatible with reasonable requirements for defense.

9. The cost of the arms competition is a continuing indictment of its role in international politics. The distortions in resource allocation by the superpowers and other nations—large and small, rich and poor—fit Pope John Paul's description of "a structure of sin." He rightly describes present global patterns of military spending as a process leading toward death rather than development. We will support efforts to redirect budgetary choices in the United States toward greater attention to the poor at home and abroad.

The conditions just specified are aimed at containing the nuclear competition, reducing its risks, enhancing chances for arms reduction and ultimately using arms control as a step toward nuclear disarmament. These measures were central to *The Challenge of Peace* and this Report seeks to update and refine our recommendations for reducing dangers of the nuclear age. . . .

This Report is written at a time when a complementary strategy must be pressed. We are skeptical about escaping the strategic and moral dilemmas of the nuclear age through technology (either in space or by more accurate weapons). The complementary strategy which needs to be pressed is a creative and sustained effort to reshape the political dimension of U.S.-Soviet relations. Such an effort should seek to relativize the nuclear component of this relationship. . . .

To contain the nuclear danger of our time is itself an awesome undertaking. To reshape the political fabric of an increasingly interdependent world is an even larger and more complicated challenge. . . .

We are convinced that the present time is better served by those willing to risk falling short of a large vision than the alternative risk of being satisfied with small achievements which fail to address the dangers or the opportunities of the moment. In that spirit we submit this Report on the meaning of *The Challenge of Peace* in 1988.

5 GLOBAL SECURITY WITHOUT NUCLEAR DETERRENCE: THE NECESSITY FOR ALTERNATIVES

Robert Johansen

. . . More and more people are ready, without knowing quite how to go about it, to relinquish their dependence on nuclear weapons. They are silently admitting to themselves, "I do not want to be defended by nuclear weapons." This new realism springs from a recognition that nuclear weapons offer extremely low utility at an extremely high cost. . . .

Not many US nuclear experts, pundits, and politicians—those who have learned too well what *cannot* be done in international affairs—have yet paid attention to this undercurrent, because they are not sensitively attuned to forces outside the mainstream of security thinking. Nonetheless, the doubt about "nuclearism"[1] filters through much of recent US public life: We find traces in the US Catholic bishops' "strictly conditioned moral acceptance of nuclear deterrence" in their pastoral letter of 1983; the Methodist bishops' rejection of the use of nuclear weapons in 1986; the House of Representatives' imposition, despite its uncourageous retraction in 1986, of restraints on presidential freedom to test new weapons in 1985, 1986, and 1987; and even the willingness of some people to embrace Star Wars as a desperate gamble to rid our world of nuclear terror.

The underlying moral objection to and practical dissatisfaction with nuclear weapons arises from two forces: frustration with arms control negotiations and nuclear diplomacy which, as currently practiced, will simply never produce a warless world, and the belief that in a war-prone world some government may eventually be propelled, as the United States once was, to use nuclear weapons in combat. Paradoxically, people's confidence that there is no *immediate* threat of nuclear war seems to free them sufficiently of fear to enable a growing support for the shelving of nuclear deterrence—if a relatively unrisky way out of the balance of terror can be found. But progress toward denuclearization is certainly not inevitable. Indeed compliant acceptance of nuclear deterrence until one day it is too late to reverse events leading toward war still seems more likely. . . .

Note: Some footnotes have been deleted, and others have been renumbered to appear in consecutive order.

WHY SHOULD THE US AND SOVIET GOVERNMENTS SEEK ALTERNATIVES TO NUCLEAR DETERRENCE?

Recent efforts to enhance nuclear deterrence by developing new weapons have in fact exacerbated already dangerous security conditions and stimulated the arms competition. Such efforts have obstructed negotiated efforts to move away from those conditions, have reinforced the psychological patterns that lead to war, and have deepened the most negative characteristics of the balance of power system. With or without the Strategic Defense Initiative, nuclear deterrence cannot provide sufficient security to make it a wise or tolerable policy for very long. The prospects for long-term avoidance of war are too low. The costs, if war occurs, are suicidally high.

First, nuclear deterrence encourages a chronic arms buildup. It heightens the desire of national officials to gain a technological or psychological edge over their rivals. As a result, both superpowers are probably less secure today than they were five years ago; they will, if present plans for armament continue without restraint, be less secure five years from now than they are today. During the past decade of declining international security, the United States has enormously increased its destructive capability and the sophistication of its arsenals. To have poured additional money into weapons would only have militarized US policy and the code of international conduct even more, with a further demise of security likely.

Current arms competition reflects the instability of nuclear deterrence. Despite arsenals large and sophisticated enough to destroy almost any conceivable set of targets many times over, the Reagan administration, with Congressional support, [believed] that new nuclear weapons and delivery systems need to be tested and manufactured. The arms buildup careens toward the acquisition of more stealthy nuclear arms and a war-fighting capability. Acquiring instruments to fight, rather than merely to deter, nuclear combat is not a trend that began with the coming to power of the Reagan administration and the conservative political swing in the United States. Republicans and Democrats, whether through votes in Congress or budget requests from the White House, have together bought the same weapons and strategic doctrine. A war-fighting capability is the logical outcome, not of a conservative presidency, but of an international security system based on competing national armaments, an ever-changing military technology, and the constant threat inherent in nuclear deterrence.

However different the Strategic Defense Initiative may appear in theory, in practice it is not a departure from the war-fighting tradition. The construction of a space-based anti-missile force that is massive and yet is of less than complete effectiveness will not lead to the elimination of nuclear weapons. If such a force is deployed in conjunction with the Minuteman III, MX, and Trident D-5 missiles, with stealth bombers and cruise missiles, and with anti-submarine warfare it will, in Soviet minds, move the United States one step closer to a war-fighting posture. The goal of such a strategic doctrine has always been to enable the United States to destroy a substantial portion of the Soviet Union's intercontinental nuclear weapons while limiting the damage Moscow's missiles can inflict on the US arsenal.

Second, permanent readiness to threaten and conduct all-out war—a necessary condition of nuclear deterrence—obstructs negotiations to reduce US–Soviet military competition. Because of constant maneuvering for technological and deployment advantages in weaponry in order to make the deterrent threat more credible, arms control negotiations seldom succeed. Even in the moments of their greatest success—the 1963 test ban treaty, the SALT I and Interim Agreement of 1972, and the SALT II treaty of 1979—arms control negotiations have not substantially slowed the arms buildup. With the possible exception of earlier anti-ballistic missile deployments, arms agreements have not halted the deployment of a single new weapons system since 1945. Indeed negotiations frequently have legitimized an arms buildup and speeded the testing or deployment of new destabilizing weapons, such as multiple-warhead missiles in the early 1970s and weapons for space warfare more recently, which can then be used for bargaining chips or for leverage in negotiations.

Third, nuclear deterrence has not eliminated, and sometimes has heightened, the psychological influences and irrational behavior that in the past have led to war. A relationship based on profound military threat and on a dehumanizing image of an enemy, which seems a psychic necessity to justify massive destruction, encourages diplomatic confrontation on a broad scale, and stimulates forward-based military deployments that exacerbate the sense of military threat. To be sure, nuclear deterrence has probably moved governments in the nuclear era to be more cautious than their predecessors in considering large-scale war as a reasonable option. But even in the pre-nuclear age most leaders seldom *wanted* a major war. If they initiated combat, it was with the hope that war would remain limited or would end quickly. They favored war when they thought—mistakenly as it often turned out—that they could wage it without being defeated.

Although imprudent, this traditional posture toward war still abounds. Leaders know that their self-destruction is not rational. But occasionally they think *war* can be rational, because with enough weapons and bravado war will not destroy *them.* Yet numerous psychological studies demonstrate that political leaders often choose to threaten or use force because they are insensitive to readily available information suggesting that their plans will not work.[2]

In their belief that war can be kept limited, contemporary leaders resemble their predecessors throughout history who occasionally decided to fight wars, even though the conflicts eventually, unexpectedly, destroyed their architects.[3] The mere passage of four decades since 1945 without direct combat between major powers provides little reassurance of permanent peace. Recall that in the past eight decades the German, Italian, Austro-Hungarian, Russian, and Japanese governments initiated wars in which they were eventually destroyed. To be sure, they did not have to face the prospect of a nuclear winter before they mobilized. But they did face, and mistakenly dismissed, the prospect of self-destruction before they chose to fight the particular war that later became suicidal for each.

That political leaders (like all human beings) occasionally do not behave rationally underscores a fatal flaw for nuclear deterrence that no exponent can provide satisfying reassurance against recurrence. Indeed, nuclear deterrence adds unprecedented anxieties to crisis decision-making. Nuclear deterrence no doubt produces caustic effects on rationality. It is impossible to demonstrate that the probabilities of war stemming from irrational calculations have been generally diminished by nuclear deterrence. Irrational behavior never can be eliminated from processes that are as filled with psychological shadows as are the power relationships that exist within government institutions and among nations. For example, although there is evidence that the use of even 10 percent of the US and Soviet nuclear arsenals would make the northern hemisphere uninhabitable, there is no evidence that battle plans intend to restrict launchings to a "fair" share of that 10 percent. There is ample evidence of official willingness to destroy the hemisphere in order to save it.

Given these problems for which nuclear deterrence provides no answer, it strains credibility to claim that today's international security system is substantially less war prone than ever before. War may be somewhat less rational than ever, but that does not make war significantly less likely—especially when national security managers emphasize that the key to preventing war is to be willing to fight it, and to express that willingness even though to do so appears to be irrational. When decision-makers operate from within a logic that scorns those who do not accept the "rationality of irrationality" as the key to war prevention, nuclear deterrence may appear stable in the short run, but in the long run there must be a positive probability of its failing; otherwise it would cease to deter. The threat to use nuclear arms remains credible only with occasional use.

Finally, nuclear deterrence probably never deserved the widespread support it has received over the past 40 years. Although it is frequently credited with keeping peace since 1945, or at least with preventing superpower war, there is in fact no substantial evidence that the international system has become more stable with nuclear weapons than it would have been without them. It seems highly unlikely that the Soviet Union ever intended to attack Western Europe, or that it would have developed that intention if nuclear weapons had not existed. There is no evidence that it ever contemplated an attack on the United States itself. So it is difficult to substantiate the claim that nuclear weapons have kept the US–Soviet peace since 1945.

Soviet efforts to influence West Europeans politically or to intimidate them diplomatically were more pronounced soon after World War II, when the Soviet Union was relatively weak and the United States wielded an overwhelming nuclear superiority, than later when *mutual* deterrence made the threats by the United States to retaliate less plausible. Intimidation, therefore, to the extent that it existed in events like the Berlin crisis and the construction of the Berlin wall, was dampened by the development of friendlier economic and political relations between eastern and western Europe, not by growing US military strength or nuclear deterrence.

Rather than produce a durable peace, nuclear deterrence and the problems that attend it reinforce the most dangerous features of the balance of power system: pressure for arms buildups; competition for allies and overseas influence everywhere on the planet; anxiety about controlling territory, sea lanes, airspace, and natural resources; pursuit of power as an end in itself; and a reluctance to use legal and political means of peaceful settlement. This system has never kept the peace for the length of time that is now required to avert catastrophe.

"Balance" of power, of course, is really a misnomer for the prevailing security system. Because there is no reliable way to determine whether the United States and the Soviet Union are at an exactly equal position on the balance scales, neither side really wants an equality of power. Just to be safe, each wants a predominance of power in its favor. Each adversary threatens the other sufficiently that both are driven endlessly to pile up more weapons.

In addition to the well-known military rivalry that accompanies the balance of power, recent scientific studies of war suggest there is a less visible long-term cycle in the present international system which brings war periodically, somewhat similar to long business cycles.[4]

These studies challenge the conventional wisdom that the long 40-year period of peace since 1945, compared to the pre-nuclear 20-year period following World War I, is a result of nuclear deterrence. The 40 years of peace since World War II may be only one peaceful segment of a much longer cycle that later will include global war if the cycle is not interrupted. The forces that caused a decline in Britain's 19th and early 20th century dominance of the international system led to both World War I and World War II. Within the perspective of a century-long cycle, these wars may be seen as two segments of the same global war and geopolitical changes from which the United States emerged as the new dominant power. The international stability since 1945 appears to be the phase that normally follows a period of global war and major readjustment such as occurred, with one interlude, from 1914 to 1945.

According to this view, the stable phase of the international system following a world war of readjustment has made nuclear deterrence safe; nuclear weapons have not made the international system safe. Peace has made nuclear deterrence tolerable; nuclear deterrence has not brought the peace. But as the world moves into the declining phase of the long cycle, war prevention will prove more difficult. That difficulty will increase, assuming the normal cycle is not interrupted, even with a vast array of US weapons. This phase seems evident now in the declining role the United States is playing as a world economic and political leader, while Washington squanders its economic capacity on wasteful military spending and its moral leadership on military adventures . . .

Because a substantial amount of historical evidence and empirical analysis challenges the conventional wisdom that nuclear deterrence has "worked," the idea that the balance of power system *ought* to be changed has become widely recognized in theory, although largely ignored in practice. Even the eminent architect of political realism, Hans Morgenthau, said, in one of his last public addresses, that without some form of world governance, catastrophe could not be avoided.[5] Inis Claude, in his celebrated study of the balance of power, concluded, "the suitability of the world for the operation of the balance of power system has been steadily diminishing for well over a century. All the most fundamental tendencies . . . in recent generations run counter to the requirements of a workable system of balance of power."[6] There is a gradually widening recognition that if the traditional balance of power is here to stay, then the human species is not.

HOW CAN GOVERNMENTS SAFELY MOVE BEYOND NUCLEAR DETERRENCE?

To move beyond deterrence requires diplomatic initiatives to overcome the three central problems that current nuclear policies exacerbate: a *condition* of insecurity caused by the arms buildup and the erosion of existing arms restraints; a *process* of arms control negotiations that, unless given a much broader security focus, will only continue its barren record; and a balance of power *system* that impedes steps toward regional and global security mechanisms in which the likelihood of war could be substantially reduced.

To alleviate unstable military conditions, initiate a fruitful arms control process, and open the door to transformation of the present code of conduct and international system, three policy-making guidelines apply. First, it is important to distinguish as sharply as possible between policies that increase *arms* and policies that increase *security*. The choice between whether to enhance military power or "security power" is crucial. Yet it is a distinction seldom made in practice. More arms do not automatically produce more security. Increasing the threat to one's opponent will often decrease one's own security: a more threatening US military posture is only one step removed from additional threats poised against the United States.

Current efforts to bolster nuclear deterrence are based on the outworn assumption that it remains useful to threaten massive destruction of one's adversary. As the United States tried to enhance deterrence by deploying Pershing II and ground-launched cruise missiles in Europe, for example, it was a foregone conclusion that the Soviet Union would put additional missiles closer to the United States and its European allies . . . . These weapons give the West shorter warning times in the event of war. The Soviet Union may also put other systems on hair trigger and disperse command and control.

Such steps increase the possibility that decisions may be made hastily or mechanically, on the basis of rigid orders laid down in advance, or without proper authorization.

If [US] officials would reverse their priorities and seek security advantages rather than military advantages, they would find greater leeway in negotiations with Moscow. Because it is not essential for security to maintain precise equality in numbers of US and Soviet weapons, officials could prudently compromise on insignificant numerical differences in order to achieve an agreement to halt the arms buildup. For example, as [the agreement] to eliminate intermediate range missiles [underscores], either Moscow or Washington could have increased its security back in 1983 if it had simply accepted the other's proposal on Euromissiles in return for a complete halt to the nuclear arms buildup in Europe. Similarly, at Reykjavik the president could have reduced Soviet arsenals by 50 percent in only 5 years by merely adhering to the anti-ballistic missile treaty which the United States had negotiated, ratified, and honored for 14 years. That would have been easy to do if security advantages had taken priority over the vain pursuit of future military advantages.

Second, it is important to emphasize the difference between reducing *arms* and reducing *the role of military force* in international relations. If . . . government officials focus narrowly on limiting arms, they will not make significant or lasting progress, because nations will not give up their arms as long as they rely on them for security. Even if arms control negotiations could be surprisingly successful and lead to drastic cuts in all US and Soviet nuclear arms, the outbreak of a conventional war would probably lead both governments quickly to reassemble nuclear weapons.

There is little reason to believe that the human race can forever avoid catastrophies, perhaps including a nuclear winter, unless we eliminate the prospect of nuclear war. And the risk of nuclear war cannot be substantially reduced without eliminating major conventional war as well: if large scale, conventional war occurred, there would be a serious danger of escalation from conventional to nuclear combat. . . .

Thus it does not seem possible to lift the nuclear sword from our heads unless we move toward the elimination of all war, nuclear and conventional. To accomplish this requires a vision not of a world without conflict, but of a world without war. . . .

Third, it is important to shift focus away from military hardware, to acknowledge *all* threats to human security, and to identify broad, multilateral programs for combatting these threats. They include severe economic insecurity, deprivation of human rights, and environmental decay, as well as the danger of war or conquest. Because the United States has overestimated military threats and underestimated nonmilitary threats, it has mistakenly stressed military solutions and largely ignored nonmilitary solutions. It has overemphasized go-it-alone policies, and underutilized multilateral opportunities to institutionalize more cooperative, internationalist solutions. This approach has reinforced the militarization of foreign policy and of international relations generally. . . .

In short, a security policy capable of moving beyond deterrence must focus on the overriding goal for our time: to reduce the role of military power in world affairs. . . .

To lay the groundwork for security without nuclear deterrence, it is not necessary to convince governments at this time to accept some grand blueprint for global security. It is sufficient to demonstrate that there are sensible steps that can be taken now—steps that will not jeopardize anyone's national security in the short run, but that can open a path toward a new international security order in the long run. To move away from nuclear deterrence does not mean an end to nonnuclear forms of deterrence, nor an end to the need to prevent military aggression and expansion. It also certainly does not mean an end to the nation-state. The demise of nuclear deterrence cannot achieve in the foreseeable future the total elimination of the threat of isolated nuclear accidents or the danger of deliberate, unauthorized use of one or several crude, clandestinely fabricated nuclear weapons. But the danger of abusing the nuclear genie can be reduced to a much lower level with the proposed approach for gradual demilitarization than the danger the world will face if a new security order is not constructed.

To move beyond nuclear deterrence means that deterrence by nuclear weapons would gradually be replaced with deterrence by nonnuclear means. These at first would presumably be both military and nonmilitary. The military determinants of the present international balancing process would be gradually reduced as the nonmilitary determinants—international monitoring and enforcement, economic incentives for demilitarization, political checks and balances, and international legal procedures—would be strengthened. Eventually deterrence could rely solely on nonmilitary means, including, of course, a transnational adaptation of the legal processes and police enforcement that play a central role in dispute resolution in all societies. . . .

NOTES

1. Nuclearism is defined here as unwarranted faith in the efficacy of nuclear weapons for maintaining security. . . .

2. Robert Jervis, *Perception and Misperception in International Politics* (Princeton: Princeton University Press, 1976); Ralph K. White, *Fearful Warriors: A Psychological Profile of U.S.–Soviet Relations* (New York: Free Press, 1984); D. Goleman, "Political Forces Come Under Scrutiny of Psychology," *The New York Times*, April 2, 1985.

3. I refer to the many statements by officials and their advisers affirming that it is possible to fight and prevail in a limited nuclear war. See, for example, Colin S. Gray and Keith Payne, "Victory is Possible," *Foreign Policy*, No. 39, Summer 1980, pp. 14–27. The classified Defense Guidance Statement requires commanders to prevail over the Soviet Union, even after fighting a protracted nuclear war. See Richard Halloran, "Pentagon Draws Up First Strategy for Fighting a Long Nuclear War," *The New York Times*, May 30, 1982. . . .

4. See David Wilkinson, *Deadly Quarrels: Lewis F. Richardson and the Statistical Study of War* (Berkeley: University of California Press, 1980); Francis A. Beer, *Peace Against War* (San Francisco: Freeman, 1981); George Modelski, "The Long Cycle of Global Politics and the Nation-State," *Comparative Studies in Society and History*, Vol. 20, April 1978, pp. 214–235;

. . . and J. David Singer and Melvin Small, *The Wages of War, 1816–1965: A Statistical Handbook* (New York: Wiley, 1972).

5. Statement in his plenary address before the International Studies Association, Los Angeles, March 19, 1980.

6. Inis Claude, *Power and International Relations* (New York: Random House, 1962).

6 THE LONG-TERM FUTURE OF DETERRENCE

Joseph S. Nye, Jr.

Can nuclear deterrence last forever? To answer yes requires heroic assumptions. . . .

Generally speaking, nuclear strategists have ignored the question of the long-term future of deterrence. The rational models of deterrence theory tend to be static and ahistorical. However, when a president announces not merely a hope but also a massive program to make nuclear weapons "impotent and obsolete" and asks "How long, after all, can the American people hold to a strategy that threatens innocent lives?" strategists cannot continue to duck the question. Many analysts complain about the alleged lack of technical or political realism in the president's proposal, but few have sketched alternative visions or even seriously addressed the problem of how to think about the long term.

The Strategic Defense Initiative (SDI) is only one among a number of relevant utopias that can be compared in terms of their intrinsic desirability, their political and technical conditions for stability, and the relative feasibility of processes for their attainment. It is time that strategic studies move out beyond static models and address more adequately questions about the long-term future of deterrence. . . .

EVIDENCE, PROBABILITY, AND METAPHORS

Deterrence seems to have worked for [over] forty years. Prodeterrence strategists make too much and the antinuclear critics make too little of the absence of any war between the superpowers for [more than] the past four decades. The simple form of the pronuclear argument begs the difficult causal question of ascertaining what would have been the case in the absence of nuclear deterrence, and more important, it also begs the question of why the future should resemble the past. For those who believe that catastrophic failure is inevitable, it is no answer to say simply that deterrence has worked in the past.

At the same time, the argument that deterrence has worked is not without

Note: Some footnotes have been deleted, and others have been renumbered to appear in consecutive order.

merit. Four decades without war among the great powers is a remarkable period of peace in modern Western history. (The record is forty-three years between 1871 and 1914.) There is good reason to believe that nuclear weapons contributed to the prudence that kept leaders out of war during the past forty years.[1] . . . Today, modern leaders know the horrible devastation that would result from any nuclear war. In the words of the [1985] Summit communique, "recognizing that any conflict between the U.S.S.R. and the U.S. could have catastrophic consequences, they emphasized the importance of preventing any war between them, whether nuclear or conventional."

This is only partial comfort, however. . . . Even if nuclear deterrence has lasted for nearly four decades, it is difficult to believe it will last forever. Some dire fears, such as C. P. Snow's 1960 prediction that nuclear war within a decade was a mathematical certainty, have proved wrong. It has been argued that Snow's exaggeration will be justified if nuclear war takes place in the next hundred years.[2] But the difference between a decade and a century can make all the difference in the world when it comes to deciding what can be done to avoid nuclear war.

Some antinuclear critics object to the whole approach to deterrence in terms of probability. For example, the sociologist Todd Gitlin argues that "since deterrence works only if it works forever, it is an all-or-nothing proposition, so applying the language of probability to it is misleading."[3] But his argument is not compelling. Gitlin seems to assume that failures of deterrence or inevitable accidents must lead to all-out nuclear war, but this is far from self-evident. Indeed, a case can be made that an accident or a partial failure of deterrence may be the prelude to major changes that reduce risks or reliance on nuclear deterrence in the long term. Even if he were right about catastrophe, however, it is odd for Gitlin to discount "microscopic probability" by asking, "Do we feel secure playing Russian roulette if the revolver has a hundred chambers?" Perhaps not, but if he had to play, I doubt that he really would not care whether a revolver had one hundred chambers rather than six! And if he readmits probabilistic reasoning, then it can also be applied to the question of relative risks between unilateral disarmament ("refusing to play") and trying to increase the number of chambers in a world in which the game of nuclear deterrence already exists.

Other antinuclear critics use the concept of probability to "prove" that deterrence will inevitably fail. With a series of trials over time, even a low probability approaches a certainty. The probability of at least one successful event in a series of trials is equal to $1 - (1 - p)^n$. Thus, if we flip a coin once, the chances of getting tails once is 50 percent. If we flip a (true) coin ten times, the chance of seeing tails at least once is 99.9 percent. Using this approach to the distribution of probabilities, Bradford Lyttle concludes that the average daily chances of nuclear war during the past thirty years (10,950 days) was probably not higher than .0006 percent. But Lyttle goes on to argue that even if the daily chances of one missile's being launched are only one in a hundred million, the probability of such an event passes 50 percent within fifty years.[4] Douglas Lackey points out that a one-in-a-hundred chance of nuclear war in the next forty years becomes a 99 percent probability after eight thousand years.

Although such calculations can be useful numerical reminders, we cannot conclude very much about deterrence from them. They assume that probabilities are constant and that events are independent of each other. The metaphor of a flipped coin is misleading. Human interactions are more like loaded dice. The odds change; and the outcome of one set of events may greatly change the odds of the next event. In fact, frightening events like the Berlin and Cuban missile crises may drive the odds of war down in their immediate aftermath. A diplomatic rapprochement, such as occurred between the United States and China in the 1970s, can have a similar effect. New technologies may cut either way. It seems unlikely that the odds of nuclear war future generations face will be the same as ours. . . .

The likelihood of nuclear war rests on both independent and interdependent probabilities that relate different aspects of the process by which war might occur. Purely accidental war might be conceived of in terms of independent probabilities; but if the numbers are low enough, they may not matter. If we are speaking of eight thousand years, for example, humankind may have concerns other than nuclear war. The longer the period, the greater the chance that other things will have changed, and that an accident will have a different meaning in that changed context. In short, even when we have independent probabilities (as we might approximate in the case of pure accidents), the significance of the events they lead to must be seen in the context of the interdependent probabilities involved in human history. As Paul Schroeder has put it, "Murphy's Law does not apply to history." That is not an argument for optimism, but it is "an argument *against* a certain extremely popular kind of crippling pessimism."[5] Those who use simple probabilistic arguments to argue that abolition of nuclear weapons is the only policy that is both moral and realistic build their case on shaky grounds. . . .

What are the risks of nuclear war? This is a critical question, but unfortunately there is no fully satisfactory answer. . . . Despite our inability to be precise, we are bound to make crude estimates of whether the probability [of nuclear war] is high or low. It seems more plausible to assume that the probabilities are relatively low than that they are very high. There are both rational and accidental models of the causes of war, and both models seem to have low probabilities in the nuclear age. As McGeorge Bundy has written, "In light of the certain prospect of retaliation, there has been literally no chance at all that any sane political authority, in either the United States or in the Soviet Union, would consciously choose to start a nuclear war."[6] As for pure accident, the prospects seem low. In Michael Howard's view, it is hard to find any historical evidence of a purely accidental war. Technical progress during the past two decades has reduced the prospects of purely accidental onset of nuclear war.[7]

Unfortunately, it is also difficult to be precise about trends in probability over time. For example, is the current situation more or less risky than the period of previous concern, that is, 1958–1962? Those who argue that nuclear risk was higher in 1962 point to such technical improvements as permissive action links; improved command, control, and communication; national technical means of verification; and such political factors as United States and Soviet experience in managing crises. Those who argue that the risk is higher in the current period point to the loss of United States nuclear superiority, the greater Soviet capability to support forces in third world areas, the deployment of vulnerable weapons and support systems that place a premium on preemption, doctrinal stress on protracted war fighting, and the deterioration of political dialogue.

In examining such arguments, it is interesting to note the mixture of technical and political factors, and the mixture of arguments that rest on assumptions about rational factors and those that stress nonrational and accidental factors. Policy responses vary accordingly.

Within a rational actor framework, the insanity of large-scale nuclear war (i.e., the extreme disproportion between political ends sought and the consequences of the military means used) suggests that nuclear war is very unlikely. At the same time, political conflict will occur, and we will need to deter a variety of Soviet actions. Hawks argue that the danger of nuclear war comes from a Soviet miscalculation of the credibility of capability of our commitment. The way to reduce risk and to enhance deterrence is to add nuclear capability so that it is clear we cannot be beaten at the end of a multiple move game (or escalation ladder).

The rational actor model can also lead to other conclusions. Many doves tend to believe that provocation is a greater danger than is temptation in the onset of war, and that the hawks' unrestricted armament could create such provocation. Although the historical evidence that arms races lead to war is more shaky than prevalent views admit, there are historical cases, most prominently American policy toward Japan in 1941, in which one country intended to deter another, but succeeded only in provoking the second country to initiate war.[8] The proper response in such cases is reassurance, although hawks and doves differ on the relative dangers of provocation versus appeasement and on the proper balance to be struck between deterrence and reassurance.

A third view of the probability of the onset of nuclear war rests on a nonrational model that includes such factors as psychic stress, misperception, bureaucratic pathologies, and accidents. Owls worry about loss of control more than wrong intention. Although pure accidents under normal conditions are extremely unlikely, the probability of accident and inadvertent initiation can rise dramatically in a situation of nuclear crisis. At such times, the safety catches that make accidents unlikely are deliberately released, psychic stress is increased, and there is little time to correct mistakes. Such crises also present the rare situation in which, on an expected value definition of rationality, it might make sense to initiate war. If one were absolutely convinced that the other side was about to launch a nuclear attack, it might seem better to strike first rather than second.

In short, the interaction of nonrational and rational factors in crisis situations that might involve escalation and preemption seem the most likely causes of dramatic rises in the probability of nuclear war. Although all three models of the potential onset of nuclear war capture important aspects of causation, many strategists have focused too much on policies of deterrence and reassurance related to intentions, and too little on situations in which intentions may be irrelevant or so constrained that rational choice becomes virtually meaningless.

TECHNOLOGICAL AND POLITICAL UTOPIAS

It does not follow from the proposition that the system of deterrence might fail someday that nuclear holocaust is either imminent or inevitable. Nonetheless, any chance of holocaust or species extinction is so horrible that we would be wise to reduce our reliance on nuclear weapons as much as possible in a way that does not raise the current risks of nuclear war. Given the fallibility of human reason and human organizations, and the inevitable spread of nuclear technologies to more countries (and possibly terrorist groups), it would seem wise gradually to reduce our reliance on nuclear weapons. Whether this can ever lead to abolition of weapons is impossible to say. Certainly, it would be impossible to abolish nuclear knowledge without burning all books and all scientists. The prospect for that solution may have passed when the Pope failed to burn Galileo! However, even if the knowledge of nuclear weapons is an inescapable part of the trajectory of human history, there is nothing inevitable about the number of weapons and the centrality of their role in military and political relations among nations.

Robert Tucker argues that "the first, and indeed the last thing that needs to be said in any moral assessment of deterrence, is that it should not be regarded as a temporary arrangement. . . . Its justification now cannot be made to turn on a prospect that from the vantage point of the present must appear as near utopian. . . . Deterrence, it appears, will remain a part of our 'condition' for as far as we can presently see."[9] Tucker is correct to caution us against overly optimistic attempts to escape deterrence in the near term; such utopian thinking could have highly immoral, unintended consequences. But he would be wrong if he were to discourage long-term utopian thinking. We simply know too little about the distant future to make such categorical assertions, and a little dose of utopian thinking now about the distant future may involve few short-term risks, while helping us to set our policies in a direction in which currently improbable solutions become possible some time in the future. Almost by definition, the current probabilities of utopian solutions are low, but they may become higher for future generations. We simply do not know. In any case, we should avoid foreclosing such prospects and take proportionate risks to keep such possibilities open.

How might one envisage moving toward less reliance on nuclear weapons and lower risks of nuclear war in the future? Two centuries ago, Immanuel Kant suggested that peace among nations might come about as a result of three things: the increasing destructiveness of war; the spread of republican governments; and the growth of commerce and trade. In the short run of two centuries, Kant proved wrong. Extensive trade and enormous destructive capability did not prevent Europe from destroying itself in World War I. But perhaps a century and a half was too short to test the validity of Kant's prescriptions. Unlike 1914, when many leaders (and their citizens) glorified and desired war, nuclear devastation has made war far less attractive today. Although the evidence is not conclusive, it is almost impossible to find instances of war in this century among republican (i.e., constitutional liberal representative) governments.[10]

Trying to predict long-term change would be foolish, although one can sketch rough outlines of broad paths of change that might lead to a future with less reliance on nuclear weapons. Roughly speaking, there are technological paths and political paths. The latter are the more promising, but the former are now receiving more attention.

Among the most dramatic technological changes of the past decade has been the increase in the accuracy with which weapons can be delivered. This accuracy range has reduced the nuclear destructive power needed to destroy particular targets and has increased the precision with which some military targets can be separated from civilian ones. In addition, there have been important improvements in the identification of changing targets and the flexibility of the weapons that might attack them. These changes cut two ways. On one hand, they permit greater discrimination and the possibility of counter combatant targeting; on the other, they give rise to the temptation to think of nuclear weapons as militarily useful in battle. From an owlish perspective, this concept would be seriously mistaken. But the same improvements in accuracy and identification of targets can be used to improve the capabilities of conventional weapons and allow them to replace battlefield nuclear weapons. In other words, if wisely applied, the technology of accuracy could help reduce reliance on battlefield nuclear weapons and on city-burning strategic weapons. However, technology alone will not determine that outcome.

The technological promise that has received greatest attention in recent years is the prospect of effective defense against ballistic missiles. President Reagan expressed a desire to escape from the dilemmas of nuclear deterrence in his speech of March 1983. However, escape from deterrence requires a leak-proof defense, not only against ballistic missiles but also against bombers and cruise missiles. Such a perfect defense seems unlikely. Some who doubt the technological feasibility of such a task have urged that the New Strategic Defense Initiative Organization in the Pentagon concentrate on the lesser task of defending missiles rather than cities. But this is a rationale that would enhance rather than replace deterrence.

Moreover, the feasibility of a utopia is more than a matter of technology. It also has a political dimension. Even if the complex defense technology can be developed and combined into a system that has to be perfect without ever having been tested under the stress of nuclear war, can we get from here to there without going through a transition period in which the nuclear predicament of both sides would be worse? Will improving defenses stimulate a massive increase in offensive weapons as the other side tries to prove it can still overcome the defenses? If it appears we are about to perfect a defensive system in a few years that would effectively disarm the Soviet deterrent, would they take more risks during crises in the short run because they saw the likelihood that these risks would pay off politically becoming bleaker and bleaker with the passage of time?

These questions do not mean that there should not be a significant research program on strategic defense. Quite the contrary. The prospect of enhancing deterrence, and perhaps, in the long term, of being able to save a large number of lives in case deterrence fails, justifies considerable efforts. The value of such an initiative will depend on the consequences, not the motives. It may be "better to defend than to avenge," but only if the consequences of *trying* to defend do not increase the risk of nuclear conflict in the meantime. Those consequences are likely to be determined not by our intentions, but by the types of technology chosen (how it will affect crisis stability) and the political state of United States–Soviet relations (will the introduction of defense be in a cooperative or an antagonist setting?).

The political path lacks the glamour of the technological one, and as many technologists have discovered, politics is harder than physics. But political change is the key factor in the long-range future. Further, political change may take a number of forms. There may be changes in relations between the United States and the Soviet Union; there may be changes in the growth of international institutions and cooperation among states; there may be changes in domestic political and social attitudes toward the sovereign state and its defenses.

Sometimes political relations between states change quickly—witness the change in relations between the United States and China in less than a decade. Because such rapid changes are often related to the existence of a common enemy, it would be unwise to expect a similarly rapid change in United States–Soviet relations.

There are several deep-seated reasons to expect tension in United States–Soviet relations. First, as de Tocqueville already saw in the nineteenth century, the enormous size and resources of the Russian and American nations foreshadowed a future bipolar rivalry. Then in 1917, the Bolshevik Revolution added a layer of deep ideological incompatibility. When the Second World War destroyed the multination balance of power existing before 1939, it left a bipolar structure of world power centered on the United States–Soviet rivalry. The accumulation of vast nuclear arsenals overshadowing those of all other nations has consolidated that special relationship. From a power politics point of view, the probability of tension is built into the very structure of the relationship.

Nonetheless, at different times, there have been lesser degrees of hostility. It is worth remembering that the worst outcome has not occurred. Despite hostility, there has also been prudence in managing the world's first nuclear balance of power. The destructiveness of nuclear weapons introduced a disproportion between most ends that the superpowers seek and the principal military means at their disposal.

This situation has led to the evolution, by a process of trial and error, of some primitive rules for avoiding or managing crises. The rules are so primitive that they might more correctly be called prudent practices. Indeed, they began well before the onset of detente in the 1970s and survived its demise. As described by Stanley Hoffmann, "One such informal rule was the non-resort to atomic weapons. A second rule was the avoidance of direct military clashes between armed forces. A third element was the slow (and for America) painful learning of limited wars ... calculated so as to limit the risks of escalation, even if those constraints made a clearcut victory or a rapid settlement impossible. Later came the beginnings of nuclear arms control between Washington and Moscow."[11] Rudimentary as these rules or prudent practices are, they are significant if one believes that a stable balance of power requires a degree of moderation in the actors' behavior, as well as a military balance. . . .

Beyond the United States–Soviet relationship, there may be other political changes that will affect the role of nuclear weapons in world politics. That the development of cooperation among states rests on self-interest rather than goodwill is encouraging because it implies that cooperation is consistent with realistic premises. There may continue to be a gradual development of international regimes that govern various dimensions of economic and social interdependence among states. In some cases, these regimes may involve a gradual growth of institutions. In other instances, economic integration among states may reduce the degree of potential conflict, as it has between ancient enemies such as France and Germany. The development of transnational institutions and contacts may gradually transform domestic attitudes toward sovereignty and the use of violence to defend the state. After all, the modern territorial state that replaced looser feudal loyalties has only been the dominant institution since the Peace of Westphalia in 1648. It is not implausible to think it may give way to other institutional forms, if we look forward for an equivalent period.

Of course, this Kantian view of the distant future is only one among a vast number of possible outcomes. Other benign (or horrendous) outcomes are also possible. The important point is that we should not let our imaginations be captured solely by images of imminent nuclear holocaust or by cynical views of the immutability of our dependence on nuclear weapons, for both images tend to stifle the modest efforts we can and should make now so that a Kantian type of future will be somewhat more probable for coming generations to develop. Similarly, we should not let the current debate about a single technological utopia like SDI so dominate our thinking that we fail to evaluate its various dimensions in relation to alternative visions of the long-term future.

NOTES

1. John Lewis Gaddis, "The Long Peace," *International Security*, Vol. 10 (Spring 1986).

2. Thomas Powers, *Thinking about the Next War* (New York: Knopf, 1982), p. 17.

3. Todd Gitlin, "Time to Move beyond Deterrence," *The Nation*, December 22, 1984, p. 676.

4. Bradford Lyttle, *The Flaw in Deterrence* (Chicago: Midwest Pacifist Publishing Center, 1983), pp. 8–11. Note that Lyttle's numbers depend on the number of missiles that could be accidentally launched. Nuclear war need not follow.

5. Paul Schroeder, "Does Murphy's Law Apply to History?" *The Wilson Quarterly*, Winter 1985, p. 88.

6. McGeorge Bundy, "To Cap the Volcano," *Foreign Affairs*, Vol. 47, 1969.

7. Michael Howard, *The Causes of Wars* (London: Unwin Paperbacks, 1983); and Paul Bracken, "Accidental Nuclear War," in *Hawks, Doves and Owls*, ed. Graham Allison, Albert Carnesale, and Joseph Nye (New York: Norton, 1985).

8. Graham Allison, Albert Carnesale, and Joseph S. Nye, eds. *Hawks, Doves and Owls* (New York: Norton, 1985), chapter 8.

9. Robert W. Tucker, "Morality and Deterrence," *Ethics*, April 1985.

10. See Michael Doyle, "Kant, Liberal Legacies and Foreign Affairs" *Philosophy and Public Affairs*, Vol. 12, nos. 3 and 4.

11. Stanley Hoffmann, *Primacy or World Order* (New York: McGraw-Hill, 1981), p. 11.

7 SOVIET NUCLEAR STRATEGY AND ARMS CONTROL UNDER GORBACHEV: NEW THINKING, NEW POLICY

Peter Zwick

One of the most hotly debated questions among professional Soviet watchers is whether new Soviet leaders make a difference. Implicit in this question is whether the Soviet Union is too constrained by ideological, historical, or bureaucratic rigidity for new leaders to fundamentally alter existing policy. Although the question may seem counterintuitive in view of the fact that Soviet policy making has been controlled by a relatively few, strong personalities—Lenin, Stalin, Khrushchev, and Brezhnev—it forces us to think about what is really new and different about any incoming Soviet leader and how the West should respond.

The rise of Mikhail Gorbachev to power has given this question new urgency. In addition to the remarkable domestic changes incorporated in *perestroika* (restructuring) and *glasnost* (openness), Gorbachev has surprised the world with an avalanche of foreign policy initiatives. Without underestimating the importance of improved Sino-Soviet relations, the withdrawal of Soviet forces from Afghanistan, or Soviet "détente" in Western Europe, the most significant Gorbachev initiatives have been in Soviet policy toward the United States in general, and in the area of arms control in particular.

Gorbachev has not only made original and sweeping arms control proposals of his own but has accepted major American offers, all of which have resulted in significant progress in almost all aspects of nuclear weapons reductions. So rapid and dramatic have some Soviet shifts been that many in the West worry that Gorbachev has some "trick up his sleeve," and that the West is stepping into an arms control trap that ultimately favors the USSR from which it will be unable to extricate itself. The concern is that in their desire to rid the world of the nuclear nightmare Western leaders are incorrectly imputing to Gorbachev the same desire.

Is Gorbachev serious about arms control? Is this a *new* Soviet foreign policy? Or is it the same long-standing goal of enhancing Soviet military power and shifting the "correlation of forces" in favor of the USSR?

While it would be foolish to suggest that U.S. policy should be based solely on trust of Gorbachev, it has become clear that Gorbachev is indeed serious about arms control and that he has made fundamental changes in Soviet nuclear strategy that have far-reaching impact on Soviet arms control strategy. To be sure, the foundations for Gorbachev's approach are to be found in evolving Soviet military doctrine, but Gorbachev's conclusions represent a significant break with past strategy and may offer the U.S. and the world an unprecedented opportunity for real arms control.

GORBACHEV'S NEW THINKING ON NUCLEAR STRATEGY

Gorbachev's nuclear strategy and approach to arms control are part of what has become known in Soviet circles as the "new thinking" (*novoye myshleniye*). The "new thinking" is the foreign policy equivalent of *perestroika* in domestic affairs, but no less important. While some observers still question whether the "new thinking" will be fully translated from declaratory policy into action, there remains little doubt that Gorbachev is serious about its implementation.

According to Gorbachev, the foundation of his "new thinking" is that "We made ourselves face the fact that the stockpiling and sophistication of nuclear armaments means that the human race has lost its immortality. It can be regained only by destroying nuclear weapons."[1] While the elements of "new thinking" cover the entire gamut of Soviet foreign policy, those that pertain specifically to nuclear strategy and arms control may be summarized as follows:

1. Peaceful coexistence must continue in a "civilized" and "polite" manner.
2. The USSR can no longer seek to preserve its security solely through military power. Political means must also be employed.
3. There is nothing to be gained from a military conflict with the United States.
4. Traditional nuclear deterrence theories must be replaced by nuclear disarmament.
5. There is little chance for socialist transformation in the West; if it does occur it will probably be peaceful.
6. A comprehensive system of international security based on mutual security achieved by political agreement must replace the current system of security based on military competition.

What inspired Gorbachev to adopt this "new thinking"? First, he appears to believe that traditional Soviet and American approaches to nuclear arms are immoral and ultimately suicidal. There is, according to Gorbachev, "evil inherent in the ideology and policy of nuclear deterrence," because, "deterrence is a policy of blackmail and threats ... [which] means subordination of politics to the interests of militarism."[2] Those who remain skeptical of Gorbachev's peaceful motives may be more convinced by his other argument that "we need lasting peace to concentrate on the development of our security and to proceed to improve the life of the Soviet people."[3]

Whether motivated by moral or economic considerations, Gorbachev's new thinking on nuclear strategy has resulted in new Soviet positions on virtually every aspect of nuclear arms control. Ironically, this occurred at precisely the same time that U.S. strategic policy was being re-evaluated and redirected by President Reagan. Even more surprisingly, Reagan and Gorbachev came to many of the same conclusions, although in some crucial areas their responses were quite different.

THE EVOLUTION OF
SOVIET STRATEGIC DOCTRINE

To fully appreciate the changes in the Soviet position it is useful to review briefly the evolution of Soviet strategic doctrine. In particular, we must assess the goals of Soviet nuclear strategy with respect to the possibility of fighting and winning a nuclear war, an issue that has divided Western experts on the motives of Soviet military policy and often confused the debate on the appropriate American response.

The first major shift in the Lenin-Stalin view of war was Khrushchev's 1956 declaration that the Soviets no longer considered war inevitable. This pronouncement did not, however, rule out the possibility of war and left open the question of what kind of war, nuclear or conventional, it would be. That doctrinal issue was resolved in 1959, when Khrushchev declared that if a war between the USSR and the United States did break out it would inevitably become a nuclear war, no matter how it started. This viewpoint required that the Soviet Union use nuclear weapons in the earliest stages of a conflict in order to inflict massive damage to the war-fighting capabilities of the United States. Since conventional forces were of marginal utility under this doctrine, Khrushchev shifted spending priorities from conventional arms toward strategic nuclear forces.

The transfer of power from Khrushchev to Brezhnev brought major change in Soviet military doctrine. In 1966, Soviet strategic planners reversed their earlier position on the inevitability of escalation to nuclear war and declared that it might be possible to avoid nuclear war in an East-West conflict, especially one that began in Europe. Soviet thinking on this issue was shaped by NATO's adoption of a "flexible response" strategy in Europe, which called for step-level escalation. Strong pressure from the Soviet military establishment for a new look at the role of conventional weapons and forces contributed to this reversal of military doctrine. Under the 1966 doctrine, the role of Soviet strategic forces became nuclear deterrence rather than preemptive destruction.

The adoption of a "limited war" doctrine in 1966 did not, however, rule out the possibility that nuclear war could occur. It merely gave the Soviets some conventional options prior to the use of nuclear options. Soviet doctrine with respect to nuclear "war-fighting" and "war-winning" did not change in 1966. Both Party and military leaders continued to believe that a nuclear war was "fightable" and would result in victory for socialism. Soviet military doctrine continued to assert that nuclear war was merely the extension of conventional war and that a nuclear war was "winnable." Soviet strategy, therefore, included defense, both active (interceptors and anti-missile systems) and passive (civil), as a means of keeping damage to a minimum. Thus, if deterrence failed, Soviet military strategy provided for the capability to wage and win nuclear war.[4]

Although Soviet military doctrine continued to combine elements of "war-fighting" and "war-winning," the Soviet Union entered into a series of arms control agreements with the United States that were based on the contrary American doctrine of "mutual assured destruction" (MAD). This American theory of nuclear deterrence held that only the certainty of total destruction would deter the use of nuclear weapons. MAD as a deterrence theory relied on both adversaries having massive offensive strategic nuclear capability and agreeing not to deploy defensive systems that could protect against nuclear devastation.

The Soviet willingness to enter into MAD-based agreements, such as the 1972 Anti-Ballistic Missile (ABM) and Strategic Arms Limitation (SALT) agreements, which conflicted with its traditional doctrine, is difficult to explain. One explanation is that the Soviets were being duplicitous. Another more probable explanation is that Brezhnev was willing to adjust Soviet national security policy in order to achieve economic benefits in the larger context of détente.

Nevertheless, the inconsistency of a Soviet military doctrine that included "war-fighting" and "winnability" with a deterrence theory based on mutual vulnerability to massive retaliation was apparent and troubling to Western leaders, especially those suspicious of Soviet motives. Brezhnev began the process of resolving this obvious contradiction in a speech delivered in the city of Tula in January 1977. In it Brezhnev questioned the basic principles of existing Soviet military doctrine by repudiating for the first time the notion that victory in nuclear war is possible. He went on to assert that the Soviet Union had rejected military superiority for equality with the United States and that Soviet nuclear forces were purely defensive.

Brezhnev formalized the new Soviet military doctrine at the Twenty-sixth CPSU Congress in 1981 when he said, "To try to prevail over the other in the arms race or to count on victory in a nuclear war is dangerous madness." If the USSR could no longer count on the inevitability of victory in nuclear war, then pursuit of military superiority over the United States became meaningless. Brezhnev said as much: "The military-strategic equilibrium that exists between the USSR and the US and that exists between the Warsaw Treaty and NATO objectively serves to preserve peace on our planet. We have not sought, and do not now seek, military superiority over the other side." Brezhnev went on to say that any nation that started a nuclear war with the USSR would be committing suicide because "retaliation is unavoidable." In other words, Brezhnev adopted the MAD theory of deterrence.

There is evidence nonetheless of opposition within the Soviet Union to this doctrinal shift. Some analysts see the conflict as the reflection of a debate between civilian and military factions over the utility of war in the nuclear era. Brezhnev's 1977 appointee as Chief of the General Staff, Marshal Nikolai Ogarkov, was one of the most vocal critics of the change and was eventually removed from his post in 1984 because of the conflict.[5] Despite Ogarkov's fall, many analysts believe that the military continued to reject MAD and that the doctrine was not incorporated into operational Soviet nuclear strategy. That is to say, the structure of Soviet forces remained oriented to war-fighting.[6] Others see it as a conflict between "diplomacists" who believe that progress can only be achieved through accommodation, and "unilateralists" who believe that only Soviet military power can guarantee Soviet strategic gains.[7]

Despite this resistance to change, Gorbachev forcefully reiterated Brezhnev's position on the impossibility of winning a nuclear war in his Twenty-seventh Party Congress address. Speaking as much to his own military establishment as to the Reagan administration, Gorbachev declared: "The nature of current weaponry leaves no state with any hope of defending itself using solely military-technical means—through the creation of a defense. . . . Ensuring security is becoming more and more a political task, and it can be accomplished only by political means." Gorbachev went on to explain, "this means recognizing that winning the arms race, like winning a nuclear war itself, is no longer possible."

Just prior to the Party Congress, on January 15, 1986, Gorbachev made a major announcement on Soviet nuclear policy. He declared that the Soviet Union was prepared to enter into a process with the United States and the other nations of the world that would lead to the elimination of *all* nuclear weapons by the year 2000. There was undoubtedly propaganda value associated with such a grandiose offer, but in terms of Soviet military doctrine Gorbachev's proposal was a repudiation of nuclear-based security.

These pronouncements and proposals are perfectly consistent with Gorbachev's "new thinking," which substitutes the complete elimination of nuclear weapons for their use as a deterrence. The problem with this "new" theory is that while it is patently true that there can be no *nuclear* war without nuclear weapons, Gorbachev's formulation begs the question of how *war* will be avoided in a nuclear-free world and raises legitimate concerns in the West about Soviet conventional superiority. All that the "new philosophy of foreign policy" has to say on this subject is that: "After the elimination of nuclear weapons, stability in the world will be maintained primarily with the help of political and legal means, international means included, while military means will be based on reasonable sufficiency to repel attack."[8]

Skeptics have suggested that there is no substance to Gorbachev's proposals and they have no effect on military doctrine. Opponents of total nuclear disarmament have argued that even if Gorbachev is sincere, his proposals are a ploy to establish Soviet military superiority in conventional forces.[9] Gorbachev seems to be having enough difficulty convincing his own colleagues of the wisdom of his views to suggest that they are serious proposals to be taken seriously. On the whole, they are couched in enough realistic reservations to suggest that Gorbachev does not expect full implementation of his proposals, but sees them as goals to be striven for if not achieved. Finally, Gorbachev has proposed the reduction and elimination of nonnuclear weapons, which suggests that he is not simply attempting to gain conventional superiority through nuclear disarmament. For example, he has called for the banning of chemical weapons, and with respect to conventional arms has said that the WTO nations "are prepared for a decisive scaling down of the military confrontation of the two blocs in a zone stretching from the Atlantic to the Urals."

The equivocation in Gorbachev's statements on nuclear disarmament address concerns within the Soviet military as well as skepticism in the West. For example, in his Twenty-seventh Party Congress address, Gorbachev reiterated Brezhnev's unilateral Soviet commitment not to use nuclear weapons first, but modified it with the warning that the USSR "will adhere to that commitment *as strictly as possible*." He also acknowledged that there were indeed "scenarios" for nuclear attack against the Soviet Union (by the United States), and agreed that "we have no right to disregard them." Gorbachev also conceded to military concerns about opening Soviet installations to outside inspectors by saying, "Disarmament without verification is impossible, but verification without disarmament makes no sense either." Finally, with respect to the Soviet response to the American escalation of the arms race, Gorbachev assured his audience, "The Soviet Union does not lay claim to greater security, but it will not settle for less."

These assurances that he would not ignore or surrender the military security of the USSR notwithstanding, Gorbachev's analysis led him to the conclusion that "Striving for military superiority —objectively cannot bring anyone political gain." Reiterating his antinuclear theme, Gorbachev insisted that "True equal security in our age is guaranteed not by the highest possible but the lowest possible level of strategic balance, from which it is necessary to completely exclude nuclear . . . weapons." "Thus," he said, "objective—I emphasize objective—conditions have evolved in which the struggle between capitalism and socialism can proceed *solely and exclusively in forms of peaceful competition and peaceful rivalry*." His reference to "objective" conditions was an obvious attempt to undercut those at home and abroad who continued to argue that it was technically possible for one nation to gain nuclear superiority.

Gorbachev lent credence to his antinuclear policy with a sixteen-month unilateral moratorium on nuclear testing. But, in light of continued U.S.

testing, Gorbachev eventually renewed the Soviet testing program, presumably under pressure from his own military.

Until nuclear weapons are eliminated, there remains one very important respect in which Soviet military doctrine is not totally inconsistent with a "war-fighting" strategy. The one problem with MAD deterrence theory is that it does not answer the question: What happens if, despite all good intentions, the political effort to avoid nuclear war fails; if the nuclear deterrent fails to deter? What will the Soviet Union do if the unthinkable happens? Soviet military doctrine continues to allow that if deterrence fails, the USSR must be defended. Soviet leaders may not be able to rely on victory, or even be able to achieve it, but they continue to believe that it is possible to avoid total annihilation, and, more important, to deny the United States a victory. In that context, Soviet military strategy includes a "war-fighting" capability, but this is far different from the notion that nuclear war is "winnable."

Soviet defensive strategy is not aimed at the establishment of a first strike capability (i.e., the ability to preemptively destroy the American nuclear arsenal without retaliation). Rather, Soviet defensive preparations are intended to increase the probability of survival if a nuclear war occurs. Here, historical factors must play a very strong role in Soviet calculations. In view of Soviet wartime experiences, it would be unthinkable for Soviet leaders, civilian or military, to devise a military doctrine that did not include some effort to protect the civilian population and reduce the potential damage to the Soviet homeland. The objective possibility of survival in a nuclear war is secondary to the need for the Soviet leaders to appear to be doing something to ensure some level of protection.

Soviet military doctrine incorporates "war-fighting" and defensive elements as fall-backs if MAD deterrence fails rather than as substitutes for MAD. There is no evidence that today's Soviet political leadership believes that it is possible to fight and win a nuclear war or that nuclear war can achieve the ultimate ideological goal—a socialist world. The Clausewitzian view that war is merely the violent extension of politics has been repudiated as a principle of Soviet national security policy in the nuclear age.

SDI AND ARMS CONTROL

This major change in Soviet nuclear doctrine is reflected in current Soviet arms control policy. Owing to the aforementioned shift in U.S. strategic doctrine under President Reagan, Soviet-American arms control negotiations began to focus for the first time on reductions in nuclear arsenals rather than on limits in growth. However, at the same time that U.S. and Soviet policies began to converge on the goal of arms reduction, they began to diverge on the issue of nuclear deterrence.

The superpowers first reversed position on deterrence theory when Brezhnev adopted MAD at virtually the same time that the United States moved toward "war-fighting" capability under [Jimmy] Carter's Presidential Directive 59. Then, when Gorbachev's "new thinking" abandoned nuclear deterrence entirely in favor of a nuclear free world, Reagan initiated a plan—the Strategic Defense Initiative (SDI)—for making nuclear weapons obsolete through technological innovation rather than voluntary renunciation. The issue dividing Reagan and Gorbachev became how best to eliminate nuclear weapons. The problem was that each saw the other's plan as unworkable at best and threatening to his nation's security at worst.

For his part, President Reagan saw SDI as a means to ensure against nuclear attack by creating a virtually impenetrable shield over the United States. This defensive system would purportedly make offensive strategic weapons obsolete without threatening the security of the Soviet Union. Furthermore, once developed, the United States originally offered to share SDI technology with the USSR, thereby ensuring that neither side had an unfair advantage. However, Gorbachev has remained adamantly opposed to SDI and has consistently tied any agreement on offensive strategic systems to some limit on SDI.

Why would Gorbachev object to the development of a purely defensive system, which by most estimates could never operate at the level of effectiveness necessary to guarantee absolute protection against nuclear attack? To understand Gorbachev's reservations about Reagan's approach, the defensive potential of SDI must be considered in the light of what might conceivably result from any possible agreement on offensive weapons. We must ask what Gorbachev would ask: What level of nuclear arms reduction is achievable, and how would a strategic defense system affect Soviet security under these lower levels of offensive strategic weapons?

While it is important to understand what SDI could do, it is equally important to understand what it could not do. Contrary to President Reagan's publicly expressed hopes for SDI, virtually all SDI experts agree that it will not eliminate the need for offensive nuclear weapons. The United States might gain an increased margin of security through a defensive system, but it could not rely exclusively on a defensive shield to deter nuclear attack.

While current technological limits should not be used to evaluate SDI's potential as a defensive shield, projections can be made on the basis of current technology for the remainder of the twentieth century. The question that must be addressed is not whether SDI can ever be a perfect defense against all offensive nuclear weapons, but what its effect would be on arms control, even if deployed in a less than perfect form.

The proposed strategic defense system will be a space- and land-based network that can destroy Soviet intercontinental missiles within five minutes of launch, or their multiple warheads after they and decoys have been deployed in space. Computer programs must be written to control and coordinate the system that can accommodate virtually any Soviet launching strategy or sequence. Projections of software and hardware capability into the next century make this a dubious undertaking at best.

More important, perhaps, is what SDI is not anticipated to be able to defend against. The challenge of destroying missiles launched from submarines, where 25 percent of Soviet strategic nuclear forces are currently based and whose exact locations are unknown until their missiles are airborne, is far beyond the near-term capability of SDI. Further, if those submarines are close off shore and launch their missiles in a low, sub-stratospheric trajectory, the anticipated system is not designed to stop them. As both the United States and the Soviet Union have substantial submarine launching capability, it is inconceivable that the United States expects to depend exclusively on SDI in the foreseeable future, and Gorbachev knows that.

Similarly, SDI is not intended to produce a defense against nuclear attack by strategic bombers carrying either gravity bombs or cruise missiles equipped with nuclear warheads. The deployment of the Stealth bomber, which is undetectable by radar, would mean that no known defense could effectively thwart a nuclear attack from these bombers. Hence, sharing SDI technology with the USSR will not reduce the risk of nuclear attack from this source.

What all this means is that SDI will not be a 100 percent effective defense against the types of weapons it is designed to stop, and it cannot be a 100 percent effective defense against *all* offensive nuclear weapons. In short, SDI could not be relied upon as the sole deterrence against nuclear attack by either side, and some form of offensive retaliation would have to be maintained to guarantee the national security of both superpowers. SDI may be an "insurance policy," but it does not provide "all risk" coverage.

The promise of SDI to eliminate the need for offensive strategic nuclear weapons must also be evaluated in the context of political considerations, particularly the Soviet-American rivalry in Europe. When President Reagan refused to join General Secretary Gorbachev in his renunciation of first use of nuclear weapons, he did so on the grounds that if the United States were to repudiate first use of nuclear weapons, the Soviet Union would have a free hand to exercise its superiority of conventional military force in Europe. With the total elimination of all intermediate-range nuclear forces in Europe, the American strategic nuclear deterrence becomes even more crucial. In other words, American offensive strategic nuclear capability is an essential guarantee of European security. Total abrogation of the right or ability to use offensive nuclear weapons might be construed as an invitation to Soviet aggression in Europe and elsewhere in the free world.

In view of Reagan's ongoing mistrust of Soviet motives, Gorbachev must have realized that Reagan had no intention of abandoning all offensive strategic nuclear weapons. Furthermore, Gorbachev must know that even if any American president were inclined to remove America's nuclear umbrella from Europe, the NATO governments would never permit that to happen. A passive defense, such as that provided by SDI, could not guarantee Western European security.

The issue of whether the President was actually prepared to accept total nuclear disarmament at Reykjavik raised a mild furor when Reagan briefed congressional leaders on the Reykjavik negotiations. The president, echoing statements made by top members of the American team immediately following the Reykjavik collapse, reportedly told Congress that he had offered to eliminate *all* nuclear weapons at Reykjavik. Subsequently, White House spokesmen claimed that the President had been misunderstood. What he had agreed to, they said, was a 50 percent reduction of *all* nuclear weapons in the first stage (five years) and the complete elimination of intercontinental ballistic missiles in the second stage. This would have left the United States with strategic bombers and cruise missiles as a nuclear deterrent against Soviet aggression in Europe.

Secretary of State [George] Shultz's exact words at Reykjavik were: "The agreement that might have been said, 'During the ten-year period in effect, all offensive strategic arms and ballistic missiles would be eliminated.'" General Secretary Gorbachev reiterated this interpretation in an address to the Soviet people on October 22: "The President did, albeit without special enthusiasm, consent to the elimination of all—I emphasize—all, not only certain offensive strategic arms, to be destroyed precisely over ten years, in two stages." By way of substantiating Gorbachev's contention, the Soviet foreign ministry took the unprecedented step of releasing the text of their notes taken at the meeting, which quoted the President after he learned that Gorbachev was proposing the elimination of all nuclear weapons as saying, "Apparently we misunderstood you. But if that is what you want, all right." The President's spokesman responded with the official post-summit position: "The President discussed it, but it was not formally tabled."

Exactly what was on the table in the final hours at Reykjavik may never become completely known. What is clear, however, is that both sides appear to accept the possibility that offensive strategic weapons can be significantly reduced in the short term. A fifty percent reduction over a five or even ten year period would indeed be a remarkable achievement. However, as remarkable as it might be, it would still leave a very large number of nuclear weapons in place—as many as 6,000 warheads on each side.

The reality of arms control for Gorbachev, then, is simply this. Even under the best of circumstances, in ten years the United States and the Soviet Union could significantly reduce but not eliminate their offensive strategic nuclear arsenals. Great Britain, France, and China will still have independent strategic nuclear forces, and some smaller states will also join the nuclear club. The U.S. will not eliminate its offensive nuclear weapons, even if SDI is ready to be deployed by 1996 (an extremely optimistic timetable), because the USSR will still be perceived as a threat to European security, and nuclear attack from weapons that SDI could not stop would be possible.

With this reality in mind, the crucial fact about SDI for Gorbachev is that its potential effectiveness increases in inverse proportion to the number of warheads it must defend against. In other words, *arms reduction will increase the value of SDI*. It is patently easier to locate and destroy 5,000 than 10,000 warheads, and easier still to defend against 3,000 or 300. The smaller the number of offensive strategic weapons there are, the more vulnerable Soviet forces are to even a rudimentary American strategic defense system.

At a minimum, what Gorbachev hopes to accomplish by restricting research and testing of SDI is to ensure that mutual reductions in offensive weapons will not unilaterally increase Soviet vulnerability. Without such a guarantee, Gorbachev cannot possibly agree to substantial reductions in the Soviet nuclear arsenal, even if they are matched by equivalent American cutbacks.

On the assumption that Gorbachev understands that an arms control agreement could result in fewer nuclear weapons by 1996, but not their elimination, his objection to SDI becomes obvious. If Gorbachev were to permit the United States to research and test SDI and then to decide unilaterally whether to deploy the system in ten years, while at the same time agreeing to substantial reductions in offensive weapons knowing that their elimination is impossible, he would be guaranteeing American military superiority. In effect, the United States would have a "first strike" capability, which means that the U.S. could launch a nuclear attack against the USSR and defend against any retaliation. That, in a nutshell, is why Gorbachev opposes SDI.

FUTURE PROSPECTS FOR ARMS CONTROL

Gorbachev's opposition to SDI did not, however, prevent him from continuing to make substantive proposals on strategic arms reductions. With the signing of the INF agreement in December 1987, Gorbachev shifted the focus once again to strategic weapons. In response to U.S. demands that an arms control agreement would have to include a restructuring of the Soviet strategic forces away from ICBMs, which American negotiators consider the most dangerous system, Gorbachev proposed that each side adopt a formula that would allow no more than 60 percent of warheads in any single leg of the strategic triad. This would reduce Soviet land-based warheads to 3,600 from 6,470, even with no reductions in delivery systems. The initial American reaction was to reject this proposal on grounds that it would impose unacceptably low limits on American SLBMs, which in the American view are less dangerous because they are smaller and less accurate than Soviet land-based, heavy missiles. The Soviets made other proposals, including the banning of mobile, land-based missiles and the limiting of sea-launched missiles to submarines, with a total of 400 warheads.

What is clear from this agenda is that Gorbachev is serious about arms control and will pursue it vigorously, but not to Soviet disadvantage. Flexibility on SDI on both sides will be the key to success.

Gorbachev's "new thinking" on nuclear strategy has indeed been followed by a new nuclear policy. Whatever his motives—moral, security, or economic—Gorbachev has made a significant difference in this crucial area of Soviet foreign policy. Whether this is a long-term commitment or just a "window of opportunity" will depend in part on the success of the first initiatives. There are undoubtedly members of the Soviet hierarchy who have misgivings about Gorbachev's "new thinking," just as there are those who oppose *perestroika*. If Gorbachev's current strategy does not succeed in reducing the perceived American threat, including SDI, he, or his successor, will be forced to return to the traditional Soviet approach of security through military strength.

The issue for future American policy makers is whether there is more security in a defensive shield against a massive Soviet nuclear arsenal or in significantly reduced nuclear arsenals on both sides. Gorbachev's "new thinking" has opened new opportunities as well as new challenges of an unprecedented nature. Gorbachev has made a difference in Soviet policy; the question that remains is whether he will make a difference in U.S. policy.

NOTES

1. Mikhail Gorbachev's Address to Participants in the International Forum, "For a Nuclear Free World, for Survival of Humanity," *Information Bulletin* (April 1987): 7.

2. Speech by Mikhail Gorbachev at the Dinner in Honor of Margaret Thatcher, Prime Minister of Great Britain, *Information Bulletin* (June 1987): 3.

3. Ibid., p. 4.

4. Richard Pipes, "Why the Soviet Union Thinks it Could Fight and Win a Nuclear War," *Commentary* 64 (July 1977): 21–34.

5. George C. Weickhardt, "Ustinov Versus Ogarkov," *Problems of Communism* 34 (January–February 1985): 77–82.

6. Tsuyoshi Hasegawa, "Soviets on Nuclear-War-Fighting," *Problems of Communism* 35 (July-August 1986), p. 79; and Benjamin Lambeth, *Has Soviet Nuclear Strategy Changed* (Santa Monica, CA: Rand Corporation, 1985).

7. Dan L. Strode and Rebecca V. Strode, "Diplomacy and Defense in Soviet National Security Policy," *International Security* (Fall 1983): 91–116.

8. Ye. Primakov, "A New Philosophy of Foreign Policy," *Pravda*, July 10, 1987, p. 3, translated in *The Current Digest of the Soviet Press* 34 (August 12, 1987): 1.

9. See, for example, James Schlesinger, "Reykjavik and Revelations: A Turn of the Tide," *Foreign Affairs* 65 (1986): 426–46.

8 U.S. NUCLEAR STRATEGY: CHARACTERISTICS AND COMMON CRITICISMS

U.S. Office of Technology Assessment

The overall strategic objective of [current U.S.] nuclear strategy is, and consistently has been, to avoid nuclear attack . . . while preserving other national interests. To accomplish this, our strategy has attempted to achieve three major goals:

- deter the Soviets from nuclear attack on the United States by convincing them that the outcome would be unacceptable to them;

- convince the Soviets that we will attempt to preserve our national interests by means short of nuclear war, but that attacks on those interests might well lead to nuclear war; and

- terminate nuclear war, if it cannot be avoided, at the lowest possible level of violence and on terms most favorable to us.

We strive to deter nuclear attack by fostering a perception among the Soviet leadership that they would suffer unacceptable losses in a nuclear war, and that under no circumstances would such a war leave them better off in terms of achieving their geopolitical objectives than they otherwise would have been. For this strategy to be credible, we must also foster the perception among the Soviets that we are not only willing to fight a nuclear war if necessary, but that nothing they could do could make us incapable of doing so. However, we also do not want our forces to be structured in such a way as to give the Soviets increased incentive to strike first in a crisis. We therefore strive to balance potential war-fighting capability against crisis stability.

In the event of attack, U.S. strategy incorporates two broad elements. We would seek to deny the Soviets success in achieving the goals motivating such an attack, and we would threaten retaliation. The *perception* of these capabilities contributes to deterring attack; the *possession* of these capabilities is intended to make possible the termination of hostilities on favorable terms if they cannot be avoided. These elements apply both to deterring a Soviet first strike and to deterring and responding to subsequent Soviet actions. This discussion stresses "intending" to terminate hostilities, rather than success-

Note: Some footnotes have been deleted, and others have been renumbered to appear in consecutive order.

fully doing so, because it is by no means obvious that any plan for initiating even limited use of nuclear weapons can avoid the destruction of the societies of both parties to the conflict.

We would accomplish these elements, denial of success and retaliation, with offensive and passive defensive means. We deny the Soviets success in attacking military installations by means of a variety of passive measures such as hardening them and making them redundant (e.g., ICBM silos), dispersing them (e.g., air and naval forces), and hiding them (e.g., ballistic missile submarines). We do not attempt to deny success to attacks on our cities, on economic targets, or on "soft" military targets. We threaten retaliation by maintaining survivable offensive forces that are capable on balance of riding out attack and then reaching and destroying Soviet military and civilian assets. In short:

- The survival of the United States depends on rational behavior of the Soviet leadership. We seek to deter them from attacking, but if they intend to destroy the United States and suffer the consequences, we cannot prevent them from doing so.

- Deterrence rests primarily on offensive forces. We rely more heavily on the threat of retaliation than we do on denial of success.

- We rely on the use of passive defenses, not active ones, for the survivability of our offensive forces. . . .

While catastrophic failure of this strategy would be clear, its success is hard to quantify. "We can never really measure how much aggression we have deterred, or how much peace we have preserved," wrote Secretary of Defense Weinberger [in 1984]. "These are intangible—until they are lost."

COUNTERVAILING STRATEGY

In 1980, after having conducted a comprehensive review of U.S. strategic policy, President Carter issued Presidential Directive 59 which formally codified a "countervailing" strategy. As described by Secretary [Harold] Brown in . . . 1982, the countervailing strategy is based on two fundamental principles:

> The first is that, because it is a strategy of deterrence, the countervailing strategy is designed with the Soviets in mind. Not only must we have the forces, the doctrine, and the will to retaliate if attacked, we must convince the Soviets, in advance, that we do. Because it is designed to deter the Soviets, our strategic doctrine must take account of what we know about Soviet perspectives on these issues, for, by definition, deterrence requires shaping Soviet assessments about the risks of war. . . . We may, and we do, think our models are more accurate, but theirs are the reality deterrence drives us to consider. . . .
>
> The second basic point is that, because the world is constantly changing, our

strategy evolves slowly, almost continually, over time to adapt to changes in U.S. technology and military capabilities, as well as Soviet technology, military capabilities, and strategic doctrine. . . .

Seeking to incorporate flexibility and encompassing many options and target sets, the countervailing strategy continues to be the basis for U.S. strategic nuclear policy.

STRATEGIC STABILITY

American nuclear strategy has [also] placed high priority on strategic stability. Most often, the term "stability" used alone has stood for *crisis stability,* which describes a situation in which, in times of crisis or high tension, no country would see the advantages of attacking first with nuclear weapons as outweighing the disadvantages. Crisis stability depends on the force structures and doctrines of both sides and on each side's perception of the other. The lower the degree of crisis stability, the greater the risk that a power would preempt if it perceived that it were likely to be attacked. This is not to argue that it is U.S. policy to consider a preemptive strike, but Soviet perceptions of such a possibility might increase a Soviet inclination to preempt under some circumstances. President Reagan's Commission on Strategic Forces (the Scowcroft Commission) stated that:

> . . . stability should be the primary objective both of the modernization of our strategic forces and of our arms control proposals. Our arms control proposals and our strategic arms programs . . . should work together to permit us, and encourage the Soviets, to move in directions that reduce or eliminate the advantage of aggression and also reduce the risk of war by accident or miscalculation. . . .

U.S. FORCE REQUIREMENTS AND POSTURE

[According to Secretary of Defense Weinberger, present] U.S. countervailing strategy places five specific requirements on strategic nuclear forces:

1. Flexibility: ". . . A continuum of options, ranging from use of small numbers of strategic and/or theater nuclear weapons aimed at narrowly defined targets, to employment of large portions of our nuclear forces against a broad spectrum of targets."

2. Escalation Control: ". . . We must convince the enemy that further escalation will not result in achievement of his objectives, that it will not mean 'success,' but rather additional costs."

3. Survivability and Endurance: ". . . The key to escalation control is the survivability and endurance of our nuclear forces and the supporting communications, command and control, and intelligence (C^3I) capabilities."

4. Targeting Objectives: "We must have the ability to destroy elements of

four general categories of Soviet targets." These are strategic nuclear forces, other military forces, leadership and control, and the industrial and economic base.

5. Reserve Forces: "Our planning must provide for the designation and employment of adequate, survivable, and enduring reserve forces and the supporting C^3I systems both during and after a protracted conflict."

To attempt to satisfy these requirements, the United States maintains a *triad* of strategic offensive weapons systems consisting of long-range bombers, submarine-launched ballistic missiles (SLBMs), and land-based intercontinental ballistic missiles (ICBMs). These systems carry thousands of nuclear warheads in ballistic missile reentry vehicles, bombs, cruise missiles, and short-range air-to-ground missiles. There are thousands more nonstrategic nuclear warheads including those in artillery shells, bombs carried by tactical air forces, short- and medium-range rockets, and intermediate-range rockets and cruise missiles. . . .

COMMON CRITICISMS OF U.S. NUCLEAR STRATEGY

This nation's strategic nuclear doctrine has continually evolved, but it has not been dramatically changed in the last 20 years. Despite this consensus, various analysts have suggested either further modifications or major revisions to it to redress perceived weaknesses. In many cases, differing recommendations stem from differences in fundamental premises and values. They may also arise from different predictions of future capabilities and intentions. Much of the strategic debate, therefore, is really a debate about which assumptions more closely reflect (or will reflect) reality.

Few are pleased that the U.S. deterrent posture relies heavily on threatening the use of weapons of mass destruction. What is debated is not whether deterrence by threat of nuclear retaliation is a good thing, but whether there is a viable and preferable alternative. Some analysts believe that existing strategy, although imperfect, is the best available under the circumstances. They argue that it should in essence be continued, perhaps strengthened in various ways or carried out (with the aid of arms control agreements) at substantially smaller force levels. Others who basically agree with the premises underlying current strategy foresee difficulty in maintaining its viability in the face of continual technological evolution, particularly on the part of the Soviet Union. Some of the latter see a potential role for ballistic missile defense in enhancing the U.S. deterrent posture.

Still others hold fundamentally different assumptions [from] those on which current strategy is based. Their concern is to modify existing strategy in accordance with a different set of premises.

MAINTAINING CURRENT STRATEGY

Technological evolution influences strategy both by changing what is seen as possible ("technology push") and what is viewed to be necessary ("requirements pull"). On the "technology push" side, for example, many believe that we now have the potential to develop ballistic missile defenses which are considerably more capable than could be considered years ago. . . .

Technology is also advancing in areas other than ballistic missile defense, and contributes to the "requirements pull" that some believe will mandate changes to our strategy. In particular, Soviet ability to harden and make mobile elements of their land-based strategic forces, and their efforts towards hardening command and control facilities and other targets, all serve to degrade the ability of U.S. forces to place these targets at risk. In addition, although there is as yet no reason to believe that the Soviets will ever be able to reliably detect U.S. ballistic missile submarines when on patrol, it cannot be ruled out that some as-yet-unknown technology might someday threaten SLBM invulnerability. Space systems today are able to enhance the effectiveness of terrestrial forces, and this ability will no doubt be accentuated in the future. Combined with political factors such as the Soviet ability to proliferate military forces taken with what is perceived to be U.S. reluctance to do the same, these actual and possible technological trends lead some analysts to question whether the "countervailing strategy" can be maintained without significant change into the indefinite future. . . .

ALTERNATIVE U.S. STRATEGIES

In addition to those advocating modifications to current strategy, there are those who differ with basic assumptions central to that strategy and who therefore offer alternatives. Three such alternatives are presented below.

One group believes that current strategy does not sufficiently recognize what they see as the inherent opposition between minimizing the risk of nuclear war, on the one hand, and preparing to fight one, on the other. Therefore, they see that the balance mentioned previously between war-fighting capability and crisis instability is swinging dangerously towards instability, and that weapons systems that could improve the ability to fight a nuclear war could also make such a war more likely to occur. Alternatively, they may believe that existing plans for prosecuting a nuclear war overestimate the probability that those things which the war would be defending would survive the war at all. These analysts recommend that the United States pursue a strategy which we will label "retaliation only."

A second group of strategists believes instead that present strategy does not sufficiently recognize the essential equivalence between deterring war and preparing to fight war. Moreover, existing strategy does not offer a coherent picture of what it would consider victory, and it cannot be expected to effectively deter an opponent who, it is argued, would have a very clear conception of his strategic objectives in war. These strategists advocate adopting what might be called a "prevailing" strategy.

Finally, there are strategists who think that this country should not and need not accept having its continued survival contingent on the decisions of others. They argue that no matter how strong our deterrent strategy can be made, should it fail (whether due to accident, miscalculation, or just poor design), the results would be catastrophic. They moreover argue that we have, or will have, the means to develop defenses (possibly augmented by stringent offensive force limitations) which can remove, or substantially reduce, the ability of others to destroy this country. Discussion of such "defense dominant" strategies concludes the alternatives presented below.

Retaliation-Only

"Retaliation-only" strategists question whether any military utility at all can be derived from nuclear weapons which justify the risks inherent in planning to use them in battle, short of retaliating against nuclear attack. Although their prescriptions for change differ [as noted in Selection 16], they are based on a fundamental premise similar to that stated by Robert McNamara:

> I do not believe we can avoid serious and unacceptable risk of nuclear war until we recognize—and until we base all our military plans, defense budgets, weapon deployments, and arms negotiations on the recognition—that *nuclear weapons serve no military purpose whatsoever. They are totally useless—except only to deter one's opponent from using them.*

Accordingly, "retaliation-only" strategists adopt the principle of "no first use" of nuclear weapons, which in some versions would be stated publicly and in others would be left silently ambiguous. Starting with that premise, retaliation-only strategists can go in two different directions. In the first, a variety of nuclear weapons with flexible targeting options would be retained in order to display the capability of responding in kind to any level of nuclear attack. There would be no immediate requirement to reduce the number of warheads existing today (although should Soviet forces be reduced, U.S. forces could be reduced accordingly). However, nuclear forces under this strategy would differ qualitatively from today's forces in that weapons would not be given prompt hard-target kill capability—a capability needed in order to conduct a successful preemptive attack on enemy nuclear forces. Attacks on a wide variety of military forces would still be possible under such a strategy using those weapons having slow hard-target kill capability. This strategy would therefore be able to maintain some degree of war-fighting potential, but would significantly lessen the degree to which that potential could be used (or would appear capable of use) in a first strike.

In the second variation, often called *minimum deterrence*, only those weapons which would be needed to threaten a number of high-value targets—

cities, for example—would be retained. The number and nature of those targets would be selected to threaten enough destruction to deter a potential attacker from initiating a nuclear strike. Opinions differ as to the exact size of "minimum," but no definition of a minimum deterrent would require thousands of warheads on a multiplicity of delivery vehicles.

What would be essential in either version would be that the nuclear weapons that were retained include (in the first case) or constitute (in the second) an invulnerable, second-strike force. The size of this force would be determined in the first case by being able to retaliate for whatever form of attack had been executed initially, and in the second by being able to destroy with high confidence that set of targets judged to provide minimum deterrence. To the extent that the retaliatory weapons were vulnerable, or to the extent that a potential attacker possessed defenses, the second-strike force would either need to expand in size or increase its invulnerability and penetrativeness in order to maintain a minimum deterrent threat.

Should the Soviets acquire defenses so effective that even this minimum deterrent retaliation could not be executed with high confidence, and were the United States unable to penetrate, evade, or neutralize these defenses effectively, then the fundamental premise of promising nuclear retaliation for nuclear attack could not be assured, and strategies based primarily on the threat of retaliation would no longer be viable. On the other hand, if the United States and the Soviet Union had equal offensive and defensive capabilities (and if the survivability of offensive forces did not depend on defenses), retaliation might still be credible. However, uncertainties in each side's evaluation of the opposing side's defense might make assuring an equivalent retaliation difficult.

Since a "retaliation-only" strategy explicitly denies use of nuclear weapons in response to conventional attack, some other way of fulfilling U.S. defense commitments to its NATO allies must be found (e.g., augmentation of conventional forces in Europe). Furthermore, a "minimum deterrence" strategy, presumably using far fewer weapons than are presently in the U.S. arsenal and probably embodying a much more limited repertoire of nuclear responses, must ensure that all opponents remain firmly convinced that any use of nuclear weapons will be met with a retaliatory response. If retaliatory threats are not credible, then potential attackers may gamble that retaliation might not be carried out and they may not be deterred successfully.

One suggested implementation of a "retaliation-only" deterrent strategy (similar to minimum deterrence as described above in its force employment policy but not necessarily in the size of its arsenal) would eliminate all tactical and theater-level nuclear weapons. It would retain only an invulnerable, second-strike force of central strategic weapons which would not be given the combination of yield, accuracy, and quantity needed to pose a threat to the retaliatory capability of the other side. Their survivability would be critical, and it could be enhanced by deploying them in a redundant manner similar to that of the present triad. Flexibility in responding to nuclear attack could be maintained, in that the attacked nation would have options ranging from delivering a single retaliatory weapon to launching its entire strategic arsenal.

Critics of "retaliation-only" strategists believe that there may not be effective alternatives to the threat of first use to deter attack on NATO, that such strategies (in particular the "minimum deterrence" approach) would not credibly deter attack since potential adversaries might not believe the United States would actually carry out its retaliatory threats, and that such strategies do not provide sufficient opportunity to terminate hostilities on favorable terms should deterrence fail.

Prevailing

A quite different proposed change to current doctrine would push in the opposite direction from the recommendations of "retaliation-only" strategists, toward the formulation of more credible plans for the use of nuclear weapons in wartime. These strategists believe that, in a world where adversaries possess nuclear weapons and may well believe in their military utility, it is not sufficient for the United States merely to seek to deny the enemy his political and military goals should war break out. Credible deterrence requires that we plan in the event of war to "secure the achievement of Western political purposes at a military, economic, and social cost commensurate with the stakes of the conflict."[1]

Where some see the uncertainties inherent in estimating outcomes of nuclear war to be so great, and the potential damage so devastating, that there is little to be gained in trying now to affect the nature of a post-war world, a "prevailing" strategy focuses specifically on the conduct of a nuclear war, and is based on consideration of how such a war might end. It would agree with the countervailing school (and the "no prompt hard-target kill" option of the "retaliation-only" school) that ". . . the deterrent effect of our strategic forces is not something separate and apart from the ability of those forces to be used against the tools by which the Soviet leaders maintain their power. Deterrence, on the contrary, requires military effectiveness."

However, to change from the current strategy towards a prevailing one, the United States ". . . must set its planning sights considerably beyond developing a defense posture that will simply deny victory to the enemy. To prevail in stressful circumstances the United States must be able to defend itself against nuclear attack."[2]

Credibility that deterrent threats would actually be carried out would result not so much from flexibility in strategic planning or response options as it would from the "Soviet belief, or strong suspicion, that the United States could fight and win the military conflict and hold down its societal damage to a tolerable level."[3] As a result, such credibility that we would use nuclear weapons to retaliate would be greater than it is in our current, undefended posture.

Clearly, determining "tolerable" levels of damage "commensurate with the stakes of the conflict," in addition to predicting potential levels of attack, will be needed in order to specify the defensive capability required by such a strategy. Effective air defense, civil defense, and ballistic missile defenses would all be required were defending a major portion of population and economic and industrial infrastructure to be a high priority. Offensive force requirements for such a strategy would depend on the set of targets in the Soviet Union (their number, hardness, and location), and would depend critically on the level to which these targets were defended.

"Prevailing" strategists directly address the problem of extended deterrence by recommending sufficient damage-limitation capability (passive defense, active defense, or preemptive attack) to make believable the threat that the United States would use central strategic forces in circumstances other than responding to nuclear attack. If the Soviet Union were convinced that a defended United States believed it could use tactical or even strategic nuclear weapons in defense of NATO Europe without leading to unacceptable devastation of the United States, the Soviets might be more likely to believe that conventional attack against NATO would lead to the use of nuclear weapons against the Soviet Union.

One essential factor in establishing defense requirements for a prevailing strategy is determination of how much damage to the United States can be tolerated in pursuit of those objectives that strategic nuclear forces will be employed to attain or preserve. Another is the degree of U.S. military superiority such a strategy would require, and whether such a strategy would be viable without it. From 1945 until the early 1960s, U.S. strategic superiority was such that this country had the capability to adopt a "prevailing" strategy; adopting one today in the light of existing Soviet forces poses an entirely different set of challenges.

Critics of "prevailing" strategies argue that the United States has no guarantee of being able to attain or maintain the degree of military superiority necessarily to implement them, and that these strategies are equivalent to destroying the Soviet "deterrent," which the Soviets have the will and the technology to prevent.

Defense Dominance

The "countervailing," "retaliation-only," and "prevailing" strategies described so far are characterized by the policies they recommend for employing offensive forces. Although there are also differences between them in the roles that defenses play, it is primarily the role of the offense that distinguishes them. In contrast, defenses supplant, more than they augment, offensive forces in "defense-dominant" strategies. President Reagan's speech of March 23, 1983, and his Strategic Defense Initiative, have greatly stimulated discussion about the feasibility of attaining such a long-term goal. However, since a defense-dominated world is "too distant a technical prospect to be a very active player in the U.S. strategy debate as yet,"[4] there is not so widely developed a body of strategic thought on this alternative as there is concerning some of the others.

Proponents of "defense-dominant" [strategies] see defenses as lessening both the probability of nuclear war and the damage that would be done by such a war, should it occur. They also see such strategies as being moral, in that defending through active defense is preferable to defending through terrorism—the ultimate mechanism by which deterrence through threat of retaliation operates. In a "defense-dominant" world, the probability of war would be lessened since the attacker, less certain of achieving his objectives, would be less likely to attack in the first place. Two factors would lessen the attacker's confidence in success. For one, it would be much more difficult to destroy all his intended targets, directly frustrating his objectives. Probably more importantly, though, he would not be able to plan an effective attack since he would not know *in advance* which warheads will penetrate the defense. Defenses will contribute uncertainty to an attack in addition to defeating part of it. In addition, if war nevertheless were to break out in a "defense-dominant" world, its consequences might be less severe than they would be in any of the other cases described here.

In a way, "defense-dominant" and "retaliation-only" strategists share a common goal: a world in which the only plausible use for a strategic nuclear weapon is in retaliation for the use of another. However, adherents of the "retaliation-only" strategy believe that we are already in such a world although our offensive strategy does not recognize it, and that BMD might destabilize the situation; supporters of the former believe that the Soviet Union, at least, finds "military utility" in ballistic missiles and that only BMD can ensure that all sides will perceive the use of nuclear weapons as truly and clearly irrational for all sides. Moreover, they argue, at the very highest levels of defensive capability, even an irrational decision by the Soviets would not lead to the destruction of U.S. society. Indeed, if defense dominance became total, we could consider [a] strategy of "assured survival" in which retaliation became unnecessary because we had confidence that no Soviet nuclear attack of any kind could succeed.

However, to the extent that defenses on both sides lessen the utility and the probability of preemptive nuclear attack, they will interfere with any other roles assigned to offensive strategic forces. This is, after all, the point. In particular, if conventional attack on Europe is deterred by the ultimate threat of escalation to central strategic exchange, then lessening the effectiveness of strategic forces may lessen their deterrent value, possibly increasing the likelihood of conventional war in Europe. A "defense-dominant" strategy, like a "retaliation-only" one, must solve the problem of deterring conventional attack without nuclear weapons.

Unless a defense can be deployed which is so effective that the Soviet nuclear arsenal becomes irrelevant, the Soviet response will be the key to the success of a "defense-dominant" strategy. Such a strategy will either attempt to force the U.S.S.R. to unilaterally avoid strategies which the United States believes to be particularly dangerous, or it will seek cooperation with the Soviet Union in order to be implemented in a coordinated, mutual manner.

The degree to which the Soviet Union, and other nuclear powers, would cooperate in a transition to a defense-dominated world is therefore crucial. The Soviets will choose to cooperate in such a transition either if they conclude that such a world is preferable to the present situation, or if they decide that defensive measures will prove to be so cost-effective that they recognize the futility of offensive/defensive competition. In either case, they might be expected to be amenable to regulating the defensive buildup and controlling offensive arms.

Critics of "defense-dominant" strategies argue that it is by no means clear that defensive technologies capable of supporting such strategies can be developed, that such strategies raise the risk of both preemptive nuclear attack and conventional war, and that nobody knows how a coordinated transition to defense-dominance could ever be carried out. . . .

NOTES

1. Colin S. Gray, *Nuclear Strategy and Nuclear Planning*, Philadelphia Policy Papers (Philadelphia, PA: Foreign Policy Research Institute, 1984), p. 2.
2. Ibid., p. 2.
3. Ibid., p. 3.
4. Ibid., p. 3.

9 THE OBJECTIVES OF BALLISTIC MISSILE DEFENSE: A STRATEGIC ISSUE

Robert M. Bowman

. . . President [Reagan] challenged the scientific and engineering community with "the development of an intensive effort to define a long-term research and development program aimed at the ultimate goal of eliminating the threat posed by nuclear ballistic missiles." He also held out the hope of rendering nuclear weapons "impotent and obsolete" and asked if it wasn't better to "save lives, rather than avenge them." These statements, along with some of the clarifications issued later, indicate a desire to replace the policy of deterrence through the threat of retaliation with a new policy of pure defense. Indeed, in his "Star Wars" speech, he clearly acknowledged the fact that the systems he was talking about, if combined with offensive systems, would be threatening and destabilizing. Clearly, he was talking about the kind of defensive system that would allow us to (indeed, *require* us to) discard our offensive systems.

The systems requirements and technological demands of such a defensive system are staggering. The allowable leakage rate would be something like 0.01% or less. The system would have to be itself invulnerable, impervious to countermeasures, and absolutely reliable. Moreover, it would have to provide such a defense against not only ballistic missiles, but all other means of delivery (cruise missiles, light aircraft, sailboats, diplomatic pouches, . . .) as well.

So far, numerous study groups both in and out of government have declared such a system an impossibility. Impossible or not, it is a worthy objective and worthy of serious consideration. . . .

As a first step in a rational discussion of BMD—before looking at system requirements and technology challenges [which are discussed in Part II of this book—*eds.*]—it is necessary to look at the various possible objectives of a BMD program, and the strategic issues associated with each. . . .

BMD OBJECTIVES

There are four possible objectives for ballistic missile defense:

1. to replace a policy of deterrence by the threat of retaliation with a policy of assured survival based on a near-perfect defense against all types of of-

fensive weapons (as proposed by the President in his "Star Wars" speech of March 23, 1983.)

2. to enhance deterrence by reducing the vulnerability of our retaliatory offensive forces,

3. to complete a disarming first strike capability by providing a shield against the 5% of enemy missiles surviving our MX, Trident II, and Pershing II attack, and

4. to limit the damage to our country should deterrence fail, by reducing the number of warheads getting through.

Each of these four objectives results in its own unique set of system requirements and associated technology challenges. Each also presents its own political and diplomatic challenge. The first, in particular, faces the diplomatic problem of managing the transition from the current offense-dominated to a defense-dominated strategy without passing through an unstable situation. Implementing it would have to be done so that at no time did the combination of offensive and defensive capabilities bring about the situation sought for in objective 3, the disarming first strike.

The fourth possible objective for a BMD system (limiting the damage should deterrence fail) is particularly troublesome. Such an objective is legitimate, provided the system implementing it doesn't increase the likelihood of deterrence failing. And since the system requirements are very similar to those for objective 3, the chances of it doing so are very good. Damage-limiting is essentially preparing to fight and win (or at least survive) a nuclear war. There is almost unanimous agreement now that a nuclear war cannot be won and must not be fought. Scientists are arguing over whether even people in the southern hemisphere, thousands of miles from the battle, can survive. Since it is not clear that damage-limiting will do any good, we should not allow it to increase the likelihood of war occurring in the first place.

Having now enumerated the possible objectives of BMD, let us turn to the strategic implications of each.

BMD TO REPLACE DETERRENCE

The following is quoted from the beginning of a typical position paper on Ballistic Missile Defense:

> There can be no perfect defense against nuclear ballistic missiles. Avoidance of nuclear conflict must therefore always be our nation's primary security objective, whether through arms control or deterrence. To deter war we must continue to convince any potential attacker that on balance his losses would be unacceptable.

Having thus disposed of the President's initiative, the rest of the paper was devoted to systems serving other objectives. Rather than take that easy way out, however, let us take an honest look at BMD to replace deterrence and

defense . . . Such claims are wildly optimistic, particularly if they were attempting to deal with 1000 or so missiles. But if they were faced with only 70, their task would be immensely simpler (though probably still impossible). From the point of view of Soviet reactions, however, it isn't the real capability of the system that counts, but the worst fears of Soviet planners faced with them. If *we* only had 70 missiles and were faced with the Soviet deployment of a "Star Wars" defense, would we still have confidence in the ability of our retaliatory capability to deter a Soviet first strike? Hardly.

Even if we believe that the United States would never initiate a nuclear war, we must acknowledge that Soviet *fears* are real. When faced with such a capability, those fears could cause the Soviets to launch a desperation preemptive attack. . . .

. . . We should conclude that, in addition to being morally repugnant, a BMD system for first strike is probably unobtainable. Hopefully, the Soviets will come to the same conclusion and quit worrying—but I wouldn't bet on it.

The above analysis points up one fact quite clearly. . . . A BMD system for replacing deterrence looks exactly like a BMD system for first strike. The only difference is in whether or not you discard your offensive weapons—*before you complete the defense.*

BMD FOR DAMAGE LIMITING

It must be reiterated here that *prevention* of nuclear war is and must be our overriding objective. Nothing should be done to compromise that objective. Having said that, let us consider what the system requirements would be on a BMD system for limiting damage to this country should deterrence fail.

If more than 50 warheads were to fall on the United States we would lose most of our people and probably cease to function as a society. It might not take even that many. I think we could agree that unless a BMD system could reduce the number of warheads impacting to this level, it's probably not worth having. So we would be looking for a system that would stop 199 out of every 200 missiles. . . .

The strategic situation in which this system would operate, however, would be very different, for we would have retained our offensive deterrent forces. Potential adversaries would still fear us. They would see a system in place as capable as one which could shield us from retaliation after we conducted a first strike. They would therefore be under intense pressure to preempt. If they restrained, they would at least be on a hair trigger. Our space-based layered defense would, of necessity, be under computer-automated response. The chances of a software error, a computer malfunction, or a response to a natural event initiating war would be immense.

The net result of attempting to implement such a system would therefore be an enormous increase in the likelihood of war occurring and little if any improvement in our chances of surviving it.

We must conclude therefore that a BMD system for damage limiting makes no sense whatsoever.

CONCLUSIONS

We have examined the four possible objectives for BMD systems and have concluded that the last two should be rejected out of hand. To pursue an extremely effective defensive shield while retaining offensive weapons carries an enormous danger of provoking war or causing one by accident, while yielding very little hope of providing sufficient protection to enable the nation to survive.

The first two objectives, on the other hand, are worthy of closer scrutiny.

The first, BMD to replace deterrence, seems to be impossible, but is a legitimate objective of long-range basic research. It would demand a permanently invulnerable system with a leakage rate of better than 0.01% and could only be based on scientific phenomena as yet undiscovered. None of the technologies proposed to date have any chance of meeting these requirements.

The second, BMD to enhance deterrence, does not seem to be required by a rational look at the strategic situation, but could be implemented at a reasonable cost within the constraints of the ABM Treaty and without increasing the danger of war. It does not require any space-based elements beyond existing launch detection and early warning systems, which are required in any event. Such a system would not be impacted by a treaty banning space weapons.

If the United States is going to pursue BMD, it is absolutely essential that the objective of such a program be clearly defined and that the nature of the program is in keeping with its objectives. . . .

10 OFFENSE AND DEFENSE IN THE POSTNUCLEAR SYSTEM

Andrew C. Goldberg

The term *postnuclear* increasingly is being used to describe the developing East-West military relationship. That the postwar world of nuclear deterrence is fading is an idea sparked in great measure by serious attempts to formulate policies that would extract nuclear weapons from superpower relations. U.S. arms-control proposals have enshrined radical reductions and zero options as organizing concepts, and Washington's efforts to develop ballistic missile defenses have had at least the declaratory goal of making nuclear weapons impotent and obsolete. Hence, to the extent that so many of the United States' postwar relationships—particularly with Europe—rest on the talismanic character of nuclear escalation, these developments are sufficient cause for anxiety and reappraisal.

The success or failure of these schemes for denuclearization is less immediately important than the radical alteration of the U.S. political discourse over nuclear strategies that they represent. This fact may have profound effects on the disposition of U.S. forces and doctrine beyond the year 2000. Thoughts of the future of the nuclear system provoke two fundamental questions. First, what are the basic trends affecting the deployment and use of strategic offensive and defensive systems? Second, what should be the appropriate mix of U.S. offensive and defensive systems under a regime in which nuclear offensive weapons are constrained sharply?

THE BALANCE TODAY OR THE BLESSINGS OF ANXIETY

For three decades the North Atlantic Treaty Organization (NATO) and the Warsaw Pact lived with two facts of life: a seemingly intractable mutual vulnerability to nuclear attack and the inescapable anxieties provoked by this condition. For NATO, the fears were particularly acute. The perceived nonnuclear superiority of the Soviet Union seemed to demand the availability of a nuclear riposte. As Soviet nuclear forces grew to rival those of its adversary, the search for usable nuclear options became increasingly tortuous and problematic.

Note: Footnotes have been deleted.

Nevertheless, U.S. leaders have learned to adapt to their nuclear neurosis rather well. The presence of abundant and diverse forces on both sides seems to preclude any recourse to their use. Therefore, the general availability of inconceivable destructiveness creates a perception that all are equally afraid. Thus, while U.S. leaders retain fears of nuclear war they also find it difficult to comprehend how an opponent could contemplate an attack that risks triggering holocaust.

This tension between fear and psychological denial (which has spawned another new term—existential deterrence) allows the opportunity for a variety of strange and not so wonderful manifestations. It enables U.S. policymakers to bemoan simultaneously the perilous state of deterrence in Europe while proclaiming the certainty of a nuclear response to Soviet aggression. It prompts an insistent effort at deploying weapons such as intermediate-range nuclear forces for the purpose of linkage, yet provides the basis for just as insistently removing them. It fosters demands for the procurement of additional weapons, such as the MX, but opens the possibility of slowing, truncating, or killing such programs without altering the general balance of terror.

Until very recently there were no compelling reasons to assume that nuclear circumstances would change markedly. U.S. forces would continue to grow and to modernize and they would be distributed within the traditional triad. Critical choices—whether to buy fixed or mobile ICBMs, manned bombers or cruise missile carriers—could be sidestepped or postponed, as long as the overall force structure possessed the luxury of size, diversity, and almost unrestricted access to the enemy homeland.

In [the late 1980s] U.S. forces [seemed] able to survive a Soviet first strike and to respond against a wide array of targets. Despite the furor of the 1970s and early 1980s over vulnerability in the fixed components of the triad, the actual ability of U.S. strategic forces to retaliate against the USSR appears to be substantial and growing. The most accessible targets for this force comprise the most critical elements of Soviet military and political power, such as Soviet general purpose forces (ports, terminals, barracks, and large naval targets), Soviet leadership assets, and Soviet war support industries.

The most difficult targets to threaten are the hardened Soviet strategic forces, a fact that still provokes tormented discussion in the United States. The persistent desire for this capability is militarily justifiable. In an offense-dominated world, the only way to reduce damage—short of maintaining mutually held rules of limited engagement—is to destroy the forces of the other side before they can be used. This goal probably will remain elusive, even with the acquisition of weapons capable of destroying even the hardest targets. This is because both sides are shifting even greater numbers of warheads to more survivable basing modes, such as land mobility and submarines.

First, assuming the Soviets are willing to brave the dangers of nuclear war in the first place, they likely will try to implement as much of their major targeting missions as possible on the very first strike. Substantial, perhaps irreparable, damage to the United States, therefore, can be expected from the outset of the Soviet campaign, unaffected by what the United States might do subsequently.

Second, even if the United States sought to prevent Soviet commanders from undertaking follow-on strikes utilizing Soviet unfired or reloaded strategic launchers, U.S. actual ability to limit damage using surviving U.S. forces would remain highly suspect. Surviving numbers of hard-target warheads would have to be more substantial than is projected currently to cover effectively not only those silos that are filled but also those that are empty in order to prevent their reuse. Moreover, there is a strong likelihood that Soviet weapons withheld from a first strike would be launched on warning or in preplanned subsequent strikes rather than be allowed to fall prey to U.S. counterblows.

Compounding this problem, finally, is the inescapable fact that a large and growing portion of strategic forces will be difficult, perhaps impossible, to target on a second strike regardless of whether or not the United States ultimately procures the ability to destroy a large number of fixed, hardened Soviet targets. Increasing Soviet investment in submarine-based forces, land-mobile systems, and a large number of alert, cruise missile–carrying bombers will provide the Soviets with the opportunity to conduct subsequent strikes of considerable magnitude on U.S. territory.

U.S. decision makers, consequently, still are faced with the inability to limit damage or control escalation by the use of offensive nuclear forces alone, regardless of how refined the targeting policy may be. At the same time, they possess a force that can deny an aggressor any reasonable prospect of victory.

A BRAVE NEW WORLD?

The elusiveness of assured survival and damage limitation, which in the 1970s led to the articulation of limited nuclear targeting concepts, now propels U.S. decision makers toward expectations of a new world of radical arms control and strategic defense. Although there is no political consensus within the United States or among its allies on the value of either option, the two complement each other in some significant ways.

A central obsession of U.S. leaders is the threat posed by intercontinental ballistic missile (ICBM) forces because their speed and accuracy make them archetypical first-strike weapons. Reducing these forces—and eventually eliminating them—would reduce the principal instrument of surprise attack. As former Arms Control and Disarmament Agency director, Kenneth L. Adelman, noted [in 1986], "If we move away from these hair trigger weapons we may improve stability." Deterrence then would rest on slower flying, air-breathing delivery vehicles, such as bombers and cruise missiles, which are considered less useful for a first strike.

Defenses against ballistic missiles fit neatly into this scheme. As deployed offensive capabilities decline, the viability of defenses rises. If such offensive weapons were reduced to zero, defenses still could be retained against the prospect of cheating.

The dilemmas associated with this policy course are, however, most profound and fall into three categories. First, if nuclear weapons, particularly ballistic systems, pose problems of stability, they also provide disincentives to aggression. From the outset, U.S. nuclear forces capable of attacking deeply into Eastern Europe and the USSR have had the mission of flexibly responding to Soviet aggression. Abandonment or substantial neutralization of these forces potentially increases Soviet confidence that the United States would not be prepared to stem Soviet aggression in Eurasia.

The second factor is that offensive reductions and defensive deployments, if not properly balanced, may create far greater instabilities than they resolve. A regime of massive, relatively secure, arsenals and no defenses is insensitive to cheating because marginal changes do not affect the basic retaliatory balance. Smaller arsenals that are potentially less diverse and less survivable offer more opportunity for assault.

Nuclear relationships, finally, are likely to become more, rather than less, confusing in the future. Radical arms control may reduce some classes of weapons, such as ballistic missiles, but may not constrain others, such as cruise missiles, which could appear in new or more unusual varieties. It also will not necessarily cover such other parties as France, the United Kingdom, and the People's Republic of China. All of these parties may choose to create, retain, or multiply nuclear forces that the superpowers choose to abandon. Arsenals, therefore, may not necessarily decrease but, instead, may mutate, with unknown consequences. All of these considerations influence possible U.S. force development choices as well as the formulation of its deployment policies.

ALTERNATIVE FUTURES

It is important to recognize that force restructuring and strategic defense will alter dramatically relationships among the entire range of deterrent forces. This means not only those weapons that comprise the triad but also peripheral attack systems, such as sea-launched cruise missiles (SLCMs) based on submarines or surface ships.

To picture such a world, one usefully may consider three possible futures that were spawned by the October 1986 summit. In Future I, the superpowers eschew deep cuts in offensive systems and proceed to break out of the Anti-Ballistic Missile (ABM) Treaty with deployment of defenses sometime beyond the mid-1990s. Future II is derived from . . . Soviet proposals [made in the late 1980s] in which strategic defenses are not deployed, an arms-control agreement emerges that sharply reduces strategic and theater nuclear weapons, and (eventually) eliminates ballistic missile weapons. Future III is arms control à *l'américaine*—offensive forces are configured as in Future II, but with the addition of strategic defenses.

Future I

In contemplating Future I, it is increasingly difficult to imagine any strategic ballistic missile defense shield that, in the near term, can end mutual vulnerability at high levels of offensive nuclear armament. Many prominent defense spokesmen continue to subscribe to the belief that exotic Strategic Defense Initiative (SDI) systems eventually will obviate mutual vulnerability. The weight of evidence, however, indicates that through combinations of direct countermeasures, new tactics, and alternative offensive systems, an attacker will penetrate for the foreseeable future any defense system. Thus, whatever the opponent holds dear—the economy, the social fabric, and the ability to wage war—will remain open to massive nuclear attack.

Ballistic missile defense offers two advantages in such a future. At the strategic and theater levels it may frustrate or foreclose attacks by relatively small numbers of nuclear warheads (in the tens to low hundreds). At the theater level, they also may blunt substantially the use of non-nuclear missiles against major military targets because the acceptable leakage rates for defenses are higher when faced with such less destructive weapons.

The advantages of this ballistic missile defense (BMD) regime to the United States and major allies are compelling. First, a layered defense—including mid-course and perhaps some boost-phase coverage—would serve as a hedge against the accidental launch of missiles. Second, defenses provide insurance against exotic attacks against command and control sites or other limited-use options. Finally, BMD at the strategic and theater levels constrains the threats posed by third party ballistic missile arsenals—those belonging to China, for example, or the incipient ballistic forces of Third World states.

However, the disadvantages cut to the heart of the current U.S. policy of extended deterrence. Because of their accuracy, speed, and flexibility of employment, ICBMs are the weapons of choice for limited nuclear operations. Given the Soviet conventional preponderance, NATO may need to employ limited nuclear attacks as a means of communicating a willingness to escalate and as a way of destroying a relatively small number of targets that may have decisive impact on the Soviet campaign.

Even low-level deployments of Soviet BMD would compromise the U.S. ability to execute such attacks. If U.S. planners drastically increase the size of the attacking force to saturate the defense, they run the risk of having the Soviets misinterpret the character and aims of the attack. In essence, limited nuclear attacks cease to appear limited. If, however, U.S. forces assault only targets that are defended poorly, the menu of militarily and politically useful targets may be constricted sharply. In either case, it is very clear that the demands of U.S. limited targeting policy—therefore NATO's policy of flex-ible response—may be weakened seriously by the advent of BMD.

Futures II and III

If Future I represents a reinforcement of mutually assured destruction, Futures II and III easily could disrupt deterrence. This is primarily due to the fact that military perturbations—whether in the form of numerical cheating or technological breakthroughs—are felt more readily at much smaller levels of force deployments.

Arms reductions themselves may not be disruptive, yet they will not guar-antee strategic stability. It is quite possible to imagine a world of smaller, more vulnerable arsenals, in which both parties are in hair trigger, launch-on-warning postures. The addition of asymmetric deployments of ballistic missile defenses to this equation may create compelling incentives for a first strike at a time of crisis. Hence, any arms reduction regime must focus on forces that are not merely smaller but more secure.

Future II is obviously a world without strategic defense but that functions within the shadow of ABM breakout. Missile forces are reduced substantially and perhaps eventually eliminated. Air-breathing systems, by extension, as-sume a greater importance. Verification under these conditions becomes a major chore. Many strategic targets, such as the few remaining ICBMs, bomber bases, and communication centers, could be held at risk by even a few ICBMs that are kept hidden. In many ways, therefore, survivability issues become even more profound than at present.

Employment and targeting problems also may be acute. A trimmed ICBM force, for example, may find it difficult to perform limited targeting in defense of Europe as well as carry out major retaliatory missions. Because ICBMs provide a hedge against major failures in the submarine and bomber forces, U.S. leaders may be reluctant to expend weapons needed for major dramatic retaliation on targets that are deemed marginal.

Flexibility could be diminished in the submarine-launched ballistic missile force as well. Assuming that the Trident force remains the primary submarine system in the next 15–20 years, deep reductions would lead to a smaller number of boats on patrol. From the current 31 vessels, Reykjavik-style cuts could reduce such a force to as few as twelve (depending on how many ICBMs and air-launched cruise missiles [ALCMs] are retained). Because the full num-ber of Tridents will not be kept "on station" at any one time, the actual force complement could reside only in six to nine Tridents.

A smaller strategic submarine force could be one that is more vulnerable to antisubmarine warfare, when the ICBM force also is declining. While one cannot foresee any technical breakthrough in the near future that will make strategic submarines more exposed to attack, the amount of buffering against such a situation could decline readily.

Evisceration or total elimination of the ballistic missile force inevitably increases reliance on air-breathing systems. This means, first, that greater attention would have to be paid to the survivability of bomber bases. Traditionally, ICBMs and bombers mutually reinforced their survivability. Basically, it was impossible for the Soviets to strike ICBMs and bombers at the same time, guaranteeing that the surviving leg would respond. As the ICBM force disappears, bomber forces could fall prey to any hidden Soviet ICBMs or sea-launched ballistic missiles (SLBMs), as well as to SLCMs launched near the U.S. coastline.

The second problem is associated with the conduct of operations. In principle, any target that can be destroyed by a ballistic missile also can be eliminated by a bomber or cruise missile. In practice, the pace of warfare is slower (due to the much greater travel times of air-breathing weapons), and the penetration problems are greater. This means that air-breathing systems are inappropriate for limited nuclear operations requiring speed (such as attacks on large Soviet troop concentrations and mobile missiles). They are also subject to greater risks of inattention: while one might be confident that some percentage of targets would be destroyed, one could not know in advance which particular targets would be eliminated. Additionally, if the Soviets are able to concentrate on a single enemy force, it will be more difficult to ensure high-confidence penetration of the Soviet homeland.

The third future—deep ballistic missile cuts and strategic defense—is an extreme extension of the second. All the aforementioned characteristics apply, but with one crucial difference. Future III posits a process of transition in which offensive ballistic missile arsenals decline as strategic defenses grow. The nightmare scenario under these circumstances is that within some range of deployment there would be enormous advantages to striking first at an opponent's defensive systems (by destroying or jamming sensors, command and control assets, and launchers) and offensive systems, so that surviving residual capabilities would be soaked up by one's own partial defense. Thus, it is in the third future where the most complex instability may emerge. . . .

CONCLUSION

It may be inevitable that the United States and the USSR will enter a new strategic future, shaped by deep offensive reductions and strategic defenses. Regardless of the configuration of the strategic balance, however, it should not be referred to as postnuclear. Indeed, the relationship within the nuclear family of states may mutate radically. Therefore, whatever the perceived advantages of altering the current pattern of mutual deterrence, it is apparent that many positive features of the current balance now taken for granted may be sacrificed.

Each conceptual future outlined in this essay may enhance some aspects of deterrence, but almost certainly at the price of reduced flexibility. Each future nuclear configuration may reinforce inhibitions against preemptive attacks during a crisis, but, in turn, may complicate further the task of protecting U.S. allies against non-nuclear aggression. Ultimately, the United States will be forced into making wrenching choices in the acquisition of weapons for each leg of the strategic triad. In short, each future would have some important liabilities.

Regardless of the chosen future, certain core requirements for U.S. deterrent policy will be necessary. First, any major configuration of the strategic balance makes it more, rather than less, necessary to ensure the survivability of each element of the nuclear force. Second, one must avoid enslaving U.S. arms-control policy to any grandiose expectations surrounding ballistic missile defense. Under the most optimistic assumptions, BMD simply will reinforce deterrence, not eliminate it. Finally, if the United States wants to preserve limited nuclear options, it will have to pay much greater attention to the development of peripheral attack systems. The United States and the USSR may have the opportunity to restructure the outline of the current strategic balance. U.S. policymakers must be careful not to turn this possibility into massive chaos to the ultimate detriment of national security.

Part II: Weapons

Science and technology have created the means to destroy humankind. Controlling the use of weapons of mass destruction has thus become a necessity. To meet this objective, a variety of proposals have been advanced. Some, such as the "no first use doctrine,"[1] the call for a "nuclear freeze,"[2] and the advocacy of a nuclear "build down,"[3] which were articulated in the 1980s, have commanded support for relatively short periods of time. Others, such as the arms control negotiations symbolized by the Strategic Arms Limitation Talks (SALT) and the Strategic Arms Reduction Talks (START), have been relatively more enduring and have perhaps exerted a relatively more potent impact and generated a more dedicated following. But, regardless of their duration or influence, all efforts to control or dismantle weapon systems share in common the purpose of preventing a nuclear exchange.

The selections in Part II of *The Nuclear Reader* are concerned primarily with the *control* of nuclear weapons. If, as suggested in the essays in Part I, nuclear weapons are to serve political purposes, then policymakers must ensure that the mere existence of weapons of mass destruction does not become threatening, with the weapons themselves becoming the causes of instability and the irritants leading to their use. In other words, policymakers must control the weapons and not permit the weapons to control them.

Invariably, questions about how to limit arms focus on whose arms would be controlled and how, which immediately raise the question "Who's ahead?" The question is simple enough, but the answer is complex and inherently ambiguous, with the inevitable result that discussions of the numbers making up the nuclear balance are profoundly colored by the political persuasion of strategic analysts, who differ widely in their assessments of real or imagined strategic asymmetries.

Historically, the simplest measure of the "strategic balance" between the United States and the Soviet Union has been the number of strategic launchers—ICBMs, SLBMs, and intercontinental bombers—each side possesses. By this simple measure, the Soviet Union is ahead. In mid-1988 it possessed nearly 2,500 launchers (1,386 ICBMs, 936 SLBM, and 260 bombers), compared with less than 2,000 for the United States (1,000 ICBMs, 624 SLBMs, and 362 bombers) (The Arms Control Association, Fact Sheet, May 1988). On the other hand, the United States possessed over 13,000 strategic nuclear warheads, compared with fewer than 11,000 for the Soviet Union.

129

Because each American launcher is able to carry more warheads than is their Soviet counterparts, it is clear that numbers of warheads, not numbers of launchers, is more important.

Other variables must also be considered. Among them is the *equivalent megatonnage* of each superpower's nuclear weapons. This is effectively a measure of weapons' destructive power. Recent data published by the United States Joint Staff[4] suggest that the disadvantages of the United States relative to the Soviet Union on this particular measure of their strategic forces began to be reversed in the 1980s and will return to a more favorable balance by the 1990s. Similar data on another important variable, namely "throw-weight," which measures roughly the size of a payload a ballistic missile is able to hurl toward a distant target, give advantages to the Soviet Union at the present time, although the importance of the advantage is not entirely clear.

Our first selection in Part II of *The Nuclear Reader*, written by Marie Hoguet and titled "Beancounting and Wargaming: How to Analyze the Strategic Balance," seeks to add balance to the debates that invariably surround quantitative estimates of launchers, warhead numbers, destructive power, and payloads. Hoguet warns that the weapons at issue are enormously destructive—a point that cannot possibly be given too much emphasis—but she also warns that comparisons of the superpowers' nuclear balance are often superficial, indeed, artificial, "because they omit so much relevant information and fail to disclose their underlying assumptions." Her warning ought to be heeded in order to avoid drawing unwarranted conclusions from the evidence and arguments presented by many strategic analysts, including those whose assessments are presented in the essays that follow.

Our next essay, "First Strike Weapons at Sea: The Trident II and the Sea-Launched Cruise Missile," covers a topic that illustrates the endemic nature of these problems of interpretation. It has been included in *The Nuclear Reader* for precisely the reason that sea-launched missiles are an emergent weapons system of incredible destructive power about which underlying assumptions are notoriously open to question. In Part I we drew a distinction between countervalue and counterforce nuclear weapons. For two decades or more this conceptual distinction reflected technological realities—land-based ICBMs were more accurate than sea-based intercontinental missiles and therefore might be considered counterforce weapons. The initial rationale behind the U.S. decision to build the MX ("Peacekeeper") missile, for example, was premised on the belief that Soviet ICBM forces had achieved the accuracy necessary to nullify the retaliatory (second-strike) capacity of the U.S. Minuteman missile force. Sea-based missiles, on the other hand, have historically been insufficiently accurate to pose a serious counterforce threat to the Soviet Union. Instead, U.S. submarines pose such a costly (countervalue) threat of retaliation against Soviet cities as to deter effectively a potential Soviet temptation to launch a (counterforce) preemptive strike. Now, however, as U.S. nuclear submarine forces increase the accuracy of their weapons so as to pose a counterforce threat to the Soviet Union—as described in "First Strike Weapons at Sea"—the strategic calculus changes radically. No longer do sea-based missiles guarantee the mutual-hostage relationship of the superpowers' respective populations. Instead, they now threaten the very basis of the balance of terror presumed to account for the absence of nuclear war between the United States and the Soviet Union for more than four decades. For, if U.S. SLBMs, which are invulnerable to Soviet retaliatory strikes, can now devastate Soviet ground-based missile forces (which constitute roughly 70 percent of their strategic nuclear forces), what prevents the United States from launching a decisive, preemptive first strike?

Implicit in this question is how nuclear weapons are to be managed so that they serve rather than thwart the political objectives of deterrence for which they presumably were constructed. Put differently, we might ask: Is it possible to control nuclear weapons—indeed, perhaps to eliminate them—so that they are never used unintentionally or, one hopes, intentionally?

One path to the elimination of both threats is complete nuclear disarmament. But the political obstacles to this solution are formidable. The reason disarmament is not a realistic policy objective is simple: Nuclear weapons are a consequence, not a cause, of the conflicts of interest that divide states. Therefore, under prevailing global circumstance, states will never unilaterally and voluntarily dispose of the means of defense. To do so would expose the nation to unacceptable risks and sacrifice the military intruments that enable states to coerce their adversaries. Nor is there much basis for states to agree to mutual disarmament, for this presupposes precisely the kind of trust that is lacking, as evidenced by the presence of arms.

But states have been willing to engage in *arms control* negotiations. As noted above, recent examples involving the United States and the Soviet Union include the *Strategic Arms Limitation Talks* (SALT), the *Strategic Arms Reduction Talks* (START), the *Intermediate Nuclear Force* (INF) negotiations, the *Antisatellite* (ASAT) *and Space Weapons Negotiations*, and the efforts to conclude a *Comprehensive Test Ban Treaty* and a *Threshold Test Ban Treaty*.

Arms control is distinguished from disarmament in that "it accepts conflict among nations as an inevitable part of contemporary international politics and views military force as a necessary (and legitimate) instrument of national policy."[5] Accordingly, it seeks more modest objectives than does disarmament.

The theory of "arms control" is based on the rather modest notion that decisions to acquire certain types or quantities of weapons can aggravate political conflicts and thereby *in themselves contribute to the risk of war*. This is not to say that weapons decisions are a primary or even secondary cause of conflict; only that such decisions are one factor which influence the relative probabilities that political conflicts are resolved peacefully, remain unsettled, or result in war. . . . [A]dverse effects can be reduced, or at least contained, both through unilateral decisions to avoid deployment of "destabilizing" weapons and, more important, through international negotiations on agreements to mutually avoid deploying certain types of weapons or to place other types of agreed mutual limitations on weaponry.[6]

If the objectives of arms control are so modest, then the record of its accomplishments should be long and rich—but it is neither. In our next selection, "National Security Policy and Arms Control," Robert L. Pflatz-graff, Jr., considers the record and concludes that "There are few examples of lasting arms limitation for those accords that are negotiated represent . . . the codification of a particular set of political relationships existing at any one time. As political conditions change, so does the basis for the arms limitation agreement."

Pfaltzgraff is not only pessimistic about the promise of arms control but also critical in the sense that he sees negotiated disarmament and arms control agreements as "an adjunct to national security policy that cannot form an alternative to adequate defense. . . ." In this sense he applauds the Reagan administration's conviction during most of its eight-year tenure "that the security needs of the United States could *not* be met by a policy in which arms control played the central element." In this regard the Reagan administration departed from the Nixon, Ford, and Carter administrations, all of which placed negotiated arms agreements with the Soviets at the center of their national security policies. Reagan also departed from his predecessors by undertaking the largest peacetime military buildup in United States history. During the first seven years Reagan was in office, the United States spent $2 trillion on the military, which amounts to $21,000 for each American household.

The Reagan rearmament program was based on the convictions that during the 1970s the military position of the United States vis-á-vis the Soviet Union had deteriorated markedly, and that it was necessary to bargain with the Soviet Union from a position of strength. The Soviets had in fact abruptly suspended all arms talks with the United States in the early 1980s when the NATO allies decided to proceed with the deployment of intermediate-range nuclear forces (INF) in Europe, only to return to the negotiating table later where an agreement completely eliminating INF weapons was concluded. Whether the agreement signed by President Reagan and General Secretary Gorbachev during the Washington summit in December 1987 was indeed the result of the Reagan administration's tough posture toward the Soviet Union generally and toward arms control in particular cannot be known with certainty. What is clear is that the United States and its Western allies achieved virtually all of the objectives they had sought. Furthermore, the INF accord is a truly historic agreement for two reasons. First, it calls for the elimination of an entire class of launch vehicles, and thus contains elements of disarmament, not simply the control of existing arms (although, significantly, at the insistence of the United States the agreement does not call for the destruction of the nuclear warheads on the INF launchers that will be destroyed). And second, it contains an elaborate verification regime, including on-sight inspections in both the United States and the Soviet Union to ensure against cheating.

Verification—inspection, as it was called earlier in the history of arms control—has often been a point of contention between East and West. Electronic surveillance via satellites and other so-called national technical means permitted verification of compliance with the 1963 partial test-ban treaty, for example, but it is arguably inadequate to monitor recent technological innovations in weaponry and its testing. For example, national technical means presumably would be unable to determine whether dual-capable delivery systems—cruise missiles that can deliver either conventional or nuclear warheads, for example—were in violation of an arms accord. The verification regime built into the INF treaty may thus set a precedent for future agreements that seek to grapple with ever more complex technical issues.

Despite the overwhelming support for the INF treaty in the United States and abroad (a result in no small part of the belief that the United States has retreated from what many believed to be the dangerously militant anti-Sovietism of the early Reagan years), the treaty is not without its critics. Some view it as little more than symbolic, as it deals with an infinitesimally small number of nuclear launchers (and keeps the warheads intact). Others believe the loss of intermediate-range forces plays into the hands of the Soviet Union by contributing to the decoupling of American security guarantees to Europe by making it less likely that the United States will use its strategic nuclear weapons against the Soviet Union itself in the event of a Soviet conventional attack against Western Europe. At the same time, however, it is generally acknowledged that Warsaw Pact conventional forces are far superior to NATO's, and that nuclear weapons are therefore an integral element of the deterrence of the Soviet Union and, ultimately, the defense of the West.

Many of the issues raised by the INF accord are addressed in our next two essays. In the first, "Lessons of the INF Treaty," written by Lynn E. Davis, the author provides the historical background leading up to the treaty and draws from it important insights that may influence future arms control negotiations between the superpowers. One strand of thinking addresses NATO's long-held concern about the credibility of the United States deterrent threat. The other concerns the motives and style of the new Soviet leadership, which Davis describes as posing "a formidable challenge" to the Atlantic Alliance. Because NATO is fundamentally a pluralistic security community in which domestic politics and varying perceptions of the meaning of national security affect its members' approach to intra-alliance issues and how to cope with the Soviet "threat," Davis concludes that "the most important lesson of the INF treaty" is that "the West needs to define strategic and arms control objectives which are mutually consistent and serve alliance interests." The implication is that the INF negotiating experience was deficient in both respects.

In "Defending Post-INF Europe," Jeffrey Record and David B. Rivkin move beyond the lessons of the INF negotiations to inquire into the treaty's implications for NATO strategy and the military defense of Western Europe which the INF treaty portends. The conclusions derived from their analysis, which juxtaposes the domestic contraints faced by many NATO members against the presumed needs of the alliance in the absence of the deterrent threat that the intermediate-range weapons eliminated by the INF treaty poses, are disconcerting. Record and Rivkin believe that the necessity of conventional force modernization which the INF accord implies cannot be met, and that ultimately "the non-nuclear military balance in Europe in the post-treaty era will be even more unfavorable to NATO than it is today."

An alternative to conventional force defense is continued reliance on nuclear weapons. Importantly, Record and Rivkin emphasize that the INF agreement does not mean that Europe will become a nuclear-free zone. On the contrary, thousands of nuclear weapons will remain on the continent, but the authors are skeptical about whether the remaining weapons have the same deterrent value as the intermediate-range weapons eliminated by the INF treaty. In the final analysis, then, the authors conclude that the INF accord is a step toward European denuclearization whose implications for the Atlantic Alliance are not well understood but imply that "NATO will have to learn to live with a lower order of both deterrence and defense in Europe in the post-INF treaty era than that to which it has become accustomed."

The role that nuclear weapons should play in the defense of Western Europe is an issue that has plagued the Atlantic Alliance for decades. The central issue is how to ensure the credibility of the United States pledge that it will come to the defense of Western Europe in the event of a conventional or nuclear attack. The credibility question is stated in its starkest form with the question "Would the United States be willing to trade New York City or Washington for Bonn or Paris?"

Theater nuclear weapons—what the Reagan administration preferred to call intermediate-range nuclear forces—were designed historically to provide the critical link between conventional forces and the American strategic nuclear deterrent. And the NATO strategy known as *flexible response* explicitly calls for the NATO allies to be the first to use nuclear weapons should it become apparent in a conflict that the Warsaw Pact's conventional forces are gaining the upper hand.

Thus, the long-standing doctrine of the United States and its NATO allies maintains that the common defense rests on the strategy of initiating the use of nuclear weapons should their conventional or non-nuclear forces be threatened with defeat in Europe. To depart from this doctrine by embracing a no-first-use policy would require that NATO's conventional forces be built up to the level necessary to balance the Warsaw Pact forces. Such a buildup is unlikely given the historic unwillingness of NATO's members to pay the cost of meeting the conventional challenge, as Record and Rivkin explain. As a consequence NATO has strong incentives to rely on nuclear weapons to provide the decisive deterrent to a Soviet attack on Western Europe. To abandon the first-use strategy would imply a decoupling of the United States from the defense of Europe because it would undermine the deterrent value of U.S. strategic nuclear weapons. "This linkage is considered the ultimate deterrent to Soviet attack against Western Europe."[7]

In our sixth selection in Part II, "The Military Role of Nuclear Weapons: Perceptions and Misperceptions," Robert S. McNamara, a former American Secretary of Defense, addresses the question of whether nuclear weapons in Europe serve a military purpose. McNamara surveys the development of NATO's doctrine of *flexible response*, to which he contributed, and concludes that the force posture necessary to support it was never developed. Hence the emergence of NATO's reliance on the threatened first use of nuclear weapons. McNamara argues that the threat is no longer credible militarily or politically, and concludes:

> I do not believe we can avoid serious and unacceptable risk of nuclear war until we recognize—and until we base all our military plans, defense budgets, weapon deployments, and arms negotiations on the recognition—that *nuclear weapons serve no military purpose whatsoever. They are totally useless—except only to deter one's opponent from using them.*

McNamara thus strongly disagrees with the logic of both the deployment of nuclear weapons and the proposition that nuclear weapons may represent the decisive obstacle to a Soviet invasion of Western Europe.

McNamara's prescription for shoring up Western defenses and maintaining the link between European and American security through a credible posture of extended deterrence is the familiar—but politically problematic—one of placing greater reliance on conventional military forces, including reliance on a new generation of high-tech weapons and acceptance of accompanying strategies that such a reliance would require. However, such weapons might increase rather than diminish the risk of conventional war—and ultimately nuclear war. This is the thesis of Michael T. Klare's "Breaching the Firebreak." The *firebreak* in this context refers to the psychological barrier separating conventional from nuclear war, much like the physical barriers that fire fighters build to keep forest fires from racing out of control. Klare worries that the firebreak between nuclear and conventional war is being crossed from both sides—by a new generation of "near-nuclear" conventional weapons whose destructive capabilities approximate those that could result in a limited nuclear conflict, and by a new generation of "near-conventional" nuclear weapons whose destructiveness does not greatly exceed that of the most powerful conventional weapons. Once the firebreak between conventional and nuclear warfare is breached, Klare warns, the prospect for controlling escalation is remote. It follows logically, if ironically, that reliance on conventional weapons to enhance extended deterrence in Europe may hasten rather than avert a nuclear Armageddon.

In 1986 President Reagan and Soviet General Secretary Gorbachev met in Reykjavik, Iceland, where, in the course of the negotiations, Reagan reportedly agreed to the goal of eliminating *all* ballistic missiles. Exactly what was said at Reykjavik may never be known for certain, but the revelation that the President of the United States was committed to abolish the very weapons on which the security, through deterrence, not only of the United States but also of all of its allies in Western Europe, the Far East, and elsewhere had depended for a generation, was startling. An agreement to eliminate ballistic missiles was not reached at that time, but the discussions did infuse new meaning into the proposition that the United States had previously advanced in the START negotiations, namely, that the time has come not simply to limit the growth of nuclear launchers and stockpiles but actually to reduce them. The popular phrase "deep cuts" refers to the goal of reducing to approximately 6,000 the number of strategic weapons in each superpower's arsenal, or about half their current level. (The number of tactical nuclear weapons is unknown but apparently far in excess of the number of strategic weapons and is beyond the purview of the START negotiations.) Our next two selections ask what deep cuts might mean for deterrence, crisis stability, and ultimately war prevention.

In the first, "Deep Cuts and the Risks of Nuclear War," by Joseph S. Nye, Jr., the author argues that any assessment of the effects of deep cuts on the strategic balance "depends on how deep the proposed cuts are and how they relate to one's definition of deterrence." Even if strategic nuclear weapons are maintained not only to guard against the threat of war by chance but also the possibility of the deliberate use of nuclear weapons, Nye continues, effective counterforce targeting would permit significant reductions in strategic forces without having significant negative effects on deterrence. And because "such reductions would help enhance the survivability of land-based forces," deep cuts may be not only tolerable but actually preferable.

Another well-known nuclear arms expert, John D. Steinbruner, comes to an analogous conclusion by speculating that in some distant future as few as 3,000 weapons may be adequate to meet the deterrent purposes of the superpowers. But he also casts his analysis in the context of American domestic politics, with the implicit warning that questions of doctrine, strategy, and "sufficiency" are often driven by a logic far removed from what a "rational" point of view might recommend.

Managing the superpowers' arms race is one approach to the control of nuclear weapons; preventing their spread to other countries is another. Today only six countries are known to have a nuclear weapons capability: the United Kingdom, France, China, India, and the two superpowers: Two others, Israel and South Africa, are also widely believed to have acquired a nuclear weapons capability. Thus the spread of nuclear capability has clearly not been rapid; yet the prevention of proliferation of nuclear weapons has been on the global agenda since the 1950s when, following successful Soviet and British atomic tests, it became apparent that the United States could not retain a monopoly over nuclear know-how and that other states would seek to acquire, either clandestinely or openly, a nuclear weapons capability. As many as thirty countries are now believed to be on the threshold of joining the nuclear club.

How threatening is nuclear proliferation? Some analysts see *horizontal proliferation*, that is, the spread of weapons to non-nuclear states, as less threatening than *vertical proliferation*, the continued improvement and stockpiling of weapons by the now-nuclear states. This view is premised on the assumption that the nuclear stalemate between the United States and the Soviet Union, captured in the concept of mutual assured destruction, explains the absence of war between the great powers since 1945. The lesson seems clear: The possession of nuclear weapons could induce the same degree of caution and restraint in others, thus having a stabilizing effect on world politics that would reduce rather than increase the probability of violent international conflict.[8]

In "Pinioning the Genie: International Checks on the Spread of Nuclear Weapons," Ian Smart reviews the history of diplomacy leading to the Non-Proliferation Treaty (NPT) of 1968 and the threats to the preservation of the regime created by it. Smart perceives increased challenges to non-proliferation, but promise in the willingness of the Third NPT Review Conference in 1985 to prevent a total collapse of the non-proliferation regime. He also warns, however, that "either agony or apathy could easily lead back to re-newed conflict, pitting the self-serving abuse indulged in formerly by representatives of certain developing non-nuclear-weapon countries against the naive arrogance displayed in the past by some nuclear exporters and nuclear weapons states." Non-proliferation—and, perhaps ultimately, international stability—depend on the binding of consensual support for non-proliferation into the mid-1990s, when the rules embodied in the current NPT agreement are scheduled for reevaluation and, potentially, legal termination.

To this point our discussion has focused on arms control and war prevention insofar as they relate to offensive weapons. Defensive weapons have commanded little attention since 1972, when the United States and the Soviet Union agreed to limit their deployment of anti-ballistic missile (ABM) systems. That accord effectively legitimized mutual assured destruction as an approach to strategic stability, as it proscribed the superpowers' ability to mount an effective defense against an adversary's second-strike capability. Since then, as our previous selections make clear, technological developments may nonetheless have eroded the foundations of stable deterrence based on assured destruction.

Proponents of ballistic missile defense (BMD) see in these same technological developments the possibility of shifting from an offense-oriented conception of deterrence to a defense-oriented one that promises a far greater measure of national security. President Reagan committed the United States to the search for such a "Star Wars" approach to defense in 1983, when he called upon the scientific community to devise defensive means of rendering the "awesome Soviet missile threat" "impotent and obsolete."

The doctrinal implications of the Strategic Defense Initiative (SDI) were introduced in Part I. Here we focus on two related but somewhat distinct issues: the technical feasibility of strategic defense, and the transition from

Figure II-1 First Phase of Pentagon's Ballistic Missile Defense

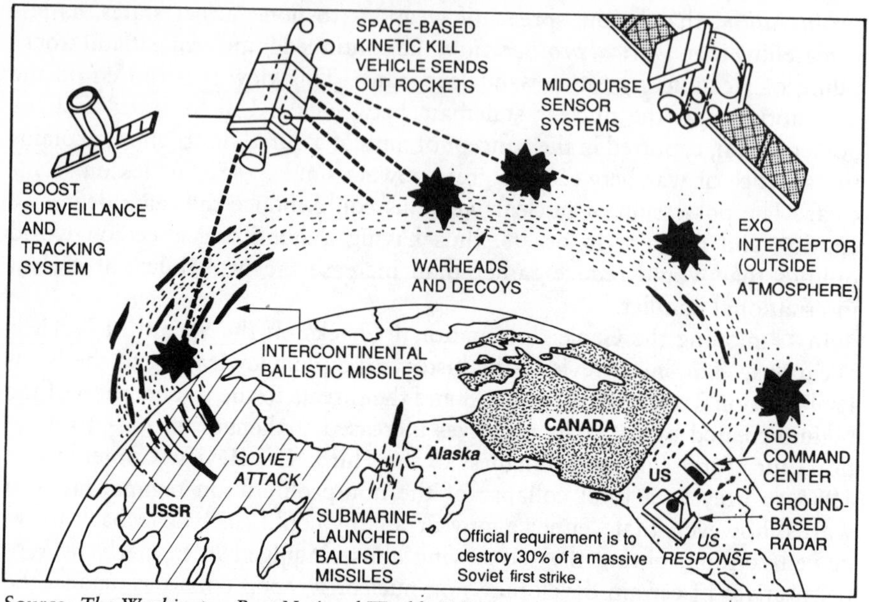

Source: *The Washington Post National Weekly Edition.* April 4–10, 1988, p. 9.

a nuclear world described by "assured destruction" to one characterized as "assured survival."

The technical feasibility of SDI has commanded considerable attention. The questions range from the types of as-yet-unknown weapons that would be necessary to defend effectively against a determined attack against the United States or its allies to the development of a new generation of computers and related software with the ability to make the millions and millions of precise calculations that would be essential to an effective ballistic missile defense. Robert S. McNamara gives a concise yet understandable discussion of many of these and related issues in "The Star Wars Defense System: A Technical Note."

McNamara concludes his discussion with the observation that research on anti-ballistic missile defense should continue—although it is clear he is doubtful about the long-term prospects of its effectiveness. Interestingly, SDI as President Reagan first conceived the program was also seen as essentially a research effort. That is, the president challenged the scientific community to determine whether SDI could prove technically feasible in years to come. Presently, however—in typical bureaucratic fashion—it is clear that many of those involved in the initial research thrust have come to advocate an early (mid-to-late-1990s) deployment of a defensive system even though it is clear that such a system would fall short of the "protective shield" once envisioned. A "layered defense," similar to the artist's conception shown in Figure II-1, would permit a good deal of "leakage," but it would also afford some measure of protection for American land-based missile forces, which for long have been considered most vulnerable to a Soviet nuclear attack. As the figure suggests, the official requirement is to destroy some 30 percent of a massive Soviet first strike. Regrettably, however, the remaining 70 percent that would penetrate the American BMD would cause horrendous death and destruction.

Many analysts who have considered the strategic and practical implications of SDI have concluded that the transition from an offense- to a defense-dominated deterrent system would be the most dangerous, as it would create the opportunity to launch a preemptive strike against the adversary for any number of different reasons without fear of receiving a devastating retaliatory strike. Charles L. Glaser weighs these considerations in "Managing the Transition from Offense to Defense." Like many other observers, Glaser is less than sanguine about the transition, concluding that "The fundamental problems lie in the technical infeasibility of near-perfect defenses, in the political infeasibility of extensive superpower cooperation and, possibly most important, in the dangers inherent in a world of highly effective defenses."

Nowhere is the question of effective deterrence and defense more important than in Europe. If nuclear war occurs, it may not start in Europe, but it would inevitably engulf the continent, with Germany a certain geographic focal point. Consequently, averting war of any kind, conventional or otherwise, has for decades dominated the thinking of European statesmen and scholars. Many of the conclusions reflected in current declaratory strategy in the United States and Western Europe are the product of this thinking. Nonetheless, a series of less orthodox ideas, often reflected in European professional journals, have also gathered support. These seek goals not unlike those championed by the advocates of SDI because, in a similar manner, they prefer a world in which defense, not offense, is the dominant mode of thinking about military force in the contemporary world. The ideas are diverse, as suggested by such terms as alternative defense, common security, civilian-based defense, defensive-defense, nonprovocative defense, and the like. Stephen J. Flanagan surveys many of these varied approaches in "Nonprovocative and Civilian-Based Defenses," which serves as a fitting conclusion to Part II of *The Nuclear Reader*, where weapons have been our dominant concern. Flanagan is not entirely unsympathetic to the concerns of those whose ideas he canvasses, but, not unlike Glaser, he highlights the most difficult question of all—how do we get from here (offensive dominance) to there (defensive defense)?

NOTES

1. In 1982 four eminent, former high U.S. officials—McGeorge Bundy, George F. Kennan, Robert S. McNamara, and Gerald Smith—called for a declaratory policy of "no first use" in "Nuclear Weapons and the Atlantic Alliance," *Foreign Affairs* 60 (Spring 1982): 753–68. See also the recommendation of the Union of Concerned Scientists in Kurt Gottfried, Henry W. Kendall, and John M. Lee, "'No First Use' of Nuclear Weapons," *Scientific American* 250 (March 1984): 33–41, and P. Terrence Hopmann, "The Path to No-First-Use: Conventional Arms Control," *World Policy Journal* 1 (Winter 1984): 319–37.

2. The case for a nuclear freeze was made by one of its early advocates in Randall Forsberg,

"A Bilateral Nuclear-Weapons Freeze," *Scientific American* 247 (November 1982): 52–61. See also Harold Feiveson and Frank von Hippel, "Freeze on Nuclear Weapons Development and Deployment: The Freeze and the Counterforce Race," *Physics Today* 36 (January 1983): 36–49.

3. *Build-down* proposed, as an alternative to no first use, that the United States and the Soviet Union destroy one or more of their existing weapons for each new one they build. Alton Frye discusses this proposal, which at one time was embraced as a negotiating position by the Reagan administration, in "Strategic Build-Down: A Context for Restraint," *Foreign Affairs* 62 (Fall/Winter, 1983–1984): 293–317.

4. *United States Military Posture FY 1989* (Washington, D.C.: U.S. Department of Defense, 1988), pp. 43–44.

5. Barry M. Blechman, "Do Negotiated Arms Limitations Have A Future?" in Charles W. Kegley, Jr., and Eugene R. Wittkopf, eds., *The Global Agenda: Issues and Perspectives* (New York: Random House, 1984), p. 126.

6. Blechman, pp. 125–26.

7. Jonathan Dean, "Beyond First Use," *Foreign Policy*, Fall 1982, p. 37.

8. For an elaboration of this argument, see Kenneth N. Waltz, "Toward Nuclear Peace," in Robert J. Art and Kenneth N. Waltz, eds., *The Use of Force* (Lanham, Md.: University Press of America, 1983), pp. 573–601. For a rebuttal, see Joseph S. Nye, Jr., "Sustaining the Non-Proliferation Regime," in the first edition of *The Nuclear Reader* (New York: St. Martin's Press, 1985), pp. 187–200.

11 BEANCOUNTING AND WARGAMING: HOW TO ANALYZE THE STRATEGIC BALANCE

Marie Hoguet

Sooner or later most discussions of the arms race lead to the question of "who's ahead"—which side has more, or bigger, or better nuclear weapons; whose build-up has been more unprecedented; and what it all means for our defense policies. Many teachers and students have seen graphs and charts comparing the numbers of U.S. and Soviet intercontinental ballistic missiles (ICBMs), submarine-launched ballistic missiles (SLBMs), warheads, bombers and so on.

Comparisons of U.S. and Soviet nuclear forces are both inevitable and necessary in considering our relative strengths and weaknesses. But very often they are misleading because they omit so much relevant information and fail to disclose their underlying assumptions. They tend to give an incorrect impression of precision where in fact it is impossible to be precise.

There are two basic approaches to comparing U.S. and Soviet nuclear forces. The first and more familiar approach compares the characteristics and destructive potential of the two sides' weapons. Sometimes called "beancounting," it looks at specific weapons or characteristics of weapons and attempts to show, often in graphic form, what the U.S. and the Soviet Union each has in the discrete categories. This approach provides a static picture, a snapshot, of the various components of each side's forces at a particular time, in peacetime. Or it can provide a picture of the change in the quantity of these components over a certain period of time. This approach does not, and cannot, show how these components would interact in a war, or what extrinsic factors would affect their performance or importance in actual combat.

Let us look at one of the more frequently encountered comparisons—the one between U.S. and Soviet ICBMs and SLBMs—and note some of its limitations. A typical graph depicts a small forest of the many different kinds of Soviet missiles and a more modest array of the U.S. missiles. It will show that Soviet ICBMs and SLBMs are larger, more varied, and more numerous than their U.S. counterparts. One's intuitive conclusion, on seeing such a graph, would be that the Soviets are better armed and stronger.[An example of such a figure, which is not part of Hoguet's essay, is shown at the end of it in Figure II-2—*eds.*]

But this sort of graph does not reveal that U.S. *Minuteman* missiles, which make up the vast bulk of our ICBM arsenal, are smaller because superior technology in miniaturizing explosive devices and guidance systems and in using more efficient, less bulky solid fuel propellants allowed the U.S. deliberately to scale down the size of its missiles. (If size itself were important, the U.S. would not be phasing out of its arsenal its largest ICBMs, the gargantuan *Titans*.) Nor does such a graph show that the variety of the U.S.S.R.'s ICBMs and SLBMs is in no small part attributable to the Soviets' persistent problems in producing one reliable model in which they have confidence. This graph gives no indication, moreover, of the qualitative differences between the Soviet and American ICBMs and SLBMs—differences which are at least as significant as differences in quantity, size and variety. For example, a submarine's ability to glide silently through the water and thus evade detection and destruction is a critically valuable feature. And the U.S.'s SLBM-carrying submarines can move much more quietly than Soviet submarines.

One frequently sees charts showing the relative increase in the number of U.S. and Soviet ICBMs and SLBMs over a particular span of time. [As an example, see Figure II-3 following this selection—*eds.*] This too can create a misleading effect. A graph showing the tremendous growth in the number of Soviet missiles and the much flatter growth of the U.S. arsenal from 1970 to 1980, for example, suggests a truly alarming Soviet build-up. However, a graph including the period from 1950, say, to 1980, would reveal that the U.S. too engaged in an enormous build-up—but in the decades preceding the Soviet effort. The point here is simply that the choice of period can radically alter the message of a graph comparing quantities of weapons over a span of time.

Another common way of comparing nuclear forces is by counting the number of warheads. Initially, both U.S. and Soviet missiles carried only one warhead apiece. Each missile could therefore be aimed at only one target. In the early 1970s, however, first the U.S. and then the Soviet Union mastered the technology of multiple independently targetable reentry vehicles, or MIRVs, which allows one to load onto a single missile a number of warheads, each of which can be programmed to strike a different target. (The reentry vehicle of a missile basically contains the explosive device or warhead.)

By now, most of the superpowers' missiles are MIRVed, carrying between 3 and 14 warheads on each missile. Counting each side's ICBMs and SLBMs has therefore become an even less useful exercise than before, because it does not tell one how many bombs each side can deliver with these systems. So graphs comparing the number of deliverable warheads have become more common.

This measure, however, has its own limits. It is very difficult to determine just how many warheads the various delivery systems actually carry. The Strategic Arms Limitation Treaty of 1979 between the U.S. and U.S.S.R. . . . put ceilings on the numbers of reentry vehicles that ICBMs and SLBMs may carry. But in order to make their forces as versatile as possible, both the U.S.

and the Soviet Union deploy their missiles with differing numbers of war-heads, as well as differing megatonnage, range, and guidance systems. Thus in many cases missiles carry fewer than the maximum permitted them by SALT II. Bombers too vary in the amounts and kinds of warheads they carry. Comparisons of each superpower's warheads can therefore be based only on educated guesses.

Comparisons of numbers of warheads, like comparisons of delivery systems, also do not tell one about qualitative differences. The effectiveness—that is, the destructive potential—of a weapon is a function of the weapon's explosive power and its accuracy and must be judged in relation to the kind of target it is intended to destroy. A weapon with a certain combination of explosiveness and accuracy may be devastating against a "soft" civilian or military target such as a city or submarine base, but ineffective against a "hardened" target such as a missile silo or command-and-control bunker buried deep in reinforced concrete and steel. The importance of accuracy is thus especially great in relation to hard targets, which are built to withstand enormous explosions unless they occur almost precisely on point. *Accuracy*, therefore, is a key variable in comparing U.S. and Soviet forces.

Like the number and distribution of each side's warheads, however, accuracy can only be estimated. These estimates are based on observations of test firings of missiles. But there are too few tests for any particular model to permit an exact evaluation of its accuracy; the tests cannot be conducted over the path that the missile would have to follow if ever actually used; and weather and wartime conditions can also cause unpredictable variations. In addition, when observing Soviet missile tests, we cannot be sure how accurate the missiles are because we do not know the precise point at which they are aimed. And since estimates of accuracy are in turn used in other, more complex qualitative measurements of weapons' capabilities, the uncertainties inherent in assessments of accuracy are compounded in any subsequent measurements. . . .

The second basic approach to weighing U.S. and Soviet nuclear forces seeks to approximate, in a very theoretical way, what could happen in "actual attack situations." It attempts to predict, through a series of calculations—computer wargames—how the superpower forces would interact in a nuclear war. These are often called *force exchange* comparisons, and they seek to measure the ability of one side to attack military targets of the other side, the ability of the other side to retaliate, and the outcome of the exchange. Force exchange analysis allows a more sophisticated comparison of the two sides' forces, but depends entirely on the validity of the many underlying assumptions.

Sometimes these assumptions are stated explicitly. For example, one scenario seeks to determine the outcome of a surprise nuclear attack. It assumes that at the time of the attacker's initial strike, the other side's forces are on normal peacetime alert during which certain percentages of its ICBMs, SLBMs and bombers are kept fully readied to respond to the attack. Another scenario assumes that the other side has received warning of a likely attack and thus has readied a higher percentage of its forces to survive and retaliate. Many other factors, however, may enter into the calculations but are unlikely to be articulated.

Furthermore, as Harold Brown noted in the 1982 [Department of Defense] Annual Report, force exchange analysis also omits from its calculations certain "real, important, yet hard-to-quantify factors such as leadership, motivation, C3 (command, control and communication facilities), training and maintenance." It does not attempt to treat the military and political context in which such exchanges occur, or the military plans and tactics which would of course come into play in any real combat situation.

Beyond these important but unquantifiable factors is yet another range of very significant elements in comparing the military capabilities of the two superpowers. Alliances, industrial capacities, natural resources, population, geography, national morale, and political leadership and values all must figure in any realistic consideration of two potential adversaries' ability to wage war against each other. And although it is impossible to quantify these factors in a way that relates them meaningfully to an overall military balance assessment, they must nonetheless be borne in mind. Similarly, one must remember that while force exchange analyses have an artificial, even surrealistic, air, they are not merely theoretical constructs. Although abstract themselves, these analyses are based on real weapons—and weapons so powerful and so numerous that, if ever used, they would only serve, in Winston Churchill's oft-quoted phrase, to "make the rubble bounce." . . .

Figure II-2 Pictoral Representation of Soviet and American Strategic Nuclear Launch Vehicles

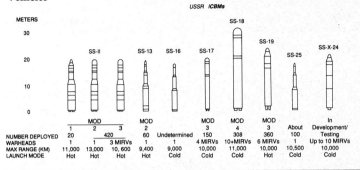

USSR *ICBMs*

	SS-II			SS-13	SS-16	SS-17	SS-18	SS-19	SS-25	SS-X-24
		MOD		MOD		MOD	MOD	MOD	About	In Development/Testing
	1	2	3	2		3	4	3		
NUMBER DEPLOYED	20	420		60	Undetermined	150	308	360	100	
WARHEADS	1	1	3 MIRVs	1	1	4 MIRVs	10+MIRVs	6 MIRVs	1	Up to 10 MIRVs
MAX RANGE (KM)	11,000	13,000	10,600	9,400	9,000	10,000	11,000	10,000	10,500	10,000
LAUNCH MODE	Hot	Hot	Hot	Hot	Cold	Cold	Cold	Hot	Cold	Cold

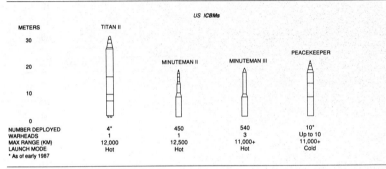

US *ICBMs*

	TITAN II	MINUTEMAN II	MINUTEMAN III	PEACEKEEPER
NUMBER DEPLOYED	4*	450	540	10*
WARHEADS	1	1	3	Up to 10
MAX RANGE (KM)	12,000	12,500	11,000+	11,000+
LAUNCH MODE	Hot	Hot	Hot	Cold

* As of early 1987

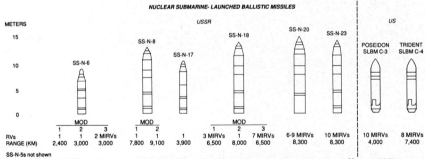

NUCLEAR SUBMARINE- LAUNCHED BALLISTIC MISSILES

USSR   US

	SS-N-6			SS-N-8		SS-N-17	SS-N-18			SS-N-20	SS-N-23	POSEIDON SLBM C-3	TRIDENT SLBM C-4
		MOD		MOD			MOD						
	1	2	3	1	2		1	2	3				
RVs	1	1	2 MIRVs	1	1	1	3 MIRVs	1	7 MIRVs	6-9 MIRVs	10 MIRVs	10 MIRVs	8 MIRVs
RANGE (KM)	2,400	3,000	3,000	7,800	9,100	3,900	6,500	8,000	6,500	8,300	8,300	4,000	7,400

SS-N-5s not shown

Source: *Soviet Military Power 1987* (Washington, D.C.: Government Printing Office, 1987), pp. 30, 33.

Figure II-3 Soviet and American Launcher and Reentry Vehicle Deployment, 1971–1987

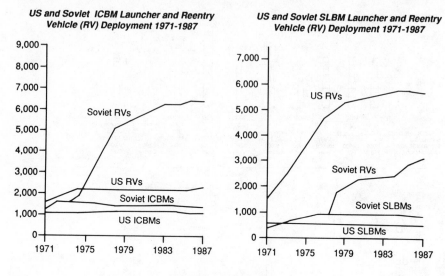

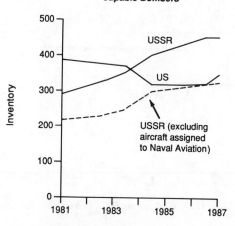

* US forces include B-52, FB-111, and B-1B; Soviet forces include BEAR, BISON, and BACKFIRE.

Source: *Soviet Military Power 1987* (Washington, D.C.: Government Printing Office, 1987), pp. 29, 31, 37.

12 FIRST STRIKE WEAPONS AT SEA: THE TRIDENT II AND THE SEA-LAUNCHED CRUISE MISSILE

Center for Defense Information

U.S. RETALIATORY CAPABILITY

In order to deter a Soviet attack, the U.S. maintains a strategic nuclear force of bombers, land-based intercontinental ballistic missiles (ICBMs) and a fleet of submarines carrying submarine-launched ballistic missiles (SLBMs). The U.S. is also placing nuclear-armed sea-launched cruise missiles (SLCMs) on submarines and surface ships. In addition to these forces the U.S. has a significant number of nuclear weapons on aircraft carriers and nuclear-armed aircraft in Europe. This combination of planes, ships, submarines and missiles is capable of delivering over 14,000 nuclear weapons on Soviet territory.

If the Soviet Union ever decides to attack the U.S., it is *possible*, but by no means certain, that it would be able to destroy most of our 1000 land-based ICBMs. But it is *certain* that the Soviet Union would be able to destroy only a few and perhaps none of the 20 U.S. ballistic missile submarines that are at sea at all times.

U.S. Nuclear Delivery Systems	Number of U.S. Nuclear Weapons
1000 ICBMs	2,268
640 SLBMs	5,632
386 Bombers	4,626
125 SLCMs	125
800 Forward-based aircraft	2,000
TOTAL:	14,651

Because submarines are hidden in the depths of the world's vast oceans, they are extremely difficult to detect. This means that if the Soviets ever are foolish enough to attack the U.S., we can retaliate with over 3000 nuclear explosions on Soviet territory with our SLBMs alone. Each of these explosions would have at least 3–7 times the explosive power of the bomb that destroyed

Hiroshima in 1945. Clearly, the U.S. already has a robust retaliatory force with which to deter a Soviet attack.

Nuclear Warfighting

U.S. strategic nuclear forces currently do not have the capability to eliminate in a surprise attack most of the Soviet Union's means of retaliation. [Several] years ago, however, the U.S. began development of the MX, a land-based missile with sufficient accuracy and destructive force to destroy Soviet land-based missiles in their silos. The Soviet Union has over 60 percent of its strategic nuclear warheads on its land-based missiles. Their destruction in a U.S. surprise attack would severely inhibit the Soviet Union's ability to retaliate.

. . . The first 10 out of a planned 100 MX missiles became operational in December 1986. Each missile carries 10 nuclear warheads. . . .

TRIDENT II: FIRST STRIKE MISSILE

Under President Reagan, Congress . . . provided billions of dollars for the development and testing of another nuclear war fighting missile to augment the MX missile. The new missile is to be placed in the Trident submarine and it will also have, if deployed, sufficient accuracy and destructive power to destroy Soviet missiles in their silos. The new Trident II (D-5) is scheduled for initial operation in 1989. . . . Each missile will carry at least 8 nuclear warheads.

Each submarine will carry twenty-four of these missiles. . . . The Navy plans to have a total of about 20 Trident submarines by the end of the century . . . with a total of about 4,800 Trident II missile warheads by the late 1990s. . . .

The Trident II will carry nuclear warheads that are more destructive than any of those currently deployed on U.S. SLBMs. Each Trident II missile is expected to have either ten to twelve 100 kiloton warheads or eight 475 kiloton warheads. The latter are nearly 5 times as destructive as those carried by current U.S. SLBMs. . . .

The Trident II will be much more accurate than any of its predecessors. In 1987, Dr. Lawrence Woodruff, the Deputy Under Secretary of Defense for Strategic and Theater Nuclear Forces, reported that the Trident II "will have better than twice the accuracy" of existing U.S. SLBMs.

Surprise Attack Weapon

With its increased accuracy and destructive power the Trident II (D-5) will have a far different military role from that of the current SLBM force. Secretary of Defense Weinberger has stated, "The D-5's significant increase in accuracy and payload over today's Poseidon (C-3) and Trident I (C-4) missiles will provide the SSBN [nuclear-powered ballistic missile submarine] force with the capability to hold hardened targets at risk . . . Trident II (D-5) will be effective against most of the hardened military targets, including missile silos and launch control facilities."

The Trident II will have a "kill" probability against hardened targets that is more than 5 times that of any existing U.S. SLBM. A 1986 Congressional Budget Office . . . study states that with its combination of increased accuracy and destructive power, one 475 kiloton warhead on the Trident II missile will have about an 80 percent chance of destroying even the hardest targets in the Soviet Union. A single Trident I (C-4) warhead, by contrast, has only about a 15 percent chance of destroying such targets.

Illusory Goal

The combination of the land-based MX missile and the new submarine-based Trident II missile will give the U.S. a very evident capability to launch a surprise attack against the Soviet Union with sufficient destructive force to prevent the Soviets from retaliating against the U.S. with a significant number of their land-based missiles. Approximately two-thirds of the Soviet Union's strategic nuclear warheads are atop these land-based missiles.

In theory, after initiating a surprise attack with Trident II and MX missiles in which most of the Soviet Union's retaliatory forces are destroyed, the U.S. could then defeat most of the surviving remnants of the Soviet forces with its new "Star Wars" ballistic missile defense systems. The Trident II-MX-Star Wars combination could be seen as giving the U.S. a first strike nuclear war-fighting capability.

Nevertheless, even if the U.S. achieved the capability to eliminate 90 percent of the Soviets land-based missiles and other nuclear forces such as strategic bombers, the U.S.S.R. would still retain more than enough nuclear weapons to devastate the U.S. in retaliation. Ten percent of Soviet ICBM warheads plus all the Soviet SLBMs at sea, would give the Soviet Union a surviving retaliatory force of over 1,000 nuclear warheads. Even the most ardent supporters of Star Wars admit that the system would not be leak proof. A 90 percent effective system, which is clearly optimistic, would allow at least 100 nuclear warheads to explode on U.S. territory. Such a catastrophe would destroy the U.S. as a functioning society.

These conservative figures are based on existing Soviet nuclear forces, not on the greatly expanded forces that are likely to come about if the U.S. continues to pursue its present course. The first strike capability that the Reagan Administration [sought] is illusory and attempts to gain such a capability will never result in the desired political benefits. In the 1960s, for example, when the U.S. still had so-called "strategic superiority" over the Soviets, it was unable to translate that into political or military clout in the Vietnam war.

Short-Lived Advantage

The U.S.-Soviet nuclear arms competition is driven by fear and mistrust, not by logic. Neither side will accept being put at any sort of disadvantage in terms of nuclear hardware. If the U.S. arms its submarines with the Trident II missile, it may achieve a nuclear warfighting capability that the Soviets [will] not have for some time. In the past, however, U.S. advantages in strategic nuclear weapons have always been short-lived. The Soviets will be under great pressure to acquire the same silo-busting capability for their missile submarines and could possibly acquire such capability much earlier than it now appears likely.

As former Secretary of Defense Robert McNamara has pointed out, "our newest submarine force will soon carry missiles accurate enough to destroy Soviet missile silos. When the Soviets follow suit, as they surely will, their offshore submarines will, for the first time, pose a simultaneous threat to our command centers, our bomber bases and our Minuteman ICBMs."

Increased Danger

If we proceed to arm our missile submarines with super-accurate, silo-busting missiles and the Soviets eventually do the same, we will enter a new and much more dangerous era in the nuclear arms competition.

In a period of crisis, with both nations armed with offensive first strike weapons, such as the Trident II and the MX, each side may become convinced that the other is about to launch a surprise attack. If this mutual suspicion exists then one or the other may decide to strike first to beat the other to the punch. U.S. and Soviet leaders may conclude that if they wait too long to "push the button" most of their nuclear weapons would be destroyed. ICBMs can hit their targets in under 30 minutes, SLBMs in under 15. This means that the warning of a surprise attack would be minimal. Leaders would have literally only five to ten minutes to decide whether to launch their retaliatory forces before they were destroyed.

The deployment of the Trident II would increase the pressure on Soviet leaders to try to beat the U.S. to the punch by launching their nuclear weapons first. Because the Trident II can destroy Soviet means of retaliation in a matter of minutes, its deployment increases the likelihood of a Soviet decision in a crisis to preempt an anticipated U.S. attack or to "use 'em before they lose 'em." *The development and deployment of the Trident II increases the likelihood of a nuclear war starting in situations in which neither the U.S. nor the U.S.S.R. originally intended to initiate nuclear attack.*

Accidental Nuclear War

The introduction of Trident II missiles into the U.S. nuclear arsenal will increase pressure on the Soviet Union during times of tension to adopt a policy of launching their nuclear weapons at the first indication of an attack, even before that indication can be confirmed as valid. This means that the Soviets might base a decision to launch their land-based ICBMs on the early indication of a perceived attack rather than on the confirmed evidence of a real attack.

False warnings are not uncommon. Between 1977 and 1984, the satellites and radars that make up the U.S. early warning system generated over 20,000 false indications of a Soviet missile attack. More than 5 percent of these were serious enough to merit a second look. Certainly, the Soviet early warning system creates many false warnings as well. Just one of these false warnings could result in the Soviet Union launching its nuclear weapons, even though no U.S. attack was underway. *The deployment of the Trident II, by putting Soviet nuclear forces on a hair-trigger in a crisis, would increase the likelihood of an accidental nuclear war caused by a technical malfunction.* . . .

THE DANGERS OF SLCMS

In addition to the upcoming deployment of the Trident II, the Navy has begun deploying nuclear sea-launched cruise missiles (SLCMs) on surface ships and attack submarines. These jet-powered missiles will further serve to transform current U.S. naval weapons from retaliatory forces to warfighting forces, further increasing the risk of nuclear war. . . .

Today's nuclear-tipped SLCM, first deployed in June 1984, has a range of 1,500 miles. The Tomahawk Land Attack Missile/Nuclear (TLAM/N), as the nuclear SLCM is called, is one variant of three types of SLCMs. There are also two SLCMs armed with conventional (non-nuclear) warheads: the Tomahawk Land Attack Missile/Conventional (TLAM/C) and the Tomahawk Anti-Ship Missile (TASM).

The deployment of nuclear SLCMs on surface ships and attack submarines constitutes a significant change in the military situation at sea. As Rear Admiral Stephen Hostettler, Director of the Joint Cruise Missiles Project, pointed out in 1984, the wide-spread deployment of SLCMs makes the Soviet Union now "consider every battlegroup ship a potential threat."

Rear Admiral Larry Blose, Director of the Cruise Missiles Project, noted in 1987 that with Tomahawk cruise missiles "the Navy is moving from 15 offensive strike platforms (aircraft carriers) to more than 195 strike platforms." The deployment of 3,994 SLCMs, of which 758 will be nuclear, by the mid-1990s on up to 198 battleships, cruisers, destroyers, and attack submarines changes the military picture at sea. It significantly increases the number of U.S. naval nuclear weapons and the number of systems capable of delivering them.

Surprise Attack Weapons

The nuclear-tipped SLCM, despite its relatively slow speed, could be used as a first strike weapon. It is not a weapon's fight time that matters, but how much warning the other side has that it is coming. If there is very little warning time for the country being attacked to react, then it will not be able to launch its retaliatory forces before they are destroyed. Because they are small and fly at low altitudes, SLCMs are difficult to detect and track on radar. In addition, their relatively cool exhaust is unlikely to be picked up by heat-detecting, infrared, early warning satellites. Furthermore, SLCMs based on surface ships or submarines may not have far to travel. A SLCM launched from a ship within 140 miles of Soviet territory could hit coastal air bases in 15 minutes, even faster than an ICBM.

In addition to short warning time, SLCMs have the accuracy and the destructive power to destroy hardened targets. In testimony in 1985 before a Senate subcommittee, Rear Admiral Hostettler stated that the Navy was "staying close to" its goal of being able to deliver SLCMs within 250 feet of their targets. The nuclear SLCMs have a yield of 200 kilotons, which combined with this accuracy, is sufficient to destroy hardened targets. . . .

SLCMS Create Verification Problems

SLCMs are small and easily concealed. Furthermore, it is virtually impossible for the Soviet Union to distinguish nuclear SLCMs from non-nuclear SLCMs by satellites. It is also difficult to determine whether they are designed to attack ships or targets on land. As the Arms Control and Disarmament Agency (ACDA) conceded in 1978, "verifying the number of [sea-launched cruise] missiles deployed would be difficult" and then added, "restrictions on cruise missile types and missions are particularly difficult to verify."

For these reasons, SLCMs create serious problems for the verification of arms limitation agreements. . . . *Without constraints on SLCMs in the near future, it will be extremely difficult for the United States and the Soviet Union to assess and monitor the number of each other's nuclear weapons,* thus vastly complicating negotiations for limits on or reductions in nuclear weapons.

Blurring the Distinction between Nuclear and Conventional Weapons

SLCMs will be deployed on existing ships and submarines, warships designed primarily for non-nuclear warfare. This poses numerous problems. If a vessel engaged in a conventional battle is about to be destroyed, its commander may elect to use all his weapons, including his nuclear SLCMs, and thus a conventional battle could escalate to a nuclear war.

Some of the SLCMs will be deployed on attack submarines with which communications are relatively poor. In critical situations, submarine commanders might believe that they do not have enough time to get authorization to launch their nuclear weapons and decide to use them. Poor judgment in such a case could result in a minor conflict escalating to a nuclear war.

Even if the U.S. Navy is engaged in routine maneuvers with ships that do not carry nuclear SLCMs, the Soviets may assume otherwise. In such situations, Soviet commanders may fear that Soviet military forces are endangered and decide to preempt what they perceive to be an impending U.S. attack. Surface ships carrying nuclear SLCMs make attractive targets. They are big and vulnerable and can be attacked with tactical nuclear weapons without danger of killing civilians. Ironically, such attacks might be made by either side under the misguided belief that they would not escalate to a general nuclear war.

Operating in a Dangerous Environment

SLCMs operate in an unpredictable and dangerous environment. Naval forces have some unique characteristics which make the sea a likely place for a nuclear war to start. These characteristics include the lack of physical restraints over naval nuclear weapons, frequent confrontational encounters between U.S. and Soviet vessels, and relatively poor communications with submarines.

Unlike U.S. Army and Air Force nuclear weapons, which have devices requiring the insertion of secret presidential codes before they can be used, *most U.S. Navy nuclear weapons have no effective restraints to prevent their unauthorized use.* This means that a relatively small number of people in a ship or submarine crew could decide to initiate the use of nuclear weapons without permission of the President or the Secretary of Defense. Although the U.S. has developed several measures to try to inhibit the unauthorized use of nuclear weapons, the Navy has resisted the application of these measures in its nuclear weapons.

Permissive Action Links (PALs) are electro-mechanical locks on U.S. intercontinental ballistic missiles (ICBMs), air-launched missiles and bombs, and battlefield nuclear weapons which require the insertion of the correct code before they can be unlocked and their nuclear warheads can be armed. Sea-based nuclear weapons, however, have no effective restraints and can be fired without authorization by submarine and ship crews.

The vast international seas, which cover about 70 percent of the earth's surface, have no boundaries and few rules governing the behavior of ships and submarines. U.S. and Soviet vessels often play "chicken" with each other. This dangerous behavior has been described by Admiral Elmo Zumwalt, former Chief of Naval Operations, as: "an extremely dangerous, but exhilarating, running game . . . that American and Soviet ships had been playing with each other for many years. Official [U.S.] Navy statements have always blamed the Russians for starting this game, but as any teen-aged boy knows, it takes two to make a drag race." . . .

SOVIET RESPONSE TO TRIDENT II AND SLCMs

U.S. technological advantages in weapon systems are always short-lived. During the SALT I negotiations, the U.S. decided not to constrain MIRV (multiple-independently targetable reentry vehicles) technology because it was ahead of the Soviet Union in that area. The Soviets subsequently developed their own MIRV technology, giving them, too, the capability to place numerous weapons on a single missile. The net result was diminished security for both nations.

If we do not move toward agreement with the U.S.S.R. to constrain the development of more accurate SLBMs, the Soviet Union will develop SLBMs with first strike capability and thereby jeopardize U.S. retaliatory forces. U.S. fears of a disarming Soviet first strike will increase. . . .

13 NATIONAL SECURITY POLICY AND ARMS CONTROL

Robert L. Pfaltzgraff, Jr.

In the international system there is a long history of efforts to limit war by limiting armaments. The inherent problem with the focus of such efforts upon armaments arises from the fact that the causes of wars are far more complex than the mere possession of weapons. If wars were caused simply by the possession of weapons, their elimination would remove the specter of war from human behavior. Nevertheless, a variety of attempts have been made to limit the means available to engage in warfare. In the discourse on arms limitation we have essentially two basic terms: (1) arms control—the exercise of *restraint* on the development, deployment, or use of a particular weapon or category of weapons; and (2) disarmament—*reductions* in the number of a particular weapon or category of weapons. Arms control and disarmament can be undertaken unilaterally, bilaterally, or multilaterally. There are many more examples of unilateral arms control or disarmament than at the bilateral or multilateral levels. There may be arms control or disarmament with or without agreement. Moreover, arms limitations have historically been imposed by the victor on the vanquished. Thus, arms control and disarmament can be unilateral, bilateral, multilateral, by formal agreement, by tacit agreement, or by no agreement. Arms control or disarmament can pertain to weapons already deployed or those yet to be deployed. The object of arms control and disarmament agreements can be the restriction of weapons at one of several stages: R&D, engineering, production, testing, deployment, and use. The object can be either weapons (hardware) or personnel.

There are few examples of lasting arms limitation agreements, for those accords that are negotiated represent, like treaties in general, the codification of a particular set of political relationships existing at any one time. As political conditions change, so does the basis for the arms limitation agreement. What is important is the political context within which the arms control agreement is developed. The absence of political tensions, or the diminution of such conflict, enhances the prospect for successful arms limitation. If arms are not the principal cause of war, but instead the symptoms of a more deeply rooted set of divisive political issues, the scope for arms limitation agreements as the basis for international security is indeed restricted. Two historical examples will suffice: The Rush-Bagot Agreement of 1817 between the United States and Great Britain—still in existence—drastically limited naval vessels on the Great Lakes and Lake Champlain to a few ships on each side. The permanence of the agreement resulted from the fact that after the Treaty of Ghent ending the War of 1812 the United States and Britain evolved a political relationship in which their basic interests converged rather than diverged. In 1921, the United States concluded with Britain, France, Italy, and Japan the Washington Naval Treaty, whose purpose was to forestall an arms race in naval vessels among the victorious allies of World War I. The agreement coincided with the interests both of Britain and the United States, but failed as a result of the commitment of Japan to naval expansion as part of her imperial policies from 1931 to the end of World War II and as a result of Hitler's determination to break out of the arms limitations that had been imposed upon vanquished Germany in the onerous Versailles Treaty.

It was the quickening pace of armaments development, including technological innovations, that led to an increased interest in the limitation of armaments, from the Hague Conventions of 1899 and 1907 to the Geneva Protocol of 1925, prohibiting the use in warfare of chemical weapons, the Threshold Test Ban Treaty of 1963, the Non-Proliferation Treaty of 1968, the ABM Treaty and the SALT I Interim Agreement on Offensive Systems of 1972, the SALT II Treaty concluded in 1979, and the START negotiations of the early 1980s.

The ABM Treaty, signed by the United States and the Soviet Union in May 1972, limited each side first to two sites for the protection of its fixed land-based strategic force and subsequently to one site. The SALT I Interim Agreement on Offensive Systems, signed by both superpowers, placed *quantitative* limitations on ICBM and SLBM *launchers*. The Interim Agreement codified a U.S.-Soviet strategic nuclear relationship in which the Soviet Union had *quantitative* superiority in numbers of launchers, while the United States retained a technological advantage (*qualitative*) in such areas as warhead design, propulsion, and accuracy. In anticipation of the likelihood that the Soviet Union would narrow and eventually eliminate the *qualitative* advantage possessed by the United States, the Congress passed the Jackson Resolution calling upon the U.S. government to negotiate a SALT II Treaty providing for equal aggregates of launchers.

By the end of the decade of SALT (1969–1979), the security problems facing the United States seemed greater than at the beginning. The vulnerability of the U.S. strategic nuclear force, or a major portion of it, was greater after SALT than it had been before the beginning of the SALT process a decade earlier. Not long after the signing of the SALT I Interim Agreement, the Soviet Union had begun to deploy a series of new generation strategic systems—including the SS-18 with a size or throwweight more than four times that of the Minuteman, the most accurate portion of the U.S. triad of strategic forces. Although the United States had already begun to place multiple warheads in its strategic force, the large size and the larger number of Soviet systems, together with the rapidity of the Soviet MIRV deployment, increased dramatically the vulnerability of the U.S. fixed, land-based strategic force to possible attack.

The deficiency of SALT I was that it failed in its most important strategic goal: to stabilize deterrence by diminishing the vulnerability of strategic forces to possible attack. But the problem was even more serious. The ABM Treaty had for all practical purposes eliminated the possibility of an American strategic defense of ICBM silos that were becoming more vulnerable as a result of the growing accuracy of Soviet strategic forces. If the United States was to restrict drastically its ability to defend some of its most important deterrence elements, it followed that an effective agreement on offensive systems would need to have as one of its principal features restrictions on Soviet offensive systems, including ICBMs, sufficient that they could not attack the targets that we were prohibited from defending. In fact, the Soviet Union had sought *only* an ABM Treaty during the first years of the negotiations. The Interim Agreement on Offensive Systems perhaps was the best of a bad bargain. In this sense the SALT process had been fatally flawed.

Like the SALT I accords, the SALT II Treaty seemed to codify an emerging strategic balance (or imbalance favoring the Soviet Union) that included the huge new Soviet fourth-generation systems—not only the SS-18, but also the SS-17 and the SS-19. In fact, the Treaty legitimized the deployment of the huge Soviet SS-18, a system that the United States was prohibited specifically from deploying—not that we would necessarily want to do so—but it suggests that in this respect the Treaty was an unequal agreement between the United States and the Soviet Union. To many of its critics, moreover, the SALT II Treaty seemed to codify the aggregates of strategic forces at too high a level (2250 launchers for each side). In March 1977 the Carter Administration had briefly tried, but failed, to achieve an agreement providing for substantial reductions in heavy Soviet ICBMs (the SS-18), from 308 to 150, and other "deep cuts." When the Soviet Union resisted, the Carter Administration abandoned this approach.

At the end of the 1970s there was growing disillusionment with arms control, especially evident in the opposition that existed to the SALT II Treaty which had failed in any readily discernible fashion to reduce the momentum of the Soviet strategic-military buildup that coincided with the decade of SALT. The SALT II Treaty faced serious problems in achieving Senate ratification even before the Soviet invasion of Afghanistan in December 1979. Early in 1980 Carter withdrew the Treaty from Senate consideration. Among the lessons of the 1970s should have been an understanding of the inability of arms control agreements, in themselves, to shape a strategic environment satisfactory to the security needs of the United States. Paradoxically, but understandable in light of the fact that historic memories are short, if nonexistent, by the early 1980s the United States found itself once again in the position of looking to arms control as an important means of enhancing national security and expecting more from arms control than it can deliver.

The Reagan Administration came to office, not opposed to arms control, but nevertheless convinced that the security needs of the United States could *not* be met by a policy in which arms control played the central element. The approach to strategic arms limitations chosen by the Reagan Administration was set forth in the acronym START, in which the principal criterion for evaluating the effectiveness of arms limitations proposals and agreements was their contribution to strategic stability. In turn, this meant that the United States would henceforth attempt to use arms control negotiations, not as a desirable end in themselves, but instead as a means of reducing the capability available to the Soviet Union to attack the strategic forces of the United States—the problem that SALT had failed to address satisfactorily.

Furthermore, the Reagan Administration recognized that the unit of account—launchers—which had been included in SALT I and only partially addressed in SALT II, had to be altered in START. After SALT I, the Soviet Union had developed a cold-launch technique, whereby the missile silo could be reloaded. The cold launch meant that the missile would be ignited after it left the silo, which therefore would not be burned up and from which additional missiles could be launched, thus presenting formidable problems of verification. Hitherto one silo had been equated with one missile. Presumably, the Soviet Union was producing and storing clandestinely a large number of additional missiles. Otherwise, why would it wish to have reloadable silos?

The Reagan Administration sought a START policy providing for a substantial *reduction* in the numbers of warheads and launchers, as well as in the size of missiles, although the principal reductions were sought in numbers of warheads. Conceptually, the greater reduction in warheads, contrasted with launchers, would represent an increase in survivability (putting fewer eggs into more baskets). The Reagan Administration . . . sought symmetrical reductions in warheads, missiles, and throwweight based on an agreement that is verifiable. The Soviet Union accepted the idea of limits on warheads but at a higher level than that sought by the United States (5,000).

Meanwhile, in 1977 the Soviet Union had begun the deployment of the SS-20, a highly accurate multiple-warhead missile targeted principally against Western Europe, but also deployed against targets in Asia. In 1979, NATO reached unanimous agreement to deploy a total of 572 ground-launched cruise missiles and Pershing II missiles unless agreement could be reached with the Soviet Union to dismantle the Soviet SS-20s. In November 1981, the Reagan Administration proposed the zero-zero option: the United States would forgo deployment of its new-generation force if the Soviet Union would dismantle its SS-20s. A second proposal put forward by the United States— the interim solution—would have provided for equivalency between the United States and the Soviet Union in warheads deployed at whatever agreed level, as long as it was lower than the existing Soviet deployment or the planned American deployment. In late 1983, the Soviet Union broke off the two sets of arms control negotiations after having failed in its effort to use such negotiations to prevent the deployment of the U.S. forces that had been authorized by the NATO decision of 1979.

On March 23, 1983, President Reagan delivered a speech, calling for research and development to ascertain the feasibility of building a strategic defense that would render less usable the strategic nuclear forces of either side. The Strategic Defense Initiative (SDI), as it has been termed, comes at a time when technologies, especially those of electronics and microminiaturization, have reached a stage in which it may be technically feasible in the next generation to deploy various forms of defensive capabilities, whose principal effect would be to render obsolete much of the huge investment that the Soviet Union has made in strategic offensive systems and which the United States is not prepared to match. With the SDI would come the possibility of transforming a conception of deterrence based upon assured *destruction* into a conception of deterrence based upon assured *survival*. Nuclear missiles would be destroyed by a *nonnuclear* device *after* they had been launched against their designated targets.

While we [have debated] the wisdom of deploying one type of new land-based system . . . the Soviet Union [has tested] at least two new ICBMs and [deployed] other advanced strategic forces as well. If present strategic force levels favor the Soviet Union, the current dissensus in the United States about the future of the land-based part of our strategic force holds the potential of widening further the gap in favor of the Soviet Union in the years ahead.

It is asked what difference it would make if the Soviet Union had a wider measure of superiority in strategic forces, for the United States could simply respond to a Soviet attack that destroyed our land-based strategic force by attacking Soviet cities with our residual, sea-based force. There are several problems with this approach. It represents a failure in the concept of deterrence, for the basis for deterrence rests upon the survivability of strategic forces. It would have been the inability of the United States to ensure the *survivability* of at least a large portion of its strategic force that would have led to the hypothesized Soviet attack. Further, the use of American retaliatory forces against Soviet cities would invite a response-in-kind against American population centers. Knowing in advance that the Soviet Union possessed a superior nuclear force that itself was largely invulnerable to a retaliatory strike, an American President would have great difficulty in ordering such an attack, whose effect would probably be the annihilation of our society.

Another deficiency in this approach lies in the assumptions that it makes about the future invulnerability of the sea-based leg of our triad of strategic forces. It has been generally assumed that submarines would remain largely immune to attack. Yet research is underway to develop the means to detect and destroy submarines. Therefore, it cannot be assumed that submarine-based forces will always be survivable. In short, the problems of survivability of strategic forces as a basis for deterrence are likely to grow in the next decade. As a result, it will become more urgent to develop the means somehow to ensure, or at least to enhance, the invulnerability of our forces.

As at the time of the SALT I negotiations, the Soviet Union prefers to negotiate a strategic arms agreement that would prevent the United States from deploying a strategic defense capability without placing effective limitations on the massive offensive forces already deployed by the Soviet Union. Stated somewhat differently, the Soviet Union wishes to reach agreements that focus on American systems *yet* to be deployed, rather than Soviet systems *already* deployed. This is a persistent element of Soviet arms control policy. Its latest manifestation is to be found in the Soviet propaganda campaign calling for the "demilitarization" of space, by which is meant to prevent the eventual deployment of a strategic defense, part of whose components might be based in space, while the Soviet Union continues to deploy missiles that fly through space en route to their targets. This is an old Soviet approach to arms control negotiations and broader diplomatic behavior as well—what is mine is mine, what is yours is negotiable, as President Kennedy once put it.

The gradual movement from an emphasis on assured destruction to assured survival based upon a strategic defense would represent a concept of deterrence linked more clearly to ethical standards acceptable to Western pluralistic societies. The ability technologically to deploy a strategic defense more cheaply than the cost of deploying additional offensive systems would provide a conceptual basis for achieving deep reductions in offensive forces that were no longer useful or cost-effective as part of a deterrence posture. In any event, the continued deployment of new generations of offensive missile systems might become counterproductive. To be sure, there remain many unanswered questions about strategic defense as a contribution to deterrence stability. What is certain, however, is the fact that merely the discussion of strategic defense for the first time provided a viable approach to reductions in the large numbers of offensive weapons possessed by both sides—but in much larger numbers by the Soviet Union in the form of counterforce, highly accurate systems of the kind that would be used to launch a first strike. Thus, we may be on the verge of a rethinking of deterrence theory and force mixes—moving from an offense-dominant to a defense-oriented strategic environment which offers fascinating possibilities for the development of a concept that reconciles the needs of deterrence with ethical standards appropriate to societies whose purpose is the preservation of peace in freedom and justice.

In brief, arms control or disarmament by international agreement represents an adjunct to national security policy that cannot form an alternative to adequate defense programs. Like international treaties generally, or contractual agreements in domestic life, arms control accords usually codify some already existing set of relationships or levels of military forces. This problem presently faces the United States as a result of the differing stages of the U.S. and Soviet strategic programs. To freeze American and Soviet nuclear forces at present levels, even if it were fully verifiable (which it is not), would lock the United States into a condition of inferiority. It would perpetuate a strategic relationship that is unsatisfactory as a result of the huge Soviet buildup of the last decade, while depriving the United States of the ability to take necessary steps to improve the survivability of its own forces. The enhancement of such survivability is not synonymous with an increase in numbers of weapons. In fact, the United States has been reducing rather than increasing such numbers. The United States has 8,000 fewer warheads and a fourth less megatonnage today than it had in the 1960s.

Arms control agreements pose formidable problems of verifiability. Here, we have another major difference between the United States and the Soviet Union. It is far easier for the Soviet Union to verify U.S. compliance with an arms control agreement than it is for the United States to make certain that the Soviet Union is complying with such an agreement. The Soviet Union is a "closed society" permeated by a tradition of secrecy. There is no free press, nor do the advocates of arms control have the opportunity to criticize Soviet policy. This stands in sharp contrast to the United States, where abundant information is available about our defense programs. In a real sense, as a pluralistic society with representative political institutions and a probing, free press and electronic media, we largely verify ourselves.

Although the quest for equitable arms control accords with the Soviet Union will continue, we should harbor no illusion that they furnish, in themselves, any real substitute for a defense capability based on peace through strength in the imperfect world in which we live in the late twentieth century.

14 LESSONS OF THE INF TREATY

Lynn E. Davis

The Intermediate-range Nuclear Forces (INF) Treaty . . . is certainly a success if measured against the West's proclaimed arms control objectives during the 1980s. In the face of opposition from both the Soviet Union and West European peace movements, NATO carried out its 1979 decision to deploy intermediate-range nuclear missiles in five West European countries. Later, after the deployment was completed, NATO succeeded in securing Soviet agreement to all of its arms control goals, including the global elimination of Soviet SS-20 missiles and acceptance of very intrusive verification measures.[1]

Nevertheless, the INF treaty has provoked considerable unease in the West, by its provisions as well as by its implications for the future. Will NATO's strategy of flexible response remain credible? Will the imbalance between conventional forces in Europe now become more dangerous? Will the treaty unleash political forces leading to the denuclearization of the continent and American disengagement from NATO? It would be both ironic and tragic if this NATO success became the vehicle for a future alliance crisis.

The story of the negotiation of the INF treaty is well known.[2] What is important now is to consider the critical lessons of the INF experience.

II

The INF saga began in the late 1970s as a result of two West European worries. First, the Soviets were deploying new SS-20 missiles, which were mobile, accurate, equipped with multiple warheads, and targeted on Western Europe. Second, the Americans were ignoring European interests in negotiating the second Strategic Arms Limitation Talks (SALT II) Treaty, seeking limits only on the nuclear threat to the United States. President Carter's inept handling of the neutron bomb affair in 1978 exacerbated European concern, rekindling doubts about the American commitment to Europe and the credibility of the American nuclear guarantee.

Finding it difficult to address these underlying doubts directly, West Europeans and Americans focused on confronting the expansion of the Soviet

Note: Some footnotes have been deleted.

162

nuclear threat to Europe and the deficiencies in the U.S. nuclear arsenal in Europe. In 1979 NATO decided to modernize its nuclear capabilities by deploying 572 Pershing 2 and ground-launched cruise missiles, and simultaneously to begin negotiations to reduce the Soviet SS-20 threat.

NATO governments argued that the capability to strike the Soviet Union with systems based on land in Western Europe was necessary in order to convey to the Soviet Union a real sense of risk from any aggression on the continent, and that only a new generation of INF missiles could provide such an assured capability. Because of their range, these missiles would also allow the United States to threaten the Soviet Union without immediately subjecting its territory to an all-out nuclear war. Critics of the INF deployment, on the other hand, suggested that the missiles were provocative and could undermine deterrence by theoretically permitting the United States to confine a war within Europe and to postpone or even avoid using its strategic nuclear weapons.

Underlying the 1979 decision was also the view that an American willingness to use its nuclear weapons would depend importantly on the location and type of nuclear weapons—hence the attraction of missiles based in Europe, compared with strategic weapons based at sea. An alternative view is that a decision to use nuclear weapons will be based on how Americans assess their interests and vulnerabilities rather than on the particular kind of nuclear weapon system. How one judges the strategic consequences of eliminating all U.S. INF missiles therefore depends in large part on which of these competing theories one believes. Supporters of the treaty argue that NATO's strategy of flexible response does not depend on any single weapon system.

The missiles represented a response to the political and military situation at the time. But their deployment created such serious divisions over nuclear weapons within many West European countries that NATO may in the future find it desirable, or even necessary, to look for alternatives to new U.S. nuclear weapons in Europe to assure the credibility of the American nuclear guarantee.

III

Soviet actions played a central role in the INF drama. Without the prior Soviet deployment of the SS-20s, NATO would almost certainly not have decided to deploy American INF missiles. After 1979 the Soviets undertook a varied but sustained campaign to prevent the U.S. deployment and, although their initial tactics failed, the Soviets succeeded in the end through the INF treaty. What changed was not their objective but their willingness to pay the U.S. price.

The Soviets initially sought to persuade Western publics that NATO, by introducing new INF missiles, was upsetting the balance of forces in Europe. They claimed that a rough equivalence existed if U.S. forward-based aircraft and British and French nuclear systems were included in comparative calculations of strength. They called for a freeze on new INF deployments but showed no willingness to give up their own sizable monopoly. When the first U.S. INF missiles were deployed in 1983, the Soviets walked out of the Geneva negotiations and announced that they would station SS-12 missiles in East Germany and Czechoslovakia. After negotiations resumed in 1985, Secretary Gorbachev—to most everyone's surprise—changed tactics and over the next two years acquiesced, in turn, to American demands for an agreement covering missiles and not aircraft, to establishing equal ceilings, to eliminating all INF missiles in Europe, to excluding limits on British and French nuclear forces, to including collateral constraints on shorter-range missiles, to banning INF missiles in Asia, and to requiring on-site inspections.

The Soviets were obviously determined to prevent the United States from deploying any INF missiles in Europe. Moscow argued that the missiles were destabilizing because of their long range and accuracy and, in the case of the Pershing 2, because of its short flight time. How seriously the Soviets viewed this threat is difficult to assess, particularly as U.S. strategic nuclear weapons pose a similar threat. A long-standing Soviet goal, however, is for the United States to withdraw all its nuclear weapons from Europe. The eventual Soviet willingness to eliminate all its SS-20s suggests that this was the overriding Soviet motivation. Soviet strategic nuclear weapons and medium-range aircraft can threaten all the targets currently covered by their INF missiles. Nevertheless, under the treaty the Soviets will destroy hundreds of existing ballistic missiles, thereby removing the threat that initially provoked the 1979 NATO decision.

The Soviets certainly saw opportunities for creating divisions in the West through their INF initiatives. Their intransigence in the years leading up to the U.S. missile deployments, their walkout from the negotiations and their attempt to link INF with the Strategic Defense Initiative (SDI) in the end all failed to destroy NATO's solidarity. But it was a close call, and the political debate in Europe over INF has left serious wounds. Finally, Gorbachev probably saw the treaty as a means to enhance his international stature, to promote political and economic relations with the West and perhaps to free up, over time, resources in the Soviet Union for his economic reform.

The INF experience has shown what a formidable challenge the new Soviet leadership poses for the West and has demonstrated Gorbachev's personal skill and dexterity as a participant in Western public debate. He succeeded in putting the West on the defensive through his initiatives, even though he was the one making concessions. The treaty also shows that the Soviets, to promote their fundamental objectives, were willing to pay a high price; the West must be prepared for the possibility that the Soviets will agree to radical Western demands. As for Soviet strategic objectives, the INF experience suggests that there has been no significant change, for through the treaty they have taken a step toward their goal of removing all U.S. nuclear weapons from Europe. . . .

IV

Drawing the correct conclusions from the INF experience is certainly important, but the West does not have the luxury of calm reflection. The treaty has provoked a debate over how best to promote peace and security in Europe over the next decade. Americans and West Europeans are both questioning past strategies and approaches. . . .

The problem is that while Americans and West Europeans are both searching for a new approach to promoting peace and security in Europe, the West has no real alternative but to proceed on the basis of its current strategy. The Soviet Union and its allies will continue to possess large numbers of nuclear and conventional weapons, and with these they will be able to threaten Western Europe. The West too will have nuclear and conventional forces and in its military strategy will wish to have flexibility and options. American interests in Europe will remain vital, and West Europeans cannot alone provide for their own defense. Changes can therefore only be made on the margin of what is the current strategy of flexible response. Some changes are, nevertheless, inevitable.

In thinking about how best to proceed, the West needs to appreciate what the INF treaty will in fact mean for Europe. While eliminating all their intermediate- and shorter-range missiles, the United States and Soviet Union will each retain thousands of other strategic and theater nuclear weapons. These can all be modernized. The United States will have some 4,600 nuclear weapons deployed in Europe, including dual-capable aircraft, short-range missiles and artillery. Some 320,000 American soldiers are currently stationed in Europe, along with equipment for two or three more army divisions.

What is uncertain is how the West wishes to respond to growing pressures on both sides of the Atlantic to reduce reliance upon U.S. nuclear and conventional forces for the defense of Western Europe. Lacking is an overall approach defining a consistent set of strategic and arms control policies.

If the past is any guide, few will be attracted to defining an overall approach to these issues. Immediate problems always take priority. . . .

The most important lesson of the INF treaty is therefore quite simple: the West needs to define strategic and arms control objectives which are mutually consistent and serve alliance interests. An important first step would be to design an overall approach to assuring the security of Western Europe based on new judgments as to the respective roles of Americans and West Europeans.

NOTES

1. The United States and the Soviet Union agreed to destroy within three years an entire class of deployed intermediate- and shorter-range missiles: for the Soviet Union some 1,700 SS-4/5, SS-12, SS-20 and SS-23 missiles, and for the United States some 800 ground-launched cruise missiles and Pershing 1A and 2 missiles.

2. See Strobe Talbott, "The Road to Zero," *Time*, Dec. 14, 1987.

15 DEFENDING POST-INF EUROPE

Jeffrey Record and
David B. Rivkin, Jr.

A substantial denuclearization of Europe is at hand. It takes the form of the U.S.-Soviet treaty that eliminates two entire classes of nuclear missiles (though not their warheads) now deployed in Europe and the U.S.S.R. The Intermediate-range Nuclear Forces (INF) Treaty has profound implications for conventional deterrence and defense on the Continent. It is also likely to have major repercussions for NATO's cohesion, arms control negotiations and the future of U.S.-European relations.

Critics and skeptics . . . contend that any degree of denuclearization of Europe not tied in some way to a redress of the conventional military balance, which continues to favor the Soviet Union, could make Europe safe for conventional warfare on a scale not witnessed since 1945.

Even partial denuclearization, it is asserted, would work against NATO by removing many of the very weapons that the alliance for almost forty years has judged an effective and comparatively cheap means of deterring the Soviet Union's use of its numerically superior and geographically advantaged conventional forces in Europe.

Finally, critics are concerned over the treaty's direct and unfavorable impact on future modernization of NATO's conventional defenses. The treaty bans deployment of *all* ballistic and cruise missiles—non-nuclear as well as nuclear—with ranges from 500 to 5,500 kilometers. Such a ban forecloses to NATO the preferred, long-term means of implementing its declared Follow-on Forces Attack (FOFA) strategy, which calls for deep interdiction strikes using conventional munitions on Soviet air bases, communications centers and westward-moving ground reinforcement echelons in Eastern Europe. Critics further point out that removal of theater nuclear missiles and banning of non-nuclear missiles will compel the alliance to allocate a significantly larger portion of its deployed tactical air power, already severely burdened by non-nuclear operational requirements, to theater nuclear strike missions.

Supporters insist that the treaty is a major arms control breakthrough that could help promote a comprehensive strategic arms agreement. It is further claimed that removal from Europe of U.S. Pershing 2 and Soviet SS-20 ballistic missiles, along with other ballistic and cruise missiles, will enhance

Note: Some footnotes have been deleted, and one has been renumbered to appear in appropriate order.

166

conflict stability on the Continent by lowering the chances that a war in Europe, an admittedly remote possibility, would escalate to nuclear Armageddon. It is also argued that reduced reliance on NATO's nuclear "crutch" will at long last prompt greater NATO investment in Europe's conventional defenses, plagued for decades by deficiencies regarded as tolerable only in the presence of a robust theater nuclear deterrent.

Critics, however, manifest little confidence in NATO's willingness and ability to offset denuclearization by improving the alliance's conventional defenses. The history of NATO has in fact been a history of heavy reliance on nuclear weapons, driven in part by a congenital reluctance of NATO's European members to fund anything other than the minimal conventional force improvements believed necessary to keep the Americans happy. Since the early 1960s, the United States has sought conventional defenses in Europe that would be capable, in the event of war, of shifting the onus of escalation onto Moscow, or at least raising the nuclear threshold. The Europeans, in contrast, have resisted acquiring a strong conventional defense, in part for fear that it would serve to decouple the U.S. strategic deterrent from Europe's defense by eliminating equitable nuclear risk-sharing among alliance members.

Thus, deficiencies in the alliance's conventional force posture continue to be tolerated, notwithstanding the loss of strategic nuclear superiority vis-à-vis the Soviet Union in the 1970s, and even the prospect of substantial theater denuclearization. General Rogers has declared that NATO's present conventional forces probably could not mount an effective defense of the alliance's central front for more than a few days. . . .

II

The INF treaty places a premium not only on invigorating NATO's conventional forces but also on the need to give greater attention to actual war-fighting capabilities as opposed to deterrence. This, in turn, suggests the need for both higher conventional force levels . . . and resolution of NATO's major problems with its non-nuclear force posture.

But herein lies the rub: it is highly likely, for reasons mostly having little to do with the INF treaty, that the non-nuclear military balance in Europe in the post-treaty era will be even more unfavorable to NATO than it is today. National force contributions, including those of the U.S. Army Europe, to the defense of the critical central front are far more likely to shrink (and shrink substantially) than to grow during the next ten years. There are, moreover, few grounds for believing that qualitative conventional force improvements will exceed the characteristically minimal and routine.

Significantly, defense budgets have not kept pace with inflation in many NATO countries, and for some countries budgets have declined in real terms. . . . Given the well-entrenched demands of West European welfare states and the projected sluggish growth of Western economies, sizable increases in NATO defense budgets are most unlikely.

These budgetary trends are reinforced by diminished perceptions of the threat. The new Soviet leadership has succeeded in greatly changing the Western public's assessments of the Soviet Union. Gorbachev has manifested both a keen appreciation of the importance of Western public opinion and an ability to manipulate it. . . .

Demographic trends throughout NATO are also adverse. The most unsettling are in the Federal Republic of Germany, which has the lowest fertility rates in the world and whose 495,000 men under arms form the core of the alliance's forward defenses. There is virtually no possibility that the *Bundeswehr* can maintain its present strength beyond the early 1990s. The size of Germany's male population of military age (women are barred by law from bearing arms) has been dropping sharply for years and will continue to do so for the remainder of the century. The German army requires an annual replenishment pool of 225,000 new conscripts. Only 125,000 will be available by the early 1990s, however. This means that by 1995 the *Bundeswehr* could shrival to a force two-thirds its present strength (i.e., to 335,000).

Though the present German government has mandated a number of remedial measures, . . . Ministry of Defense officials privately concede that these measures offer no long-term solution to the manpower crunch. . . .

There may be reductions in other national force contributions. There are no prospects for Belgian or Dutch force expansion; indeed, Belgium . . . is considering a reduction in the poorly equipped 30,000-man force it deploys in Germany. . . .

Nor can a robust British Army of the Rhine (BAOR) any longer be taken for granted. British defense expenditure is declining in real terms, and for the first time in decades defense expenditure as a percentage of gross national product is headed downward. . . . Some German Ministry of Defense officials believe that at least one of the BAOR's three divisions will be withdrawn from Germany within the next ten years.

Even the future of U.S. forces in Europe is in doubt. A number of factors seem to be converging on behalf of a sizable reduction in the American force presence in Europe by the end of the century. These factors include: (1) mounting political pressures on the U.S. defense budget, which has been declining in real terms since the Reagan Administration's first term; (2) growing demands on U.S. armed forces in the Persian Gulf and other places outside the NATO area; (3) adverse demographic trends that call into question the all-volunteer force's ability to recruit and retain sufficient numbers of qualified people over the next decade; (4) rising public and congressional anger over what is perceived to be Europe's continued unwillingness to bear its fair share of the common defense burden; (5) continuation of a comparative disinvestment in conventional force modernization and expansion; and (6) the possibility that a new American president would consider a strategic reallocation of U.S. forces overseas.

There is also the unpleasant fact that some of our NATO allies are no longer prepared to tolerate a significant U.S. force presence on their soil. . . .

Moreover, within the traditionally Eurocentric American foreign policy establishment there is growing division over the strategic wisdom and moral validity of continuing to maintain a large force presence in Europe which, together with forces withheld in the United States for Europe's reinforcement, consumes about one-half of all U.S. defense expenditure.

Until the 1980s, calls for pulling some or all U.S. troops out of Europe came almost exclusively from liberals, libertarians, and Midwestern and Rocky Mountain isolationists. . . .

Today, however, prominent members of America's foreign policy elite have joined the ranks of those who favor a reduction in America's present investment in Europe's defenses. Henry Kissinger, condemning Europe's excessive reliance on nuclear deterrence at the expense of needed improvements in conventional defenses, has talked of "a gradual withdrawal of a substantial portion, perhaps up to one-half, of our present ground forces" in Europe. Zbigniew Brzezinski, bemoaning Europe's continuing status as "an American military protectorate some thirty years after Western Europe's economic recovery" from World War II, and wishing to build up U.S. military strength for Persian Gulf contingencies, has called for a withdrawal of up to 100,000 U.S. troops from Europe. Neoconservative commentator Irving Kristol, arguing that "NATO subverts Western Europe's will to resist and interferes with America's responsibilitiies as a global power," has proposed a U.S. "withdrawal from that commitment and the reconstitution of NATO as an all-European organization that would boost the morale of West European nations by affirming their independence and national identity." . . .

III

An alternative to needed conventional defense reform would, of course, be a program to restore NATO's theater nuclear forces to a pre-INF treaty level of prowess and credibility. This is probably an impossible order to fill, however, given the treaty's elimination of NATO's most deterring theater weapons.

The alliance's declared strategy of flexible response . . . has traditionally rested upon strategic nuclear, theater nuclear and conventional forces—the so-called NATO triad. To be sure, INF aside, NATO still has some 4,600 nuclear weapons in Europe. The vast majority of them, however, are specialized or short-range weapons, including maritime nuclear depth charges, atomic demolition munitions, artillery shells with ranges of only a few miles, and aircraft-deliverable weapons. The longest-range ground-launched missile system remaining in NATO's inventory is the aging LANCE (of which there are but 88 in Germany) with a range of less than 70 miles. Nuclear-armed aircraft, of course, are theoretically capable of striking deep into Eastern Europe and even western Russia. But their ability to penetrate formidable Soviet air defenses is far from certain and, in case of war, NATO's tactical air power would be overwhelmed by conventional mission demands. Overall, then, the INF treaty, by eliminating those theater nuclear weapons having the most deterrent value, moves the alliance far down the road to a diad. . . .

Given current sentiments about nuclear weapons among allied publics, the most that NATO probably can hope to do with regard to nuclear forces in Europe is to avoid a further slide toward denuclearization. Yet, even that objective may be difficult to attain. The alliance is deeply split over the issue of what to do with NATO's remaining nuclear forces, and Moscow can be expected to prey on these differences. . . .

The two focal points of post-INF nuclear force modernization that have sparked controversy are tactical missiles and nuclear artillery shells. As far as the former are concerned, NATO has been considering replacing its aging Lance tactical missiles in West Germany with a force of several hundred longer-range missiles. There are also some 2,000 nuclear shells for 155-millimeter and 8-inch artillery tubes that need to be replaced. Less politically contentious are potential improvements in NATO's long-range nuclear delivery systems not covered by the INF treaty. . . .

Any major weakening of NATO's tactical nuclear forces—as a result of negotiated reduction or German refusal to permit modernization of weapons deployed in Germany—would also complicate conventional defense. Tactical nuclear weapons compel the Soviets to operate with tactically dispersed forces, thus facilitating conventional defense. This effect of tactical nuclear weapons cannot be fully duplicated by NATO's long-range nuclear forces. . . .

NATO's overall focus in the years ahead should be on maintaining a smaller, modernized force of tactical nuclear weapons and on bolstering its long-range nuclear systems which are not covered by the INF treaty. Such a program, if successfully implemented, would not restore theater nuclear deterrence to a quality now conveyed by the Pershing 2 and ground-launched cruise missiles; nor would it excuse conventional defense improvements. It would, however, stop any slide toward further denuclearization.

IV

As for strengthening NATO's conventional defenses, the option of active-duty force expansion would seem out of the question for the reasons already discussed. There has nevertheless been a proliferation of suggestions on how to . . . [solve] . . . the alliance's old defense problems. The starting point for most reform proposals is the claim that NATO spends more on defense than the Warsaw Pact, but ends up with less to show for it because of inefficient resource allocation. This places a premium, it is argued, on greater national force specialization within NATO, with some allies concentrating on developing air and naval power, and others furnishing the bulk of the ground forces. In addition, it is claimed, greater investment ought to be made in mobilization infrastructure and reserve forces to generate an ability to mobilize rapidly. . . .

Many defense reform ideas have considerable conceptual merit. Yet, for a variety of political and bureaucratic reasons, they are unlikely to be adopted by the alliance. As John Hawes, a senior State Department official, recently observed: "There is no quick fix to NATO's problems; if there were, NATO would have adopted it long ago. NATO, for example, is not going to replace forward defense with heavily offensive or dispersed defensive strategies. Nor is NATO going to radically change its force structure."[1]

Prospects for greater Anglo-French and Franco-German military cooperation have also been cited as a means of strengthening both deterrence and defense in Europe. . . .

. . . But prospects for truly effective European defense cooperation remain severely constrained by Germany's singular military relationship with the United States, France's refusal to place its forces under NATO's integrated military command and Great Britain's special nuclear ties to the United States. There are also the overall political constraints inherent in NATO, which make timely mobilization in response to an ambiguous strategic warning unlikely. Moreover, any attempt to bolster the European pillar of the alliance must start from a recognition that NATO's overall conventional defense "pie" is likely to be smaller in the post-INF treaty era than it is today. European defense cooperation will have to run hard just to stay in place.

What about technological remedies? Theoretically, NATO might make do with smaller conventional forces if it could achieve a decisive technological advantage over the Warsaw Pact in conventional arms. No affordable revolutionary technological miracle appears in sight, however. Moreover, the alliance has already demonstrated an unwillingness or inability to fund fully the acquisition of even those so-called emerging technologies deemed indispensable to its declared goal of achieving a robust FOFA capability against the Warsaw Pact.

Furthermore, it must be assumed that the Soviets will undertake, as they have in the past, whatever technological and operational countermeasures they deem necessary to prevent a decisive qualitative breakthrough by NATO. During the past twenty years NATO's technological lead over the Soviet Union in conventional weaponry has been eroding, not growing. In fact, in key categories of ground warfare technologies, such as reactive armor and mobile antitank systems, the Soviets now enjoy a decided edge over NATO. This is not to argue that NATO should cease to pursue such potential breakthrough technologies as low-observables, robotics, railguns and anti-theater ballistic missile systems; rather, it is simply to recognize that the history of

NATO provides no basis for believing that technology can solve the alliance's long-standing conventional force deficiencies.

V

The conclusion is that NATO is highly unlikely to make the conventional force improvements seemingly dictated by the INF treaty. This leaves open only one road to redressing the non-nuclear military balance in Europe: reduction of the Soviet threat. Such a reduction could come about via either unilateral actions by Moscow or arms control negotiations. Yet, there is little apparent prospect for unilateral Soviet action or an East-West arms control agreement that would reduce or eliminate the threat of a Warsaw Pact invasion of Europe. . . .

. . . Soviet attitudes toward stabilization of the conventional force balance in Europe cannot be simply extrapolated from recent Soviet theater nuclear arms control decisions. It is most unlikely that Moscow, even though it decided to forgo some of its nuclear options, is now prepared to relinquish its conventional warfighting options as well. And no matter how low the probability of war in Europe may be in Soviet eyes, it is difficult to believe that Moscow would now be ready to rely indefinitely on a deterrence-only posture, with no provisions made for the failure of deterrence. It is also difficult to see what inducements there are for Moscow to give up its offensive conventional warfighting options since NATO has no offensive options of its own that it can exchange in a trade. . . .

. . . The Warsaw Pact enjoys considerable conventional superiority in Europe, and Moscow is fully aware of the fact that NATO cannot expand its active-duty conventional forces—indeed, that those forces are likely to shrink. . . . Gorbachev does face considerable economic pressures, but the Soviets can unilaterally reduce their forces, cut defense spending and still retain a range of warfighting options against NATO. East European political considerations also could impose major constraints on Gorbachev's ability to pull forces out of Europe. Thus, Soviet reductions in forward-deployed forces would have to be modest in size and gradual. In short, it is likely that the Soviets, for the foreseeable future, will merely seek to "repackage" their military superiority in Europe.

VI

. . . The [NATO] alliance has yet to grapple with the INF treaty's specific long-term implications for conventional deterrence and defense. There is general agreement within NATO that the INF treaty's substantial denuclearization calls for a compensatory reinvigoration of conventional defenses. However, demographic, political, budgetary, and force deployment trends on both sides of the Atlantic portend a worsening of the non-nuclear military balance on the Continent. Thus, [arms control] negotiations could become an alibi for not implementing conventional force improvements.

The arms control process contains additional potential pitfalls for the alliance. Attractive Soviet proposals are likely to strain the cohesion of the alliance and to heighten tensions between conservative NATO governments and opposition parties.

These issues aside, NATO appears to have trouble developing a broad conceptual vision of what kind of conventional arms control regime would be beneficial to its security. NATO has to maintain a certain force-to-space ratio along the inter-German border; it cannot afford major reductions in forward-deployed forces. Yet . . . small reductions, even if tilted in NATO's favor, would further worsen the conventional balance. Any reductions in U.S. forces would also entail problems. Rebasing U.S. ground forces from Europe to the United States is likely to be costly and will encourage Congress to reduce the authorized strength of the U.S. Army.

Some commentators have proposed establishing common ceilings on tanks and artillery in central Europe. . . . Yet, it is unclear whether a mutual disengagement from central Europe would appreciably change the magnitude of the Soviet military threat. . . .

All of this means that NATO will have to learn to live with a lower order of both deterrence and defense in Europe in the post-INF treaty era than that to which it has become accustomed. The alliance has painted itself into a corner, and the paint will not dry. Though willing to accept a substantial denuclearization of its European defenses, it is unwilling or unable to put its non-nuclear defenses in order. Nor can NATO expect the Soviet Union to offer a way out.

These admittedly pessimistic conclusions, however, should be placed in proper perspective. A lower quality of deterrence does not mean that chances of a future war in Europe are appreciably greater than they are today. NATO remains a remarkable alliance, and one which, despite periodic changes in both conventional and theater nuclear force balances, has managed to prevent the outbreak of war in Europe. There is no reason, barring major mistakes by Western decision-makers and force planners, to doubt that it will continue to do so.

NOTE

1. "Improving the Balance of Conventional Forces in Europe," speech presented Mar. 27, 1987, at a National Defense University symposium, "The Future of Conventional Defense Improvements in NATO."

16 THE MILITARY ROLE OF NUCLEAR WEAPONS: PERCEPTIONS AND MISPERCEPTIONS

Robert S. McNamara

. . . There are three quite contradictory and mutually exclusive views of the military role of nuclear weapons:

- Such weapons can be used in a controlled or selective way, i.e., they have a war-fighting role in defense of the NATO nations. Therefore, a strategy of "flexible response," which has been the foundation of NATO's war plans since 1967, including possible "early first use of nuclear weapons," should be continued. Underlying this policy is the belief that NATO can achieve "escalation dominance"—i.e., NATO can prevent the Warsaw Pact from extending the use of nuclear weapons beyond the level NATO chooses, with the implication that a nuclear war once started can remain limited.

- Any use of nuclear weapons by the United States or the Soviet Union is likely to lead to uncontrolled escalation with unacceptable damage to both sides. Therefore, nuclear weapons have no military use other than to deter first use of such weapons by one's adversary.

- Although initiating the use of nuclear weapons is likely to lead to uncontrolled escalation, with devastation of both societies, the threat of such use by NATO acts as a deterrent to both Soviet conventional and nuclear aggression. It is not practical to build up an equivalent deterrent in the form of conventional forces; therefore the threat of early use of nuclear weapons should never be withdrawn.

I propose to examine these views by exploring four questions:

- What is NATO's present nuclear strategy and how did it evolve?

- Can NATO initiate the use of nuclear weapons, in response to a Soviet attack, with benefit to the Alliance?

- Even if the "first use" of nuclear weapons is not to NATO's advantage, does not the threat of such use add to the deterrent and would not the removal of the threat increase the risk of war?

Note: Some footnotes have been deleted, and others have been renumbered to appear in consecutive order.

- If it is not to NATO's advantage to respond to a Soviet conventional attack by the use of nuclear weapons, can NATO's conventional forces, within realistic political and financial constraints, be strengthened sufficiently to substitute for the nuclear threat as a deterrent to Soviet aggression?

II

Questions of the military utility of nuclear weapons are addressed most realistically in the context of the possibility of warfare in Europe. Throughout the postwar period the security of Europe has been the centerpiece of U.S. foreign policy; it is likely to remain so indefinitely. In no other region have the two great powers deployed so many nuclear weapons. In no other part of the world are military doctrines which specify the use of nuclear weapons granted such wide-ranging credibility.

The use of nuclear weapons has been an integral part of NATO's military strategy since virtually the inception of the Alliance.

Shortly after the North Atlantic Treaty was ratified in 1949, estimates were made of the size of the Soviet military threat as a basis for developing NATO's military strategy and force structure. Believing that the U.S.S.R. could muster as many as 175 divisions against Western Europe, NATO military planners concluded that the Alliance would require 96 of its own divisions—which were larger than those of the Soviet Union—in order to mount an adequate defense. This estimate was accepted by the NATO ministers in February 1952 at their annual meeting in Lisbon.

It soon became clear, however, that the member nations were not willing to meet these so-called Lisbon force goals. Instead, the Alliance turned consciously to nuclear weapons as a substitute for the financial and manpower sacrifices which would have been necessary to mount an adequate conventional defense. . . .

Nor was this new emphasis only rhetorical. A Presidential Directive (NSC-162/2) ordered the Joint Chiefs of Staff to plan on using nuclear armaments whenever it would be to the U.S. advantage to do so. Changes were made in the organization and plans of the U.S. Army so that it would be better able to fight on nuclear battlefields. By late 1953, substantial numbers of tactical nuclear weapons—artillery shells, bombs, short-range missiles, nuclear mines, and others—were beginning to be deployed in Europe. The buildup of NATO tactical nuclear weapons continued steadily, peaking in the mid-1960s at around 7,000. Although large numbers of conventional forces were retained on the continent, until the early 1960s their only purpose was seen to be to contain an attack long enough for nuclear strikes to defeat the aggressor. . . .

By December 1954, the NATO ministers felt comfortable enough with the nuclear strategy to reduce the force level objective from 96 to 30 active divisions. Two years later, the Alliance formally adopted the policy of "massive retaliation" in a document known as MC 14/2.

Whether the balance of nuclear forces between the Warsaw Pact and NATO, as it was developing during the mid-1950s, justified adoption of NATO's nuclear strategy is arguable. But its merit had become questionable to many by the early 1960s. Soon after taking office in January 1961, the Kennedy Administration began a detailed analysis of the policy's strengths and weaknesses.

These studies revealed two major deficiencies in the reasoning that had led to the adoption of MC 14/2: first, the relative balance of NATO and Warsaw Pact conventional forces was far less unfavorable from a Western perspective than had been assumed (the power of Soviet forces had been overestimated and that of NATO forces underestimated); and second, there was great uncertainty as to whether and, if so, how nuclear weapons could be used to NATO's advantage.

President Kennedy, therefore, authorized me as Secretary of Defense to propose, at a meeting of the NATO ministers in Athens in May 1962, to substitute a strategy of "flexible response" for the existing doctrine of "massive retaliation."

The new strategy required a buildup of NATO's conventional forces, but on a scale that we believed to be practical on both financial and political grounds. Instead of the early massive use of nuclear weapons, it permitted a substantial raising of the nuclear threshold by planning for the critical initial responses to Soviet aggression to be made by conventional forces alone. The strategy was based on the expectation that NATO's conventional capabilities could be improved sufficiently so that the use of nuclear weapons would be unnecessary. But, under the new doctrine, even if this expectation turned out to be false, any use of nuclear weapons would be "late and limited."

Our proposal of the new strategy was the result of the recognition by U.S. civilian and military officials that NATO's vastly superior nuclear capabilities, measured in terms of numbers of weapons, did not translate into usable military power. Moreover, we understood that the initial use of even a small number of strategic or tactical nuclear weapons implied risks which could threaten the very survival of the nation. Consequently, we, in effect, proposed confining nuclear weapons to only two roles in the NATO context:

- deterring the Soviets' initiation of nuclear war;
- as a weapon of last resort, if conventional defense failed, to persuade the aggressor to terminate the conflict on acceptable terms. . . .

The revised strategy proposed to deter aggression by maintaining forces adequate to counter an attack at whatever level the aggressor chose to fight. Should such a direct confrontation not prove successful, the strategy proposed to escalate as necessary, including the initial use of nuclear weapons, forcing the aggressor to confront costs and risks disproportionate to his initial objectives. At all times, however, the flexible response strategy specified that efforts should be made to control the scope and intensity of combat. Thus, for example, initial nuclear attacks presumably would be made by short-range tactical systems in an attempt to confine the effects of nuclear warfare to the battlefield. Even so, the strategy retained the ultimate escalatory threat of a strategic exchange between U.S. and Soviet homelands to make clear the final magnitude of the dangers being contemplated.

"Flexible response" has remained NATO's official doctrine. . . . Its essential element, however—building sufficient conventional capabilities to offset those of the Warsaw Pact—has never been achieved. Indeed, during the late 1960s and early 1970s, the Alliance may have fallen farther behind its opponent. Although NATO has made considerable strides in improving its conventional posture in more recent years, most military experts believe that the conventional balance continues to favor the Warsaw Pact; they thus conclude that an attack by Soviet conventional forces would require the use of nuclear weapons, most likely within a matter of hours. NATO's operational war plans reflect this belief. The substantial raising of the "nuclear threshold," as was envisioned when "flexible response" was first conceived, has not become a reality. . . .

III

Doubts about the wisdom of NATO's strategy of flexible response, never far from the surface, emerged as a major issue in the late 1970s; debate has intensified in the ensuing years. The debate hinges on assessments of the military value of nuclear weapons.

The nuclear balance has changed substantially since the Kennedy Administration first proposed a strategy of flexible response. Both sides have virtually completely refurbished their inventories . . . and vastly [improved] the performance characteristics of both the weapons themselves and their delivery systems. . . .

It will be recalled that the strategy [of flexible response] calls for the Alliance to initiate nuclear war with battlefield weapons if conventional defenses fail, and to escalate the type of nuclear weapons used (and therefore the targets of those weapons), as necessary, up to and including the use of strategic forces against targets in the U.S.S.R. itself. Given the tremendous devastation which those Soviet strategic forces that survived a U.S. first strike would now be able to inflict on this country, it is difficult to imagine any U.S. President, under any circumstances, initiating a strategic strike except in retaliation against a Soviet nuclear strike. . . .

In short, a key element of the flexible response strategy has been overtaken by a change in the physical realities of the nuclear balance. With huge survivable arsenals on both sides, strategic nuclear weapons have lost whatever military utility may once have been attributed to them. Their sole purpose, at present, is to deter the other side's first use of its strategic forces.

Thus, given that NATO would not be the first to use strategic nuclear weapons, is it conceivable that the first use of tactical weapons would be to its military advantage?

The roughly 6,000 NATO nuclear weapons . . . deployed in Europe consist of warheads for air-defense missiles, nuclear mines (known as atomic demolition munitions), warheads for shorter-range missiles, nuclear bombs, and nuclear-armed artillery shells. . . . [N]uclear artillery shells comprise the largest portion of the stockpile, about one-third of the total. They are also the weapons which cause the greatest worry.

There are two types of nuclear artillery shells in the NATO inventory: those for 155mm howitzers and those for 203mm cannons. Both the howitzers and cannons are dual-capable: they can be used to fire shells containing conventional explosives as well as nuclear weapons. The precise ranges of these systems are classified, but most accounts put them at around ten miles. Because of the short range of nuclear artillery, the guns and their nuclear shells tend to be deployed close to the potential front lines of any conflict in Europe—there are, in effect, approximately 2,000 short-range nuclear warheads concentrated at a few sites close to the German border. . . .

In terms of their military utility, NATO has not found it possible to develop plans for the use of nuclear artillery which would both assure a clear advantage to the Alliance and at the same time avoid the very high risk of escalating to all-out nuclear war. . . .

Two problems stand in the way.

First, since the assumption is made that NATO will be responding to a Warsaw Pact invasion of Western Europe, and since the artillery has short range, the nuclear explosions would occur on NATO's own territory. If a substantial portion of the 2,000 nuclear artillery shells were fired, not only would the Warsaw Pact likely suffer heavy casualties among its military personnel, but large numbers of NATO's civilian and military personnel also would likely be killed and injured. There also would be considerable damage to property, farmland, and urbanized areas.[1]

Moreover, there is no reason to believe that the Warsaw Pact . . . would not respond to NATO's initiation of nuclear war with major nuclear attacks of its own. These attacks would probably seek most importantly to reduce NATO's ability to fight a nuclear war by destroying command and control facilities, nuclear weapon storage sites, and the aircraft, missiles, and artillery which would deliver NATO's nuclear weapons. Direct support facilities like ports and airfields would likely also be attacked in the initial Warsaw Pact nuclear offensive. Thus the war would escalate from the battlefield to the rest of Western Europe (and probably to Eastern Europe as well, as NATO retaliated).

What would be the consequences of such a conflict? In 1955 an exercise called "Carte Blanche" simulated the use of 335 nuclear weapons, 80 percent of which were assumed to detonate on German territory. In terms of immediate casualties (ignoring the victims of radiation, disease, and so forth), it was estimated that between 1.5 and 1.7 million people would die and another 3.5 million would be wounded—more than five times the German civilian casualties in World War II—in the first two days. This exercise prompted Helmut Schmidt to remark that the use of tactical nuclear weapons "will not defend Europe, but destroy it."[2]. . .

Have the more modern weapons deployed on both sides in the 1970s changed the likely results of nuclear war in Europe? Not at all! A group of experts were assembled recently by the U.N. Secretary General to study nuclear war. They simulated a conflict in which 1,500 nuclear artillery shells and 200 nuclear bombs were used by the two sides against each other's military targets. The experts concluded that as a result of such a conflict there would be a minimum of five to six million immediate civilian casualties and 400,000 military casualties, and that at least an additional 1.1 million civilians would suffer from radiation disease.[3]

It should be remembered that all these scenarios, as horrible as they would be, involve the use of only a small portion of the tactical nuclear weapons deployed in Europe, and assume further that none of the roughly 20,000 nuclear warheads in the U.S. and U.S.S.R.'s central strategic arsenals would be used. Yet portions of those central forces are intended for European contingencies: the United States has allocated 400 of its submarine-based Poseidon warheads for use by NATO; the Soviet Union, it is believed, envisions as many as several hundred of its ICBMs being used against targets in Europe.

Is it realistic to expect that a nuclear war could be limited to the detonation of tens or even hundreds of nuclear weapons, even though each side would have tens of thousands of weapons remaining available for use?

The answer is clearly no. Such an expectation requires the assumption that even though the initial strikes would have inflicted large-scale casualties and damage to both sides, one or the other—feeling disadvantaged—would give in. But under such circumstances, leaders on both sides would be under unimaginable pressure to avenge their losses and secure the interests being challenged. And each would fear that the opponent might launch a larger attack at any moment. Moreover, they would both be operating with only partial information because of the disruption to communications caused by the chaos on the battlefield (to say nothing of possible strikes against communications facilities). Under such conditions, it is highly likely that rather than surrender, each side would launch a larger attack, hoping that this step would bring the action to a halt by causing the opponent to capitulate. . . .

It is inconceivable to me, as it has been to others who have studied the matter, that "limited" nuclear wars would remain limited—any decision to use nuclear weapons would imply a high probability of the same cataclysmic consequences as a total nuclear exchange. In sum, I know of no plan which gives reasonable assurance that nuclear weapons can be used beneficially in NATO's defense.

I do not believe the Soviet Union wishes war with the West. And certainly the West will not attack the U.S.S.R. or its allies. But dangerous frictions between the Warsaw Pact and NATO have developed in the past and are likely to do so in the future. If deterrence fails and conflict develops, the present NATO strategy carries with it a high risk that Western civilization, as we know it, will be destroyed.

If there is a case for NATO retaining its present strategy, that case must rest on the strategy's contribution to the deterrence of Soviet aggression being worth the risk of nuclear war in the event deterrence fails.

IV

The question of what deters Soviet aggression is an extremely difficult one. To answer it, we must put ourselves in the minds of several individuals who would make the decision to initiate war. We must ask what their objectives are for themselves and their nation, what they value and what they fear. We must assess their proclivity to take risks, to bluff, or to be bluffed. We must guess at how they see us—our will and our capabilities—and determine what we can do to strengthen their belief in the sincerity of our threats and our promises.

But most difficult of all, we must evauate all these factors in the context of an acute international crisis. Our problem is not to persuade the Soviets not to initiate war today. It is to cause them to reach the same decision at some future time when, for whatever reason—for example, an uprising in Eastern Europe that is getting out of control, or a U.S.-Soviet clash in Iran, or conflict in the Middle East—they may be tempted to gamble and try to end what they see as a great threat to their own security.

In such a crisis, perceptions of risks and stakes may change substantially. What may look like a reckless gamble in more tranquil times might then be seen merely as a reasonable risk. This will be the case particularly if the crisis deteriorates so that war begins to appear more and more likely. In such a situation, the advantages of achieving tactical surprise by going first can appear to be more and more important.

As I have indicated, the launch of strategic nuclear weapons against the Soviet homeland would lead almost certainly to a response in kind which would inflict unacceptable damage on Europe and the United States—it would be an act of suicide. The threat of such an action, therefore, has lost all credibility as a deterrent to Soviet conventional aggression. The ultimate sanction in the flexible response strategy is thus no longer operative. One cannot build a credible deterrent on an incredible action.

Many sophisticated observers in both the United States and Europe, however, believe that the threat to use tactical nuclear weapons in response to Warsaw Pact aggression increases the perceived likelihood of such an action, despite its absolute irrationality. They believe that by maintaining battlefield weapons near the front lines, along with the requisite plans and doctrines to implement the strategy that calls for their use, NATO confronts the Warsaw Pact with a dangerous possibility which cannot be ignored.

In contemplating the prospect of war, they argue, Soviet leaders must perceive a risk that NATO would implement its doctrine and use nuclear weapons on the battlefield, thus initiating an escalatory process which could easily get out of control, leading ultimately to a devastating strategic exchange between the two homelands. It is not that NATO would coolly and deliberately calculate that a strategic exchange made sense, they explain, but rather that the dynamics of the crisis would literally force such an action—or so Soviet leaders would have to fear.

Each step of the escalation would create a new reality, altering each side's calculation of the risks and benefits of alternative courses of action. Once U.S. and Soviet military units clashed, perceptions of the likelihood of more intense conflicts would be changed radically. Once any nuclear weapon had been used operationally, assessments of other potential nuclear attacks would be radically altered.

In short, those who assert that the nuclear first use threat serves to strengthen NATO's deterrent believe that, regardless of objective assessments of the irrationality of any such action, Soviet decision-makers must pay attention to the realities of the battlefield and the dangers of the escalatory process. And, in so doing, they maintain, the Soviets will perceive a considerable risk that conventional conflict will lead to the use of battlefield weapons, which will lead in turn to theater-wide nuclear conflict, which will inevitably spread to the homelands of the superpowers. . . .

[At this point, the author comments on the intermediate-range nuclear forces scheduled for demolition under the 1987 U.S.-U.S.S.R. INF agreement. Interestingly, even in the absence of the agreement, McNamara concludes that] "A president would be unlikely to launch missiles from European soil against Soviet territory." . . .

There are additional factors to be considered. Whether it contributes to deterrence or not, NATO's threat of "first use" is not without its costs: it is a most contentious policy, leading to divisive debates both within individual nations and between the members of the Alliance; it reduces NATO's preparedness for conventional war; and, as I have indicated, it increases the risk of nuclear war.

Preparing for tactical nuclear war limits NATO's ability to defend itself conventionally in several ways. Nuclear weapons are indeed "special" munitions. They require special command, control and communications arrangements. They require special security precautions. They limit the flexibility with which units can be deployed and military plans altered. Operations on a nuclear battlefield would be very different than those in a conventional conflict; NATO planning must take these differences into account.

Moreover, since most of the systems that would deliver NATO's nuclear munitions are dual-purpose, some number of aircraft and artillery must be reserved to be available for nuclear attacks early in a battle, if that became necessary, and are thus not available for delivering conventional munitions.

Most important, though, the reliance on NATO's nuclear threats for deterrence makes it more difficult to muster the political and financial support necessary to sustain an adequate conventional military force. Both publics and governments point to the nuclear force as the "real deterrent," thus explaining their reluctance to allocate even modest sums for greater conventional capabilities.

To the extent that the nuclear threat has deterrent value, it is because it in fact increases the risk of nuclear war. The location of nuclear weapons in what would be forward parts of the battlefield; the associated development of operational plans assuming the early use of nuclear weapons; the possibility that release authority would be delegated to field commanders prior to the outset of war—these factors and many others would lead to a higher probability that if war actually began in Europe, it would soon turn into a nuclear conflagration.

Soviet predictions of such a risk, in fact, could lead them to initiate nuclear war themselves. For one thing, preparing themselves for the possibility of NATO nuclear attacks means that they must avoid massing their offensive units. This would make it more difficult to mount a successful conventional attack, raising the incentives to initiate the war with a nuclear offensive. Moreover, if the Soviets believe that NATO would indeed carry out its nuclear threat once they decided to go to war—whether as a matter of deliberate choice or because the realities of the battlefield would give the Alliance no choice—the Soviets would have virtually no incentive not to initiate nuclear war themselves.

I repeat, this would only be the case if they had decided that war was imminent and believed there would be high risk that NATO's threats would be fulfilled. But if those two conditions were valid, the military advantages to the Warsaw Pact of preemptive nuclear strikes on NATO's nuclear storage sites, delivery systems, and support facilities could be compelling.

The costs of whatever deterrent value remains in NATO's nuclear strategy are, therefore, substantial. Could not equivalent deterrence be achieved at lesser "cost"? I believe the answer is yes. . . .

V

Writing in [*Foreign Affairs* in 1982] General Bernard Rogers, the [former] Supreme Allied Commander in Europe, stated that major improvements in NATO's conventional forces were feasible at a modest price.[4] These improvements, he said, would permit a shift from the present strategy requiring the early use of nuclear weapons to a strategy of "no early use of nuclear weapons." General Rogers estimated the cost to be approximately one percent per year greater than the three percent annual increase (in real terms) which the members of NATO, meeting in Washington, had agreed to in 1978.

... Recently, an international study group also analyzed the possibilities for moving away from NATO's present nuclear reliance.[5] The steering committee of this "European Security Study" ... concludes that NATO's conventional forces could be strengthened substantially at very modest cost—a total of approximately $20 billion which would be spent over a period of five or six years. For comparative purposes, note that the MX missile program is expected to cost $18 billion over the next five years.

The European Security Study stated that to constitute an effective deterrent, NATO's conventional forces did not have to match specific Soviet capabilities. Rather, these forces need only be strong enough to create serious concerns for Warsaw Pact planners whether or not their attack could succeed.

To accomplish this, the study concluded, NATO's conventional forces would have to be able to:

- stop the initial Warsaw Pact attack;

- erode the enemy's air power;

- interdict the follow-on and reinforcing armored formations which the Pact would attempt to bring up to the front-lines;

- disrupt the Pact's command, control, and communications network; and

- ensure its own secure, reliable, and effective communications.

The report outlines in detail how NATO could achieve these five objectives utilizing newly available technologies, and accomplishing with conventional weapons what previously had required nuclear munitions. These technological advances would permit the very accurate delivery of large numbers of conventional weapons, along with dramatic improvements in the ability to handle massive quantities of military information. ...

In the meantime, immediate steps could be taken to reduce the risk of nuclear war. For example:

- Weapons modernization programs designed to support a strategy of early use of nuclear weapons—such as those to produce and deploy new generations of nuclear artillery shells—could be halted.

- The Alliance's tactical nuclear posture could be thoroughly overhauled, with an eye toward shifting to a posture intended solely to deter the first use of nuclear weapons by the Warsaw Pact. Such a shift would permit major reductions in the number of nuclear weapons now deployed with NATO's forces in Europe; no more, and probably less, than 3,000 weapons would be sufficient. Those weapons which raise the most serious problems of release authority and pressures for early use—atomic demolition munitions and nuclear air defense systems—could be withdrawn immediately. Nuclear artillery could be withdrawn as the program to improve the conventional posture was implemented.

- The creation of a zone on both sides of the border in Europe, beginning in the Central Region, within which no nuclear munitions could be deployed, could be proposed to the Soviets.[6] The agreement to create such a zone could be verified by on-site inspections on a challenge basis. The Soviet Union has stated officially that it supports a nuclear-free zone, although it proposed that the width of the zone be far greater than is likely to be acceptable to NATO. If agreement could be reached on the size of the zone and adequate methods established to verify compliance with the agreement, such an agreement could build confidence on both sides that pressures for early use of nuclear weapons could be controlled. . . .

VI

. . . Having spent seven years as Secretary of Defense dealing with the problems unleashed by the initial nuclear chain reaction [over] 40 years ago, I do not believe we can avoid serious and unacceptable risk of nuclear war until we recognize—and until we base all our military plans, defense budgets, weapon deployments, and arms negotiations on the recognition—that *nuclear weapons serve no military purpose whatsoever. They are totally useless—except only to deter one's opponent from using them.* . . .

. . . [I]f we are to reach a consensus within the Alliance on the military role of nuclear weapons—an issue that is fundamental to the peace and security of both the West and the East—we must face squarely and answer the following questions.

- Can we conceive of ways to utilize nuclear weapons, in response to Soviet aggression with conventional forces, which would be beneficial to NATO?
- Would any U.S. President be likely to authorize such use of nuclear weapons?
- If we cannot conceive of a beneficial use of nuclear weapons, and if we believe it unlikely that a U.S. President would authorize their use in such a situation, should we continue to accept the risks associated with basing NATO's strategy, war plans, and nuclear warhead deployment on the assumption that the weapons would be used in the early hours of an East-West conflict?
- Would the types of conventional forces recommended by General Rogers . . . and the European Security Study serve as an adequate deterrent to non-nuclear aggression by the U.S.S.R.? If so, are we not acting irresponsibly by continuing to accept the increased risks of nuclear war associated with present NATO strategy in place of the modest expenditures necessary to acquire and sustain such forces?

- Do we favor a world free of nuclear weapons? If so, should we not recognize that such a world would not provide a "nuclear deterrent" to Soviet conventional aggression? If we could live without such a deterrent then, why can't we do so now—thereby moving a step toward a non-nuclear world?

NOTES

1. A 100-kiloton tactical nuclear weapon would be needed to destroy approximately 50 to 100 armored fighting vehicles (e.g., tanks) in dispersed formation, the equivalent of a regiment. Such a weapon would create general destruction (of structures and people) in a circle with a diameter of 4.5 miles (an area of 15 square miles). A blast circle of this size, in typical Western European countries, would be likely to include two or three villages or towns of several thousand persons. In addition, depending on the nature of the weapon and height of burst, a much larger area could be affected by fallout. Several hundred of such tactical nuclear weapons would be required to counter an armored development in Europe. See Seymour J. Deitchman, *New Technology and Military Power*, Boulder (Colo.): Westview Press, 1979, p. 12.

2. Helmut Schmidt, *Defense or Retaliation?* New York: Praeger, 1962, p. 101; Schmidt's comment and the exercise result are cited in Jeffrey Record, *U.S. Nuclear Weapons in Europe*, Washington: Brookings, 1974.

3. *General and Complete Disarmament: A Comprehensive Study on Nuclear Weapons: Report of the Secretary General, Fall 1980*, New York: United Nations, 1981.

4. General Bernard W. Rogers, "The Atlantic Alliance: Prescriptions for a Difficult Decade," *Foreign Affairs*, Summer 1982, pp. 1145–56.

5. *Strengthening Conventional Deterrence in Europe*, Report of the European Security Study, New York: St. Martin's Press, 1983.

6. Such a proposal was made in the Report of the International Commission on Disarmament and Security Issues, *Common Security: A Program for Disarmament*, London: Pan Books, 1982.

17 BREACHING THE FIREBREAK

Michael T. Klare

Despite the impressive upsurge in public concern over the nuclear arms race, . . . new conventional and tactical nuclear weapons programs have systematically begun to erode the time-honored firebreak between nuclear and non-nuclear combat, raising the likelihood of nuclear war.

The notion of a nuclear firebreak is based upon a major premise of current military thought: that a full-scale nuclear war, should one ever occur, would probably result from a conventional conflict that exploded out of control, prompting one side to use nuclear arms in a desperate bid to stave off defeat. The only existing barrier to such escalation is a moral and psychological firebreak—the widely shared perception that nuclear weapons are different from all other weapons, and that their use could unleash a chain reaction of strikes and counterstrikes leading to total world destruction. So long as this firebreak remains wide and secure, so long as the distinction between nuclear and conventional arms remains sharp and unambiguous, potential combatants will retain an incentive to stay on the non-nuclear side of the divide, no matter what their prospects are on the conventional battlefield. But if that distinction were to fade or disappear, the inhibition against nuclear escalation would decrease and the risk of global annihilation would skyrocket.

This, unfortunately, is the situation today. As a result of innovations in both nuclear and conventional weaponry, as well as in U.S. military strategy, the continued existence of the nuclear firebreak is in jeopardy. NATO's May 1984 decision to develop conventional arms with a destructive potential akin to that of low-yield "tactical" nuclear weapons, the stockpiling of very-low-yield "neutron" shells for the 8-inch howitzers now deployed among U.S. forces in Europe, the continued development of neutron ammunition for even smaller and more widely dispersed artillery pieces, substitution of "dual-capable" (nuclear- and conventionally equipped) aircraft and cannons for the non-nuclear weaponry now in U.S. combat arsenals, and the adoption of such strategies as the "AirLand Battle Doctrine" that stress the "integration" of nuclear and non-nuclear forces on the future battlefield—these are only a few of the changes in U.S. force structure and military strategy that represent a systematic assault on the stability of the firebreak. If this process is not stopped, the gap between conventional and nuclear arms will rapidly close

Note: Some footnotes have been deleted, and others have been renumbered to appear in consecutive order.

and the risk of cross-firebreak escalation will greatly increase. And because the likelihood of our preventing the use of strategic nuclear arms becomes practically nonexistent once *any* type of nuclear arms has been used, the erosion of the firebreak poses a threat to world survival as great as the introduction of new, counterforce strategic weapons.

Thus protection of the firebreak is absolutely essential to the prevention of nuclear escalation. But the nuclear divide also serves other crucial functions. By placing limits on the explosive capacity of conventional weapons, the firebreak confines the destructive violence of those non-nuclear conflicts that do occur. Furthermore, by inserting a break or pause into the process of escalation, the firebreak offers combatants a moment of "breathing time" during which to negotiate an end to conflict, or at least to impose limits on the scale of military violence. These are compelling reasons to develop strategies for keeping the firebreak intact and stable.

THE ESSENCE OF THE FIREBREAK

Since the dawn of the atomic era, nuclear theory has held that there is a fundamental divide between nuclear weapons and all other types of weapons, and that once this gap is crossed, one enters a realm of unimaginable violence and slaughter. "As time goes by and the size and destructive power of nuclear arsenals increase," Assistant Secretary of Defense Alain C. Enthoven noted in an early discussion of this concept, "total war between nuclear powers will more and more mean total destruction." There is, then, "an important distinction, a 'firebreak' if you like, between nuclear and non-nuclear war, a recognizable qualitative distinction that [all] combatants can recognize and agree upon."[1]

This concept of an inherent disjunction between nuclear and non-nuclear conflict has become more and more important as the world's nuclear stockpiles have expanded and the risk of uncontrollable escalation has increased. Although some U.S. strategists have tried to argue that one can identify a *second* firebreak between "limited" nuclear war and full-scale thermonuclear combat, most theorists now agree that such a distinction would rapidly vanish once nuclear weapons of any sort were used in combat. "It is time to recognize that no one has ever succeeded in advancing any persuasive reason to believe that any use of nuclear weapons, even on the smallest scale, could reliably be expected to remain limited," McGeorge Bundy, George F. Kennan, Robert S. McNamara, and Gerard Smith declared in a joint 1982 article in *Foreign Affairs*. "The one clearly definable firebreak against the worldwide disaster of general nuclear war is the one that stands between all other kinds of conflict and any use whatsoever of nuclear weapons."[2]

But while invested with critical importance by most military analysts, the firebreak remains an essentially theoretical construct: although the successful avoidance of nuclear war since 1945 suggests that the firebreak is operant, no empirical data exist by which to calculate the firebreak's durability under varying degrees of stress. Nonetheless, one can identify certain factors that contribute to its long-term stability. In particular, the firebreak appears to consist of two basic elements—one moral and psychological, the other military and technological.

The moral and psychological component of the firebreak relates to the uniquely destructive nature of nuclear weapons: any decision to use them would represent an unprecedented threat to human life. . . .

The military and technological component of the firebreak relates to the role nuclear weapons would play during the actual fighting of a war; any decision to use them would represent a significant break or *discontinuity* in the progressive escalation of military violence. While a non-nuclear conflict can escalate in small stages from a low-intensity conflict to a full-scale conventional war, it cannot continue to escalate in this incremental fashion across the firebreak without a conscious decision to employ a whole new category of weapons and tactics—a decision fraught with immense risks and uncertainties. This discontinuity provides combatants with a readily identifiable boundary, or "pause," at which to limit the escalation of conflict. . . .

Obviously, these two components must both be operant for the firebreak to perform effectively: the gap in destructiveness is needed to provide a pause during the process of escalation, and the moral dimension is needed to convert that pause into a durable restraint. Moreover, for the firebreak to remain secure, the perceived distinction between conventional and nuclear weapons must remain sharp and clear and the gap in destructive potential between the two types of weapons must remain wide. Conversely, any softening of this distinction between nuclear and conventional arms, or any closing of the gap in their relative destructive power, would narrow the firebreak and increase the risk of nuclear escalation. . . .

THE ERODING FIREBREAK

The current deterioration of the nuclear firebreak results from many factors working in tandem. To a large degree, of course, it is a product of sheer technological momentum: scientists and engineers are continuously upgrading conventional and nuclear arms, thus encroaching on the firebreak from both sides. But the firebreak's erosion also reflects a deliberate attempt by the United States to establish new options for military action. Because recent shifts in the world power equation have diminished America's perceived capacity for "escalation dominance"—the ability to control the degree and tempo of escalation so as to ensure American supremacy at any level of military violence—U.S. leaders have sought new weapons and tactics designed to enhance military flexibility and control. And because maintenance of a large gap between conventional and nuclear firepower limits the potential for new escalatory options, this search has produced a sustained assault on the firebreak.

In essence, this emphasis on escalation dominance represents a concerted U.S. drive to reverse the disadvantageous military developments of the post-Vietnam era. Other countries—including many Third World nations—now possess large arsenals of modern conventional arms that may prevent the United States from dominating non-nuclear battlefields in the future to the same extent that it did in the past. Accordingly, U.S. military leaders seek new conventional arms that will outperform anything in existing enemy arsenals. Even with such weapons, though, U.S. forces may not be assured of ultimate victory. Thus the Pentagon is placing ever more reliance on the first use of tactical nuclear arms to overcome superior enemy forces. But since the use of such arms could invite a massive nuclear counterattack, U.S. strategists seek to minimize the risk of retaliation by introducing low-yield nuclear arms that would produce less damage than the "city busters" now in the U.S. arsenal. To justify all these moves and to invest them with a consistent strategic logic, the Pentagon has adopted a new combat doctrine stressing the "integration" of nuclear and non-nuclear forces on the battlefield. . . .

Near-Nuclear Conventional Weapons

In order to provide U.S. forces with a significant combat advantage over potential adversaries—many of whom now possess arms as sophisticated as those in U.S. hands—the Department of Defense seeks to acquire a whole new generation of extremely lethal, high-tech conventional weapons. These armaments include guided bombs and missiles possessing very high accuracy, like the precision-guided munitions (PGMs) or "smart bombs" first employed during the Vietnam War, as well as "cluster" munitions capable of devastating relatively large areas. When combined with new explosive mixtures and fragmentation effects, these new weapons would possess a destructive potential comparable to that of low-yield nuclear munitions.

Among the most vocal advocates of such "near-nuclear" conventional weapons are [former] NATO Commander-in-Chief General Bernard W. Rogers and his staff. Confronted by what they perceive as an overwhelming Warsaw Pact advantage in conventional firepower, and under considerable political pressure to reduce NATO's reliance on the first use of nuclear weapons, these leaders want to acquire large numbers of high-tech conventional arms that could be substituted for tactical nuclear arms in strikes on critical Warsaw Pact bases and formations. . . .

Such weapons, once deployed, are expected to play an important role in NATO's new "Follow-on Force Attack" (FOFA) strategy, formally adopted in November 1984. The brainchild of General Rogers, FOFA calls for NATO to strike enemy forces and installations deep inside Warsaw Pact territory at the very onset of an East-West conflict, with the aim of destroying the Pact's second and third waves of attacking forces before they can reach the front lines. Under this strategy, . . . Allied forces are to attack critical Warsaw Pact facilities, such as airfields, command-and-control centers, and communications and logistics bases, deep inside Eastern Europe and as far as the westernmost reaches of the Soviet Union. This strategy, Rogers claims, will allow NATO's front-line forces to repel the first wave of invaders without having to face a devastating second-echelon attack by superior enemy forces—an attack that would, under existing conditions, prompt the early use of tactical nuclear weapons by the West.

NATO officials argue, with some passion, that by permitting Allied forces to sustain higher levels of conventional combat without resorting to the use of nuclear weapons, introduction of the new high-tech conventional arms would stiffen the West's defense against Warsaw Pact attack and "raise the nuclear threshold." But [these] . . . claims . . . are dubious. By diminishing the gap in destructive power between nuclear and non-nuclear weapons, such initiatives will undermine the military and technological basis of the firebreak; by suggesting that conventional munitions can be substituted for nuclear ones, they will weaken the firebreak's moral and psychological component as well. Indeed, by narrowing the firebreak and using the new arms in strikes against critical Soviet installations, the Rogers Plan could ultimately *lower* rather than raise the nuclear threshold in Europe.

Aside from the question of the firebreak, there is another significant issue here—the growing intensity of non-nuclear combat. By introducing conventional arms with vastly increased explosive power, military officials are ensuring that future non-nuclear wars will be increasingly violent and destructive. . . .

What makes this . . . all the more frightening is the prospect that these weapons will be introduced into the arsenals of a great number of countries, including many in the Third World. While the major arms suppliers once restrained their sales of high-tech arms to Third World buyers, today they tend to offer their most advanced and sophisticated armaments. This trend has already contributed to the intensity of local wars in Lebanon and the Persian Gulf, and is likely to increase the destructive magnitude of future conflict. Because a superpower war is most likely to emerge out of a limited conflict in the Third World, the growing proliferation of high-tech conventional arms increases the risk that such encounters will escalate out of control and thereby trigger a nuclear confrontation.

Low-Yield Tactical Nuclear Munitions

Just as the firebreak is being threatened on the conventional side by the development of near-nuclear conventional arms, it is also being eroded from the nuclear side through the introduction of low-yield nuclear munitions with near-conventional damage capabilities. Such munitions are intended as replacements for existing tactical nuclear weapons (TNWs) that have been deployed in large numbers throughout Western Europe since the 1950s. Often described as "battlefield" nuclear munitions, such arms are intended for attacks on discrete military forces and installations—arms depots, command and control centers, tank formations—and are designed to be fired by regular combat forces using standard weapons delivery systems such as artillery guns, tactical aircraft, and guided missiles. While many older warheads of this type are in the multi-kiloton range—capable of destructive effects comparable to those produced by 1,000 or more tons of TNT—the newer TNWs are generally lower in yield or confine their lethal effects to radiation, thus reducing the potential for "collateral damage" to nearby structures and civilian populations.

The development of low-yield, enhanced-radiation (ER) tactical nuclear munitions—"neutron" weapons—has been a significant Pentagon objective since the early 1970s, when many Western defense analysts began to question the utility of existing TNWs. Because such arms would produce widespread collateral damage, and because they were intended for targets in densely populated areas of Central Europe, these experts worried that NATO leaders might balk at using them in response to a conventional Warsaw Pact assault. Since the usefulness or "credibility" of existing TNWs as a deterrent to such attack rested on the assumed *certainty* of their being used, such doubts, once uttered, automatically robbed TNWs of utility. To overcome this apparent dilemma, American strategists proposed the replacement of existing nuclear warheads with new, reduced-yield warheads that would produce less collateral damage and whose use would presumably be easier to authorize in a crisis. . . .

Supposedly, the introduction of such weapons will ultimately reduce the risk of nuclear escalation by enhancing the perceived credibility of NATO's first-use nuclear deterrent. . . . These military innovations will, however, narrow the gap in destructive power between nuclear and non-nuclear arms, thus eroding the military and technological foundation of the firebreak.

As is the case with near-nuclear conventional munitions, low-yield tactical nuclear weapons undermine the moral and psychological foundation of the barrier. By suggesting that tactical nuclear weapons are not much different from the most powerful conventional arms, this strategy is clearly intended to diminish the moral *unacceptability* of nuclear combat. Consider, for instance, General Andrew J. Goodpaster's 1973 testimony before the Joint Atomic Energy Committee:

> Achievable new weapons of lower yields could increase military effectiveness while reducing possible collateral damage, thereby increasing their utility as well as the *acceptability in NATO planning* for employment in the NATO countries and the adjacent areas in which they would most likely be used.

Such views, while consistent with NATO's first-use deterrence policy, obviously represent a significant threat to the survival of the firebreak.

Dual-Capable, "Trans-firebreak" Weapons

In addition to this erosion of the firebreak from both the conventional and nuclear sides, there is yet another form of encroachment: the growing deployment of delivery systems that carry both nuclear and non-nuclear warheads. Such dual-capable systems can also be described as "trans-firebreak" weapons, since they only need to undergo a change of loading to cross the gap from conventional to nuclear warfare. Weapons of this sort include tactical aircraft (F-4s, F-15s, F-16s, A-6s, and A-7s) that can carry nuclear as well as non-nuclear bombs, artillery systems that can fire nuclear as well as non-nuclear shells, and tactical missiles (Lance, Terrier, ASROC, Tomahawk, and Nike-Hercules) equipped with both conventional and nuclear warheads. . . .

. . . Dual-capable systms are systematically replacing older, non-nuclear weapons in the military inventory. . . .

This proliferation of dual-capable systems, which also appears to be under way in the Soviet Union, represents a multiple threat to the firebreak. First, the growing availability of such systems among frontline units diminishes the problems involved in moving from the conventional to the nuclear realm—thus narrowing the "pause" or discontinuity that separates one from the other. Moreover, the very advocacy of dual capability tends to implant the view that conventional and nuclear weapons are essentially *interchangeable*—thus eroding the moral and psychological barrier to escalation.

The threat represented by these weapons is heightened by the fact that many are deployed near the front lines in Europe, Korea, and along the Sino-Soviet border. If a conventional war broke out in any of these areas, and if one side made rapid inroads into the territory of its opponent, the losing side could be faced with a "use-them-or-lose-them" dilemma, a choice between firing off its nuclear warheads and risking their capture by approaching enemy units. A comparable situation could also arise at sea: rather than risk the loss of its nuclear-armed ships to enemy submarines or surface vessels, the United States or the Soviet Union might launch a preemptive nuclear strike against its adversary's fleet. In either case, such action would require little more than a change in the loading of dual-capable systems. The transition from conventional to nuclear combat would be easy to accomplish.

Dual-capable systems pose yet another threat to the stability of the firebreak: the danger of unintended escalation arising from uncertainty in the mind of an adversary about the type of threat he faces. Because it is impossible to determine whether dual-capable systems are carrying nuclear or non-nuclear munitions until they are actually fired, a combatant, upon detecting a large-scale attack by such systems, may adhere to "worst-case" logic and respond with a nuclear strike of his own—without waiting to see what sort of loading is on the attacking systems. This danger is particularly severe in the case of the Tomahawk sea-launched cruise missile (SLCM), now being deployed in both nuclear- and conventionally armed versions aboard selected

U.S. surface ships and submarines. Since the nuclear and non-nuclear variants of the Tomahawk are indistinguishable from each other except under very close inspection, the Soviets would never know which type of missiles were aboard any SLCM-equipped vessels that appeared off their coast. Should a conflict erupt when such a ship was present, Soviet forces might choose to attack it with nuclear weapons rather than take the chance that it was equipped only with conventional missiles.

AirLand Battle Doctrine

Accompanying all the arms developments described above has been a parallel initiative in the strategic concepts and policies that govern the employment of troops and weapons on the battlefield. To some extent, this effort is intended to reconcile present strategies with advances in technology and shifts in the world power equation. But it is also intended to alter the configuration of U.S. forces in such a way as to endow them with a more aggressive, offensively oriented fighting stance and to promote the "integration" of nuclear and conventional capabilities in frontline combat units.

While this new stance has been incorporated into the combat doctrine of all four military services, it is most evident in the Army's AirLand Battle Doctrine (ABD). As described in the basic Army strategic handbook, *Operations* (Field Manual 100–5), ABD is designed to replace the static, defensively oriented tactics of the past with new tactics stressing fluid, aggressive battlefield maneuvers. ABD's basic premise is that well-trained, well-commanded U.S. forces can defeat superior numbers of enemy soldiers by going on the offensive, by mobilizing U.S. strength against the enemy's weak points, and by carrying the attack deep into the enemy's rear. . . .

ABD explicitly portrays nuclear munitions as one of a range of weapons that might be employed in carrying out future operations. "In execution," FM 100–5 notes, "the AirLand Battle may mean using every element of combat power from psychological operations to nuclear weapons." Moreover, "by extending the battlefield and integrating conventional, nuclear, chemical, and electronic means, forces can exploit enemy vulnerabilities anywhere." Although the manual notes the highly destructive potential of nuclear weapons, it says nothing about the crucial distinction between conventional and nuclear arms or about the vital necessity of avoiding the use of the latter. If anything, the emphasis lies in the opposite direction. Consider, for instance, this passage on field artillery: "The fire support system destroys, neutralizes, or suppresses surface targets. . . . When nuclear weapons are available, the fire support may become the principal means of destroying enemy forces."

This portrayal of nuclear arms as legitimate instruments of firepower is all the more disturbing in light of the high premium placed on *offensive* military action. "AirLand Battle offensives," FM 100–5 states, "are rapid, violent operations that seek enemy soft spots, remain flexible in shifting the main effort, and exploit successes promptly." Particular emphasis is placed on the "deep attack"—that is, strikes against the enemy's rear that are designed to cripple his follow-on forces and to disrupt his command, control, communications, and logistics capabilities. Needless to say, nuclear arms are considered ideal for such operations: "Nuclear weapons are particularly effective in engaging follow-on formations or forces in depth," the manual suggests, "because of their inherent power and because of reduced concerns about [U.S.] troop safety and collateral damage."

In some respects, AirLand Battle Doctrine echoes General Rogers's Follow-On Force Attack strategy in its emphasis on offensive action and on attacking the enemy's critical rear-area forces and installations. But there are also differences between the two strategies, and these differences are significant. To begin with, FOFA calls for the use of high-tech conventional arms in deep-strike attacks, while AirLand envisions the use of both nuclear and non-nuclear arms. Second, and more important, FOFA is designed exclusively for combat in Europe, while ABD—although certainly developed with Europe in mind—is considered applicable to any combat situation in which U.S. troops encounter well-equipped enemy forces. Thus, FM 100–5 clearly indicates that ABD tactics could be used in jungle and desert, as well as in temperate environments, and that U.S. forces must be prepared for a wide range of unpredictable "contingency" operations in the Third World. Because such "contingencies" may entail combat with relatively powerful enemy forces, ABD envisions the use of tactical nuclear arms to ensure U.S. success.

Adoption of the AirLand Battle Doctrine also represents a very significant threat to the moral and psychological component of the firebreak. Not only does the ABD suggest that nuclear weapons are not remarkably different from other types of munitions, but it explicitly extols the use of such arms in certain combat situations. By advocating offensive thrusts deep into enemy territory, moreover, it heightens the risk that small and uncertain incidents will explode into major conflicts.

While ABD is the most elaborate of the new U.S. strategic doctrines, it is not the only one to threaten the stability of the firebreak. Similar initiatives in the naval area—notably the strategic concepts advanced by [former] Navy Secretary John F. Lehman, Jr. and thus known as the "Lehman Doctrine"—also narrow the nuclear/non-nuclear divide. By proposing naval offensives in "high-threat areas" on the periphery of the Soviet Union, and by advocating the deployment of Tomahawk SLCMs on a wide range of U.S. combat vessls, Lehman [revamped] naval strategy in much the same way that ABD has transformed Army strategy. And just as the employment of ABD tactics would tend to increase the risk of cross-firebreak escalation on land, so would implementation of the Lehman Doctrine tend to narrow the firebreak at sea.

The Lehman Doctrine also accords closely with yet another doctrinal innovation of the Reagan era: the strategy of "horizontal escalation," which prescribes responding to a Soviet offensive in an area where the United States does not have a large military presence with counterattacks on other fronts—presumably those with inadequate Soviet defenses. . . .

These developments pose an extremely grave threat to the survival of the firebreak. Each, in its own way, erodes both the moral and psychological, and the technological and military foundations of the barrier. Furthermore, each of these developments interacts with the others in such a way as to magnify the danger: the simultaneous introduction of near-nuclear conventional weapons and conventional-like nuclear arms confuses the nuclear/non-nuclear distinction; the adoption of AirLand Battle Doctrine increases the perceived advantage of dual-capable, trans-firebreak weapons. Indeed what one now observes is the *convergence* of trends that, if not reversed, will soon consume what little remains of the nuclear divide.

This prospect is especially frightening in light of the current U.S. drive to restore the perceived utility of military force as a foreign policy instrument. Although the United States has always retained the option of using nuclear arms to safeguard U.S. forces conducting interventionary operations—often using this option as an implied threat with which to intimidate rival powers—the firebreak has heretofore proved strong enough to withstand the pressures for escalation. But if the divide continues to narrow and U.S. forces are repeatedly sent into combat abroad, conventional conflict may soon overwhelm what little remains of the nuclear barrier.

Needless, to say, this danger is made all the more acute by the growing proliferation of high-tech conventional arms and nuclear-arms technology in the Third World. Should the United States or the Soviet Union choose to intervene in some future Middle Eastern or Asian conflict, the fighting could leap rapidly to the very edge of the firebreak; if at that point one side faced a major setback, and if it possessed trans-firebreak weapons and a strategy favoring their use, the last remaining barrier to escalation could disappear. There is every reason to expect that the result would be nuclear conflagration.

SECURING THE FIREBREAK

Until now, nuclear arms control and disarmament initiatives have generally focused on the uppermost rungs of the ladder of escalation—the most powerful and destructive strategic nuclear weapons. Yet because a barrier against the escalation of conventional conflict is a prerequisite for the prevention of nuclear war—and because military and strategic developments now threaten this time-honored nuclear firebreak—the superpowers must also reorient their policies to preserve this divide between nuclear and non-nuclear combat. This means that the United States and the Soviet Union must begin to consider limiting weapons at the mid-range of the escalatory spiral, where the firebreak separates conventional conflict from nuclear nightmare. . . .

NOTES

1. Alain C. Enthoven, "American Deterrent Policy," in Henry Kissinger, ed. *Problems of National Strategy: A Book of Readings* (New York: Praeger, 1965), pp. 123–24.

2. McGeorge Bundy, George F. Kennan, Robert S. McNamara, Gerard Smith, "Nuclear Weapons and the Nuclear Alliance," *Foreign Affairs*, Vol. 60, No. 4 (Spring 1982), p. 757.

18 DEEP CUTS AND THE RISKS OF NUCLEAR WAR

Joseph S. Nye, Jr.

Many military strategists warn against assuming that reducing the number of weapons is necessarily the same as reducing risks of nuclear war. They worry that deep reductions could have destabilizing effects on the strategic balance and actually raise risks. How one draws a balance between these pros and cons depends on how deep the proposed cuts are and how they relate to one's definition of deterrence. Deterrence depends on some prospect of use, but how great, what type, and how it might be affected by reductions is a matter of considerable controversy.

There are two distinct ways that nuclear use could occur: deliberately or inadvertently. Consequently, there are two forms of deterrence. One relies on credible threats of deliberate use; the other relies upon the chance of inadvertent use, or what has been called "the threat from chance." The two types can be labelled deliberate deterrence and inherent deterrence, respectively. Those who believe that inherent deterrence is sufficient can accept very deep cuts without great concern. As long as there are enough weapons to pose a threat to cities and civilization, deterrence will exist. Those who believe that some degree of deliberate deterrence is also necessary must carefully examine the manner in which reductions would affect the ability to threaten particular military targets. In fact, a continuum exists between these two types of deterrence with many strategists falling somewhere in between.

Those who wish to maximize deliberate deterrence often push weapons acquisitions that may not be very good in terms of survivability and crisis stability in the hope of increasing the credibility of deliberate use. For example, in debating the merits of a small mobile missile versus the MX, a Defense Department official argued that "more killing power could be bought for less money by buying more MX's." Senator Albert Gore replied that the "MX is the cheapest way to build raw strategic inventory, but Midgetman is the cheapest way to build survivable inventory."

The issue of targeting affects one's views of reductions. If one targeted cities only, one could settle for a few hundred large, invulnerable weapons. But as a deliberate strategy, the destruction of cities lacks credibility, appears genocidal and, if nuclear winter theory is even partly correct, could be suicidal. On the other hand, a strategy of prompt attacks against Soviet silos may increase rather than limit damage to the United States if it leads the

Soviets to a policy of launching on warning those missiles that might otherwise have been withheld.

The question of how much and what type of counterforce capabilities are necessary for deterrence underlines differences among strategists regarding the wisdom of significant reductions. For those who stress deliberate deterrence, even modest cuts may remove the capacity to threaten necessary targets. They believe that deterrence requires the United States to threaten four areas: Soviet ICBM silos; facilities supporting the political leadership at the local and central levels; Soviet economic targets related to postwar recovery; and Soviet general-purpose forces. If deterrence requires such an extensive target list, then significant reductions will be difficult. But even those who believe, as I do, that inherent deterrence buys much of what is needed, are reluctant to rely on it alone at this stage in the evolution of U.S.-Soviet relations. Americans simply know too little about what deters the Soviets, particularly in a severe crisis. Soviet force deployments and doctrines indicate that counterforce targeting plays a significant role in Soviet military thinking. If maintaining some counterforce options is prudent insurance, then reductions must be consistent with such options.

The most appropriate targets for deterrence are the Soviet military forces that might invade Europe or other areas the U.S. wishes to defend. By threatening to destroy such forces, one threatens to deny the Soviets their military objective, and to punish their military while leaving cities largely unharmed. The cities' continued existence, moreover, provides an incentive to negotiate a termination of war. Such counter-combatant targeting could require improvements in target acquisition and retargeting capabilities, and several thousand survivable weapons. Even if the number were doubled to hedge against a Soviet surprise attack, a robust counter-combatant strategy fits well within the 5,000–6,000 weapons that would remain if fifty percent reduction proposals were implemented.

Not only are the current reduction proposals unlikely to have significant negative effects on deterrence, but such reductions would help enhance the survivability of land-based forces such as the Midgetman missile. Though some of the benefits are modest, even modest gains are welcome. The largest gains are likely to come in the political area, both in terms of reversing the sense of momentum that worries the public and in improving U.S.-Soviet relations.

One can defend this point while also agreeing with the skeptics that reducing the risks of nuclear war and reducing reliance on nuclear weapons is not necessarily the same as reducing the number of nuclear weapons. For example, the shift from bombers to missiles led to a major reduction of weapons (from bombs to missile warheads) in the early 1960's, but it also shortened response time from eight hours to 30 minutes. Even a reduction in the number of destabilizing weapons (assuming agreement on definitions) could change the structure of military forces, but it would not affect the operation of these forces. It is the command, control, and operations of these forces during crises that is most clearly related to the probability of nuclear war. This would remain true even after deep cuts. Arms control measures that affect operational practices and the actual use of nuclear forces might do more than structural arms control to reduce the risk of nuclear war. Moreover, political steps to prevent and manage crises may do more than deep cuts to improve the U.S.-Soviet relationship and lessen risks.

The most important measures are those that lengthen the fuses rather than cut the numbers. To borrow from standard terminology in nonproliferation, "timely warning," and "time for diplomacy to work," rather than the number of weapons, should be the measures of successful arms control and force structures. The U.S. might aim for stable, limited second-strike counter-combatant capability. Beyond a certain level of cuts, the assurance of enough time and control to allow considered response is a more important avenue to explore than ever deeper reductions in numbers. One of the dangers of the deep cuts philosophy is the possible diversion of attention and investment from what ought to be America's top priority—putting time for presidential consideration of options back into deterrence systems. . . .

Since there is no purely technical fix to the dilemmas of deterrence, we are forced to the realization that only a long-term political strategy of societal engagement and a jointly managed balance of power offer a real promise of escaping the dilemmas of deterrence and keeping the threat of war low and proportionate to the values the U.S. hopes to protect. After all, it is not the weapons that are the greatest threat. It is the hostility in which they are embedded that poses the greatest danger. . . .

19 THE EFFECT OF STRATEGIC FORCE REDUCTIONS ON NUCLEAR STRATEGY

John D. Steinbruner

The prospect of cutting strategic nuclear forces roughly in half has seized the attention of the U.S. and Soviet governments, and it is widely accepted that such a step would be, in principle, a good thing. There is much less clarity, however, on the question of exactly why, and that is a warning that the details may prove troublesome. At any rate, the process of deciding which weapons to remove, which to keep, and which must be redesigned will predictably force both political systems to refine their conceptions of strategic security.

The United States in particular will encounter the familiar problem of divided jurisdictions. Strategic weapons are operated by both the Air Force and the Navy, which impose significantly different institutional perspectives. The influence of these perspectives can be identified in the details of current reduction proposals. The nominal ceiling that has been agreed upon is 6,000 warheads, but the United States has advanced rules for counting that would allow a substantial number of additional weapons to be carried on bombers, reflecting the Air Force's strong traditional commitment to bomber operations. Moreover, the reductions projected would be roughly proportionate across existing categories and types of weapons, a procedure that makes more sense in preserving the balance of institutional interests than in affecting the calculus of deterrence.

Strategic weapons are purchased in the course of the budget cycle, a process that is centered in Washington and is heavily influenced by Congress and all that is involved in domestic American politics. The specific numbers that have emerged have been affected by many purposes—technical investment, industrial employment, and rival fiscal priorities, for example—that are not directly related to the prevention of war. Once purchased, however, the weapons are assigned to targets by a military organization centered in Omaha and held quite remote from public discussion and domestic politics. That organization is professionally driven to do the best it can if ever ordered to fight a nuclear war.

The overall strategic posture of the United States has been influenced by

199

these different organizations and different decision processes, and it has not been perfectly coherent. The familiar doctrine of mutual assured destruction, for example, often proclaimed in the course of debates over budget decisions to be the national strategy, has a distinctly subordinate influence on the process of assigning weapons to targets, as best can be judged from public discussion of that subject.

An agreed reduction of strategic weapons would set direct constraints on the decisions that can be made in the budget process. Congress, in ratifying an agreement, would impose those restraints on itself. That leaves open the question of how the more remote process of weapons targeting would be affected, and hence, what the ultimate strategic consequences would be. That question itself identifies a significant feature of U.S. strategic planning: there appears to be no official process for judging a sufficient level of deterrent capability.

Currently, nearly all the weapons in active inventory are assigned to targets. Those who make the assignments do so by identifying individual targets that have direct military or supporting economic value and by establishing damage criteria for each target. "Requirements" are determined by listing the identified targets, and options are created by provisions allowing categories of weapons to be withheld in the course of carrying out attacks on assigned targets. It is obvious that a lethal effect on the Soviet Union would be achieved long before every individually valuable target was destroyed—just as the death of a living body would occur well before its individual cells were dismembered. The targeting process does not attempt to judge levels of sufficiency for specified missions, however. It sets priorities among basic mission categories, but with that done, the level of target coverage is driven by the number of weapons available and the degree of confidence deemed appropriate in calculating the probable destruction of each individual target. The prospect of strategic force reductions is therefore an occasion for asking an important and officially unanswered question: how many and what types of targets must be threatened in order to achieve the desired deterrent effect? . . .

STRATEGIC MISSIONS AND CONTENDING PERSPECTIVES

There are four basic types of missions that strategic forces can attempt to perform:

a) They can attack the strategic forces of the opponent, directly reducing the capability of these forces and thereby reducing as well the damage that might be inflicted on one's own forces and society.

b) They can attack the military infrastructure of the opponent—that is, support facilities, conventional forces, and general organizational capability—thereby degrading the opponent's ability to sustain military operations.

c) They can attack the industrial capability of the opponent, indirectly reducing military potential but more immediately inflicting punishing damage to people and social organization.

d) They can attack specialized targets designed to have some leveraged effect on the opponent while reducing the weight of the attack necessary to accomplish the effect.

Though each of these potential missions can be associated with the idea of deterrence, they differ markedly in the legitimacy and effectiveness that is attributed to them by various segments of American opinion and in the degree of acquiescence that can be expected from the Soviet Union.

The first of these missions (attack on strategic forces), when projected as a strategy for the United States, has the most doubtful legitimacy, the most questionable effectiveness, the fewest domestic advocates, and the greatest Soviet resistance. In the first instance this mission either directly contradicts or significantly compromises the principle that the United States would act only in retaliation. In each individual instance an attack on a strategic weapon target must be preemptive to be effective. This strategic concept thus imposes the burden either to initiate war absolutely or to respond so rapidly that it amounts to nearly the same thing. Moreover, because of the protection of strategic weapons installations by mobility and hardening, because of the operational difficulties involved in conducting an attack with the precision and timing necessary to succeed, and because of the strong incentive for the Soviet Union to adopt any feasible countermeasure, the effectiveness of this strategy as a guiding concept for U.S. forces is heavily discounted.

Despite prevailing skepticism about our own ability to carry out a truly decisive attack on Soviet strategic forces, however, there are very prominent fears that the Soviet Union might adopt such a strategy against the United States. This imbalance in judgment is sometimes justified by citing the yield, accuracy, and warhead numbers attributed to the Soviet SS-18 ICBM. The Soviet Union appears to have a corresponding perspective—doubting the effectiveness of the counterstrategic strategy as a guiding concept for their own forces but fearing it as one that U.S. forces might use. The Soviets cite the MX ICBM and the prospective Trident II sea-launched ballistic missile as supporting evidence.

These reciprocal fears arise because each side adopts a pessimistic bias in assessing the strategic balance—exaggerating the opponent's potential and discounting their own. In fact, when the total capacities of U.S. and Soviet forces are compared using standard weapon characteristics and standard calculations without a pessimistic bias for either side, the lethality of each force used against the other is similar and well short of that required to eliminate a deterrent threat. With roughly 10,000 strategic weapons currently available, each strategic force could do substantial damage to the opponent's weapons in an initial attack, but particularly because submarines on patrol are not susceptible to swift preemptive surprise, the victim would retain thousands of warheads for retaliation (nearly 3,000 for the United States and more than 1,500 for the Soviet Union). That situation would not be substantially affected by reductions in strategic forces now being proposed. Proportionate reductions to a nominal level of 6,000 warheads would remove available warheads and eliminate opposing targets but leave the calculated outcome essentially unchanged. That fact facilitates agreement but reduces the consequences of achieving it. In particular, it means that strategic force reductions of the size and composition now being negotiated are not likely to change the habit of applying a pessimistic bias to strategic assessments and therefore not likely to conquer reciprocal fears of the counterstrategic mission.

The second of the basic strategic missions—attack on military infrastructure other than strategic weapons—is the primary focus of the theory of deterrence that prevails within the U.S. military establishment. As a broad category, these targets are considered both legitimate and effective. They do not require preemption or a rapid reaction that is nearly equivalent. They can be the focus of strict retaliation. Such retaliation is believed credible and effective in that it would eliminate the organized military capacity of the opponent. That threat is considered by U.S. military officers to be the most powerful and appropriate form of deterrence.

This deterrent threat has not been endorsed by the Soviet leadership, but neither has it been as explicitly rejected as the counterstrategic mission has been. That ambivalence undoubtedly reflects a practical attitude. Any deterrent force of substantial size will unavoidably be very threatening to the coherence of any military organization.

The third basic strategic mission calls for attacks on industrial facilities, and these are also, inevitably, major population concentrations. As a focus for the deterrent threat, this category of targets has dedicated adherents and opponents in the United States. The effectiveness of the attack is not questioned, but both its credibility for purposes of deterrence and its moral legitimacy are sharply disputed. Some believe it is both incredible and immoral to threaten civilian populations. Others argue that such a threat is unavoidable as a practical matter, once nuclear weapons are used in significant numbers, and that acknowledging this fact allows effective deterrence to be established at the lowest possible force levels. The latter argument finds some resonance with the general public, but has relatively low standing within the U.S. military establishment.

At the moment, there does appear to be some appreciable difference between the United States and the Soviet Union on this point. At least as can be judged from distant observation, the Soviet political system as a whole is more willing to be guided by a strategic concept that makes the threat of retaliation against industrial targets the principle means of deterrence. Moreover, a practical assessment again must concede that any substantial number of nuclear weapons will threaten the coherence of any industrial society.

The fourth basic type of strategic mission, focusing on targets selected to provide effective leverage at lower levels of attack, plays largely a supplemental role in the United States. In the view of most people it does not substitute for one of the three other strategic concepts as the main focus for deterrence, but rather it provides buttressing against imagined variations of a typical threat, be it particularly willful opposing decision-makers or particularly constrained circumstances to which the more general strategic threats may not adequately apply. Opinions on legitimacy and effectiveness are not as well worked out, but some identifiable positions have been established. There are some who believe that petroleum facilities or power installations are appropriate targets for a highly leveraged threat. Others imagine that the deterrent threat might not be sufficiently persuasive unless focused specifically on the opponent's political leadership.

The Soviet Union has been hostile to these arguments for reasons that extend beyond the objective of preserving the deterrent incentive of a strong retaliatory threat. The Soviets are concerned with the possibility that the interactions between the opposing strategic forces could become uncontrollable under crisis conditions. With both sides committed to an extensive process of alerting weapons in response to imminent threat, and both sides contemplating very rapid reaction to any act, the ability to contain the use of nuclear weapons is seriously doubted. For that reason, the Soviet Union resists any attempt to legitimize limited nuclear operations. Because the number of nuclear weapons to be used in such limited options is relatively small, however, this disagreement is unlikely to affect the issue of agreed force reductions.

A PLAUSIBLE OUTCOME

Whatever its ultimate fate, the current proposal for reducing strategic forces is not sufficient to settle the underlying issue of relating weapons to targets according to the presumed deterrent effect. Neither the size of the prospective reductions nor the allowed composition of the forces remaining are binding enough to preclude convincingly any of the basic missions. In particular, with 6,000 warheads available to be directed against a reduced number of launchers, and with a quarter or more of these optimized for attacking hard targets, fears of the counterstrategic mission will persist. Political debate will be energized but not resolved; active diplomacy will very likely continue in search of a more decisive outcome.

The outlines of a more decisive outcome are fairly apparent. The obvious objective would be to remove the capacity of each side to conduct an effective attack on the opposing strategic foces while leaving sufficient capability to accomplish the other possible missions. This would eliminate the most disputed element of the current balance, but would not demand complete resolution of differing opinion about the appropriate focus of deterrence. This outcome could be approximated reasonably well by force reductions to the level of 3,000 warheads, with complete elimination of the advanced multiple-warhead systems (the SS-18, the MX, and all systems of equal or better combinations of accuracy, yield, and warhead loading) and with rules allowing for mobile basing or, even more probably, for adequately secure basing in silos. Forces of that size and configuration would enable each side to be reasonably confident of their ability to retaliate against 1,500 to 2,000 targets. Attacks of that size directed against military infrastructure targets would so devastate either military organization that it could not expect to conduct coherent operations thereafter. It would inflict damage to civilian populations roughly similar to that produced by a smaller number of weapons targeted directly on industrial facilities and surrounding populations. The competing theories of deterrence would be covered to a degree that would appear to match Mr. Gorbachev's widely noted phrase, "reasonable sufficiency."

Such an outcome is unquestionably visionary by the standards of current opinion. Even advocates are likely to consider it more an eventual possibility than an immediate prospect. It contains a logic, however, that over time may be a fair match even for the unruly wanderings of American politics and United States-Soviet relations.

20 PINIONING THE GENIE: INTERNATIONAL CHECKS ON THE SPREAD OF NUCLEAR WEAPONS

Ian Smart

Some have thought it logically desirable for every nation to possess nuclear weapons. In those international relationships where they already play a role, notably between the superpowers, confronting nuclear arms is thought to have imposed caution on the strongest. Why could their unlimited proliferation not be used to infect the whole world with prudence and caution? Why should they not after all eliminate war, as so many observers in 1945 had predicted they would?

At an opposite logical extreme, far more people have wanted to see nuclear weapons themselves eliminated. Whatever their value as a deterrent, the undiscriminating horror associated with using them if deterrence fails has seemed so repellent morally as to demand nothing less than their abolition. Politically, moreover, their possession in peacetime by only a handful of countries perpetuates an international hierarchy founded in ephemeral historical circumstance and repugnant to contemporary taste. Why then should either those few countries or any other nation be allowed to keep them?

Arguments for total abolition have been strengthened progressively over more than 30 years by the unending expansion of existing nuclear arsenals. Especially in the Soviet Union and the United States, the inexorable quality of that "vertical" nuclear proliferation has been matched only by the ingenuity with which its stages are successively rationalized. The economic and political costs are high. The human dangers are higher. Whatever the motives of its different advocates around the world, therefore, the cause of nuclear abolition has fed throughout upon the weapons procurement decisions taken in Moscow and Washington.

The stimulus of superpower arms procurement has equally provoked governmental responses at both extremes of logic. Albeit in different ways, what Franklin Roosevelt used to call "me-tooism" played its part in pushing governments in London, Paris and Beijing along the nuclear weapons path. But the sheer pace of American and Soviet programs over the years drove those other governments also to acknowledge their inability to keep up with the superpowers. And meanwhile there was the fear that a bilateral nuclear deadlock would shackle the United States and Soviet Union as allies or guarantors, while forcing them to pursue their own quarrels by proxy and by means of subversion or, at most, conventional conflict.

With all this, what is so surprising is that international attitudes to "horizontal" nuclear proliferation—the dissemination of nuclear weapons to additional countries—have evolved since 1945 not from a struggle between opposed ideals but as a realist's essay in pragmatism. For a brief moment at the end of the Second World War, it seemed that common ground might be found instead in absolutism—the absolute impossibility of another war in the aftermath of Hiroshima and Nagasaki, the absolute need to internationalize nuclear energy and all its uses, as proclaimed in the 1946 Acheson–Lilienthal–Baruch Plan. Thenceforward, however, the history of non-proliferation efforts has been one in which international bickering, suspicion and fundamental disagreement have been held in check only by a series of pragmatic, and even expedient, compromises. One feature is the thread of conflict. But another and more striking feature is the recurrence of pragmatic consensus. . . .

THE CONFLICT AND THE CONSENSUS

The sequence of conflict and consensus, heated dissension and cooler reflection, is both fascinating and too long to retrace in all its detail. Major turning points nevertheless stand out. The North Atlantic Treaty in 1949, for instance, marked resignation to secular east-west division and recognition of the west's consequent security needs. But it ranked also as a crucial alternative in those circumstances to wider nuclear proliferation in the west. Eisenhower's "Atoms-for-Peace" initiative in 1953 made no reference to weapons proliferation. But it quickly became a symbol of efforts by the major powers to trade civil nuclear assistance for restrictions on the military use of nuclear fission. And the creation of the International Atomic Energy Agency (IAEA) in 1957 embodied the wider consensus needed to harmonize such national restrictions and make them internationally tolerable.

In 1961, the UN General Assembly's "Irish Resolution" on non-proliferation . . . gave a new voice to the tide of unease about nuclear weapons among smaller countries. The Partial Test Ban Treaty of 1963, reflecting the catharsis of the Cuba missile crisis, pointed both to the pressure of that popular tide on the superpowers and to their assumption in response of an almost paternal responsibility for drawing up notionally universal rules. In contrast, the 1967 Treaty of Tlatelolco, constituting Latin America as a nuclear-weapon-free zone, was a case where agreement among developing non-nuclear-weapon states left nuclear powers with little option but to conform. And the Non-Proliferation Treaty (NPT) of 1968 was different again: conceived in private by the superpowers and their closest allies, but carried thereafter through gestation by a much wider international coalition with aligned and unaligned non-nuclear-weapon states.

What runs through those two decades of international non-proliferation activity is a tantalizing dialectic of populism and paternalism. On the one hand is the worldwide sense of nuclear awe and apprehension, prompting an equally wide range of national governments from non-nuclear-weapon countries to press in the common interest for strict limits on the spread of nuclear armament. On the other hand is the special conviction of superpowers and other nuclear-weapon states that further horizontal proliferation would disturb the fragile balance they have achieved through deterrence, and that they have a special right and duty to prevent it.

The question of who should sponsor international non-proliferation rules, a privileged, benevolent, paternal caucus or a notionally universal consensus, has never been resolved definitively, and presumably never will be. Neither technique has always succeeded or always failed. What has always been clear, however, is that the question itself tends to generate political friction. Paternalism disparages the weak. Populism demeans the strong. Until the end of the 1960s, therefore, each effort to check horizontal nuclear proliferation tended to alienate one or the other. At that point, however, a corollary became the NPT's immediate success, exactly because it almost accidentally blended the two approaches. Bilateral superpower negotiations built the nucleus of an agreement. But it was consultation with allies and then general debate under United Nations aegis which elaborated and legitimized a treaty.

Only an unusual technique could have forged and sustained such an assembly of implicit compromises and explicit bargains as the NPT. No addition would be permitted to the five acknowledged nuclear-weapon states. Yet, while total disarmament was the avowed goal, no specific step would be taken in the interim to reduce that number or, therefore, to eliminate existing nuclear armament. Nuclear-weapon states gave up their right to share control of nuclear weapons in pursuit of political influence or commitment. Non-nuclear-weapon states, in return, gave up their right to acquire such arms. Non-nuclear-weapon parties also accepted international safeguards on all their present and future nuclear activities. All parties then agreed to attach analogous conditions to their nuclear exports. But all promised also to engage in the fullest possible exchange of nuclear goods, services and information for peaceful use—a provision clearly if implicitly looking toward the most advanced nuclear countries. And nuclear-weapon states themselves, again by implication, accepted that they had a special duty to seek nuclear arms control. In retrospect, it was a remarkable package. It marked the effective renunciation of both logical extremes in regard to nuclear weapons—immediate abolition as much as universal possession. But it also marked an almost unprecedented convergence of populist democracy and paternal oligarchy in the interest of halting nuclear proliferation.

AFTER THE NPT

Had the even balance of those elements been maintained in the years after the NPT entered into force in 1970, a great deal of international back-biting and some real injury to international security might have been avoided. What went wrong, and why, is another story. In brief, however, the 15 subsequent years [fell] into four short periods.

From 1970 to 1974, other international and national preoccupations, including notable progress toward nuclear arms control, combined with an unfortunate sense of post-NPT complacency to sap the momentum of non-proliferation policy. Then, in 1974, as growing fears about the spread of "sensitive" technologies for enriching uranium and separating plutonium began to strain complacency, India's nuclear test explosion came to shatter it. In reaction, the advanced nuclear countries of west and east turned back from consensus and reverted in 1975–78 to a kind of injured paternalism, seeking to legislate separately as exporters for the whole conduct of nuclear trade.

The inevitable response of resentful populism nearly completed the dismemberment of the consensus on which the NPT had been built. By 1979–80, however, a combination of circumstances—economic and energy recession and some frantic nuclear diplomacy—helped to check the decay of peaceful nuclear relations (although not to revive the flagging fortunes of nuclear arms control). From about 1982, therefore, there began to emerge the first signs of a new interest in rebuilding some wider consensus.

That chequered recent history has been punctuated by three review conferences of the NPT: in 1975, 1980 and . . . 1985. And their very different outcomes provide a crude but broadly accurate index of the general mood in regard to horizontal nuclear proliferation over the same period. In 1975, for instance, impetus surviving from the orginal treaty negotiations combined with alarm aroused by India's nuclear test in the previous year to produce a sense of common purpose and renewed urgency. Nuclear suppliers had not yet fully revealed their reversion to separate rule-making. Nuclear trade was apparently expanding. The superpowers had achieved their SALT I agreements limiting strategic nuclear arms. And the net result was a reasonably unruffled First Review Conference, culminating in a sober, substantial and generally constructive final declaration.

The Second NPT Review Conference in 1980 was a very different affair. Although third-world resentment had already passed its peak, action by the United States and other exporters to restrict nuclear trade and technology transfer more narrowly after 1974 remained a cause for bitter recrimination. More important, nuclear arms control had turned sour, with a SALT II agreement blocked by the American Senate and negotiations on a comprehensive nuclear test-ban looking increasingly futile. And, most important of all, a sequence of conflicts in Asia, Africa and Europe, from Kampuchea and Iran to Afghanistan and Poland, had strained the American-Soviet relationship to the point of inhibiting, although not destroying, their co-sponsorship of the NPT's purposes.

Of the two main committees between which the 1980 review conference's working program was largely divided, that dealing with peaceful nuclear trade and cooperation . . . came within reach of substantive agreement. But the committee discussing nuclear arms control . . . proved quite unable to bridge the gulf between third-world countries wanting to condemn lack of progress by the nuclear-weapon states and nervous efforts by American and Soviet delegates, not always in comfortable harmony, to defend a somewhat dismal record. And the result was an impasse, scantily clothed in a brief communiqué calling for a further conference in 1985, but no less a failure for all of that.

A RESURGENCE OF MODERATION

The debacle of 1980 would have been sufficient reason for worrying in advance about the Third NPT Review Conference. Despite the adherence of no fewer than 130 governments, no treaty could reasonably be expected to preserve its political dynamic, as distinct from its static legal form, in the face of two such public rebuffs. But there were other reasons to worry as 1985 approached. The SALT II treaty remained unratified. Efforts to revive arms control negotiations between the superpowers remained unrequited, while their several contributions to vertical nuclear proliferation had gathered new pace. Some of the non-nuclear-weapon states outside the NPT—Pakistan and South Africa, for example—were widely believed to be moving closer to a nuclear-weapon capability of their own. Hardly any significant addition had been made to the list of treaty parties since 1975. And the NPT's initial term of 25 years was drawing ever closer to its end. All in all, the prospect was hardly one of superficial promise.

In the event, apprehension aroused in advance by all those factors proved to be largely, although not wholly, unjustified. The Third NPT Review Conference which met in Geneva from 27 August to 21 September 1985 neither broke down in despair nor broke up in disarray. It witnessed some furious argument and hard bargaining on particular topics, notably over nuclear relations with South Africa and Israel and over continuing failure to achieve a comprehensive nuclear test-ban. In the end, however, the 86 governments taking part agreed on a turgid but generally worthy and occasionally thoughtful final declaration. And the overall effect was to leave many of the NPT's supporters more hopeful than they had been at any time since 1975. . . .

Advanced nuclear countries, and especially the leading exporters of nuclear goods and services, have persisted in their separate efforts to make or revise rules for nuclear trade in the name of non-proliferation. But they have learned to act with more discretion and discrimination than in 1975–78, when the expanded Nuclear Suppliers' Group (NSG) drew up its "guidelines" in amplification of or despite its members' NPT obligations (depending on one's point of view). Instead, with the NSG relegated to inactivity, the older and less contentious NPT Exporters' Committee (often called the Zangger Committee after its Swiss chairman) has been used to pick up obviously troublesome technical developments in the nuclear-fuel cycle for special attention.

One reason why that has helped to reassure nuclear importers . . . is that the committee's work has been running in parallel with a quite different stream of debate about peaceful nuclear cooperation. In the latter, developing as well as developed countries, nuclear recipients as well as nuclear suppliers, have been meeting in various forums under the auspices of the IAEA. Those meetings and studies, on international plutonium storage, international spent fuel management and, above all, international arrangements to guarantee the security of nuclear supplies, have been important for their substantive products. But they have been more important as a means of regenerating among non-nuclear-weapon states at large some idea of a wider international consensus in support of non-proliferation policy.

It would be too much to say that there has yet been recreated the remarkable mixture of the late 1960s, blending the benign paternalism of the strong into a larger populism. There is still some way to go before injuries inflicted on that consensus since 1970 are wholly repaired. But the Third NPT Review Conference was evidence of progress. With minds increasingly focused by the approach of 1995, when the NPT's initial term expires, most non-aligned as well as aligned NPT parties proved to be interested after all in reinforcing the treaty, even if it meant missing opportunities to score political debating points in the shorter term. And it was that circumstance, more than any other factor, which tipped the balance in favor of consensus when the time came to consider a final declaration.

The points from their final declaration which stay in the minds of review conference participants will probably be those dealing with South Africa, Israel, Iraq, Iran and a comprehensive test-ban, simply because they provoked most disagreement. In a wider perspective, however, it is quite different elements that deserve to be noticed.

There is broadly worded encouragement in the final declaration for putting "sensitive" nuclear fuel cycle processes such as enrichment and plutonium separation under international or multinational control. There is a most unusual call for governments and international agencies to help in financing nuclear power projects in developing countries—unusual because the case is advanced on non-proliferation grounds. There is a pregnant exhortation to establish "full-scope" IAEA safeguards as a necessary condition of all nuclear sales to non-nuclear-weapon states—a requirement going beyond what even nuclear exporters alone were formerly willing to accept in the 1978 NSG "guidelines." And there is an equally notable and even more innovative recommendation that nuclear-weapon states should separate their military from their civil nuclear activities and submit all the latter to IAEA inspection. . . .

LOOKING TO . . . 1995

It may be tempting after the Geneva meeting in 1985 to look with quiet confidence to the 1990 review conference, or even to the crucial date of 1995. If so, a handful of reflections may serve as an antidote.

- Technology is still evolving within the nuclear fuel cycle, and some of its twists present new challenges to non-proliferation policy. In particular, the rapid development of lasers to separate different isotopes of one element poses a major problem. Within the next few years . . . lasers will permit cheaper, quicker and less easily detectable enrichment of uranium to weapons standard, and even separation of weapons-grade plutonium from commercial spent reactor fuel. Non-proliferation rules and international safeguards must keep pace with such advances or lose their credibility.

- Capacity to enrich uranium or separate plutonium is in any case spreading. Plants in Brazil and Argentina are held back temporarily by economic stringency, but unsafeguarded developments are going ahead in Pakistan and South Africa, in addition to larger safeguarded projects in Japan and West Germany. Safeguards aside, such gradual but steady growth in the number of purely national facilities raises questions of political confidence in a non-proliferation regime, as well as of economic rationality.

- In at least some parts of the world, notably in eastern Asia, there are already signs that nuclear power development may be reviving. In any case, the amounts of plutonium-containing spent reactor fuel needing to be stored somewhere in the world are increasing at an accelerating rate. Safeguards in support of non-proliferation policy will have to cope with that quantitative pressure, as well as with new qualitative challenges.

- With the Reagan-Gorbachev [summits] accomplished, expectations of substantive progress in nuclear arms control are bound to revive. Conversely, superpower reluctance to engage in peripheral bickering is likely to fade. Soviet-American collaboration in the non-proliferation sphere was forged in the mid-1960s and has withstood every subsequent strain. Yet it would be unwise to assume that the next NPT review conference . . . will witness the same diffidence toward and between the superpowers which characterized [the 1985 conference].

- Singularly little progress has been made toward bringing the most significant "absentee" countries into the international non-proliferation regime of which the NPT, the Treaty of Tlatelolco and IAEA safeguards are the pillars. Recruiting the missing nuclear-weapon states, France and China, to the NPT would provide a major boost, even if they are already informally committed to the regime's general objectives. But a more urgent need is to bring in some of the notable non-nuclear-weapon absentees. Accession by India, Pakistan or Israel may be too much to expect (although prior Chinese accession might generate a new sort of pressure on India). But it hardly seems too much to hope that Spain might finally be brought to accede, or that the Soviet Union might induce Cuba to accept both the NPT and the Treaty of Tlatelolco (thus removing an important obstacle to Argentinian and Brazilian acceptance of the latter). Progress on at least some of those fronts . . . may be regarded as a necessary index of revived political momentum.

- Finally, the real possibility has to be faced that there will be further horizontal nuclear proliferation . . . Pakistan, Israel, South Africa, Argentina and Brazil obviously stand out among countries which might conduct an initial test explosion by that time. And the chance of further tests by India is at least as great. So is the chance that if any one of those countries moves another will follow. . . . If one reflection is calculated to dispel any complacency engendered by the Third NPT Review Conference, . . . it is the thought of how governments supporting and opposing the existing non-proliferation regime would be likely to respond in such a case.

Complacency, in fact, is exactly the wrong reaction to the state of the non-proliferation regime in the aftermath of the Third NPT Review Conference. Had the conference failed overtly, the regime would already be close to dissolution. As it is, the meeting ranks as a notable success only in relation to that alternative. At best, parties to the NPT have bought more time. That is an indispensable commodity. But there is little enough time between now and . . . 1995 to cope with the new challenges confronting non-proliferation policy or the old deficiencies it has yet to repair.

Above all, the 1985 review conference demonstrated only an initial, fragile success in bringing back together the privileged few and the many: nuclear-weapon and non-nuclear-weapon states, suppliers and recipients, rich and poor. That was the unique combination which permitted and shaped the NPT itself in the 1960s. A small step has been taken toward rebuilding it, but much more needs to be done before the structure can recover any stability. Meanwhile, either agony or apathy could easily lead back to renewed conflict, pitting the self-serving abuse indulged in formerly by representatives of certain developing non-nuclear-weapon countries against the naive arrogance displayed in the past by some nuclear exporters and nuclear-weapon states. Only unremitting efforts to build consensus on the foundations laid before and during the Third NPT Review Conference can hope to avoid that sort of relapse into the cacophony of distressed paternalism and disgruntled populism.

21 THE STAR WARS DEFENSE SYSTEM: A TECHNICAL NOTE

Robert S. McNamara

For more than a quarter of a century the United States has carried on research programs aimed at devising the means to destroy Soviet missiles before they reach their targets. Since the mid-1960s we have known how to shoot down a small percentage of the incoming missiles. The Strategic Defense Initiative (SDI), or Star Wars program, through a vastly expanded research effort, seeks to so increase the "kill" capability of an antiballistic missile system as to justify its deployment.

. . . President Reagan and Secretary of Defense Caspar Weinberger . . . suggested on numerous occasions that SDI is aimed at developing a system that would fully protect our population. However, it is generally accepted by the technicians supervising the program that such a leakproof defense is not a realistic goal for at least four or five decades, if ever. Therefore, current research is directed toward a system which, while not perfect, would be sufficiently effective to provide partial protection to our urban populations. Defense of hardened targets such as missile silos and command centers would be far simpler to devise, but the [Reagan] Administration on several occasions . . . stated that this is not the goal of Star Wars.

[At this point the author provides a simple schematic diagram of a multi-layered ABM defense system which we have deleted in favor of the more recent and detailed diagram shown in Figure II-1 on page 138—*eds.*]

The SDI, as now planned, envisions an antimissile system composed of four to seven "layers." The goal is to detect and intercept ballistic missiles in each of the stages of their flight from silos in the Soviet Union and submarines at sea to targets in the United States and Western Europe.

There are four flight stages. In the boost phase the missile is launched and its booster rocket burns. The boost phase for existing ballistic missiles ranges from three to five minutes. In the postboost phase, which lasts from two to ten minutes, a postboost vehicle (also called a bus) separates from the burned-out booster rocket and proceeds to release warheads—more than one for MIRVed missiles—and various "penetration aids" designed to fool the SDI system. In the midcourse phase, the warheads and penetration aids travel on a ballistic flight trajectory through space. Land-based intercontinental ballistic missiles require fifteen to twenty-five minutes to complete this phase of flight, while submarine launched missiles need from five to twenty minutes. Finally, missiles enter the terminal stage of flight, in which they reenter the atmosphere and, in about one minute, descend upon cities and military targets.

Can a system to shoot down missiles in each of these stages be built and made effective with foreseeable technologies?

Discussion of the technical prospects for an SDI system requires much speculation, but both proponents and opponents of the plan recognize that constructing and maintaining the system would represent the most complex technical task ever undertaken in human history.

To make Star Wars work will require successful development of a great number of subsystems. These would have to quickly detect a Soviet missile attack, track each missile and warhead in the various stages of flight, discriminate them from decoys, and destroy them. SDI command and control systems would have to be capable of coordinating human and computer decision-making. And since humans could not adequately direct the effort to destroy attacking missiles, computer hardware and software would have to provide "battle management" sufficient to coordinate the various layers of attack.

Major parts of the system would be based in space. For this we would need to build hundreds or thousands of satellites, develop adequate power sources for them, and lift them into outer space. We would need to construct thousands more sea-, air-, and ground-based missile interceptors and sensors.

But such a description does not do full justice to the magnitude of the task. The SDI has been compared to a challenge initiated by President Kennedy: putting a man on the moon. But there is a fundamental difference between the two tasks: the moon didn't fight back. The Soviet Union, on the other hand, has indicated that it will respond vigorously if we endeavor to render impotent its missile arsenal. It will attempt to overwhelm, evade, or directly attack our SDI systems.

Lieutenant General James Abrahamson, SDI's director, has recognized that the response of Soviet planners to SDI will be to try to defeat the system. Thus, SDI will have to be effective against existing and projected countermeasures in order to achieve its aim. Abrahamson flatly predicts such an outcome: "The large number of opportunities to engage the threat with [a multilayered] architecture leads to an expectation of achieving very low levels of defense leakage even if the enemy proliferates his offensive forces in response to our defense."

But ensuring an effective SDI system in the face of Soviet countermeasures would be a daunting task. The most obvious Soviet response would be to increase the number of missiles and the number of warheads carried by those missiles. The Soviets already possess more than 2,300 long-range ballistic missiles with some 9,500 warheads. But SDI cannot assume it will face only those numbers. In the absence of arms control limitations, for example, the Soviets might be able to put up to 30 warheads on its 308 SS-18 missiles, which now carry no more than 10 warheads. Experts in the SDI organization have estimated that the Soviets could deploy 30,000 to 40,000 ballistic missile warheads by the end of the century.

Numerically increasing the Soviet arsenal is only the first countermeasure to consider. There are far cheaper ways to defeat an SDI system. Both we and the Soviets are currently engaged in efforts to develop various types of penetration aids to ensure that missiles will reach their targets. As we survey the technologies under consideration for SDI, I will point out some of the countermeasures that could be developed to try to defeat them.

According to Abrahamson, "the most important" layer of the SDI system is the one that will attack missiles in their boost phase. The reason why is clear: it is in the boost phase that the Soviet missile arsenal is at its most vulnerable. Booster rockets are easier to detect and track than postboost vehicles or warheads because they emit strong infrared radiation. Boosters are also larger and more fragile and thus easier to destroy. In addition, because each booster can carry multiple warheads and penetration aids, more of the Soviet arsenal can be "killed" with less shots in the boost phase.

Boost-phase defenses face a fundamental obstacle, however: where do we deploy them? The two alternatives are to station them on satellites in outer space or to "pop them up" into space from submarines once an attack has commenced. However, neither option appears feasible in light of potential countermeasures.

As the Fletcher panel, charged by the President with laying the technical groundwork for the SDI, noted in their 1983 study, "Survivability is potentially a serious problem for the space-based components." Satellites carrying SDI sensors and interceptors would be vulnerable to attack by an array of Soviet antisatellite weapons, including nuclear space mines, homing kill vehicles, and lasers. In fact, . . . the same technologies used for antimissile weapons could produce potent antisatellite weapons. And satellites, moving in predictable orbits, are easier to target than missiles. The department manager for systems analysis at the Sandia Laboratories said in 1985: "I think boost phase [defense] may be out of the question, which is unfortunate. . . . Every time we look at it, it seems very difficult to ensure the survivability of space-based assets." Because of the criticality of an effective boost-phase layer to the overall performance of the SDI defense, the opponent might need only to punch a hole in the boost-phase layer to severely degrade the defense.

In response to the Soviet antisatellite threat, we would have to develop counter-countermeasures. We could attempt to harden our satellites against enemy blows, but such hardening would increase the weight of our systems and thus increase the cost of lifting them into space. Moreover, nuclear explosions from Soviet space mines could probably wreck our satellites, hardened or not. We could increase the number of satellites, attempt to disguise them, or give them the capability to maneuver away from enemy fire. Such efforts would create an endless and expensive cat-and-mouse game with the Soviets. We could also use the kill mechanisms—designed to shoot down Soviet missiles—to attack their hostile satellites. But this would not only magnify our weapons and battle management needs, it would also create the possibility of a preemptive strike in space: If war seemed inevitable, whoever shot first would gain a significant advantage.

The other option for the boost phase is to deploy "pop-up" weapons on submarine- and land-based missiles. But most weapons under consideration for boost-phase intercept would be too heavy to be popped up. The only viable candidate for a pop-up role is a concept called the X-ray laser, a so-called directed energy weapon. Directed-energy weapons—lasers or particle beams—create beams of energy made of a single wavelength of radiation, or of electrically neutral atoms, respectively.

The X-ray laser would focus X-rays from a nuclear bomb explosion into powerful beams of directed energy. When Soviet missiles were launched, hundreds of these weapons would be popped up. As the weapons rose into outer space, they would track the missiles. The nuclear bombs would explode, produce X-ray beams focused on the booster, whose impact would create a shock wave in its skin and destroy the missile.

In order to reach Soviet missiles in space in time to destroy them, the X-ray would have to be launched almost simultaneously with Soviet missiles. Human decision-making would thus be impossible; computers would have to give the order to fire.

Moreover, a single countermeasure—one that appears quite feasible—would decisively defeat the X-ray laser. The Soviets could develop "fast-burn" booster rockets that could burn out and release the postboost vehicle in far less than the three minutes required by current missiles. Indeed, the Fletcher panel stated that fast-burn boosters could allow the missile to complete the boost phase in one minute—before it had left the atmosphere to enter outer space. Not only would pop-up systems be unable to reach their targets with such speed; X-rays simply cannot penetrate the atmosphere.

Even a more modest reduction in boost time would cause problems for the X-ray laser. If we wanted the weapons to get a good shot at Soviet missiles in boost phase, they would have to be launched from submarines patrolling close to Soviet shores, where they might be vulnerable to Soviet attack, or on the territories of such Soviet neighbors as Turkey or China, who might not be amenable to such an arrangement. But such positioning would be necessary because the earth is round: only if the X-ray laser was launched near Soviet silo fields would it have a clear line of fire against boosters. The Pentagon has stated that a Soviet fast-burn booster—which appears feasible without drastically altering missile weight or performance—"would cast doubts" on the effectiveness of the X-ray laser for boost-phase defense.

These weaknesses in the X-ray laser concept have forced SDI officials to place their hopes for boost-phase intercept in space-based systems despite their vulnerability. The primary candidate now is a kinetic-energy weapon: a mechanism that fires at high speed a projectile (a bullet or rocket) that would simply ram into the enemy missile or warhead. The weapon, called the space-based kinetic kill vehicle, is based on less exotic technologies than many other SDI concepts. It is envisioned that perhaps five thousand of these chemical-fueled rockets would be deployed on thousands of satellites.

At least that many satellites would be required to compensate for the so-called absentee problem. To explain briefly, the kinetic-energy rockets, relatively slow and with limited range, would have to be placed in low orbits in order to reach launched Soviet boosters in time. But objects in low orbits revolve around the earth quickly—more quickly than the earth rotates on its axis—and thus cannot remain over Soviet missile-launch areas continuously. Therefore, a large number of satellites would be required to ensure that enough of their relatively short-range rockets would be within reach of Soviet missiles at all times.

Fast-burn boosters, which would negate the X-ray laser as a boost-phase weapon, would also pose severe problems for the kinetic vehicle. As I noted above, fast-burn rockets could finish their boost phase in the atmosphere. Kinetic vehicles are unlikely to perform effectively in the atmosphere, because atmospheric friction could interfere with their homing mechanisms. In fact, the kinetic vehicles, far slower than laser weapons or other directed-energy weapons, would have trouble reaching enough of even existing types of booster rockets before they burned out.

Former Secretary of Defense Harold Brown has stated that the concept of the kinetic-kill vehicle is "unpromising" because of the feasibility of effective countermeasures. Although the kinetic vehicle is being pushed as a major component not only of the boost-phase layer but also for destruction of warheads in later stages of flight, even its proponents acknowledge that the weight of the kinetic vehicle must be dramatically reduced if the system is to be feasible financially.

The prospects for other kinetic-energy weapons are even more remote. For example, the electromagnetic railgun, which would accelerate small homing projectiles at high speed, would require huge amounts of energy, and placing sufficient energy sources in space would incur huge lift requirements. The program has already encountered considerable technical problems.

Another directed-energy concept, the space-based chemical laser, was once considered promising but now has been deemphasized by the SDI. The chemical laser, like the X-ray laser, would use a concentrated beam of light to burn into the skin of the booster. However, because the chemical laser would lack the power of the X-ray laser, in order to provide sufficient heat to burn the booster, the beam, which would be up to thirty-five hundred miles from its target, would have to focus on the same point on the missile for several seconds while the missile moved at ten thousand miles per hour. In 1983 testimony to Congress, an Air Force major general provided an analogy to this task: "You want to be able to point from the Washington Monument to a baseball on the top of the Empire State Building and hold it there while both of you are moving." He concluded, "As a technologist, I view the whole thing with a fair amount of trepidation."

The space-based laser would suffer the same absentee problem facing the kinetic-kill vehicle, since its beams would not be powerful enough to reach targets from high orbit. Since only those satellites "on station" over missiles at the time of attack could respond, each satellite would have to destroy a large number of boosters and thus would have to be enormously powerful. But such a requirement suggests a need for launching extremely heavy power supplies into space.

Another laser concept, the ground-based free-electron laser, is now considered a more viable concept by the SDI organization for both boost- and postboost-phase intercept. Under this scheme, ground-based laser systems would shoot beams through the atmosphere and into outer space, where the beams would bounce off orbiting mirrors and hit attacking missiles and warheads.

Keeping the laser on the ground would eliminate the problem of lifting large power sources into space, but the free-electron laser concept presents another set of problems. The first is to develop lasers ten thousand times brighter than any existing laser. A second is to ensure that the laser beams can remain focused on their path through the atmosphere and into space. While advances have been made in this area, the problem has by no means been solved. A third problem is that clouds could block the beams, and thus a large number of widely dispersed laser stations might be required to provide a high likelihood that, in the event of attack, a sufficient number of stations would have clear skies above. Finally, space-based mirrors would face the same absentee problem confronting space-based interceptor weapons.

Moreover, one can envision various countermeasures that would undermine the effectiveness of the free-electron laser and other so-called optical lasers (such as the chemical laser). The Soviets could develop boosters that would rotate as they ascended. Since optical lasers must focus on a single point for several seconds in order to burn a hole in the booster's skin, such rotation could prevent its destruction. The Soviets could also coat each missile with an ablative shield that would absorb the heat and evaporate but leave the booster intact. In addition, fast-burn boosters would pose severe problems for optical lasers.

But perhaps the most serious problem concerns the space-based mirrors. These would be even more vulnerable than the orbiting battle stations envisioned by other SDI concepts. Such mirrors would have to be three or four times larger than any mirror ever constructed, and they could be ruined by collision with small pellets released by the Soviets.

Moving beyond the boost and post-boost phases, the SDI envisions three or four types of high-speed ground-based kinetic-energy missiles for interception of warheads in the midcourse and terminal portions of the flight. A concept called Braduskill, which would employ heat-seeking and radar guidance, is a candidate for midcourse intercept. Another type of weapon would shoot down missiles just prior to their reentry into the atmosphere, while two others would destroy them after reentry. These terminal systems would use heat-seeking guidance.

Because the "footprint"—the area over which each rocket would provide protection—would be relatively small, a highly effective SDI defense would require perhaps thousands of ground-based rocket sites across the United States and Europe. A great deal of land would be required, especially in densely populated Western Europe, which would face an array of shorter-range ballistic missiles that would not be easily engaged in earlier stages of flight.

Moreover, terminal defenses would face significant countermeasures in their effort to defend vulnerable civilian targets from the vast destructive power of nuclear weapons. The Soviets could "salvage-fuse" their warheads, so that they would explode in the atmosphere upon sensing or colliding with our interceptors—exploding with sufficient power to destroy urban populations. In addition, the Soviets could develop a maneuvering reentry vehicle (MARV) with small fins or specially configured noses that would allow the reentry vehicle to veer away from its apparent target and toward another target and thus evade the defenses. To counter MARVs we might have to arm our kinetic rockets with nuclear warheads whose explosive power could destroy Soviet reentry vehicles without a head-on collision. Thus, the final stage of the SDI defense could involve the detonation of hundreds of U.S. nuclear warheads above our country.

Despite the many difficulties with these various schemes for destroying missiles, such a task only represents one component of the challenge facing SDI. Before we can destroy Soviet weapons, we will have to track them along their flight paths and discriminate between actual warheads and the various decoys released by the postboost vehicle. As in the case of kill mechanisms, every concept for tracking and discriminating suggests another countermeasure.

The first layer of SDI's detection system might be about a dozen satellites—in geosynchronous orbit (matching the earth's rotation)—capable of detecting the infrared emissions from Soviet booster rockets. This Boost Surveillance and Tracking System would transmit the warning of attack to the next level of sensors, the Space Surveillance and Tracking System (SSTS), deployed on some one hundred to two hundred satellites in low orbit. The task of identifying the attacking missiles would be made more difficult if the Soviets constructed dummy missile silos and fake boosters that could approximate the infrared signatures of actual missile-carrying rockets. SSTS would track missiles and warheads from the boost phase through the midcourse stage of flight. Sensing in the late midcourse phase could be augmented by the Airborne Optical System, a fleet of aircraft with on-board infrared detectors.

But Soviet explosion of nuclear bombs in space would pose major problems for detection of infrared signatures. Such explosions could cripple sensors or emit enough infrared radiation to blind them. SDI technicians are concentrating much effort on "hardening" sensors against explosions and making them capable of sensing in a nuclear environment.

However, as SDI officials recognize, the reading of infrared signals, so-called passive discrimination, will be insufficient for the task of identifying warheads in the long midcourse phase. Warheads emit far less infrared radiation than boosters and are difficult to locate in the darkness of space. But the task becomes far more daunting in the face of likely Soviet countermeasures: loading up its missiles with additional warheads and myriad penetration aids.

As I noted above, the heaviest Soviet missiles could carry up to thirty warheads. The congressional Office of Technology Assessment estimates that the Soviets could deploy on its missiles some ten lightweight decoys for each warhead. Decoys could be balloonlike objects or pieces of metal or plastic. Thus, midcourse sensors might have to track hundreds of thousands of objects. The release of additional penetration aids such as chaff (fragments of metal wire) and aerosol clouds would further increase the challenge facing SDI. Discrimination of warheads from decoys would be especially difficult in the vacuum of outer space, since without the effects of "atmospheric drag," genuine and phony warheads would glide along in seemingly identical trajectories. And the Soviets could disguise their warheads to make them appear like balloon decoys.

Thus, the SDI organization is developing a concept called interactive discrimination: using beams of energy to produce observable distinctions between warheads and decoys. Gentle taps from free-electron lasers—the same weapons that might be used for destroying missiles—could induce vibrations in the warheads that might be distinguishable from those of decoys.

Another type of directed-energy weapon, the neutral-particle beam, which was considered but largely rejected as a kill mechanism, is now the SDI organization's preferred concept for interactive discrimination. In such a system, streams of neutral hydrogen atoms would be pushed into a particle accelerator and forced out as narrow beams of energy. For interactive discrimination the beams would irradiate the various warheads and decoys, and the warheads would give off distinctive radiation.

It is no accident that particle beams have essentially been rejected as a kill mechanism: the concept poses major problems that might also preclude its effectiveness as a sensing system. Particle-beam systems would require placing large, bulky, accelerators with huge power requirements on vulnerable space satellites.

Technicians have also suggested using small, colliding aerosols and pellets to separate warheads from decoys. But it has yet to be proven that interactive discrimination is a workable concept.

Tracking warheads in the terminal phase would be a less demanding task, since atmospheric drag would facilitate discrimination between reentry vehicles and decoys. But unless the system can perform the crucial task of midcourse discrimination with great effectiveness, there would be far more incoming warheads than the terminal sensors could handle. Moreover, initial Soviet attacks, perhaps with low-flying sea-launched cruise missiles, low-trajectory ballistic missiles, or with the first standard-trajectory ballistic missiles to penetrate the defense, could destroy vulnerable ground-based SDI radars. Various effects of nuclear explosions could blind those sensors even if they were not directly destroyed. The vulnerability of such radars was a prime argument against the Sentinel/Safeguard terminal antiballistic systems the United States developed in the mid-1960s.

Another fundamental task for SDI is developing battle-management and command-and-control systems sufficient to direct thousands of kill weapons at tens of thousands of targets and decoys in an extremely compressed time period and—once the Soviets exploded bombs in the atmosphere and outer space—a nuclear environment. Each layer of missile defense would have to inform the next how well it did in engaging the missile threat and how much of the threat was still traveling toward our territory. The extreme time demands, especially in the boost phase, would leave little room for human intervention, or, as a member of the Fletcher panel put it, "There is no time for man in the loop." Major advances in artificial intelligence would probably be required to allow computers to perform tasks normally reserved for humans.

Developing and maintaining adequate computer software, according to the Fletcher panel, "will be a task that far exceeds in complexity and difficulty any that has yet been accomplished in the production of civil or military software systems." Two and a half years into the SDI effort, the Pentagon reaffirmed in May 1986 that "the battle management software to be developed for the SDI may be the most complex ever attempted." SDI studies conclude that ten million to a hundred million lines of computer code would be required.

Finally, as the Fletcher panel noted, this fantastically complex software—like the SDI system as a whole—could never be fully tested short of engaging in an actual nuclear war. It would have to work the very first time.

Two additional and related SDI tasks, to which I alluded several times above, are power and space transportation.

As General Abrahamson has acknowledged, "many of the SDI systems in orbit are going to be very power-hungry." To provide sufficient power for the system, the United States would have to develop and perhaps lift into space far more power than has ever been lifted in the past. The heaviest power reactor lifted thus far was a 12-kilowatt source carried in the Skylab program. By contrast, some 10,000 to 1,000,000 kilowatts might be needed to power SDI systems. A current U.S. program, SP-100, is developing a space-based nuclear reactor of 300 kilowatts or more.

Even if we could develop sufficient power sources, we could not take for granted our ability to deploy reactors and other elements of the system in space at manageable cost. SDI lift requirements would not end with the deployment of the system, since space-based systems and mirrors would require periodic maintenance as well as upgrades to deal with new Soviet countermeasures.

Transportation costs would have to be reduced dramatically from present levels. According to a May 1986 Pentagon document, the SDI will require lifting between 20 and 200 million pounds to low earth orbit, and "at today's cost of between $1,000 and $3,000 per pound to orbit, the cost of space transportation alone could approach $60 billion."

The current state of the U.S. space program suggests that it will be difficult to focus on reducing lift costs in the coming decades. The tragedy of the space shuttle *Challenger* and subsequent failures of Titan and Delta boosters suggest long-term problems for both NASA and Air Force space programs. These events also suggest the enormous costs and risks that could be incurred by a program requiring the launch of thousands of military payloads.

The shuttle tragedy—and the Soviet nuclear reactor disaster—should also remind us of human fallibility and of the danger of relying on technology to secure our long-term safety. As I have noted, an SDI system could never be fully tested. Its sensors could misread a nuclear-reactor accident or some other phenomenon on the ground as the beginning of a missile attack and launch SDI interceptors. Some of the weapons might strike Soviet satellites and thus trigger an unintended superpower war. Or the system could massively fail in the event of an actual nuclear attack.

Finally, it is worth repeating that SDI seeks a defense against only one means of delivering nuclear weapons, the ballistic missile. Even an extremely capable Star Wars system would not protect us against a Soviet nuclear attack using bomber aircraft or air- and sea-launched cruise missiles. Mounting defenses against those means of delivery would provide additional technical challenges and costs. Even with such defenses in place, our cities would be vulnerable to nuclear attack by a smuggled suitcase bomb or a giant explosive on a Soviet merchant ship docked in one of our harbors.

Animated Star Wars film sequences may appear like elegant ballets in space. Rockets glide from their silos, only to encounter fine beams of energy from floating satellites. Elsewhere, other light beams are tapping soaring cones, producing tiny quivers. Mirrors spin and reflect beams from the ground. Rockets are lofted out of vast oceans, and aircraft glide toward the heavens to track other flying objects. Rockets rotate as they rise and glide back and forth as they descend, with other rockets rising to embrace them.

What is sometimes forgotten by the observer is that what is being depicted is not some celestial dance, but a nuclear war, one that, even if SDI performs to its full capacity, will cause immense death and destruction on earth.

This is not to say that antiballistic-missile research should not continue. It should. But deployment of any system that such research may produce, at any time in the next several decades, is unlikely to lead to anything other than a rapid acceleration of the arms race.

22 MANAGING THE TRANSITION FROM OFFENSE TO DEFENSE

Charles L. Glaser

President Reagan launched the Strategic Defense Initiative (SDI) premised on the desirability of a fundamental change in the way the United States pursues its national security objectives. The hoped-for outcome of this research program is a replacement for nuclear deterrence, which is now based on threats to inflict high levels of retaliatory damage on the Soviet Union. Many SDI proponents want to base U.S. security increasingly on the ability to deny the Soviet Union the ability to inflict extremely high levels of damage on the United States. This would require a highly effective ballistic missile defense (BMD) system, which is the focus of current SDI research, as well as a highly effective defense against Soviet bombers and cruise missiles. Two barriers are commonly seen as blocking the future success of this initiative. The first, the technical feasibility of highly effective BMD, has been the focus of much analysis and debate. The second barrier, the "transition from offense to defense dominance," has been analyzed far less, yet is generally considered to pose serious problems for the eventual achievement of the president's goal. This [selection] . . . reviews the currently limited debate on the transition and raises key issues that deserve further attention.

The conventional wisdom is that the transition to a world of highly effective defenses—that is, near-perfect defenses that eliminate the adversary's ability to inflict extremely high levels of retaliatory damage—is likely to be perilous. If true, then even if such highly effective defenses are found to be technically feasible, the United States might not want to head down the path toward so-called defense dominance.

. . . Why do analysts tend to believe the transition would be dangerous? . . . Roughly stated, both ends of the transition—high vulnerability at its beginning and relatively low vulnerability at its end—are believed to have desirable features. In between these extremes, that is, during the transition, neither the offense nor the defense dominates but instead [both] are more evenly matched; as a result, the advantages of the extremes are missing and the transition is dangerous.

When both superpowers have large offenses that are relatively invulnerable to attack, the probability of nuclear war is generally believed to be low. The probability is low because leaders know that an all-out nuclear war would

Note: Footnotes have been deleted.

be extremely costly, possibly leading to the virtual annihilation of the countries involved. . . . Much of the search for alternative worlds is motivated by the fear that we cannot avoid a nuclear war forever and, therefore, that it is imprudent to continue with policies that allow the possibility of such high costs if war occurs.

If the United States had near-perfect defenses, then the costs of an all-out war to our nation would be significantly lower than in today's world of mutual high vulnerability. Proponents of the SDI hold that the possibility of a nuclear war, although obviously still a serious concern, would be less worrisome; the United States would have high confidence that it could survive even the worst wars. President Reagan suggested a further advantage of perfect defenses: U.S. security would depend on denial of the Soviet ability to destroy the United States, not upon deterrence of such attacks. Finally, others point out that near-perfect defenses would reduce the danger posed by an irrational adversary, thereby eliminating a key flaw in the current situation.

Accepting for the moment this characterization of the endpoints, imagine the transition as the "region" between these extremes that lacks the desirable features of each extreme. At a minimum, it is not obvious that the probability of war would be low. A frequently raised fear is that severe crisis instabilities would develop as one or both superpowers lost their assured destruction capabilities. At the same time, though, if nuclear war were to occur during the transition, the damage could be quite high. Thus, the transition offers neither low probability of war nor low damage if war occurs.

To examine the accuracy of this characterization, and to shed some light on the transition more generally, this [essay] considers the following questions: What is the transition? How is the transition to be accomplished? And could the transition be made safely?

WHAT IS THE TRANSITION?

The term *transition* (as well as the term *defensive transition*) is used to refer to two significantly different phenomena. In the first, the emphasis is on getting to a world in which one or both superpowers cannot inflict "socially mortal damage" on the other—that is, to a nuclear situation in which a superpower has deployed "near-perfect defenses." This transition begins as one country's deployment of defenses eliminates the other's ability to inflict extremely high levels of damage. Given the redundant capability of the superpowers' offenses to inflict damage, just beginning the transition requires extremely effective defenses. In the second use of the term, the transition begins as one or both superpowers deploy militarily significant levels of strategic defense. Clearly, these are not the same "transition": a BMD system protecting ICBM silos could be militarily significant but have no effect on the vulnerability of superpowers' homelands.

The confusion may result in part from imprecision in the terms *offense dominance* and *defense dominance*. One view of defense dominance sees U.S. capabilities that would enable it to adopt a nuclear strategy heavily dependent on denying the Soviet Union the ability to inflict enormous damage on the U.S. homeland, thereby reducing the current role of deterrence based on credible threats to inflict large retaliatory costs. In this case, defense dominance requires near-perfect, or even perfect, defenses. Otherwise the Soviet Union would retain the capability to virtually annihilate the United States and a strategy based on denying the Soviet Union the ability to inflict damage would be inadequate. Understood this way, the transition to defense dominance is the first type of transition noted above.

If, on the other hand, one takes defense dominance to be a mix of strategic offenses and defenses weighted heavily toward defenses, then a transition does not require highly effective strategic defenses. Extensive BMD systems deployed to perform less demanding missions, for example, protecting a moderate percentage of a large number of hard targets, could significantly shift the mix of U.S. defenses and offenses toward the defense. Deployment of a thin area of defense could result in a similar shift in the mix of offense and defense. This could occur, of course, at a time when near-perfect defenses were judged technically infeasible. If defense dominance is understood to reflect simply a given mix of forces, then the transition to defense dominance is the second type noted above.

I suggest that the term *transition* be applied exclusively to the first phenomenon described above. . . . The transition region spans a tremendous distance: at one extreme, a country approaches invulnerability. The transition occurs as one or both countries cross the transition region. . . .

This definition of the defensive transition captures much of what the common use of the terms seems to imply: fundamental change; moving from one distinct type of world to another; and the possibility of danger precisely because basic elements of the strategic environment are being transformed.

In contrast, extensive, militarily significant deployments of BMD, which I will no longer refer to as a transition, might not have these effects. As long as both countries maintain redundant capabilities for inflicting damage, the nuclear situation is not fundamentally different than today's; its most important features remain unchanged. The mix of offense and defense may be radically different, but the superpowers' capabilities are not; thus, deploying defenses does not begin a transition. For example, while there is much debate about the necessity of increasing ICBM survivability, few would hold that ballistic missile defense of ICBMs would result in such a radical strategic change; nor would a defense limited to ICBMs raise the strong concerns about crisis stability that are commonly associated with a transition. . . .

Three additional comments help to clarify issues central to the transition. First, in discussing the vulnerability of the superpowers' homelands, we should distinguish between vulnerability to first strikes and to second strikes. Why countries would launch these attacks is open to question and may be a key factor in the analysis of the transition. Here I simply raise the distinction to help characterize different nuclear situations. The key point is the obvious observation that a country's vulnerability is not independent of the attack scenario—that is, it matters whether the country is struck first or second. . . . Because deterrence depends heavily upon second-strike capabilities, we should imagine the transition region beginning where vulnerability to second strikes begins to decrease. Thus, even at the outset of the transition, the vulnerability of the superpowers' homelands to a first strike could be as high as it is today.

Second, we should recognize that the concept of a transition is in itself something of a simplification. The term *transition* suggests that eventually a static endpoint is reached. Such a final state would probably never be reached, however. The superpowers' efforts to improve both their offenses and defenses can be expected to continue; even if impenetrable defenses were eventually deployed, the superpowers might find this level of effectiveness impossible to maintain.

Third, there are many possible transitions, at least in theory. The transition could be cooperative or competitive, symmetric or asymmetric. Additionally, the superpowers would face many choices about the order in which offense and defense should be deployed. Thus, questions about the security and feasibility of the transition should be understood to apply to the full range of possible transitions.

HOW IS THE TRANSITION TO BE ACCOMPLISHED?

In theory, the transition could be accomplished in two fundamentally different ways: In the first, the United States and the Soviet Union cooperate; in the second, they compete. This is a central distinction because both the requisite capability of the defenses and the relationship between the superpowers are likely to be quite different in the two cases.

In a competitive transition each country would try to reduce its own vulnerability while trying to maintain its ability to annihilate the adversary. In this case, each country would probably deploy defenses to reduce the penetrability of the adversary's offense and to expand and modify its offenses to maintain its ability to penetrate the adversary's defense. The latter capability might be valuable for attacking the adversary's strategic nuclear forces as a complement to the damage-limitation capability of the defenses, in addition to its role in the maintenance of the ability to attack the adversary's value targets. In contrast, in a cooperative transition the superpowers would likely coordinate the deployment of defenses and the reduction, or at least the freezing, of offenses.

The feasibility of these transitions depends on different factors. In a competitive transition, each country's ability to reduce its vulnerability to attack would depend on the ability of its defense (combined with the counterstrategic force capability of its offense) to defeat the adversary's offense. The weight of technical opinion now strongly suggests that the outcome of a competition between one superpower's offense and the other's defense would be the maintenance of high vulnerability to nuclear attack. In other words, a competitive transition is not feasible in the foreseeable future. . . .

If we assume that the superpowers cooperate, then a transition appears more plausible. We can hypothesize frozen or reduced offenses and increasingly large and effective defenses. At some point defenses would begin to reduce the superpowers' societal vulnerability. This stands in sharp contrast to the competitive case, in which each country's offense reacts qualitatively and quantitatively to the adversary's defense.

The key question here is: How do defenses affect the prospects for the cooperation necessary for a transition? This question quickly links the discussion of the transition with an ongoing debate about the SDI more generally. . . .

Some proponents of BMD believe that defenses reduce the utility of nuclear weapons, thereby making it easier to trade existing and less attractive offenses to build additional ones. Moreover, the argument continues, if the cost of building offenses to defeat defenses is greater than the cost of building defenses (i.e., the "cost-exchange ratio" favors the defense), then U.S. deployment of defenses might essentially force the Soviet Union to relinquish its offenses.

Opponents, however, argue convincingly that deploying BMD will not facilitate arms control, warning that if BMD reduces the Soviet Union's ability to perform strategic missions, then it will increase the size and penetrability of its force to restore these capabilities. Moreover, it would only be harder for the superpowers to limit offenses once the United States deployed BMD. A number of points support this position.

First, U.S. BMD would not reduce the value the Soviet Union places on being able to perform certain missions with nuclear weapons; rather, BMD might increase the difficulty of performing these missions. (In this case, BMD might increase the marginal utility of adding offenses.) Therefore, the utility of nuclear weapons would remain high, and the Soviet Union is likely to react to U.S. BMD with efforts to offset it.

Second, the cost-exchange argument of BMD proponents, while not without merit, suffers serious weaknesses. The cost-exchange ratio depends upon the mission that the defense is asked to perform. In the context of the transition, the mission would constitute the country's denial of its adversary's ability to inflict extremely high levels of damage. The cost of such highly effective defenses, however, probably would heavily favor the offense for the foreseeable future. For one thing, the only concepts proposed for highly effective area defense require expensive boost-phase technologies, which still appear susceptible to defeat by relatively inexpensive countermeasures. In addition, defenses become more costly as they are asked to perform more demanding missions since they must be able to defeat the full range of offensive countermeasures, which in turn makes the cost-exchange ratio more favorable to the offense. Furthermore, because each superpower would believe that its fundamental security interests were threatened by the adversary's defense, it might be expected to be willing to pay a disproportionate sum to defeat it. In other words, even if a favorable cost-exchange ratio existed, it would not be sufficient to subdue competition between one superpower's offense and the other's defense.

A likely response to these counterarguments is that if a country could protect its homeland, then it would not need to be able to threaten credibly to attack its adversary. As a result, the value of being able to perform this mission would decrease dramatically, defenses would not increase the marginal utility of nuclear weapons, countries would not be driven to invest disproportionate sums in offense, and, consequently, cooperation would ensue.

[Several] observations undermine this argument. The superpowers have not acted this way heretofore. . . .

In addition, it seems doubtful that statesmen would see a lack of utility in being able to attack their adversary, even if their own vulnerability to attack is reduced. What if one or both superpowers comes to believe that a world of mutual highly effective defenses is very dangerous? . . . Instead of feeling secure because defenses had greatly reduced its vulnerability to nuclear attack, each superpower is likely to focus on the threat posed by the adversary's offense—perhaps it will be able to defeat one's defense—and the adversary's defense—maybe it will continue to outpace one's offense. These fears might make symmetric, highly effective defenses look quite dangerous. . . .

Finally, in the unlikely event that favorable cost-exchange ratios are developed, the superpowers might compete not only to avoid the risks of the adversary's acquisition of a unilateral advantage, but also to gain a unilateral advantage. Most American analysts would prefer an invulnerable United States and a highly vulnerable Soviet Union to the lack of advantage in a world of mutual low vulnerability. Given this, what should we expect if the United States attains a highly favorable cost-exchange ratio and the Soviet Union does not? Rather than contend that U.S. deployment of defenses would strongly encourage Soviet cooperation, analysts could argue that the United States had attained the ability to gain an overwhelming strategic advantage— or at least the ability to bankrupt the Soviet Union if it insists on denying the United States this advantage. Similar arguments should be expected if the Soviet Union acquired this technical advantage. . . .

To summarize, in a competitive strategic environment, U.S. deployment of defenses will almost certainly be unable to reduce significantly its vulnerability to Soviet attack—a competitive transition is technically infeasible for the foreseeable future. The cooperative route is hardly more promising, however. Deployment of defenses is quite unlikely to encourage the cooperation of the superpowers in a transition to mutual low vulnerability to nuclear attack.

COULD THE TRANSITION
BE MADE SAFELY?

Consideration of U.S. security in a transition to low vulnerability is important, even if that transition is not an immediate probability. Many analysts believe the danger of the transition is a key barrier to the safe achievement of dramatically reduced U.S. vulnerability. Thus, the dangers deserve assessment, if only to determine whether the risks of "getting from here to there" more than offset the supposed benefits of low vulnerability to nuclear attack. In addition, this assessment can provide insights into how to manage a transition if one becomes feasible, and if the endpoint—greatly reduced vulnerability—is judged desirable.

To analyze security during a transition, we need to specify the basic nature of the transition, most importantly: whether it is competitive or cooperative; the appropriate measures of security, based on the probability of war and of the damage if war occurs; and the criteria by which the probability of war is to be assessed, which in the end must rest upon theories of the causes of war.

Whether the transition is competitive or cooperative is important for a number of reasons. In a cooperative transition the superpowers would almost certainly plan to have essentially symmetric capabilities. Anything but symmetry would appear to place one country at a disadvantage that it would be unwilling to accept. In contrast, in a competitive situation, the countries' programs would be out of sync—they would develop and deploy both offenses and defenses at different rates. Even if the countries had roughly similar technical capabilities, then, there would be times when one country or the other had a technological advantage in deployed forces. While such a transition might be characterized by a rough symmetry in capability, a country might be gaining or losing an advantage in any given period. In addition, it is possible in a competitive situation that one country would acquire and maintain a clear-cut technological advantage.

A further difference is that superpower cooperation might reduce certain dangers that would exist in a competitive transition, even a roughly symmetric one. Examples of this type of cooperation are outlined below. Finally, if cooperation were possible, the superpowers would likely have a much better relationship than in the competitive case; this would probably reduce the danger of the transition.

U.S. security depends upon both the probability of war and the damage if war occurs. . . . The probability of nuclear war depends upon the ability of the United States to deter the Soviet Union, and vice versa. In the current nuclear situation, in which most analysts agree that both superpowers have redundant large retaliatory capabilities, the key U.S. requirements of deterrence are satisfied. First, because the costs of a nuclear war far exceed the benefits of any action, the United States can deter *premeditated attacks* by the Soviet Union if threats to retaliate are sufficiently credible. Second, the incentives to launch a *preemptive attack* in a crisis are small, or nonexistent, because each superpower has the ability to inflict extremely high levels of damage in a second strike. In other words, crisis stability is high because little, if any, damage limitation is possible. Third, U.S. capabilities are characterized by a high degree of *robustness*; U.S. security is relatively insensitive to possible changes in Soviet forces. The ability of the United States to deter premeditated attacks and to maintain a high degree of crisis stability is unlikely to be compromised by a Soviet buildup of forces unless the United States does not respond over an extended period of time. In short, the United States' redundant assured destruction capability goes a long way toward satisfying the requirements of deterrence.

During a transition, U.S. security would depend upon the same factors— the ability of the United States to deter premeditated attacks, to maintain a high degree of crisis stability, and to maintain robust forces. The principal difference is that the United States may not have an assured destruction capability; this would certainly be the case in a symmetric transition. . . .

Much of the concern about the transition centers on the crisis stability of a symmetric transition: many analysts fear such a transition would be characterized by a decrease in crisis stability because both superpowers would lack assured destruction capabilities. However, the lack of assured destruction capabilities would create preemptive incentives only if forces were vulnerable. The possible danger in a transition would occur if forces remained highly vulnerable, as defenses provided protection for cities. If both countries had invulnerable forces, then there would be virtually no incentive to preempt. In practice complete invulnerability is probably unobtainable, however, and the result would be crisis instability.

A key question about a transition then, is: Could the superpowers reduce the vulnerability of their forces to a level at which preemptive incentives were very small? Before reducing the vulnerability of their homelands, the superpowers could pursue measures to increase the survivability of their forces and their command and control. ICBM survivability might be increased through a variety of means, including BMD designed to protect hard targets. Whether or not BMD would be the preferred means would depend on the feasibility and cost of other approaches. The survivability of offenses would be further increased by the deployment of increasingly effective defenses designed to protect large areas. If defenses can ever make the superpowers' homelands largely invulnerable, then they can almost certainly also make offenses highly survivable. In addition, in a cooperative transition the superpowers could agree to steps for increasing the survivability of each other's forces—for example, capping or reducing the lethality of offenses. Further, we need not assume that the superpowers maintain offenses that closely resemble today's: the reduction of societal vulnerability would increase the significance of force vulnerabilities; thus, a transition might require the restructuring of offenses. . . .

This [essay] only begins to look at security during transitions. It does suggest two important observations, nonetheless. First, a roughly symmetric, competitive transition would probably be quite dangerous. This is not primarily due to problems of crisis instability—one can at least imagine symmetric transitions in which crisis stability is kept high. The more difficult problem appears to be the lack of robustness that would unavoidably accompany a situation of mutual low vulnerability created by defenses.

Second, since robustness would decrease as a symmetric transition proceeds, the final defensive state would likely be less robust than the transition states. As a result, the probability of war could be higher once the final state is reached than during the transition. . . .

. . . One's view of the transition will be influenced by assessments of how today's situation, created by redundant capabilities to inflict high levels of damage, compares to the low vulnerability that might be created by defenses. Recognition of the weaknesses of mutual low vulnerability makes the transition look relatively less dangerous. This is of little comfort, however, since it comes at the cost of seeing that a situation in which both superpowers have near-perfect defenses, generally seen as infeasible but highly desirable, is less desirable than conventional wisdom suggests. It might not even be preferable to today's mutual high vulnerability. If this is true, then the transition is less interesting.

CONCLUSION

There are strong reasons to believe that a transition, whether competitive or cooperative, is not feasible in the foreseeable future. Stated differently, neither superpower will be able to bring its vulnerability into the "transition region." . . .

In light of this conclusion, actions that the United States might want to pursue to ensure its security during the transition cannot now be justified by the benefits they would provide if a transition were in the making. Specifically, while the United States would want to increase the survivability of its offense in preparation for a transition and might want to deploy BMD in this role, this does not support deployment in the foreseeable future of BMD to protect ICBMs and command and control.

If a transition were possible, it would most likely be quite dangerous. Although a high degree of crisis stability might be maintained throughout a transition, a symmetric, competitive transition would almost certainly lack robustness. This is not a completely overwhelming weakness only in light of the greater weakness of the final state: it would probably be even less robust since it would be more sensitive to small changes in Soviet capability.

The transition, then, is not the key barrier to increasing U.S. security by deploying highly effective defenses. The fundamental problems lie in the technical infeasibility of near-perfect defenses, in the political infeasibility of extensive superpower cooperation and, possibly most important, in the dangers inherent in a world of highly effective defenses. If the severe problems of that world could be overcome, then chances are good that the transition could also be managed safely. At present this appears impossible, however, which should greatly reduce any enthusiasm for the SDI.

23 NONPROVOCATIVE AND CIVILIAN-BASED DEFENSES

Stephen J. Flanagan

A number of Western analysts have argued that a major source of international insecurity is fear of aggression based on worst-case assessments of other states' military capabilities. . . . Among states with antagonistic relationships, military preparations, particularly those with the potential for ready application to offensive operations, are themselves part of the security problem. This assessment has been reflected in Western defense policy debates as well. The West German Social Democratic party's August 1986 policy statement, "Peace and Security," characterizes the problem this way: "Security concepts continue to be dominated by fear and the threat and counterthreat of force. . . . As long as armaments programmes and strategic planning are based on the worst-case assumption, no security problems will be solved, rather new ones will be created. The general feeling of being under threat, which is both a cause and a consequence of the arms race, can only be overcome through negotiated, inter-bloc security."

These theorists and practitioners see the situation in Central Europe as a concrete and extremely dangerous illustration of this problem. There NATO and the Warsaw Pact confront each other with what are seen as excessively large, heavily armored, and highly mobile forces that are ideally suited for offensive warfare. The military doctrines and training activities of both sides have offensive aspects that exacerbate fears of hostile action. States on both sides of the East-West divide have adopted strategies and force postures that assume that the likelihood of military aggression by the other bloc in a crisis is quite high. Thus, some analysts argue, a shift to military capabilities and doctrines that left states structurally incapable of conducting offensive military actions, or even the replacement of traditional military forces with plans for civilian-based resistance to any use of force, would stabilize European security. They contend that such a shift in national defense postures would be reassuring to domestic populations and neighboring states but credible enough to deter aggression and guarantee a country's survival if deterrence failed. . . .

. . . Several European analysts and the American scholar Gene Sharp have advocated replacement of traditional military forces with integrated strategies of nonmilitary civilian-based resistance to any aggression.[1] Sharp applies the

Note: Some footnotes have been deleted, and others have been renumbered to appear in consecutive order.

history of passive and active resistance to aggression to the contemporary security dilemma of neutral states in Europe. He characterizes that dilemma as a choice between accepting an inevitably uncertain nuclear guarantee from another power and developing a nuclear or robust conventional deterrent of their own. If deterrence failed, Sharp contends, the destructive power of both nuclear and modern conventional weapons would result in devastation that would vitiate any notion of victory. Thus he advances an alternative concept of deterrence based on a society's clear expression of its determination never to accept external domination of its political life. A state could accomplish this by preparing its populace and institutions to resist and subvert civil and military instruments of state control, if deterrence fails. Where possible, the defending country would also attempt to create international problems for the aggressor state. In essence, Sharp advocates a system in which the conquerors would grow afraid of the conquered, as Steinbeck suggested in *The Moon Is Down*, his novel about the resistance to the Nazi occupation of Norway.

As an alternative to the current structure of bipolar nuclear deterrence, a system in which states shifted to purely defensive military postures has received considerable attention among the leftist "alternative defense" community in Western Europe. It remains to be seen whether any country will be able to develop military capabilities that absolutely cannot be used aggressively or at least ones that are both deterring and nonthreatening to antagonistic states.

This [essay] outlines the principal characteristics and arguments supporting three alternative security regimes: nonprovocative defense; nonintervention and defensive defenses; and civilian-based resistance. It then considers changes in the international system that would be needed for realization of these visions. All these proposals share a central premise: that the security of individual states and regional and global stability could be enhanced if no country had any significant capability to conduct extraterritorial military operations. . . .

NONPROVOCATIVE DEFENSE

Context

Concern about the instability caused by the offensive military capabilities of modern armed forces has long been widely felt in West Germany and among the left elsewhere in Western Europe. . . . As Helmut Schmidt, hardly an advocate of alternative defense concepts, wrote in 1962, "The optimum goal of German defense policy and strategy would . . . be the creation of an armaments structure clearly unsuited for the offensive role yet adequate beyond the shadow of a doubt to defend German territory." Contemporary advocates of nonprovocative defense believe that this goal has been obscured. Indeed, they find the heavily armored, highly mobile forces of NATO and the Warsaw Pact a major source of instability and tension in Europe because of their offensive capability.... In place of the current military structures, these theorists would field much smaller military forces structurally incapable of offensive operations.

Another rationale for eliminating all offensive military potential is found in the Social Democratic party's proposal for an East-West partnership in the search for common security (*Sicherheitspartnerschaft*).... For those who hold this view, East and West face a common threat: the risk of war through miscalculation. The current politico-military situation seems inadequate for stability and lasting peace. Both alliances should support the transition to this new security partnership. Arms control agreements removing the threat of attack would be the most important instruments for developing this partnership. Ultimately, a new world political order should be based on agreed procedures for the peaceful settlement of disputes, and war should be proscribed as a means of achieving political objectives.

The member governments of the Warsaw Pact have advanced a similar assessment of the causes of instability.... NATO governments are clearly troubled by the offensive plans and capabilities of the Warsaw Pact, but are quick to point out that the Alliance has always had a defensive strategy. The problem here is that both alliances have forces that *could* be used for offensive operations, and neither believes the other has purely defensive intentions. Nor do the two have a common understanding of the scope and character of defensive operations.

Defense Military Concepts and Europe

The alternative defense debate in Europe comprises two general schools of thought, characterized as the radical and moderate approaches. The former, which tends to be unilateralist in implementation, stresses the importance of reshaping the role of the European states in NATO, developing a nonnuclear Europe, and changing the social structure. The moderate version, reflected in the thinking of the Social Democratic party, seeks to strengthen the European pillar of the Alliance and envisions using bilateral arms control to achieve phased denuclearization of all of Europe and to increase the ratio of reserve forces to standing armies....

Most nonprovocative proposals are based on concepts of territorial or area defense, in which defenders seek to exploit the natural terrain and, in some instances, urban sprawl to wear down an aggressor. They also share an assumption that defenders have decisive advantages over attackers. This assessment, based on technology and history, is not a revolutionary notion. Carl von Clausewitz argued that defense is intrinsically "the stronger form of war," and that the "advantage of the ground" rests with the defenders, who inhabit the territory and know its contours. As will be seen, however, nonprovocative defense concepts depart from Clausewitz in application.

Another common assumption of these concepts is that the most significant recent breakthroughs in military technology will augment the defender's natural advantage in future conflicts. While mobility and armor have only marginally improved an attacker's ability to advance, there have been quantum leaps in both reconnaissance capabilities, which will reduce the attacker's advantage of surprise, and the lethality of individual conventional weapons systems, which allow for a more effective dispersed defense.

Western proponents of this posture advocate exploiting some of the same technologies—new surveillance systems, precision-guided munitions (PGMs), remotely piloted vehicles, and air defenses—that NATO commanders find attractive, but the nonprovocative defenders propose to use them in a much more reactive fashion. Capabilities for deep forward strikes are seen as a threat to the Warsaw Pact that would undermine crisis stability.

A few other common characteristics of these nonprovocative defense concepts should be noted. By deploying small, dispersed forces in less populated areas and forgoing military defense of urban centers, these proposals seek to increase crisis stability by providing few targets worth pre-empting before a war starts. Similarly, because airfields and other support facilities provide tempting targets for hostile aircraft and missile attack, these concepts avoid or limit the role of air forces. Moreover, advocates emphasize that nonprovocative defense would further increase stability by developing a new kind of military balance not to be measured in traditional "bean count" fashion, but "in terms of relative chances of successfully denying an aggressor his victory, without calling destruction on the civilian population.[2]" . . .

Four general types of nonprovocative defense concepts have emerged in recent years: area defense (*Raumverteidigung*); wide area covering defense (*raumdeckende Verteidigung*); the fire barrier (*Grenznahe Feuersperre*); and integrated and interactive forward defense. All seek to deter aggression by denial. If deterrence failed, defenders would attempt to ensnare any aggressor in a web of small engagements, avoiding any decisive battle, thereby precluding a clear victory.

Horst Afheldt, one of the earliest proponents of this general approach, supports a concept of area defense that would replace NATO's large heavily armored units with static light infantry, organized in 10,000 formations of twenty to thirty men each. These small units, armed with antitank guided weapons, would each defend ten to fifteen square kilometers of territory with which they were very familiar.[3] In the forward area these units would be composed of active duty forces who would guard against surprise attack. Rear areas would be covered by local reserve units.

All these "techno-commando" units would be both difficult for the attacker to locate and unsuited for offensive operations. Conversely, any efforts by an aggressor to concentrate forces would be disrupted by precise fire from short-range artillery and rockets based in dispersed patterns deep in rear areas. Afheldt has argued that these units, armed with their ATGWs and knowledge of the terrain and supported by short-range rocket and artillery batteries, all linked together by an integrated communication system, could be effective in diminishing the size and momentum of a Warsaw Pact offensive close to the inner-German border.

A number of similar concepts have gained some political support in Europe. Former Bundeswehr Major-General Jochen Loser has proposed a "wide-area territorial defence" in which a frontier defense zone would be established 80 to 100 kilometers deep, with barriers and blocking units channeling attacking tank forces toward concentrations of fire.[4] Loser advocates deployment of a network of light infantry "shield" brigades in the forward zones currently occupied by allied forces to wear down an attacker in a series of small engagements. These shield units would cooperate with traditional Allied and German units in the transition period. Once the transarmament process was completed, however, light units would make up the bulk of the shield (for covering defenses) and sword (for repulsing attacks) forces. Loser's scheme would require a doubling of the number of brigades in the Bundeswehr by expanding the reserves. He would maintain the bulk of these units in the second echelon for counterattack against breakthroughs. Loser's concept makes extensive use of air and missile defenses, and does not rule out the ultimate use of nuclear weapons.

Norbet Hannig and Albrecht von Muller have advanced similar ideas for multilayered, nonprovocative forms of forward defense.[5] In both concepts, the first layer would be a "fire-belt" four to five kilometers wide along the inner-European divide. No NATO troops would be deployed in this *cordon sanitaire*, which would be inundated with remotely delivered fire. The next layer would be composed of small units of light infantry armed with PGMs to deal with breakthroughs. Successive layers would be defended in von Muller's plan by heavily armored but dispersed units backed up by a network of local, semimobile, territorial defense units, whereas Hannig proposes to deal with breakthroughs by redirecting 180° the missiles that constitute his fire barrier.

The West German Study Group on Alternative Security Police (SAS) has advanced a nonprovocative defense proposal called "interactive forward defense" that integrates elements of several concepts described above. The SAS proposal has three components: a static containment force composed of decentralized light infantry units employing reactive tactics; a rapid commitment force composed of mechanized infantry, armor, and cavalry forces with limited mobility; and a rear protection force to cope with penetrations and airborne assaults. The first two components would be made up of active-duty NATO units, with the latter filled out by reserve forces. As SAS chief theorist Lutz Unterseher explains, the static warfare units would maintain area control and deplete an adversary's momentum by harassing advancing units and channeling them into areas where they would be vulnerable to attack by the mechanized forces.[6]

The military thinking and some of the political goals of these German strategists are echoed in a number of other European proposals, such as those of the British Just Defence organization and the Alternative Defence Commission.[7] In advocating a denuclearized posture of "defensive deterrence" decoupled from U.S. strategic forces, the latter group concedes that the political imperatives of forward defense require NATO to retain or even expand its large standing armies, but argues that more systematic preparations for territorial defense should also be explored as an alternative.[8]

Not all nonprovocative defense proposals have come from Europe. In the United States, Richard Smoke has argued for a gradual transition in NATO, over fifteen years or more, toward a strategy that relies primarily on conventional forces "unambiguously capable only of defense" and backed up by secure, second-strike nuclear forces for deterrence of any nuclear use by an opponent. Smoke expects a continuing erosion of political support for NATO's current nuclear first-use policy. As he puts it, "democratic societies that feel relatively secure cannot forever base their strategy on what amounts to a threat of global suicide."[9] . . .

A GLOBAL NONINTERVENTION, DEFENSIVE DEFENSE REGIME

Randall Forsberg has applied some of the principles underlying nonprovocative defense concepts to explain the causes of national insecurity on a global scale. She has proposed development of "a regime in which the big powers and other northern industrial states entered into multilateral agreements not to intervene directly with their own military forces in the Third World."[10] The near-term goals of this plan are to promote self-determination in the Third World, to facilitate resolution of regional security problems by disentangling them from the East-West competition, and to reduce the risk of superpower competition that could lead to nuclear war. Forsberg does not specify how nations might be motivated to pursue this conversion, but concedes that such arrangements could only be initiated in a climate of greater East-West trust and harmony than prevails today. Over the long term, Forsberg believes, this regime would foster the development of democratic institutions and a stable peace among the big powers. This new world order would be conducive to restructuring all nations' military forces, either by negotiations or as a consequence of independent national decisions based on reduced threats to nonprovocative territorial defense roles. The nations of the world could then reduce their aggregate defense expenditures from $950 to $100 billion annually by converting their large standing armies to border guards. Ultimately the restructuring could lead to a just, stable peace that might allow for negotiated abolition of all nuclear weapons. . . .

Forsberg envisions several possible "transition paths" to this new world, involving different arrangements of six basic changes in the big powers' standing armed forces:

1. Elimination of (mostly U.S. and Soviet) nuclear war-fighting systems and the renunciation of first use of nuclear weapons.

2. Ultimate elimination of the minimum nuclear deterrent forces that would remain after the war-fighting systems were abolished.

3. Conversion of the large standing armies in the northern tier to small forces equipped with short-range weaponry, which would provide for a strong territorial defense but pose no real threat of aggression.

4. Withdrawal and dismantling of Soviet troops stationed in Eastern Europe and a "Finlandization" of that region.

5. Elimination by the industrial nations of long-range air forces and ocean-going warships.

6. Renunciation by the big powers of any future large-scale, unilateral conventional military intervention in the Third World.[11]

She freely admits that these changes would not be possible without dramatic shifts in international political relations.

The principal question for Forsberg is not whether, but *when* and *in what order* these changes should take place. . . .

CIVILIAN-BASED DEFENSE

Context

In his review of the security dilemmas of small neutral states, Gene Sharp rejects deterrence by either nuclear or large-scale conventional forces as unstable and incapable of providing a genuine defense. As Sharp puts it, "the capacity to defend in order to deter has been replaced by the capacity to destroy massively without the ability to defend.[12]" . . . Sharp argues that the reach of modern conventional weaponry vitiates the traditional notion of defense at the frontier and that the destructive power of these systems means that a protracted nonnuclear war would result in devastation of one's own territory. Thus, Sharp concludes, war and traditional preparations for war have lost much of their rationale as instruments of national policy for these states.

For Sharp, the greatest weakness of NATO's present deterrent strategy is that it can fail with catastrophic consequences. Neither a policy of no first use of nuclear weapons nor a purely conventional defense overcomes this basic flaw. As Sharp sees it, traditional military means cannot both deter and defend populations. He argues that any viable defense system should provide remedial means for protecting a society after deterrence has failed. His system of civilian-based defense is intended to provide for the security of small states in the current global situation with the tacit recognition that it has wider applications in a changed world order. . . .

Definition and Operational Characteristics

The term *civilian-based defense* (CBD) is used to describe a broad array of nonviolent political, social, economic, and psychological instruments of power. There are three general methods of civilian-based defense: nonviolent protest and persuasion; social, economic, and political noncooperation and boycotts; and nonviolent intervention. Widespread training of the population in the various tactics of civilian-based defense forms the basis for a reactive strategy that seeks to frustrate efforts of any government or hostile group to achieve political or economic aims by the use of force. . . .

There are three general ways in which CBD might be applied: as an adjunct to a strategy that used nuclear weapons, traditional conventional forces, or nonprovocative defenses; as a substitute for conventional and nuclear defense in special circumstances such as a coup d'état or defeat of military forces; or as a permanent and complete alternative defense policy. . . .

Widespread adoption of CBD is virtually unthinkable unless nuclear weapons had been entirely abolished; even then it is not clear how CBD would deter nuclear rearmament. CBD would appear to undermine the credibility of any nuclear escalation strategy backed by a minimal deterrent force. If a nuclear state had extensive CBD plans, it would imply that nuclear weapons might not be used to preclude the loss of national territory. Given that dramatic political changes would be needed for the elimination of all nuclear weapons, it might well be possible, in that context, to achieve multilateral agreement on a CBD regime as the new ultimate guarantor of each state's security. Clearly, this would be a world with an unprecedented degree of cooperation among states, and probably a greatly diminished level of perceived military threats. In this world, one can imagine CBD serving as either a substitute for conventional military defenses or as an ultimate deterrent after the collapse of a traditional or nonprovocative conventional military defense.

The process of shifting completely to CBD, or transarmament, also appears much less complicated in this nuclear abolitionist context. Most schemes for transarmament envision a very long-term snowballing process initiated by the example of several small countries, which would convince the rest of the world of the viability of CBD as they moved from partial to total reliance on this strategy for their defense. . . .

ASSESSMENTS AND UNANSWERED QUESTIONS

Nonprovocative Defense: A Preliminary Assessment

The proposals for nonprovocative defense described in this [essay] have dubious deterrent effect in themselves, because they falsely assume that the problems faced by the attacker and defender are thoroughly different. Most of these concepts leave the defender with limited capability for offensive counterattack for repulsing or evicting invading forces. A more effective deterrent would blend some elements of punishment *and* denial. A state that relies on the pure form of deterrence by denial, inherent in the nonprovocative defense concepts, runs the risk of tempting a potential agressor to wear down its defenses. A related operational shortcoming is that these concepts advocate largely reactive measures to be undertaken after an attack has begun, making them highly vulnerable to surprise attack.

Most of the current European concepts . . . focus too narrowly on the threat of heavily armored assaults. The NATO countries and most industrialized states confront multidimensional security threats, including combined air and ground force operations. According to a study by the Dutch Ministry of Defence, these antitank-oriented defense postures could be severely degraded by infantry attacks supported with artillery fire. Such defenses could also stimulate and be overtaken by a technical arms race in anti-tank guided weapons (ATGW) countermeasures and new forms of armor. These ATGW units may also be subject to piecemeal destruction by heavy mechanized forces. Finally, all of these concepts are premised on the realization of some immature conventional weapons technologies and on the unverifiable assumption that these emerging technologies are shifting combat advantage to the defense. . . .

The advocates of defensive defense have shown how their ideas would operate in the countryside, but have generally neglected to indicate how these concepts would be applied in urban settings. Instead, most have simply stated that they would avoid, as much as possible, conducting defensive operations in cities. This would be a particularly difficult feat in a country with West Germany's development density. This lacuna may be partly explained by political sensibilities in West Germany, where discussion of urban warfare is hardly popular. Theorists who have broached the urban problem . . . have suggested that civilian resistance in the cities would be the most appropriate adjunct to their territorial defense concepts. However, given the nature of the Central European landscape and most modern industrialized states, urban welfare is likely to be a significant aspect of future conflicts. Thus one of the principal dividends touted by advocates of nonprovocative defense is avoiding the massive societal destruction likely to accompany modern conventional warfare.

All these theorists agree that war would be much less likely to erupt by miscalculation if the West adopted a defensive defense posture unilaterally. Moreover, they argue, if this deterrent did fail, it would be much easier to terminate a war with less capable forces on one or both sides than currently exist. In a similar vein, it is argued that the East's incentives to pre-empt NATO militarily would virtually disappear if the West had no offensive capability. Conversely, they contend, NATO's current offensive nuclear doctrine and any offensive conventional military plans provide a conventional rationale for the sustained Soviet build-up. Finally, most advocates of this posture feel that it could, in the long run, facilitate the evolution of a new politico-military situation in Europe, and may be essential to ending the division of the continent. . . .

The moderate proponents of nonprovocative defenses advocate multilateral negotiations to achieve the desired force structures. The more radical advocates would pursue these changes unilaterally, while offering unspecified "incentives" to the East to emulate this shift in its own military posture. It is hard to envision why the East would wish to reduce its military edge in Europe after the West made such a dramatic unilateral shift. Similarly, it is difficult to envision circumstances other than mutual decline or develpment of some form of world government under which the United States and the USSR, with their global interests, would agree to adopt a defense posture incapable of projecting power. It is likely that nonprovocative defenses would have to be adopted unilaterally by various small states. Such shifts actually seem more likely when a balance of power continues to provide global or regional stability.

The Defensive Defense World

The applicability of nonprovocative and civilian-based defense strategies has been discussed thus far largely in the context of the present East-West confrontation in Europe. Their application in various future worlds . . . remains to be examined.

As the preceding discussion shows, it is difficult to establish precisely what distinguishes defensive from offensive weapons systems and strategies; these difficulties are compounded when one considers the question in global perspective. The defensive nature of any military forces rests in their application and in the perception of their likely application. Even if two large states negotiated defensive force postures and strategies vis-à-vis one another, these same capabilities might still look very threatening and provocative to a smaller third state not party to the accord.

Similarly, even if one could define a purely defensive military force, with no capability to project itself into another country, those forces might still be used for purposes of aggression. There would be no stopping the Soviet Union from loading several divisions of border guards into Aeroflot aircraft and attempting to impose its will on a less powerful third country that had also agreed to field only border guards.

Other critical questions need to be addressed, such as the militarization of society in a defensive defense world. The shift from large standing and/or professional armies to large groups of citizen-soldiers may not be attractive to authoritarian societies with marginal political legitimacy. The Soviet Union would hardly find appealing the prospect of decentralized reserve forces forming the backbone of its defenses, nor would many countries in the Third World. These reserves would represent a potential threat to governmental control and hence to domestic and possibly regional stability.

The proposition that large offensive military capabilities are in themselves a trigger of war needs more detailed analysis. It is not at all clear that a regime of defensive defenses will be more stable than our current predicament. After all, much of world military history concerns conflicts between forces that were essentially border guards.

Civilian-Based Defense

It is difficult to envision any circumstances in the next fifty years, short of nuclear abolition and universal subscription to certain norms of international behavior, whereby nonviolent civilian resistance could be the sole basis of any state's security strategy. In worlds such as our own, CBD can supplement with a limited effect nonnuclear defense postures of neutral states, particularly as a safeguard against the collapse of military resistance to external aggression. However, even in this context, history shows that it is difficult to sustain such efforts for very long or with much success in the absence of external military support. To realize a national defense strategy based solely on civilian-based resistance, a modern state would also require a degree of domestic political cooperation unprecedented in history. This level of organizing could also lead to societal factionalization, more disruptive subnational conflicts, or, if imposed in a highly centralized, coercive way, to an authoritarian social order. Negotiating this strategy into a world ordering principle might even be beyond the reach of a supranational government. Like nonprovocative defense, CBD suffers from a credibility problem due to its inability to punish an aggressor. It relies exclusively on a state's convincing an adversary that its population is willing to suffer extreme repression to deny achievement of certain political objectives. The effectiveness of this deterrent would ultimately turn on the value of the objective at issue to both the attacking and defending state. If the objective had equal value to both states, a stable political situation might result. However, an aggressor state might be motivated to attack if it sensed the defender's willingness to suffer for a principle was low.

Advocates of CBD also need to specify how their system would deal with efforts by hostile states to exert influence short of invasion. How could CBD address violations of a state's territorial integrity by another country seeking easy access to a third state? Sharp dismisses the importance of safeguarding territory, but erosion of territorial control could undermine the credibility of even a CBD deterrent posture.

Finally, neither CBD strategies nor nonprovocative defenses solve the problem of catastrophic failure, which their advocates see as the central problem with nuclear and traditional conventional deterrence. Failure of any of the three alternatives reviewed in this [essay] could also result in total societal destruction. In addition, all three postures examined here offer less convincing deterrents to aggression than do nuclear weapons or large conventional forces.

244 Stephen J. Flanagan

NOTES

1. Gene Sharp, *Making Europe Unconquerable* (Cambridge, MA: Ballinger, 1986). Other major works on these concepts include Anders Boserup, *War Without Weapons: Non-Violence in National Defense* (New York: Schocken, 1975), and Stephen King Hall, *Defence in the Nuclear Age* (London: Victor Gallancz, 1958). For an assessment of some of these concepts, see Adam Roberts, "Civilian Defense Twenty Years On," *Bulletin of Peace Proposals* 9, no. 4 (1978): 293–300.

2. [Egbert] Boecker and [Lutz] Unterseher, "Emphasizing Defense," in [Frank] Barnaby and [Marlies] ter Borg, [eds., *Emerging Technologies and Military Doctrine* (New York: St. Martin's, 1986)], p. 91.

3. Hew Strachan, "Conventional Defence in Europe," *International Affairs* (London) 61, no. 1 (Winter 1984/85): 31. See also Horst Afheldt, *Verteidigung und Frieden* (Munich: Deutsche Taschenbuch Verlag, 1979).

4. Jochen Loser, "The Security Policy Options for Non-Communist Europe," *Armada International* 2 (March/April 1982): 66–75.

5. [Albrecht A. C.] Von Muller, "Integrated Forward Defense [Outlines of a Modified Conventional Defense for Central Europe," 1985], pp. 19–25, and Norbet Hannig, "Can Western Europe Be Defended by Conventional Means?" *International Defense Review* 1 (1979): 27–34.

6. Boeker and Unterseher, "Emphasizing Defense," pp. 102–3.

7. Frank Barnaby and Stan Windass, *What Is Just Defense?* (Oxford: Just Defence, 1983).

8. Report of the Alternative Defence Commission, *Defence Without the Bomb* (New York: Taylor & Francis, 1983), pp. 8–11, 249–79.

9. Richard Smoke, "For a NATO Defensive Deterrent," unpublished manuscript, Brown University.

10. [Randall] Forsberg, "Nonprovocative Defense [A New Approach to Arms Control," unpublished paper, Institute for Defense and Disarmament Studies, October 1986].

11. Ibid., pp. 33–34.

12. Sharp, *Making Europe Unconquerable*, p. 11.

Part III: War

Nuclear war is possible. It may not be probable, but it is possible. This is the premise of the first selection in Part III of *The Nuclear Reader*. In it the six Harvard University Associates that made up the Harvard Nuclear Study Group examine alternative scenarios that might prompt the onset of nuclear war.

Six triggers or sequences of events leading to nuclear war are often discussed. One is a "bolt from the blue," a Pearl Harbor type of surprise attack by one superpower against the other (typically assumed by Americans to be a Soviet strike against the United States). Second, nuclear war might begin as a conventional conflict in Europe escalates to the point that the nuclear threshold is bridged, leading to an all-out nuclear exchange between the superpowers. Third, a regional conflict between Third World countries could draw in the superpowers, which once more may find the conflict escalating to the point that nuclear weapons are used. Fourth, war might occur by accident or miscalculation, as, for example, in a situation in which one nuclear power launches an attack on another after (mistakenly) concluding that the other had already launched a preemptive attack. Fifth, in yet another escalation scenario, a terrorist attack involving nuclear weapons could create a condition of such chaos and confusion that the superpowers decide to launch their weapons against each other. Finally, nuclear war could start following an accidental or unauthorized use of nuclear weapons.

The Harvard Nuclear Study Group examines variants of each of these possibilities and attaches rough probabilies to each. Interestingly, they conclude that the bolt-from-the-blue scenario, "commonly the most feared prospect," is also "a most unlikely scenario for the start of a nuclear war," *provided*, however, that "no Russian military leader could ever report to the Politburo that a Soviet victory in nuclear war was probable or that the damage from American nuclear retaliation could be reduced to acceptable limits." The conclusion that a surprise attack will be prevented if nuclear adversaries are convinced that the costs of war are greater than its rewards is simply another way of saying that war will be prevented if deterrence succeeds—and the authors do point toward the elements that could avert a situation so dangerous that it might tempt a surprise attack. Thus, the probability of nuclear war is closely related to the political strategies that policymakers have devised for nuclear weapons and to alternative means of managing them so that they serve political purposes rather than becoming the causes of conflict themselves.

Unfortunately, there are other sequences of events that could lead to nuclear war for which the conditions promoting deterrence are less easily identified. The slide from conventional to nuclear war would be harder to arrest because, as the Nuclear Study Group concludes, "once war begins, the balance between political and military considerations shifts decidedly toward the military side." In such situations, the principal need is to maintain the firebreak between conventional and nuclear weapons. But as the essays in Parts I and II of this book make clear, opinions differ widely on how this can best be done. Do the presence of battlefield or tactical nuclear weapons and the threat of their use make nuclear war less or more likely?

Should nuclear war break out, it is difficult to comprehend its destructive consequences. In August 1945 a single bomb dropped from a single plane killed an estimated 100,000 to 200,000 people. Yet by today's standards, the bomb that leveled Hiroshima was small indeed. "Little Boy," as the atomic or fission bomb was called, had a destructive force of thirteen kilotons (that is, thirteen thousand tons) of TNT. Today the thermonuclear or fusion (hydrogen) weapons in the superpowers' strategic arsenals are often measured in megatons (that is, millions of tons of TNT), and weapons in the kiloton range are frequently considered tactical. There are literally thousands of these spread throughout the world.

Figure III-1, created by the antinuclear organization *Ground Zero*, illustrates graphically the enormous destructive power of today's nuclear arsenals. The single dot in the center of the figure represents three million megatons—the equivalent of all the firepower used during World War II. The other dots represent the eighteen thousand megatons of firepower that now comprise the superpowers' nuclear arsenals—the equivalent of six thousand Second World Wars. Each U.S. Trident submarine alone carries the equivalent of eight times the force used in all of World War II. The destructive power represented by only two squares on the figure (three hundred megatons, or about that carried on twelve Trident submarines) is sufficient to destroy all large- and medium-sized cities in the world. It is little wonder that "overkill" is popularly used to describe what seems to be an unnecessarily large stockpile of weapons of mass destruction.

The presumption, of course, is that policymakers have no intention of using their arsenals. Indeed, there is a great distance between what is technologically possible and what is politically tolerable. As McGeorge Bundy, national security adviser to Presidents John F. Kennedy and Lyndon B. Johnson, observed:

> There is an enormous gulf between what political leaders really think about nuclear weapons and what is assumed in complex calculations of relative "advantage" in simulated strategic warfare. Think-tank analysts can set levels of "acceptable" damage well up in the hundreds of millions of lives. They can assume that the loss of a dozen cities is somehow a real choice for sane men. In the real world of real

Figure III-1 The Destructive Power of Nuclear Weapons

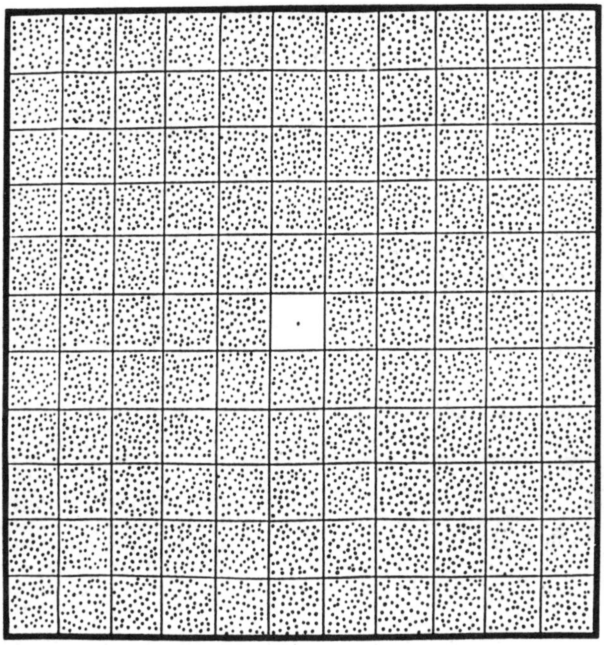

Note: Each dot represents three million megatons of explosive force.

political leaders—whether here [in the United States] or in the Soviet Union—a decision that would bring even one hydrogen bomb on one city of one's own country would be recognized in advance as a catastrophic blunder; ten bombs on ten cities would be a disaster beyond history; and a hundred bombs on one hundred cities are unthinkable. Yet this unthinkable level of human incineration is the least that could be expected by either side in response to any first strike in the next ten years, no matter what happens to weapons systems in the meantime.[1]

Nuclear war is possible nonetheless. It may not be probable, but it is possible. What would its effects be? President Jimmy Carter's National Security Council estimated that in the event of a nuclear exchange between the superpowers, the toll in lives in the United States and the Soviet Union alone would be over 250 million. The catastrophic proportions of such destruction are illustrated in Figure III-2, which shows that the expected death toll of a nuclear war would be nearly nine times greater than the number of deaths of Soviets and Americans in previous wars. And these figures do not include the tens of millions more who would suffer the ravaging effects of radiation.

A nuclear blast produces two kinds of radiation. Direct radiation occurs at the time of a nuclear explosion and, though intense, is limited in range.[2] Fallout radiation, on the other hand, which is caused when particles thrown into the air by a nuclear blast become radioactive, can extend well beyond the immediate area of a nuclear explosion, with damaging effects lasting for

Figure III-2 Estimated Soviet and American Deaths in a Nuclear War

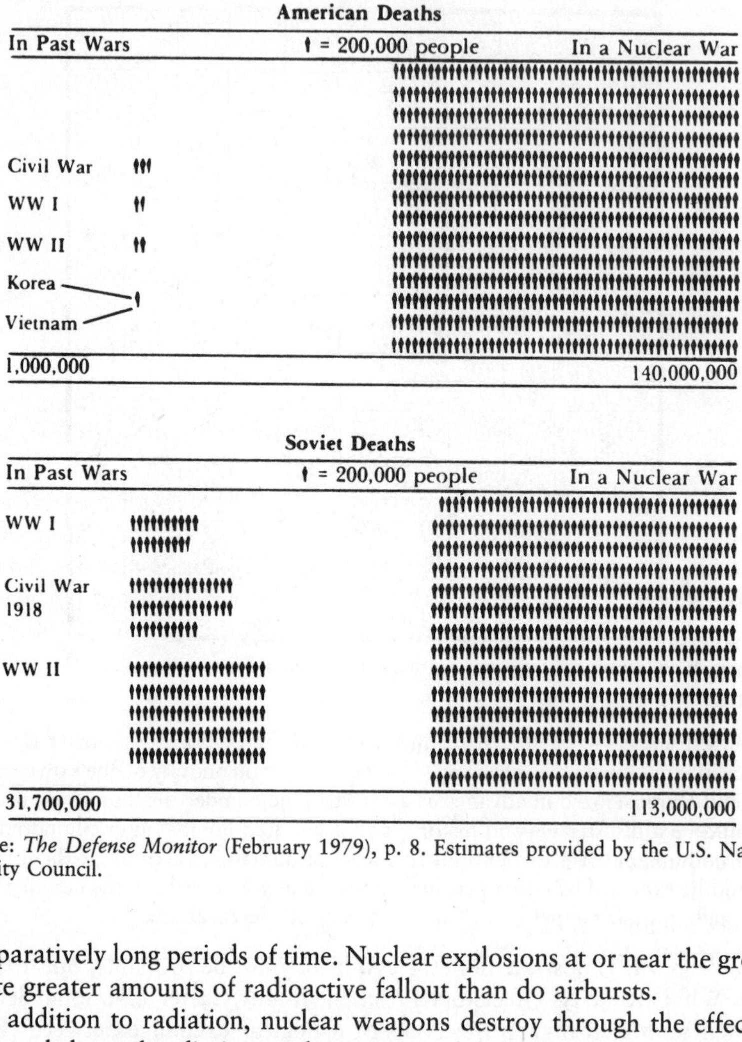

American Deaths

In Past Wars	† = 200,000 people	In a Nuclear War
		†††
		†††
		†††
		†††
Civil War †††		†††
WW I ††		†††
WW II ††		†††
Korea		†††
Vietnam		†††
1,000,000		**140,000,000**

Soviet Deaths

In Past Wars	† = 200,000 people	In a Nuclear War
WW I †††††††††† / ††††††††††		††
Civil War / 1918 ††††††††††††††† / ††††††††††††††† / ††††††††††		††
WW II ††††††††††††††††††††† (×5)		††
31,700,000		**113,000,000**

Source: *The Defense Monitor* (February 1979), p. 8. Estimates provided by the U.S. National Security Council.

comparatively long periods of time. Nuclear explosions at or near the ground create greater amounts of radioactive fallout than do airbursts.

In addition to radiation, nuclear weapons destroy through the effects of blast and thermal radiation, or heat. Most of the damage to cities, the U.S. Congressional Office of Technology Assessment concluded, would be caused by a nuclear weapon's explosive blast.

> The blast drives air away from the site of the explosion, producing sudden changes in air pressure (called static overpressure) that can crush objects, and high winds . . . that can move them suddenly or knock them down. In general, large buildings are destroyed by the overpressure, while people and objects such as trees and utility poles are destroyed by the wind.[3]

The energy released in the form of thermal radiation would cause "flash-blindness" among those who looked directly at the intense light that a nuclear explosion emits. Skin burns and fires caused by the thermal radiation's ignition of combustible materials would be extensive.

Jonathan Schell's "Nuclear Holocaust," from his popular book *The Fate of the Earth*, translates these stark figures and facts into the human tragedy they imply. He first uses the Hiroshima experience to dramatize the human horror of a nuclear holocaust. He then extrapolates from this experience, as well as from the results of U.S. nuclear tests in the years since 1945, to speculate about the consequences of a nuclear attack on New York City. Despite Schell's graphic descriptions, the extensiveness of the mass destruction is virtually impossible to comprehend. It is difficult to imagine millions of people being instantaneously vaporized, crushed, or maimed.

A counterforce attack, one directed on opposing military targets rather than on population and industrial centers, could conceivably avert the immediate level of carnage of a countervalue strike. To be sure, there would be collateral damage to the people and structures near the military installations, but it would doubtless be less than the destruction caused by a countervalue strike. In an odd sense, therefore, a counterforce nuclear attack or exchange may be preferable to a countervalue one. (A counterforce attack would likely produce more radioactive fallout, however, as groundbursts presumably would be required to destroy missiles protected by hardened silos.)

One question at issue in discussions of counterforce nuclear attacks is whether the reduced levels of destruction might make nuclear war more palatable politically. The question is often raised regarding Soviet leaders, as the level of death and destruction experienced by the Soviet Union in previous conventional wars—20 million casualties in the case of World War II, for example—might be of the same order of magnitude in the event of a counterforce nuclear attack as to encourage Soviet leaders to run the risk of "fighting" and "winning" such an engagement.

In "Civilian Casualities from 'Limited' Nuclear Attacks on the U.S. and U.S.S.R.," Barbara G. Levi, Frank N. von Hippel, and William H. Daugherty raise serious questions about such reasoning. Their estimates place the number of civilian casualties in the United States resulting from Soviet counterforce attacks in the 12 to 45 million range, with 15 to 54 million the number in the case of U.S. counterforce attacks on the Soviet Union. The precise numbers of course vary depending on the assumptions made, but in either case their conclusion regarding the effects of counterforce attacks does not materially change conclusions associated with countervalue nuclear strikes: "It would . . . seem virtually impossible for either the U.S. or the U.S.S.R. to escape their mutual-hostage relationship unilaterally with any feasible combination of strategic offensive and defensive weapons."

Related to the countervalue versus counterforce question is whether it would be possible to control a counterforce nuclear exchange so that it did not escalate to the level of an all-out, countervalue nuclear spasm, thereby permitting a limited and quite protracted nuclear war to be fought. Our next two essays address this question, and both reach negative conclusions.

In the first, "Can Nuclear War Be Controlled?," Desmond Ball, a well-known strategic analyst, reasons that "it is most unrealistic to expect that there would be a relatively smooth and controlled progression from limited and selective strikes, through major counterforce exchanges, to termination of the conflict at some level short of urban-industrial attacks." A number of considerations lead to this conclusion, not the least of which is that the number of casualties on either side would be high, even if urban and industrial targets were not struck directly. The political pressures from any kind of nuclear exchange would be enormous, and the stress under which decision makers would have to operate would be unimaginable. Consider, for example, what Zbigniew Brzezinski, national security adviser to President Jimmy Carter, described as the "utterly dumbfounding ... life-and-death decision tree" that a president of the United States might face when awakened in the middle of the night:

Time (in minutes)

- 0 Massive attack launched.
- 1 SLBMs detected.
- 2 ICBMs detected.
- 4–6 Confirmation of attack; uncertainty over scale; U.S. decision process begins.
- 6–10 First SLBMs detonate in High Altitude EMP attack; SAC launched preemptively; confirmation of scale of attack; final U.S. decision process.
- 10–12 U.S. decision needed: Ride-out or respond; first SLBMs detonate over U.S. SLBM bases and National Command Authority [political and military leaders responsible for the command of U.S. military forces].
- 12–14 Final window for initiating response; launch under attack.
- 16–20 [Soviet] Delta SLBMs launched from home ports hit SAC.
- 20–30 ICBM attack initiates possible X-ray pin-down and begins impact on targets.[4]

It is simply impossible to know how in such crisis circumstances American policymakers would respond either psychologically or operationally. Ball points out that the ability to respond at all will be seriously affected by the vulnerability of U.S. command, control, and communication (C^3) systems (the same is true of the Soviets' systems).

The Soviet Union would need to expend thousands of warheads in any comprehensive counterforce attacks against US ICBM silos, bomber bases and ... submarine facilities, and even then hundreds if not thousands of US warheads would still survive. On the other hand, it would require only about 50–100 warheads to destroy the fixed facilities of the national command system or to effectively impair the communication links between the National Command Authorities and the strategic forces.

Even if the C^3 systems were spared direct attack, the electromagnetic pulses (EMP, the pulses of electrical and magnetic energy released in a nuclear explosion) created by nuclear blasts on other targets would severely cripple, perhaps destroy, their capacity to function. As a consequence, "it is likely that beyond some relatively early stage in the conflict," the counterforce strikes "would become ragged, uncoordinated, less precise and less discriminating, and the ability to reach an agreed settlement between the adversaries would soon become extremely problematical."

An attack on an adversary's command, control, and communication systems is often described as an attempt at nuclear "decapitation." Our second article on the question, "Invitation to a Nuclear Beheading," by Barry R. Schneider, considers whether it is possible to control a nuclear war and what would be required to avert the decapitation of the United States government, specifically to ensure the survival of its key policymakers. The physical problems of protecting the government from destruction are so great as to make protection seem impossible. The same is true, of course, of the Soviet Union, where, despite a limited antiballistic missile shield and a more extensive civil defense program, the task of avoiding decapitation is no less overwhelming. The conclusion, then, is straightforward; according to Schneider, "the danger of decapitation attacks would seem to make a mockery of the idea of fighting limited nuclear wars, or protracted nuclear wars. Even if U.S. leaders somehow survived a first-wave Soviet attack, our command-control network is so perishable in a nuclear environment that a slow, tit-for-tat 'walk' up and down the escalation ladder seems unlikely." Furthermore, the vulnerability of both the United States and the Soviet Union to attacks against their leadership and command and control systems may mean that "negotiations to halt the slaughter might be impossible until both sides had expended their nuclear forces in a terrible agony of blow and counterblow."

Even if nuclear decapitation remains unavoidable, would a greater emphasis on civil defense systems protect domestic populations from nuclear annihilation? The Soviet Union has long pursued a more vigorous civil defense effort than the United States has, and the Reagan administration has sought funds from Congress that would enable it to decrease the gap with the Soviet Union somewhat on this dimension of the strategic competition.

Civil defense is appropriately considered an element of strategic competition since it is presumed by defense analysts to provide a glimpse of nuclear adversaries' intentions and expectations of nuclear war. For many analysts, the fact that the Soviet leadership has willingly pursued an active civil defense program is evidence that it expects to be able to fight and win a nuclear war. Thus one writer suggests that Soviet civil defense programs are designed to protect what are known as *cadres*, "that is, the political and military leaders as well as industrial managers and skilled workers—those who could reestablish the political and economic system once the war was over. Judging by Soviet definitions, civil defense has as much to do with the proper functioning of the country during and immediately after the war as with holding down casualties."[5]

Civil defense has not been taken as seriously in the United States as it seems to have been in the Soviet Union. In part, perhaps, this is because the United States is a more urbanized society than the Soviet Union is, and so the prospects of building an effective defense against nuclear attack and paying for it seem beyond reach. Moreover, given the known destructive force of a nuclear blast, the positions adopted by some civil defense advocates appear ludicrous. T. K. Jones, deputy under secretary of defense in the Reagan administration, for example, in 1981 told a newspaper reporter

> that the United States could fully recover from an all-out nuclear war with the Soviet Union in just two to four years. T. K. . . . added that nuclear war was not nearly as devastating as we had been led to believe. He said, "If there are enough shovels to go around, everybody's going to make it." The shovels were for digging holes in the ground, which would be covered somehow or other with a couple of doors and with three feet of dirt thrown on top, thereby providing adequate fallout shelters for the millions who had been evacuated from America's cities to the countryside. "It's the dirt that does it," he said.[6]

John M. Weinstein explores the doctrinal and practical implications of the Soviets' allegedly more sophisticated program in "Soviet Civil Defense: Strategic Implications, Practical Problems." Weinstein admits that Soviet civil defense plans take on particular significance "when viewed as a component of a Soviet warfighting strategy that also emphasizes other damage-limiting expedients." However, he is neither persuaded that Soviet defense efforts arise from the Soviet leaders' belief that it is possible to fight and "survive" a nuclear war, nor convinced that they provide any meaningful protection against a concerted nuclear attack. Indeed, the performance of the Soviet civil defense system following the explosion of the Soviet nuclear power plant at Chernobyl in April 1986, the world's most serious nuclear power accident to date, was "dismal." As a result, Weinstein concludes that "any Soviets who might have entertained thoughts about the efficacy of nuclear warfighting, the feasibility of damage-limitation, or the calculability of a successful preemptive strike will find cause to reconsider."

The United States, on the other hand, substantially increased the resources devoted to civil defense during the Reagan years as part of the administration's ambitious military modernization and rearmament program. Louis René Beres describes these efforts in "Surviving Nuclear War: U.S. Plans for Crisis Relocation" as "a natural complement to the developing U.S. nuclear war-fighting strategy of deterrence." Beres's focus is on the crisis relocation planning (CRP) developed by the Federal Emergency Management Agency (FEMA) in the early 1980s. Drawing on the experience of the daily relocation of millions of workers from their urban jobs to their suburban homes, FEMA anticipated that in the event of a nuclear crisis hundreds of millions of Americans would be moved from urban centers to rural areas, presumably a safe distance from ground zero.

Since the mid-1980s FEMA has moved quietly away from its crisis relocation plans toward an "attack preparedness plan." Due to public criticism of CRP as well as practical problems encountered during simulated efforts to actually carry out its relocation plans, the focus has moved toward (1) identifying the areas believed to be likely targets of a Soviet nuclear attack and (2) advising state and local governments in those areas to devise their own protective measures. Beres's essay nonetheless clearly identifies the problems any civil defense program will encounter; it also raises important questions about the relationship between U.S. civil defense programs and its overall military strategy not unlike those questions American policymakers have raised about Soviet strategy and intentions.

Certainly no amount of civil defense is likely to ease the catastrophic strains on the earth's ecosystem that a nuclear war would likely produce. Indeed, although it has long been asserted that a nuclear war could result in the extinction of the human species, there is now scientific evidence that lays out the path toward doomsday. The evidence is summarized in our next essay, "Nuclear War and Climatic Catastrophe: A Nuclear Winter," written by the distinguished astronomer Carl Sagan.

Based on studies of the atmosphere on the planet Mars, Sagan and his colleagues warn that a nuclear exchange—apart from the death and destruction caused by the blast, thermal radiation, and radioactivity—would spew so much dust, smoke, and poisonous gas into the atmosphere that the earth's surface would cool by tens of degrees, turning the earth into a dark, frozen wasteland incapable of sustaining humankind's delicate life-support systems.[7] Noteworthy are the claims that the climatic catastrophe would occur worldwide, even if a nuclear exchange were confined to the Northern Hemisphere. Moreover, Sagan notes that "perhaps the most striking and unexpected consequence of our study is that even a comparatively small nuclear war can have devastating climatic consequences. . . ." The threshold arsenal for triggering a climatic catastrophe, Sagan estimates, is somewhere between five hundred and two thousand deliverable warheads—a fraction of the more than [twenty-four] thousand strategic weapons already in both the Soviet and American arsenals. Indeed, the evidence suggests that only one hundred megatons of nuclear explosives would cause a nuclear winter. This is fewer than the dots contained in one single square in Figure III-1. The prescription to be derived is that every effort must be made to reduce the level of the world's nuclear arsenals below the threshold at which nuclear war might trigger a nuclear winter—and the possible extinction of humankind. The possibility of a nuclear winter also requires a fundamental reconsideration of nuclear strategy, because "if the 'nuclear winter' theory is correct, an aggressor would destroy himself, even if there were no retaliation."[8]

When the work of Sagan and his associates first appeared, it produced a storm of controversy as well as concern. Conferences were held, official studies were commissioned, special issues of scientific journals were devoted to the topic, television series were produced, and numerous books appeared, all in an effort to understand and determine the veracity of this strange, new, yet compelling vision of the impending apocalypse. Inevitably, important qualifications and caveats were added to the nuclear winter concept as scientists from around the world began to examine the relevant data and the assumptions that led to such startling conclusions. But, to our knowledge, no one has rejected the thesis outright. Even the study commissioned by the U.S. Secretary of Defense agreed there was a "threat," but it concluded that, in addition to the need for more research, strengthening deterrence would be the best response.[9]

Part of the skepticism with which some greeted the nuclear winter argument was based on the fact that many of the predictions that received the most press coverage, and hence the greatest publicity, were based on worst-case scenarios. Certainly, the predicted cold and dark could engulf the entire global habitat under some circumstances, but there are others in which the use of nuclear weapons could have comparatively localized effects as, for example, in the case of Japan in 1945.

More important to the scientific community, perhaps, was the great uncertainty regarding climatological patterns that necessarily permeated the nuclear winter hypothesis insofar as they relate to the dissipation of the smoke and dust that would precipitate the sharp drop in global temperatures causing a nuclear winter. The concluding selection in *The Nuclear Reader* is "Nuclear Winter Reappraised," by Starley L. Thompson and Stephen H. Schneider, two atmospheric scientists who have reviewed much of the work on nuclear winter since its inception. As noted, one of the important variables in research on nuclear winter has to do with how rapidly smoke and dust would dissipate into the atmosphere in such a way as to permit the sun's natural warming rays to avert a climatological disaster. Based on models that depict the earth's geography more realistically than in some of the earlier studies, Thompson and Schneider conclude that the temperature changes caused by different war scenarios would "more closely describe a nuclear 'fall' than a nuclear winter." Important conclusions that follow are that "there does not seem to be a real potential for human extinction; nor is there a plausible threshold for severe environmental effects."

Despite these comparatively reassuring conclusions, Thompson and Schneider warn that great uncertainty still surrounds knowledge about the climatological consequences of nuclear war. They also warn that just because a "plausible threshold for severe environmental effects" does not exist—like the one that led Carl Sagan to propose very sharp reductions in the levels of existing nuclear stockpiles—the uncertaintly of the environmental consequences of nuclear war continue to make urgent the task of devising policies that reduce the environmental effects of nuclear war, which includes the necessity of "reducing the total explosive megatonnage of the world's strategic arsenals." "In the final analysis, though," they continue,

> we must recognize that whatever our level of understanding of the effects of nuclear weapons, and whatever our ability to apply technical fixes to weapons, defenses or doctrines, the problem of avoiding nuclear war is not amenable to scientific solution. This problem arises more from political differences than from the latest technical capabilities. If nuclear winter has made us more aware of the urgent need to find political solutions to the arms race and the threat of nuclear war, that alone will have made the entire exercise worthwhile regardless of the scientific disposition of the remaining uncertainties.

NOTES

1. Cited in *The Defense Monitor* 8 (February 1979): 5.

2. Our discussion of the effects of a nuclear explosion is based on Office of Technology Assessment, *The Effects of Nuclear War* (Washington, D.C.: U.S. Government Printing Office, 1979), pp. 15–23. This study examines the effects of various counterforce and countervalue nuclear attacks on the United States and the Soviet Union. See also Kevin N. Lewis, "The Prompt and Delayed Effects of Nuclear War," *Scientific American* 241 (July 1979): 35–47.

3. Office of Technology Assessment, p. 16.

4. "From Arms Control to Controlled Security," *Wall Street Journal*, July 10, 1984, p. 32.

5. Richard Pipes, "Why the Soviet Union Thinks It Could Fight and Win a Nuclear War," *Commentary* 64 (July 1977): 33–34.

6. Robert Scheer, *With Enough Shovels: Reagan, Bush, and Nuclear War* (New York: Random House, 1982), p. 18.

7. These scientists' initial findings can be found in Richard P. Turco, Owen B. Toon, Thomas P. Ackerman, James B. Pollack, and Carl Sagan, "Nuclear Winter: Global Consequences of Multiple Nuclear Explosions," *Science* 222 (December 23, 1983), pp. 1283–1292. They have since been reaffirmed by the same authors in "The Climatic Effects of Nuclear War," *Scientific American* 251 (August 1984): 33–43.

8. Thomas Powers, "Nuclear Winter and Nuclear Strategy," *The Atlantic* 257 (November 1984), p. 53. See also Dan Horowitz and Robert J. Lieber, "Nuclear Winter and the Future of Deterrence," *Washington Quarterly* 8 (Summer 1985): 59–70.

9. Caspar W. Weinberger, *The Potential Effects of Nuclear War on the Climate* (Washington, D.C.: U.S. Department of Defense, 1985).

24 HOW MIGHT A NUCLEAR WAR BEGIN?

The Harvard Nuclear Study Group: Albert Carnesale, Paul Doty, Stanley Hoffmann, Samuel P. Huntington, Joseph S. Nye, Jr., Scott D. Sagan

The question is grisly, but nonetheless it must be asked. Nuclear war cannot be avoided simply by refusing to think about it. Indeed, the task of reducing the likelihood of nuclear war should begin with an effort to understand how it might start.

When strategists in Washington or Moscow study the possible origins of nuclear war, they discuss "scenarios," imagined sequences of future events that could trigger the use of nuclear weaponry. Scenarios are, of course, speculative exercises. They often leave out the political developments that might lead to the use of force in order to focus on military dangers. That nuclear war scenarios are even more speculative than most is something for which we can be thankful, for it reflects humanity's fortunate lack of experience with atomic warfare since 1945. But imaginary as they are, nuclear scenarios can help to identify problems not understood or dangers not yet prevented because they have not been foreseen. . . .

Nuclear war would most probably begin for reasons similar to those which began wars in the past. Governments might see opportunities for quick and easy gains and, misjudging enemy reactions, could take steps toward nuclear war without being fully aware of the risks involved. Governments might, under other circumstances, believe that beginning a war was the lesser of two evils, a plausible belief if the other evil is the enemy striking first. These and many other causes have led to war in the past.

Nuclear war is possible. It could occur through purposeful choice, through miscalculation, or through a variety of accidents. It could be started by a political leader, by a military commander, or by a group of terrorists. It could come as a sudden surprise in a time of peace or as the seemingly inevitable culmination of a prolonged conflict between nuclear armed nations. We chose the following kinds of scenarios (some of which are more plausible than others) to illustrate a gamut of possibilities as well as to explore popular and current concerns: (1) surprise attack by one superpower on all or part of the nuclear forces of the other; (2) pre-emptive attacks launched in desperation in time of crisis because one side believes (rightly or wrongly) that the other intends soon to strike first; (3) escalation of conventional wars to nuclear ones; (4) accidental uses of nuclear weapons resulting from malfunctions of machines or of minds; and (5) nuclear wars initiated by other nuclear armed nations or by terrorist organizations. These categories are not unique; additional scenarios involving elements from two or more categories could easily be constructed. Nor is the list of scenarios exhaustive; not all the possible paths to nuclear war can be foreseen. Murphy's law—which states that if something can go wrong, it will—applies here as in all other human activities: military plans go awry, controls fail, misjudgments occur, and one mistake often seems to lead to another, in peacetime and in war. This should not breed despair; it should serve as a constant reminder of the need to control events so that events do not control us.

SCENARIOS

The Bolt from the Blue

Imagine the following conversation. The date is November 1, [19——]; the location, inside the Kremlin.

General Secretary ——: "Comrade General, you have heard the debate. Some members of the Politburo favor your proposal for a surprise attack upon the United States. Others are highly opposed. We await your opinion. Can we go to war and win?"

General ——, Chief of Staff, Soviet Rocket Forces: "Yes! If war is to come, it must come soon, or all is lost. The counter-revolution in Eastern Europe has put our back against the wall. The American military buildup continues to threaten our socialist nation.

"But let me explain how we can triumph if we attack quickly, with all our power. The Americans suspect nothing. We have greatly improved our hunter-killer submarine force and now can closely follow all their submarines; our ballistic missile submarines can maintain adequate attack forces off the enemy's coast. In only seven minutes our submarine missiles could destroy American bombers on their runways, the American submarines in the ports, and, as importantly, American military and civilian command centers. Without orders from these command posts, the missiles in the United States will not be immediately launched and will be destroyed when our ICBMs arrive 23 minutes after the submarine missiles land on target.

"We have, of course, supreme confidence in our military strength. But if a small number of America's nuclear missiles and bombers escape destruction from our overwhelming attack, our ballistic missile defense system and our air defense system will shoot them down. We can end the capitalist threat forever. Let us decide now to end this intolerable situation, destroy them before they gain in strength and threaten us even more."

General Secretary ——: "Thank you. Comrades, the day of destiny may be upon us. How do you vote?"

Is this scenario possible? Yes. Is it likely? No. This bolt from the blue, commonly the most feared prospect, is a most unlikely scenario for the start of a nuclear war *as long as* no Russian military leader could ever report to the Politburo that a Soviet victory in nuclear war was probable or that the damage from American nuclear retaliation could be reduced to acceptable levels.

What military, political, and economic conditions would have to exist before Soviet leaders would seriously listen to the imagined general's proposal? First, nearly *all* American retaliatory forces and the entire command system would have to be highly vulnerable to a Soviet first strike. Currently, most of the Minutemen ICBMs (intercontinental ballistic missiles), U.S. bombers on airfields and submarines in port, and the American command, control, and communications network are theoretically vulnerable. But the forces that would survive a Soviet attack would still be enormously destructive. Most importantly, the American submarine force routinely at sea, which carries more nuclear warheads than does the entire Minuteman force, cannot now or in the foreseeable future be located or quickly destroyed by the Soviet navy.

Second, both Soviet ballistic missile defenses and air defenses would have to be improved greatly, perhaps beyond what is possible, before they could be expected to reduce the damage of the American retaliatory missile and bomber attacks to an acceptable level. Third, technical difficulties would plague the prospects of success in such a surprise Soviet attack: not only would it be enormously difficult to coordinate the actions of Soviet missile-bearing submarines, ICBMs, and anti-submarine warfare forces, but success would hinge on complete surprise being maintained. If Soviet strategic forces were put on full alert status, the possibility that the American intelligence network would miss the warning is exceedingly remote. Strategic Air Command bombers would be alerted and dispersed, American political leaders and military commanders could be sent to safer locations, and some submarines in port could be sent to sea. These actions would reduce still further the probability that a massive Soviet nuclear attack would be answered with only token nuclear retaliation. Finally, the United States could choose to launch its ICBMs on warning of the attack (i.e., while the attacking missiles were in flight toward their targets) or after the first attacking warheads had arrived.

The bolt from the blue is thus not likely now or any time in the foreseeable future. This scenario is, indeed, so farfetched that it is useful to consider only in one sense: it points to a set of combined circumstances which, as a matter of long-range policy, the United States must seek to avoid. There is clearly no reason that such a dangerous combination of circumstances need ever develop. The bolt from the blue could become plausible only if there was a major deterioration of Soviet-American relations and if Soviet nuclear forces, defensive preparations, and antisubmarine capabilities were greatly enhanced, while American counter-measures were unilaterally restrained.

A Limited Attack on the Minuteman Missiles

Some defense specialists believe that while American nuclear retaliatory capabilities might successfully deter surprise attacks on American cities, as well as bolt-from-the-blue attacks on all of the nuclear forces, limited attacks on portions of America's nuclear arsenal are substantially more likely. This is one of the concerns that has fueled the debate over the basing mode for the MX missile, a replacement for the vulnerable Minuteman system. The feared scenario often runs something like this:

The decision in Moscow: In a deep crisis over the status of Berlin, the Politburo decides not to launch an all-out pre-emptive attack against American forces and command centers, but only to attack the Minuteman silos. A hot-line message is sent as soon as the warheads land: first, the Soviet Union will spare American cities if the United States refrains from retaliation and, second, the United States is urged to give in to Soviet demands in Europe.

The decision in Washington: The president asks the Joint Chiefs of Staff what military options exist, now that 90% of the Minuteman force is destroyed. They say that fifteen million Americans have just died in the Soviet Attack and that an American response will likely trigger a Soviet attack on population centers. Should the president launch a retaliatory strike? Or should he give in to Soviet demands?

This Minuteman-only scenario rests upon a very questionable premise: that the Soviets would believe that the president of the United States would choose not to launch the ICBMs on warning or retaliate after 2,000 Soviet nuclear warheads have exploded here. The American submarines, moreover, could attack many Soviet military targets. A Soviet leader probably would assume that retaliation of some sort would be launched after 15 million Americans were killed. In such circumstances, it would be likely that the Soviets would try to reduce the American retaliation to whatever extent they could.

Thus, if the Soviets were to attack the United States on a large-scale basis, they would have great incentives to attack not only the land-based missiles, but also other American strategic forces and the American command, control, and communications network. There is little Soviet advantage to be gained by attacking the U.S. ICBMs alone, for they contain less than one-fourth of America's strategic nuclear warheads. It is not surprising that Soviet military doctrine, as far as American intelligence sources can determine, stresses that if nuclear war occurs, their nuclear forces would be used on a massive scale.

This Minuteman-only scenario, like the full-blown bolt from the blue, is far less likely than many other possible paths to nuclear war. These surprise attack scenarios preoccupy all too many defense analysts whose talents would be far better applied to preventing more likely dangers. And the attention of the public would be better directed to more realistic scenarios and more probable perils.

A Pre-Emptive War

Not all wars begin with coolly calculated decisions. Indeed, under certain circumstances, a nuclear war could originate from a series of hasty decisions made in the midst of uncertainty. In fact, a nuclear exchange could be precipitated by a mistaken action, originally intended to deter war, which could produce a counter-decision to launch a pre-emptive strike.

Consider the following scenario. It is the opening page of an imaginary historian's future best-seller, *The Missiles of August: The Origins of World War Three*:

What was the cause of the war? The Greek historian Thucydides, in his history of the conflict between Athens and Sparta, differentiated between the immediate causes and the underlying causes of war. The latter can be compared to the mass of combustible material; the former is the match that sets the material ablaze.

On August 2, 19——, none of the American leaders in Washington knew that they were lighting such a match. A number of years earlier, Soviet Premier Brezhnev had warned the United States that, if NATO deployed Pershing II and cruise missiles in Western Europe, the Soviet Union would "take retaliatory steps that would put the other side, including the United States itself, its own territory, in an analogous position." On the last day of July, American intelligence satellites spotted cruise missiles being unloaded onto Cuban soil from Soviet ships and on August 1 Premier Andropov announced that he would remove the missiles only if the United States withdrew the NATO deployments.

The sole surviving member of the National Security Council later reported that the president's decision to attack the Cuban dockyard and the Soviet ships was taken overnight. "We had no choice. In a few days, those missiles—we didn't know how many—would have been scattered all over Cuba. This was the only way to get rid of the missiles. We told the Soviets that there would be no attack on Russia itself. Our nuclear alert was only meant to signal our strength."

This was not the view from Moscow. Two Soviet staff officers who survived reported that the Politburo was informed that the Americans must be about to launch a nuclear attack. The head of the KGB told the Politburo that if the Americans launched first, the vast majority of Soviet ICBMs would be destroyed and eventually up to 100 million Soviet citizens might die. But if the Soviet arsenal was used immediately to destroy American nuclear forces and command centers, the casualties after retaliation would probably be "only" between 10 and 20 million. He even told the group that there was a small chance that a pre-emptive attack would "decapitate" the American giant and that no response would come.

He was wrong. The Russians thought war was unavoidable and launched first in desperation and fear. Thirty-five million Americans were killed instantly. The retaliation was perhaps smaller than the first strike the Soviets feared, but it still left 25 million Russions dead.

Perhaps, however, it is misleading to start this history with the immediate cause of the war. The deeper causes go back to 1945. At the close of the Second World War, Soviet and American relations deteriorated rapidly . . . [Even though the INF agreement between the United States and the Soviet Union [promises] removal of the Pershing II and other intermediate-range nuclear forces in Europe, the presence of other forces not covered by the agreement and anticipated replacement weapons keep preemptive war as a realistic scenario—*eds.*]

How plausible is such a pre-emptive war scenario? Although no precise probabilities can be given, of course, it is at least a possibility that in a deep and apparently irresolvable crisis the Soviets (or the United States) might launch their nuclear weapons first with full knowledge that many of its citizens might die, but fearing far worse casualties if they allowed the other side to attack first. A desperate decision indeed, but a possible one.

What conditions would increase the likelihood of such a tragic decision being made by the leaders of a superpower? First, the leaders would have to believe that the other side intended to strike first, and soon. This would require that the adversary's forces be at or moving toward (or be perceived to be at) a high state of alert—a condition likely to be met only in times of crisis. Second, the leaders would have to believe that the other side could carry out a relatively successful disarming first strike—a judgment which would depend upon the capabilities of the adversary's forces and the vulnerabilities of their own. Lastly, the leaders must be convinced that by launching a pre-emptive attack against the other side's nuclear forces, they could substantially reduce the casualties and damage that would ultimately be suffered by their own nation.

The possibility that such a scenario might happen does not, by itself, mean that the United States should never put its forces on alert in a crisis or that we should always back down in dangerous circumstances. Nor does it mean that American nuclear forces should not be aimed at Soviet weaponry. But the possibility of such an occurrence should, at a minimum, promote great caution in times of crisis, highlight the importance of clear and unambiguous military orders, and stress the need for retaliatory forces that are invulnerable and are perceived as such by both sides. Moreover, it should serve as a constant reminder that the security of both sides is diminished by either side's fear of being struck first or by either side's temptation to strike first.

Escalation: Conventional Steps to Nuclear War

It is difficult, though clearly not impossible, to outline a credible scenario in which, during peacetime, a Soviet or an American leader would decide to launch an all-out nuclear attack. It is less difficult to imagine a war occurring between the conventional forces of the two superpowers. And once American and Soviet troops met in combat, the likelihood of the use of nuclear weapons would be increased.

The process by which a war becomes incrementally more violent, either through the plans of the combatants or unintentionally, is called escalation. Escalation from conventional fighting to nuclear war has been a continuing concern of defense planners since the Soviets developed their nuclear arsenal. This fear has, thus far, produced prudence: each superpower has been reluctant to use even conventional forces against the other. Can this prudence continue indefinitely? What would happen if Soviet and American conventional forces did clash somewhere?

We do not know. And this inability to know whether conventional war would escalate to a nuclear exchange both enhances prudence and perpetuates fear. Consider two possible scenarios for nuclear conflict developing through escalation:

War in Europe

Step 1: East German workers, organized by an underground labor union, go on strike, demanding political changes in the government of their country. Martial law is imposed and riots ensue throughout the country. Russian troops help in the "police action." East Germans flee across the border into West Germany.

Step 2: Fighting breaks out between West German military units, who are aiding the refugees, and East German security forces. Soon Soviet forces join in the fighting. Two days later Soviet divisions cross into West Germany and the Soviet premier publicly warns the United States to "refrain from self-defeating threats."

Step 3: Other NATO forces—American, British, and Dutch—become involved in the fighting as the Soviets advance further into West Germany. As the Allies are being pushed back by the superior numbers of Soviet divisions, NATO leaders gather to decide on further military action. They publicly warn the Soviets to withdraw immediately or "suffer the gravest consequences." Four airfields along the Polish-Soviet border are attacked with nuclear-tipped cruise missiles, a communiqué announces, "as a demonstration of NATO resolve."

Step 4: The Soviet Union immediately fires nuclear missiles to destroy nuclear weapons sites in West Germany.

Step 5: ?? Does the war escalate to a full nuclear exchange or is a settlement possible? What would the United States do? What would the Soviet Union do next?

War in the Persian Gulf

Step 1: The Iranian Communist party overthrows the increasingly unpopular government of Ayatollah Khomeini. Civil war breaks out throughout Iran and the new government requests that Soviet troops enter the country "to help restore order." Despite American warnings against such action Soviet forces cross into Iran and move toward Teheran.

Step 2: American troops are immediately sent to southwestern Iran to protect the West's oil supply sources. Advance parties of the two armies meet and engage in combat.

Step 3: As Soviet reinforcements begin to move into Iran, the president orders aircraft from an American aircraft carrier in the Indian Ocean to "close the mountain passes" along the Soviet supply route. Told that nuclear bombs might be needed, he refuses to give weapons release authority to the local commander. "The United States will not be the first to go nuclear," the president's message concludes.

Step 4: The American military commander orders six conventional air strikes against mountain passes in Iran. The next morning, Soviet bombers fly south and attack the American carrier task force with nuclear-tipped missiles. The aircraft carrier and many of its supporting ships are destroyed instantly.

Step 5: ?? Does the president escalate further? Does the Soviet Union stop fighting? What happens next? How does the war end?

These paths to nuclear conflict (or others like them) are more likely than the previous scenarios of initial homeland-to-homeland exchanges for an obvious reason: once war begins, the balance between political and military considerations shifts decidedly toward the military side. The leader of a government is far more likely to authorize use of a small number of nuclear weapons during a conventional war than to initiate a full-scale nuclear conflict. But unless the war is somehow terminated, there will be continued incentives for further escalation.

Once a conventional war began, there would be two other factors, in addition to possible decisions to take incremental escalatory steps, that could lead to nuclear war. First, there would be increased possibilities of miscalculation leading to nuclear war. It is possible that at some stage in a conventional conflict a field commander might be given "pre-delegation of authority," the president's option of allowing commanders to decide themselves when to use tactical nuclear weapons. Once this is done, the likelihood of use through miscalculation or mistake in the "fog of battle" would greatly increase. Second, the pressures for pre-emptive nuclear strikes would likely be enhanced after the line between superpower peace and superpower war was crossed. Once the fighting began, one or both governments might decide that full-scale use of nuclear weapons was inevitable or very nearly so; thus, despite the terrible risks involved, pre-emptive attack might be chosen, on the basis that striking first is better than being stricken first, though both are worse than the unavailable option of no nuclear war at all.

The maintenance of a conventional-nuclear "firebreak"—an often used metaphor borrowed from forest fire-fighting techniques—is most strategists' goal here. If a conventional conflict between the superpowers does someday occur, every effort should be made to terminate the war without the use of nuclear weapons; escalation to full thermonuclear war should be avoided. Withdrawing tactical nuclear weapons from sites near borders, where they might be used quickly in a war, and keeping strict political control over weapons release authority widen the firebreak between conventional and nuclear war. It is not clear, however, exactly how wide such a firebreak should be because of . . . the "usability paradox": if nuclear weapons are too usable, they might be used when and in a manner not controllable by government leaders; yet if it is certain that weapons will not be used, might this not encourage conventional aggression?

Tragic Accidents

Could nuclear war begin purely by accident? Mechanical failures do occur, after all, even with (and perhaps especially with) the most sophisticated machinery. Human frailties always exist as well. And such frailties can produce highly irrational behavior at times, even when (and perhaps especially when) the psychological pressures to behave cautiously are enormous.

It is a common assumption that nuclear weapons are likely to be used, not through decisions of rational government leaders, but through mechanical or human accidents. Jonathan Schell, for example, has written that "the machinery of destruction is complete, poised on a hair trigger, waiting for a 'button' to be 'pushed' by some misguided or deranged human being or for some faulty computer chip to send out the instruction to fire."[1] Is this true? Are the following scenes possible?

The Faulty Computer Chip War

Deep inside a multimillion-dollar computer, used to process the military intelligence coming from American satellites, a 35-cent computer chip malfunctions. Suddenly the radar screens begin to flash. A thousand Soviet missiles appear to be coming over the horizon. "Oh, my God," the radar screen operator says. "This is it."

In the White House, the president is informed of the warning, now ten minutes old. "In twenty minutes the missiles will destroy our retaliatory forces, sir," his military aid informs him. As the president leaves the White House for his specially equipped command post airplane, he orders that all land-based missiles be launched immediately.

"I am not going to let our missiles be destroyed on the ground," he says as he climbs aboard the helicopter. "We'll fight. But the Russians started this war. Let the history books record that fact."

The Strangelove Scenario

Individuals under pressure cannot always withstand the strain. Sometimes men snap. Late one night, a Soviet submarine commander walks into the control room of his new *Typhoon*-class submarine and, before the astonished ensign can react, he pushes a button sending a single SLBM, with twelve nuclear warheads in the nose cone, on its way to the United Sates.

"What have you done?" the ensign cries as he tackles the commander, wrestling him to the floor.

The commander appears startled. Then he smiles, looks up, and says, "That missile is going to down a Nazi bomber. I'm teaching those fascists a lesson. Remember Stalingrad!"

Although such imaginative scenarios are often discussed, they are, fortunately, extremely unlikely if not impossible. This is not because the problem of accidental war is not a serious concern. Rather the opposite is the case: precisely because the possibility exists that nuclear weapons could be used accidentally, the United States government has devised numerous precautions to prevent such accidents. Indeed, contrary to a popular belief, the chances of an American weapon being used accidentally are probably much less today than they were in the 1950s. For along with more sophisticated and more numerous weapons, more sophisticated and more numerous precautionary policies have been developed.

Four kinds of measures intended to minimize the chances of unauthorized or accidental use are worth noting. First is the "two-man rule," which requires parallel actions by two or more individuals at several stages in the process of communicating and carrying out any order to use nuclear weapons. Second is the system of Permissive Action Links (PALs), including a highly secure coded signal which must be inserted in the weapons before they can be used. Third, devices internal to the weapon are designed to ensure that an attempt to bypass the PALs system will disarm the weapon. Finally, the nuclear warheads themselves are designed to preclude accidental detonation as a result of exposure to heat, blast, or radiation. The Soviets share our concern with unauthorized and accidental nuclear war, and there is reason to believe that they too have taken measures to prevent it.

In this light, how credible are the two scenarios outlined above? There have been, it is true, many false alarms in the American nuclear attack warning system. Some of them have been traced to such minuscule components as an inexpensive computer chip. But none of these false alerts has ever come close to leading the nation into war because the government has built redundancies into the system, precisely so that no president will ever have to rely on a single computer or single radar screen to make such important decisions. For this kind of accident to lead to war, several warning systems of different kinds (e.g., infrared sensors on satellites, and radars on land) would have to fail simultaneously. Even that by itself would be unlikely to cause the president to order an immediate launching of ICBMs. His incentives to do so might indeed be small if the missiles were relatively invulnerable and if he had other nuclear systems at sea, not under attack. It is even possible to maintain a policy of not launching missiles in a retaliatory strike until after the damage of the enemy's first strike is assessed.

Of course, it is possible that a military commander could go insane (although the stability of American officers with such responsibilities is carefully tested). An insane American officer could not, in peacetime by himself, arm and deliver the nuclear weapons under his command. In the submarine case, to give but one example, it would take the simultaneous insanity of a number of American submarine officers for an unauthorized American launch to be possible. Given the Soviets' strong propensity for tight political control of their nuclear weapons, there is no reason to believe that the chances of unauthorized Soviet use are any greater.

Thus it is a mistake to believe that a simple accident or an unstable commander could easily lead to a nuclear exchange. In reality, the probabilities of such an event are very low. This should not, however, breed complacency about the prospect of accidental war, for two reasons. First, it is only through continual concern that the likelihood of accidental use of weapons is kept so low. Second, mechanical accidents and human frailties could become increasingly dangerous in times of deep crisis or conventional war, during which time command centers could be threatened or destroyed.

There will continue to be an uneasy balance between the degree of control required to ensure that weapons are not used accidentally and the degree of "usability" required to ensure that the weapons can be used if needed. Preventing accidental use is an important goal, but it cannot be the only objective of a nuclear weapons policy. Nuclear weapons must be usable enough to provide credible deterrence, but not so usable as to invite unintended use.

Regional Nuclear War

One important reason why the world has seen nuclear peace since 1945 is that there has been no conventional war between the United States and the Soviet Union. In the future, if nuclear proliferation continues, there will be an increased danger of nuclear war breaking out between two nuclear armed Third World countries. Such an event might be more likely than nuclear war between the superpowers because many of the conditions that have led to the maintenance of nuclear peace—such as invulnerable second-strike forces, strong leadership control of nuclear weapons, and stable governments in nuclear weapons states—may be absent. The following is an imaginary future newspaper report of a nuclear war which neither Washington nor Moscow would be in a position to stop.

INDIA USES THE BOMB, PAKISTAN SUES FOR PEACE

New Delhi, India.—The Indian government this morning announced that four nuclear bombs were dropped on Pakistan late last night. At noon, a Defense Ministry spokesman in Islamabad read a declaration over the radio accepting "unconditional surrender" on behalf of the Revolutionary Islamic Council of Pakistan. Thus it appears that the week-long war between India and Pakistan has come to a sudden end.

Sources inside the Indian Ministry of Defense have revealed that India's entire nuclear arsenal was used in this morning's pre-emptive attack against Pakistan's three major military airfields and its nuclear weapons assembly facility. When the Pakistani forces crossed the Indian border last week, Radio Islamabad announced that any Indian use of nuclear weapons would be met in kind. Afetr last year's Pakistani nuclear test, the government in New Delhi took the threat seriously, the Ministry of Defense officials reported, and only decided to attack pre-emptively when Indian intelligence warned that Pakistan's weapons were being readied for use. "We had no choice," an official said. "The enemy was preparing for an attack. Fortunately, we knew where the bombs were kept, and destroyed them and their bomber aircraft simultaneously."

Meanwhile, in New York, the UN Security Council met throughout the night and . . .

Somehow this scenario appears less farfetched than most of the previously outlined scenarios for superpower nuclear war. It also appears less apocalyptic (at least from a non-Pakistani perspective). Indeed, its less-than-apocalyptic nature may be precisely the characteristic that makes it less farfetched. The dangers of this kind of nuclear war may be comparatively small today, but they will increase in the future as more countries acquire nuclear weapons. . . .

It is tempting, but incorrect, to think that a nuclear conflict between any two countries would not affect other nations. There is the possibility that one government at war would be allied to the Soviet Union and the other government to the United States, thereby raising the specter of the superpowers becoming involved in the war. Moreover, there is a danger that a nuclear armed country could use a weapon, intentionally or not, against a superpower.

Catalytic War

There is yet another way in which the superpowers could be dragged into nuclear war by the actions of a third party. Imagine the two scenarios described below:

The French Connection
A conventional conflict between NATO and the Warsaw Pact erupts and, despite the imminent collapse of the NATO front, the United States does not use nuclear weapons. The French government, however, launches a small number of its nuclear-tipped submarine-launched ballistic missiles against military targets, hoping to bring a halt to the Soviet advance. The Soviets do not know who launched the missiles, and respond by launching a nuclear attack against NATO military targets throughout Europe. The American president orders that NATO's [nuclear weapons] be used against military targets in the USSR. . . .

Mistaken Identity
A war in the Persian Gulf has broken out between the United States and the Soviet Union. After a week of conventional fighting, nuclear-tipped cruise missiles are launched against the American carrier task force. The planes are Soviet models and bear Soviet markings; they are not manned by Soviet pilots nor are they otherwise under Soviet control. Some other country has intentionally and successfully disguised its aircraft, and the Americans mistakenly conclude that it is the Soviets who have initiated use of nuclear weapons. Does the American president escalate further? What might the Soviets do in the midst of this confusion? What happens next?

Clearly, such scenarios are possible. Under a number of circumstances another nuclear power might trigger a strategic nuclear exchange between the superpowers, a war that they had thus far avoided. The possibilities of such an event are greatly increased if conventional war occurs. Few strategists place the danger of catalytic war as high as nuclear war through escalation or pre-emption, but it still is a serious concern. Indeed, during the SALT I negotiations, the Soviet Union mentioned its concern that the growing Chinese nuclear arsenal might someday be used with such results.

Nuclear Terrorism

What if a terrorist organization gained possession of a nuclear bomb? Could nuclear war occur as a result? Consider the following scenario, which was invented in the best-selling novel *The Fifth Horseman*[2]:

On a snowy December evening, the President of the United States is told by his National Security Adviser that a tape recording in Arabic has just been delivered to the White House. It appears to be a message from Muammar al-Qaddafi, President of Libya, and claims that a nuclear weapon has been placed somewhere on Manhattan. Unless the United States forces Israel to withdraw to its 1967 borders, the bomb will be detonated.

"I must further inform you that, should you make this communication public or begin in any way to evacuate New York City, I shall feel obliged to instantly explode my weapon," the message concludes.

"A man like Qaddafi has got to know we have the capability to utterly destroy him and his entire nation in retaliation. He'd be mad to do something like that," the President tells his adviser.

But what should the president do? Is nuclear terrorism possible? How could it come about?

Terrorists might gain possession of an atomic bomb in one of several ways, including theft, purchase, or manufacture. If they were to steal it, and if it were of American origin, then the Permissive Action Links should frustrate any attempt to detonate it. But it is not at all clear just how confident a president might be in the ability of the PALs to resist a concerted attempt to bypass them, especially in light of the high stakes involved. And suppose the stolen bomb was not an American one. Other current and future nuclear weapons states may not have equipped their warheads with safety systems comparable to those developed by the United States.

A terrorist organization might purchase an atomic bomb from (or be given one by) a government that shares the terrorist group's goals. Indeed, this possibility is reason enough to work to inhibit the spread of nuclear weapons to additional countries.

Finally, terrorists might fashion their own nuclear explosive device. The highly enriched uranium or plutonium essential to the project might be stolen or bought, and a crude but workable bomb assembled. . . . The task would be difficult, but not impossible. In any event, how confident could a president be that the terrorists' bomb would not work? And against whom could he threaten retaliation?

CONCLUSION: CONTINUING ISSUES

How should one think about the various paths to war outlined in this chapter? Five points need to be stressed. First, the set of scenarios presented here is not exhaustive. Surely each reader can think of other ways in which a nuclear war might begin. How probable are such scenarios? What can be done to minimize the likelihood of their occurrence? Also, the dangers of these scenarios could be compounded. Suppose, to give but two examples, mechanical failures in warning systems developed during a deep superpower crisis, or human frailty produced unstable commanders during a conventional war.

Thus, when thinking of the potential dangers to be avoided in the future, one must not assume that decisions will always be deliberate, or that accidents will always develop when they can do the least harm.

Second, this [essay] suggests that it is usually misleading to concentrate one's attention on the number of nuclear weapons when analyzing the likelihood of war. It is widely assumed that changes in the numbers of weapons in the superpower arsenals—either upward or downward—are the major determinant of the risks of war. Sheer numbers, however, matter far less than factors such as the vulnerability of weapons, the credibility of commitments to allies, and imbalances in conventional forces. In the short run, to give but one example, making command and control systems less vulnerable can be as important, and probably more so, in reducing certain risks of war than would changes in the numbers of weapons: improved command and control could reduce an enemy's incentives for a "decapitating" attack, and could improve our ability to follow a policy of "no retaliation until specifically ordered." And the long-run risk of nuclear war is likely to depend more on our ability to stem proliferation than on any other single factor. The common fixation on numbers of weapons in the superpower arsenals misses such important issues.

Third, there is no reason to assume that an all-out nuclear exchange, certainly the most frightening scenario, is either the only kind of nuclear war possible or even the most likely type of nuclear war. Nuclear war occurring through the escalation of conventional conflict appears more probable. Avoiding conventional war is, therefore, one of the most important ways of avoiding nuclear war. And maintaining strong and credible conventional forces may thus be an important component of preventing nuclear war. One should never forget that, despite the incentives to keep a conventional war limited, once fighting begins it would be difficult to control escalation to the nuclear abyss. But escalation should not be considered inevitable, for that could prove to be a self-fulfilling prophecy.

Fourth, it is noted that in none of these scenarios do leaders of the United States or the Soviet Union act insanely. But departures from rationality are not inconceivable; they must be taken into account in the design of measures to prevent nuclear war.

Finally, this glimpse at the shattered crystal ball should breed neither complacency nor despair. A horrible nuclear future is not inevitable, but only because great efforts have been made in the past to decrease its likelihood. The good news for the present is, then, that nuclear war is not probable. The bad news is that nuclear war is, and will continue to be, possible. To make sure that the possible does not become more probable is the continuing task of nuclear policy.

NOTES

1. Jonathan Schell, *The Fate of the Earth* (New York: Knopf, 1982), p. 182.
2. Larry Collins and Dominique LaPierre, *The Fifth Horseman* (New York: Simon and Schuster, 1980), pp. 13–19.

25 NUCLEAR HOLOCAUST

Jonathan Schell

Part of the horror of thinking about a holocaust lies in the fact that it leads us to supplant the human world with a statistical world; we seek a human truth and come up with a handful of figures. The only source that gives us a glimpse of the human truth is the testimony of the survivors of the Hiroshima and Nagasaki bombings. Because the bombing of Hiroshima has been more thoroughly investigated than the bombing of Nagasaki, and therefore more information about it is available, I shall restrict myself to a brief description of that catastrophe.

On August 6, 1945, at 8:16 A.M., a fission bomb with a yield of twelve and a half kilotons was detonated about nineteen hundred feet above the central section of Hiroshima. By present-day standards, the bomb was a small one, and in today's arsenals it would be classed among the merely tactical weapons. Nevertheless, it was large enough to transform a city of some three hundred and forty thousand people into hell in the space of a few seconds. "It is no exaggeration," the authors of "Hiroshima and Nagasaki" tell us, "to say that the whole city was ruined instantaneously." In that instant, tens of thousands of people were burned, blasted, and crushed to death. Other tens of thousands suffered injuries of every description or were doomed to die of radiation sickness. The center of the city was flattened, and every part of the city was damaged. The trunks of bamboo trees as far away as five miles from ground zero—the point on the ground directly under the center of the explosion—were charred. Almost half the trees within a mile and a quarter were knocked down. Windows nearly seventeen miles away were broken. Half an hour after the blast, fires set by the thermal pulse and by the collapse of the buildings began to coalesce into a firestorm, which lasted for six hours. Starting about 9 A.M. and lasting until late afternoon, a "black rain" generated by the bomb (otherwise, the day was fair) fell on the western portions of the city, carrying radioactive fallout from the blast to the ground. For four hours at midday, a violent whirlwind, born of the strange meteorological conditions produced by the explosion, further devastated the city. The number of people who were killed outright or who died of their injuries over the next three months is estimated to be a hundred and thirty thousand. Sixty-eight percent of the buildings in the city were either completely destroyed or damaged beyond repair, and the center of the city was turned into a flat, rubble-strewn plain dotted with the ruins of a few of the sturdier buildings.

In the minutes after the detonation, the day grew dark, as heavy clouds of dust and smoke filled the air. A whole city had fallen in a moment, and in and under its ruins were its people. Among those still living, most were injured, and of these most were burned or had in some way been battered or had suffered both kinds of injury. Those within a mile and a quarter of ground zero had also been subjected to intense nuclear radiation, often in lethal doses. When people revived enough from their unconsciousness or shock to see what was happening around them, they found that where a second before there had been a city getting ready to go about its daily business on a peaceful, warm August morning, now there was a heap of debris and corpses and a stunned mass of injured humanity. But at first, as they awakened and tried to find their bearings in the gathering darkness, many felt cut off and alone. In a recent volume of recollections by survivors called "Unforgettable Fire," in which the effects of the bombing are rendered in drawings as well as in words, Mrs. Haruko Ogasawara, a young girl on that August morning, recalls that she was at first knocked unconscious. She goes on to write:

> How many seconds or minutes had passed I could not tell, but, regaining consciousness, I found myself lying on the ground covered with pieces of wood. When I stood up in a frantic effort to look around, there was darkness. Terribly frightened, I thought I was alone in a world of death, and groped for any light. My fear was so great I did not think anyone would truly understand. When I came to my senses, I found my clothes in shreds, and I was without my wooden sandals.

Soon cries of pain and cries for help from the wounded filled the air. Survivors heard the voices of their families and their friends calling out in the gloom. Mrs. Ogasawara writes:

> Suddenly, I wondered what had happened to my mother and sister. My mother was then forty-five, and my sister five years old. When the darkness began to fade, I found that there was nothing around me. My house, the next door neighbor's house, and the next had all vanished. I was standing amid the ruins of my house. No one was around. It was quiet, very quiet—an eerie moment. I discovered my mother in a water tank. She had fainted. Crying out, "Mama, Mama," I shook her to bring her back to her senses. After coming to, my mother began to shout madly for my sister: "Eiko! Eiko!"
>
> I wondered how much time had passed when there were cries of searchers. Children were calling their parents' names, and parents were calling the names of their children. We were calling desperately for my sister and listening for her voice and looking to see her. Suddenly, Mother cried "Oh Eiko!" Four or five meters away, my sister's head was sticking out and was calling my mother. . . . Mother and I worked desperately to remove the plaster and pillars and pulled her out with great effort. Her body had turned purple from the bruises, and her arm was so badly wounded that we could have placed two fingers in the wound.

Others were less fortunate in their searches and rescue attempts. In "Unforgettable Fire," a houswife describes a scene she saw: "A mother, driven half-mad while looking for her child, was calling his name. At last she found him. His head looked like a boiled octopus. His eyes were half-closed, and his mouth was white, pursed, and swollen."

Throughout the city, parents were discovering their wounded or dead children, and children were discovering their wounded or dead parents. Kikuno Segawa recalls seeing a little girl with her dead mother: "A woman who looked like an expectant mother was dead. At her side, a girl of about three years of age brought some water in an empty can she had found. She was trying to let her mother drink from it."

The sight of people in extremities of suffering was ubiquitous. Kinzo Nishida recalls: "While taking my severely wounded wife out to the riverbank by the side of the hill of Nakahiro-machi, I was horrified, indeed, at the sight of a stark naked man standing in the rain with his eyeball in his palm. He looked to be in great pain, but there was nothing that I could do for him."

Many people were astonished by the sheer sudden absence of the known world. The writer Yoko Ota later wrote: "I just could not understand why our surroundings had changed so greatly in one instant. . . . I thought it might have been something which had nothing to do with the war—the collapse of the earth, which it was said would take place at the end of the world, and which I had read about as a child."

And a history professor who looked back at the city after the explosion remarked later, "I saw that Hiroshima had disappeared."

As the fires sprang up in the ruins, many people, having found injured family members and friends, were now forced to abandon them to the flames or to lose their own lives in the firestorm. Those who left children, husbands, wives, friends, and strangers to burn often found these experiences the most awful of the entire ordeal. Mikio Inoue describes how one man, a professor, came to abandon his wife:

> It was when I crossed Miyuki Bridge that I saw Professor Takenaka, standing at the foot of the bridge. He was almost naked, wearing nothing but shorts, and he had a ball of rice in his right hand. Beyond the streetcar line, the northern area was covered by red fire burning against the sky. Far away from the line, Ote-machi was also a sea of fire.
>
> That day, Professor Takenaka had not gone to Hiroshima University, and the A-bomb exploded when he was at home. He tried to rescue his wife, who was trapped under a roofbeam, but all his efforts were in vain. The fire was threatening him also. His wife pleaded, "Run away, dear!" He was forced to desert his wife and escape from the fire. He was now at the foot of Miyuki Bridge.
>
> But I wonder how he came to hold that ball of rice in his hand. His naked figure, standing there before the flames with that ball of rice, looked to me as a symbol of the modest hopes of human beings.

In "Hiroshima," John Hersey describes the flight of a group of German priests and their Japanese colleagues through a burning section of the city:

> The street was cluttered with parts of houses that had slid into it, and with fallen telephone poles and wires. From every second or third house came the voices of

people buried and abandoned, who invariably screamed, with formal politeness, "*Tasukete kure*! Help, if you please!" The priests recognized several ruins from which these cries came as the homes of friends, but because of the fire it was too late to help.

And thus it happened that throughout Hiroshima all the ties of affection and respect that join human beings to one another were being pulled and rent by the spreading firestorm. Soon processions of the injured—processions of a kind that had never been seen before in history—began to file away from the center of the city toward its outskirts. Most of the people suffered from burns, which had often blackened their skin or caused it to sag off them. A grocer who joined one of these processions has described them in an interview with Robert Jay Lifton which appears in his book "Death in Life":

They held their arms bent [forward] . . . and their skin—not only on their hands but on their faces and bodies, too—hung down. . . . If there had been only one or two such people . . . perhaps I would not have had such a strong impression. But wherever I walked, I met these people. . . . Many of them died along the road. I can still picture them in my mind—like walking ghosts. They didn't look like people of this world.

The grocer also recalls that because of people's injuries "you couldn't tell whether you were looking at them from in front or in back." People found it impossible to recognize one another. A woman who at the time was a girl of thirteen, and suffered disfiguring burns on her face, has recalled, "My face was so distorted and changed that people couldn't tell who I was. After a while I could call others' names but they couldn't recognize me." In addition to being injured, many people were vomiting—an early symptom of radiation sickness. For many, horrifying and unreal events occurred in a chaotic jumble. In "Unforgettable Fire," Torako Hironaka enumerates some of the things that she remembers:

1. Some burned work-clothes.
2. People crying for help with their heads, shoulders, or the soles of their feet injured by fragments of broken window glass. Glass fragments were scattered everywhere.
3. [A woman] crying, saying, "Aigo! Aigo!" (a Korean expression of sorrow).
4. A burning pine tree.
5. A naked woman.
6. Naked girls crying, "Stupid America!"
7. I was crouching in a puddle, for fear of being shot by a machine gun. My breasts were torn.
8. Burned down electric power lines.
9. A telephone pole had burned and fallen down.
10. A field of watermelons.
11. A dead horse.
12. What with dead cats, pigs, and people, it was just a hell on earth.

Physical collapse brought emotional and spiritual collapse with it. The survivors were, on the whole, listless and stupefied. After the escapes, and the failures to escape, from the firestorm, a silence fell over the city and its remaining population. People suffered and died without speaking or otherwise making a sound. The processions of the injured, too, were soundless. Dr. Michihiko Hachiya has written in this book, "Hiroshima Diary":

> Those who were able walked silently toward the suburbs in the distant hills, their spirits broken, their initiative gone. When asked whence they had come, they pointed to the city and said, "That way," and when asked where they were going, pointed away from the city and said, "This way." They were so broken and confused that they moved and behaved like automatons.
>
> Their reactions had astonished outsiders, who reported with amazement the spectacle of long files of people holding stolidly to a narrow, rough path when close by was a smooth, easy road going in the same direction. The outsiders could not grasp the fact that they were witnessing the exodus of a people who walked in the realm of dreams.

Those who were still capable of action often acted in an absurd or an insane way. Some of them energetically pursued tasks that had made sense in the intact Hiroshima of a few minutes before but were now utterly inappropriate. Hersey relates that the German priests were bent on bringing to safety a suitcase, containing diocesan accounts and a sum of money, that they had rescued from the fire and were carrying around with them through the burning city. And Dr. Lifton describes a young soldier's punctilious efforts to find and preserve the ashes of a burned military code book while people around him were screaming for help. Other people simply lost their minds. For example, when the German priests were escaping from the firestorm, one of them, Father Wilhelm Kleinsorge, carried on his back a Mr. Fukai, who kept saying that he wanted to remain where he was. When Father Kleinsorge finally put Mr. Fukai down, he started running. Hersey writes:

> Father Kleinsorge shouted to a dozen soldiers, who were standing by the bridge, to stop him. As Father Kleinsorge started back to get Mr. Fukai, Father LaSalle called out, "Hurry! Don't waste time!" So Father Kleinsorge just requested the soldiers to take care of Mr. Fukai. They said they would, but the little, broken man got away from them, and the last the priests could see of him, he was running back toward the fire.

In the weeks after the bombing, many survivors began to notice the appearance of petechiae—small spots caused by hemorrhages—on their skin. These usually signaled the onset of the critical stage of radiation sickness. In the first stage, the victims characteristically vomited repeatedly, ran a fever, and developed an abnormal thirst. (The cry "Water! Water!" was one of the few sounds often heard in Hiroshima on the day of the bombing.) Then, after a few hours or days, there was a deceptively hopeful period of remission of symptoms, called the latency period, which lasted from about a week to about four weeks. Radiation attacks the reproductive function of cells, and those that reproduce most frequently are therefore the most vulnerable. Among these are the bone-marrow cells, which are responsible for the production of blood cells. During the latency period, the count of white blood cells, which are instrumental in fighting infections, and the count of platelets, which are instrumental in clotting, drop precipitously, so the body is poorly defended against infection and is liable to hemorrhaging. In the third, and final, stage, which may last for several weeks, the victim's hair may fall out and he may suffer from diarrhea and may bleed from the intestines, the mouth, or other parts of the body, and in the end he will either recover or die. Because the fireball of the Hiroshima bomb did not touch the ground, very little ground material was mixed with the fission products of the bomb, and therefore very little local fallout was generated. (What fallout there was descended in the black rain.) Therefore, the fatalities from radiation sickness were probably all caused by the initial nuclear radiation, and since this affected only people within a radius of a mile and a quarter of ground zero, most of the people who received lethal doses were killed more quickly by the thermal pulse and the blast wave. Thus, Hiroshima did not experience the mass radiation sickness that can be expected if a weapon is ground-burst. Since the Nagasaki bomb was also burst in the air, the effect of widespread lethal fallout on large areas, causing the death by radiation sickness of whole populations in the hours, days, and weeks after the blast, is a form of nuclear horror that the world has not experienced.

In the months and years following the bombing of Hiroshima, after radiation sickness had run its course and most of the injured had either died of their wounds or recovered from them, the inhabitants of the city began to learn that the exposure to radiation they had experienced would bring about a wide variety of illnesses, many of them lethal, throughout the lifetimes of those who had been exposed. An early sign that the harm from radiation was not restricted to radiation sickness came in the months immediately following the bombing, when people found that their reproductive organs had been temporarily harmed, with men experiencing sterility and women experiencing abnormalities in their menstrual cycles. Then, over the years, other illnesses, including cataracts of the eye and leukemia and other forms of cancer, began to appear in larger than normally expected numbers among the exposed population. In all these illnesses, correlations have been found between nearness to the explosion and incidence of the disease. Also, fetuses exposed to the bomb's radiation in utero exhibited abnormalities and developmental retardation. Those exposed within the mile-and-a-quarter radius were seven times as likely as unexposed fetuses to die in utero, and were also seven times as likely to die at birth or in infancy. Surviving children who were exposed in utero tended to be shorter and lighter than other children, and were more often mentally retarded. One of the most serious abnormalities caused by exposure to the bomb's radiation was microcephaly—abnormal smallness of the head, which is often accompanied by mental retardation. In one study, thirty-three cases of microcephaly were found among a hundred and sixty-nine children exposed in utero.

What happened at Hiroshima was less than a millionth part of a holocaust at present levels of world nuclear armament. The more than millionfold difference amounts to more than a difference in magnitude; it is also a difference in kind. The authors of "Hiroshima and Nagasaki" observe that "an atomic bomb's massive destruction and indiscriminate slaughter involves the sweeping breakdown of all order and existence—in a word, the collapse of society itself," and that therefore "the essence of atomic destruction lies in the totality of its impact on man and society." This is true also of a holocaust, of course, except that the totalities in question are now not single cities but nations, ecosystems, and the earth's ecosphere. Yet with the exception of fallout, which was relatively light at Hiroshima and Nagasaki (because both the bombs were air-burst), the immediate devastation caused by today's bombs would be of a sort similar to the devastation in those cities. The immediate effects of a twenty-megaton bomb are not different in kind from those of a twelve-and-a-half-kiloton bomb; they are only more extensive. . . . Therefore, while the total effect of a holocaust is qualitatively different from the total effect of a single bomb, the experience of individual people in a holocaust would be, in the short term (and again excepting the presence of lethal fallout wherever the bombs were ground-burst), very much like the experience of individual people in Hiroshima. The Hiroshima people's experience, accordingly, is of much more than historical interest. It is a picture of what our whole world is always poised to become—a backdrop of scarcely imaginable horror lying just behind the surface of our normal life, and capable of breaking through into that normal life at any second. Whether we choose to think about it or not, it is an omnipresent, inescapable truth about our lives today that at every single moment each one of us may suddenly become the deranged mother looking for her burned child; the professor with the ball of rice in his hand whose wife has just told him "Run away, dear!" and died in the fires; Mr. Fukai running back into the firestorm; the naked man standing on the blasted plain that was his city, holding his eyeball in his hand; or, more likely, one of millions of corpses. For whatever our "modest hopes" as human beings may be, every one of them can be nullified by a nuclear holocaust.

One way to begin to grasp the destructive power of present-day nuclear weapons is to describe the consequences of the detonation of a one-megaton bomb, which possesses eighty times the explosive power of the Hiroshima bomb, on a large city, such as New York. Burst some eighty-five hundred feet above the Empire State Building, a one-megaton bomb would gut or flatten almost every building between Battery Park and 125th Street, or within a radius of four and four-tenths miles, or in an area of sixty-one square miles, and would heavily damage buildings between the northern tip of Staten Island and the George Washington Bridge, or within a radius of about eight miles, or in an area of about two hundred square miles. A conventional explosive delivers a swift shock, like a slap, to whatever it hits, but the blast wave of a sizable nuclear weapon endures for several seconds and "can surround and destroy whole buildings." . . . People, of course, would be picked up and hurled away from the blast along with the rest of the debris. Within the sixty-one square miles, the walls, roofs, and floors of any buildings that had not been flattened would be collapsed, and the people and furniture inside would be swept down onto the street. (Technically, this zone would be hit by various overpressures of at least five pounds per square inch. Overpressure is defined as the pressure in excess of normal atmospheric pressure.) As far away as ten miles from ground zero, pieces of glass and other sharp objects would be hurled about by the blast wave at lethal velocities. In Hiroshima, where buildings were low and, outside the center of the city, were often constructed of light materials, injuries from falling buildings were often minor. But in New York, where the buildings are tall and are constructed of heavy materials, the physical collapse of the city would certainly kill millions of people. The streets of New York are narrow ravines running between the high walls of the city's buildings. In a nuclear attack, the walls would fall and the ravines would fill up. The people in the buildings would fall to the street with the debris of the buildings, and the people in the street would be crushed by this avalanche of people and buildings. At a distance of two miles or so from ground zero, winds would reach four hundred miles an hour, and another two miles away they would reach a hundred and eighty miles an hour. Meanwhile, the fireball would be growing, until it was more than a mile wide, and rocketing upward, to a height of over six miles. For ten seconds, it would broil the city below. Anyone caught in the open within nine miles of ground zero would receive third-degree burns and would probably be killed; closer to the explosion, people would be charred and killed instantly. . . .

It it were possible (as it would not be) for someone to stand at Fifth Avenue and Seventy-second Street (about two miles from ground zero) without being instantly killed, he would see the following sequence of events. A dazzling white light from the fireball would illumine the scene, continuing for perhaps thirty seconds. Simultaneously, searing heat would ignite everything flammable and start to melt windows, cars, buses, lampposts, and everything else made of metal or glass. People in the street would immediately catch fire, and would shortly be reduced to heavily charred corpses. About five seconds after the light appeared, the blast wave would strike, laden with the debris of a now nonexistent midtown. Some buildings might be crushed, as though a giant fist had squeezed them on all sides, and others might be picked up off their foundations and whirled uptown with the other debris. On the far side of Central Park, the West Side skyline would fall from south to north. The four-hundred-mile-an-hour wind would blow from south to north, die down after a few seconds, and then blow in the reverse direction with diminished intensity. While these things were happening, the fireball would be burning in the sky for the ten seconds of the thermal pulse. Soon huge, thick clouds of dust and smoke would envelop the scene, and as the mushroom cloud rushed overhead (it would have a diameter of about twelve miles) the light from the sun would be blotted out, and day would turn to night. Within minutes, fires, ignited both by the thermal pulse and by broken gas mains, tanks of gas and oil, and the like, would begin to spread in the darkness, and a strong, steady wind would begin to blow in the direction of the blast. As at Hiroshima, a whirlwind might be produced, which would sweep through the ruins, and radioactive rain, generated under the meteorological conditions created by the blast, might fall. Before long, the individual fires would co-alesce into a mass fire, which, depending largely on the winds, would become either a conflagration or a firestorm. In a conflagration, prevailing winds spread a wall of fire as far as there is any combustible material to sustain it; in a firestorm, a vertical updraft caused by the fire itself sucks the surrounding air in toward a central point, and the fires therefore converge in a single fire of extreme heat. A mass fire of either kind renders shelters useless by burning up all the oxygen in the air and creating toxic gases, so that anyone inside the shelters is asphyxiated, and also by heating the ground to such high temperatures that the shelters turn, in effect, into ovens, cremating the people inside them. In Dresden, several days after the firestorm raised there by Allied conventional bombing, the interiors of some bomb shelters were still so hot that when they were opened the inrushing air caused the contents to burst into flame. Only those who had fled their shelters when the bombing started had any chance of surviving. (It is difficult to predict in a particular situation which form the fires will take. In actual experience, Hiroshima suffered a firestorm and Nagasaki suffered a conflagration.)

In this vast theatre of physical effects, all the scenes of agony and death that took place at Hiroshima would again take place, but now involving millions of people rather than hundreds of thousands. Like the people of Hiroshima, the people of New York would be burned, battered, crushed, and irradiated in every conceivable way. The city and its people would be mingled in a smoldering heap. And then, as the fires started, the survivors (most of whom would be on the periphery of the explosion) would be driven to aban-don to the flames those family members and other people who were unable to flee, or else to die with them. Before long, while the ruins burned, the processions of injured, mute people would begin their slow progress out of the outskirts of the devastated zone. . . .

If instead of being burst in the air the bomb were burst on or near the ground in the vicinity of the Empire State Building, the overpressure would be very much greater near the center of the blast area but the range hit by a minimum of five pounds per square inch of overpressure would be less. The range of the thermal pulse would be about the same as that of the air burst. The fireball would be almost two miles across, and would engulf mid-town Manhattan from Greenwich Village nearly to Central Park. Very little is known about what would happen to a city that was inside a fireball, but one would expect a good deal of what was there to be first pulverized and then melted or vaporized. Any human beings in the area would be reduced to smoke and ashes; they would simply disappear. A crater roughly three blocks in diameter and two hundred feet deep would open up. In addition, heavy radioactive fallout would be created as dust and debris from the city rose with the mushroom cloud and then fell back to the ground. . . . Exposure to radioactivity in human beings is measured in units called rems—an acronym for "roentgen equivalent in man." The roentgen is a standard measurement of gamma- and X-ray radiation, and the expression "equivalent in man" indicates that an adjustment has been made to take into account the differences in the degree of biological damage that is caused by radiation of different types. Many of the kinds of harm done to human beings by radiation—for example, the incidence of cancer and of genetic damage—depend on the dose accumulated over many years; but radiation sickness, capable of causing death, results from an "acute" dose, received in a period of anything from a few seconds to several days. Because almost ninety percent of the so-called "infinite-time dose" of radiation from fallout—that is, the dose from a given quantity of fallout that one would receive if one lived for many thousands of years—is emitted in the first week, the one-week accumulated dose is often used as a convenient measure for calculating the immediate harm from fallout. Doses in the thousands of rems, which could be expected throughout the city, would attack the central nervous system and would bring about death within a few hours. Doses of around a thousand rems, which would be delivered some tens of miles downwind from the blast, would kill within two weeks everyone who was exposed to them. Doses of around five hundred rems, which would be delivered as far as a hundred and fifty miles downwind (given a wind speed of fifteen miles per hour), would kill half of all exposed able-bodied young adults. At this level of exposure, radiation sickness proceeds in the three stages observed at Hiroshima. The plume of lethal fallout could descend, depending on the direction of the wind, on other parts of New York State and parts of New Jersey, Pennsylvania, Delaware, Maryland, Connecticut, Massachusetts, Rhode Island, Vermont, and New Hampshire, killing additional millions of people. The circumstances in heavily contaminated areas, in which millions of people were all declining together, over a period of weeks, toward painful deaths, are ones that, like so many of the consequences of nuclear explosions, have never been experienced.

A description of the effects of a one-megaton bomb on New York City gives some notion of the meaning in human terms of a megaton of nuclear explosive power, but a weapon that is more likely to be used against New York is the twenty-megaton bomb, which has one thousand six hundred times the yield of the Hiroshima bomb. The Soviet Union is estimated to have at least a hundred and thirteen twenty-megaton bombs in its nuclear arsenal, carried by Bear intercontinental bombers. In addition, some of the Soviet SS-18 missiles are capable of carrying bombs of this size, although the actual yields are not known. Since the explosive power of the twenty-megaton bombs greatly exceeds the amount necessary to destroy most military targets, it is reasonable to suppose that they are meant for use against large cities. If a twenty-megaton bomb were air-burst over the Empire State Building at an altitude of thirty thousand feet, the zone gutted or flattened by the blast wave would have a radius of twelve miles . . . reaching from the middle of Staten Island to the northern edge of the Bronx, the eastern edge of Queens, and well into New Jersey, and the zone of heavy damage from the blast wave (the zone hit by a minimum of two pounds of overpressure per square inch) would have a radius of twenty-one and a half miles . . . reaching to the southernmost tip of Staten Island, north as far as southern Rockland County, east into Nassau County, and west to Morris County, New Jersey. The fireball would be about four and a half miles in diameter and would radiate the thermal pulse for some twenty seconds. People caught in the open twenty-three miles away from ground zero, in Long Island, New Jersey, and southern New York State, would be burned to death. . . . People hundreds of miles away who looked at the burst would be temporarily blinded and would risk permanent eye injury. . . . The mushroom cloud would be seventy miles in diameter. New York City and its suburbs would be transformed into a lifeless, flat, scorched desert in a few seconds.

If a twenty-megaton bomb were ground-burst on the Empire State Building, the range of severe blast damage would, as with the one-megaton ground blast, be reduced, but the fireball . . . would cover Manhattan from Wall Street to northern Central Park and also parts of New Jersey, Brooklyn, and Queens, and everyone within it would be instantly killed, with most of them physically disappearing. Fallout would again be generated, this time covering thousands of square miles with lethal intensities of radiation. A fair portion of New York City and its incinerated population, now radioactive dust, would have risen into the mushroom cloud and would now be descending on the surrounding territory. . . . If the wind carried the fallout onto populated areas, then this one bomb would probably doom upward of twenty million people, or almost ten percent of the population of the United States.

26 CIVILIAN CASUALTIES FROM "LIMITED" NUCLEAR ATTACKS ON THE U.S. AND U.S.S.R.

Barbara G. Levi,
Frank N. von Hippel
and William H. Daugherty

For more than twenty years, the U.S. nuclear-weapons policy debate has been largely centered on hypothetical counterforce attacks in which the strategic nuclear weapons of the U.S. and U.S.S.R. are targeted on each other.[1] Some see a U.S. ability to threaten strategic counterforce attacks as essential to maintaining the credibility of nuclear deterrence. Others view counterforce strategies and capabilities on both sides as destabilizing and believe that, in any case, nuclear war could not be kept limited. Only infrequently considered, however, are the magnitudes of the civilian casualties that would be caused by counterforce attacks, and the implications of these casualties for escalation.

In a previous article,[2] we presented estimates of the civilian casualties that would result from a Soviet strategic counterforce attack on the U.S. involving approximately 3000 nuclear explosions. We found that 12–27 million Americans would die and that altogether 23–45 million would suffer lethal or serious non-lethal injuries from the short-term, direct effects of the nuclear explosions. In the longer term, an additional 2–20 million might develop radiation-caused cancers. The variation was due to different assumptions concerning winds and casualty models.

We also presented estimates of the casualties that would result from much smaller attacks on U.S. urban targets involving approximately 100 one-Mt airbursts. We estimated that such attacks would kill 3–11 million people if a set of 100 strategic nuclear sites were targeted; 11–29 million people if about 100 military-industrial facilities were struck; and 25–66 million people if the 100 most populous city areas were bombed. The ranges resulted from the use of two alternative casualty models.

The present article considers similar attack scenarios—but with the roles of the U.S. and Soviet Union reversed. In brief, we find very similar consequences:

Note: some footnotes have been deleted, and others have been renumbered to appear in consecutive order.

- A major U.S. attack on strategic nuclear facilities in the Soviet Union might kill 15–32 million people, kill or injure a total of 25–54 million people in the short term and cause 2–14 million people to suffer radiation-induced cancers in the longer term.

- A worst-case attack on Soviet urban areas with one hundred one-Mt airbursts would kill 45–77 million people and cause a total of 73–93 million to suffer lethal and non-lethal injuries.

We have not considered the casualties due to the indirect environmental and social disruptions resulting from such attacks, but they could be at least as great as casualties resulting from the direct effects. No consideration of strategic nuclear attacks can ignore human consequences of this magnitude. . . .

CONCLUSIONS

As this and the previous paper [show], if either the U.S. or the U.S.S.R. used its strategic nuclear forces to attack those of the other side, it would kill tens of millions of people as an unintended consequence. Despite great reductions in the average yields and increases in the accuracy of U.S. strategic warheads over the past two and a half decades, the situation is still the same as that described 26 years ago to President Kennedy by Chairman of the Joint Chiefs of Staff Lyman Lemnitzer:

> there is considerable question that the Soviets would be able to distinguish between a total attack and an attack of military targets only. . . . [B]ecause of fallout from attack of military targets and co-location of many military targets with military-industrial targets, the casualties would be many millions in number. Thus, limiting attack to military targets has little practical meaning as a humanitarian measure.[3]

In such circumstances, it would be unlikely for the Soviet Union to restrain its response. Certainly, enough of its strategic forces would survive the counterforce attack to enable it to mount a devastating counterblow. Our results, therefore, put strategic counterforce strategies in serious question.

It has also been shown in these papers that even one hundred one-Mt weapons—equivalent to about two percent of the destructive power currently in the U.S. or Soviet strategic nuclear stockpile—could devastate the urban areas of either "superpower." It would therefore seem virtually impossible for either the U.S. or the U.S.S.R. to escape their mutual-hostage relationship unilaterally with any feasible combination of strategic offensive and defensive weapons. . . .

NOTES

1. See e.g. Lawrence Freedman, *The Evolution of Nuclear Strategy* (New York: St. Martin's Press, 1981); and Fred Kaplan, *The Wizards of Armageddon* (New York: Simon and Schuster, 1983).

2. William H. Daugherty, Barbara G. Levi and Frank N. von Hippel, "The Consequences of 'Limited' Nuclear Attacks on the United States," *International Security*, Vol. 10, No. 4 (Spring 1986), pp. 3–45.

3. Reprinted in Scott D. Sagan, "SIOP-62: The Nuclear War Plan Briefing to President Kennedy," *International Security*, Vol. 12, No. 1 (Summer 1987) pp. 22–51, at 50–51.

27 CAN NUCLEAR WAR BE CONTROLLED?

Desmond Ball

For the greater part of the nuclear age, Western strategic thought focused on deterrence and other means of avoiding strategic nuclear war. The principal concerns of the strategic studies community were the conditions of viable mutual deterrence and crisis stability, the prevention of accidental nuclear war, and the promotion of nuclear non-proliferation to limit the danger of catalytic war. Virtually no consideration was given to the conduct of nuclear war in the event that deterrence failed or that, for whatever the reason, nuclear strikes were initiated. It was assumed, at least implicitly, that any significant use of nuclear weapons by either the United States or the Soviet Union against the territory or military forces of the other would inevitably develop into an all-out nuclear exchange limited only by the size of their respective nuclear arsenals.

During the last decade, however, there has been a radical shift in this thinking. Today, the principal concerns of the strategic studies community relate to the period *following* the initiation of a strategic nuclear exchange— i.e. to questions of nuclear war-fighting, such as targeting plans and policies, the dynamics of escalation during a strategic nuclear exchange, and the termination of any such exchange.

Controlled Escalation has become the central operational concept in current U.S. strategic doctrine. This concept requires the U.S. to be able to conduct very selective military operations, initially focusing on the protection of vital American interests immediately threatened, but also aimed at foreclosing opportunities for further enemy aggression; the intention is to "deter escalation and coerce the enemy into negotiating a war termination acceptable to the United States by maintaining our capability to effectively withhold attacks from additional hostage targets highly valued [or] vital to enemy leaders, thus limiting the level and scope of violence by threatening subsequent destruction."[1] Controlling escalation requires *both* adversaries to exercise restraint, and current U.S. policy is to offer a combination of measures involving a mixture of self-interest and coercion.

The capabilities for command and control, and the conditions which enable control to be exercised throughout a stategic nuclear exchange, are critical to the viability of the current U.S. strategic doctrine. Without survivable

Note: The footnotes have been renumbered to appear in consecutive order.

284

command, control and communication (C³) systems, for example, any limited nuclear operations involving control, selectivity, discrimination and precision would rapidly become infeasible. . . .

A strategic nuclear war between the United States and the Soviet Union would involve so many novel technical and emotional variables that predictions about its course—and especially about whether or not it could be controlled—must remain highly speculative.

To the extent that there is a typical lay image of a nuclear war, it is that any substantial use of nuclear weapons by either the United States or the Soviet Union against the other's forces or territory would inevitably and rapidly lead to all-out urban-industrial attacks and consequent mutual destruction. As Carl-Friedrich von Weiszacker recently wrote, "as soon as we use nuclear weapons, there are no limits."[2]

Among strategic analysts on the other hand, the ascendant view is that it is possible to conduct limited and quite protracted nuclear exchanges in such a way that escalation can be controlled and the war terminated at some less than all-out level. Some strategists actually visualize an escalation ladder, with a series of discrete and clearly identifiable steps of increasing levels of intensity of nuclear conflict, which the respective adversaries move up—and down—at will. Current U.S. strategic policy, although extensively and carefully qualified, is closer to this second position: it is hoped that escalation could be controlled and that more survivable command-and-control capabilities should ensure dominance in the escalation process. Indeed, reliance on the ability to control escalation is an essential element of U.S. efforts with respect to extended deterrence.

Escalation is neither autonomous and inevitable nor subject completely to the decisions of any one national command authority. Whether or not it can be controlled will depend very much on the circumstances at the time. The use of a few nuclear weapons for some clear demonstrative purposes, for example, could well not lead to further escalation. However, it is most unrealistic to expect that there would be a relatively smooth and controlled progression from limited and selective strikes, through major counterforce exchanges, to termination of the conflict at some level short of urban-industrial attacks. It is likely that beyond some relatively early stage in the conflict the strategic communications systems would suffer interference and disruption, the strikes would become ragged, uncoordinated, less precise and less discriminating, and the ability to reach an agreed settlement between the adversaries would soon become extremely problematical.

There is of course no immutable point beyond which control is necessarily and irretrievably lost, but clearly the prospects of maintaining control depend to a very great extent on whether or not a decision is taken deliberately to attack strategic command-and-control capabilities.

Command-and-control systems are inherently relatively vulnerable, and concerted attacks on them would very rapidly destroy them, or at least render them inoperable. Despite the increased resources that the U.S. is currently devoting to improving the survivability and endurance of command-and-control systems, the extent of their relative vulnerability remains enormous. The Soviet Union would need to expend thousands of warheads in any comprehensive counterforce attacks against U.S. ICBM silos, bomber bases and ... submarine facilities, and even then hundreds if not thousands of U.S. warheads would still survive. On the other hand, it would require only about 50–100 warheads to destroy the fixed facilities of the national command system or to effectively impair the communication links between the National Command Authorities [political and military leaders responsible for commanding U.S. military forces] and the strategic forces.

This figure would permit attacks on the National Military Command Center, the major underground command posts (including the Alternative National Military Command Center and the NORAD [North American Defense] and SAC [Strategic Air Command] Command Posts), the critical satellite ground terminals and early-warning radar facilities, the VLF [very low frequency] communication stations, etc., as well as 10 or 20 high altitude detonations designed to disrupt HF [high frequency] communications and generate EMP [electromagnetic pulse] over millions of square miles. Any airborne command posts and communication links that survived the initial attack could probably not endure for more than a few days. Soviet military doctrine suggests that any comprehensive counterforce attack *would* include strikes of this sort. U.S. strategic targeting plans involve a wide range of Soviet command-and-control facilities, and, while attacks on the Soviet national leadership would probably only be undertaken as part of an all-out exchange, it is likely that attempts would be made to destroy the command posts that control the strategic forces, or at least to sever the communication links between the Soviet NCA [National Command Authorities] and those forces at a much earlier stage in the conflict.

In fact, control of a nuclear exchange would become very difficult to maintain after several tens of strategic nuclear weapons had been used, even where deliberate attacks on command-and-control capabilities were avoided. Many command and control facilities, such as early-warning radars, radio antennae and satellite ground terminals would be destroyed, or at least rendered inoperable, by nuclear detonations designed to destroy nearby military forces and installations, while the widespread disturbance of the ionosphere and equally widespread generation of EMP would disrupt HF communications and impair electronic and electrical systems at great distances from the actual explosions. Hence, as John Steinbruner has argued, "regardless of the flexibility embodied in individual force components, the precariousness of command channels probably means that nuclear war would be uncontrollable, as a practical matter, shortly after the first tens of weapons are launched."[3] Moreover, any attack involving 100 nuclear weapons that was of any military or strategic significance (as opposed to demonstration strikes at isolated sites in northern Siberia) would produce substantial civilian casualties. Even if cites were avoided, 100 nuclear detonations on key military or war-supporting facilities (such as oil refineries) would probably cause prompt fatalities in excess of a million people.

The notion of controlled nuclear war-fighting is essentially astrategic in that it tends to ignore a number of the realities that would necessarily attend any nuclear exchange. The more significant of these include the particular origins of the given conflict and the nature of its progress to the point where the strategic nuclear exchange is initiated; the disparate objectives for which a limited nuclear exchange would be fought; the nature of the decision-making processes within the adversary governments; the political pressures that would be generated by a nuclear exchange; and the problems of terminating the exchange at some less than all-out level. Some of these considerations are so fundamental and so intemperate in their implications as to suggest that there can really be no possibility of controlling a nuclear war.

The origins of a nuclear exchange are relevant because, for example, a strategic nuclear strike by the United States or the Soviet Union against targets in the other's heartland—no matter how limited, precise, or controlled it might be—is most unlikely to be the first move in any conflict between them. Rather, it is likely to follow a period of large-scale military action, probably involving substantial use of tactical nuclear weapons, in an area of vital interest to both adversaries, and during which the dynamics of the escalation process have already been set in motion. Some command-and-control facilities, communications systems and intelligence posts that would be required to control a strategic nuclear exchange would almost certainly be destroyed or damaged in the conventional or tactical nuclear phases of a conflict. And casualties on both sides are already likely to be very high before any strategic nuclear exchange. In the case of a tactical nuclear war in Europe possible fatalities range from 2 to 20 million, assuming extensive use of nuclear weapons with some restraints, up to 100 million if there are no restraints at all.[4] The capabilities of the Warsaw Pact forces (using large and relatively "dirty" warheads) and the Warsaw Pact targeting doctrine make it likely that the actual figure would lie at the higher end of this range.

A war involving such extensive use of nuclear weapons in Europe would almost inevitably involve attacks on targets within the Soviet Union. Indeed, it has long been U.S. policy to use nuclear weapons against the Soviet Union even if the Soviet Union has attacked neither U.S. forces nor U.S. territory. As [U.S. Defense] Secretary [Harold] Brown expressed it in January 1980, "We could not want the Soviets to make the mistaken judgment, based on their understanding of our targeting practices, that they would be spared retaliatory attacks on their territory as long as they did not employ strategic weapons or attack US territory."[5] The U.S. would attempt to destroy the Soviet theater nuclear forces, including the MRBMs, IRBMs and bombers based in the western U.S.S.R., the reserve forces, and POL and logistic support facilities. Soviet casualties from these attacks could amount to several tens of millions. The prospects for controlling any subsequent strategic exchange would not be auspicious.

In addition to these technical and strategic considerations, the decision-making structures and processes of large national security establishments are quite unsuited to the control of escalatory military operations. The control of escalation requires extreme decisional flexibility: decision-makers must be able to adapt rapidly to changing situations and assessments, and must have the freedom to reverse direction as the unfolding of events dictates; their decisions must be presented clearly and coherently, leaving no room for mis-interpretation either by subordinates charged with implementation or by the adversary leadership.

These are not attitudes that are generally found in large national security establishments. In neither the United States nor the Soviet Union are these establishments unitary organizations in which decisions are made and ex-ecutive commands given on the basis of some rational calculation of the national interest. They are made up of a wide range of civilian and military individuals and groups, each with their own interests, preferences, views and perspectives, and each with their own quasi-autonomous political power bases; the decisions which emerge are a product of bargaining, negotiation and compromise between these groups and individuals, rather than of any more rational processes. The heterogeneous nature of the decision-making process leads, in the first instance, to a multiplicity of motives and objectives, not all of which are entirely compatible, and resolving them generally involves the acceptance of compromise language acceptable to each of the contending participants. The clarity of reception among the adversary leadership is con-sequently generally poor, and the reactions invariably different from the re-sponses initially sought.

The "fog of war" makes it extremely unlikely that the situation to which NCA believe themselves to be reacting will in fact correspond very closely to the true situation, or that there will be a high degree of shared perception between the respective adversary leaderships. In these circumstances it would be most difficult to terminate a nuclear exchange through mutual agreement between the adversaries at some point short of all-out urban-industrial attacks.

Of course, the pressures to which decision-makers are subject do not come only from within the national security establishment. In the event of a nuclear exchange, the national leadership would also be subject to the pressures of popular feelings and demands. The mood of horror, confusion and hatred that would develop among the population at large as bombs began falling on the Soviet Union and the United States and casualties rose through the millions would inevitably limit the national leaderships' freedom of maneu-ver. Whether the horror would force them to recoil from large-scale attacks on urban-industrial areas or the hatred would engender rapid escalation must remain an open question—but neither mood would be conducive to measured and considered actions.

The likelihood that effective control of a nuclear exchange would be lost at some relatively early point in a conflict calls into question the strategic utility of any preceding efforts to control the exchange. As Colin Gray has argued, it could be extremely dangerous for the United States "to plan a set of very selective targeting building blocks for prospective rounds one, two and three of strategic force application" while rounds four and five entailed massive urban-industrial strikes.[6] Implementation of such a plan, no matter how controlled the initial rounds, would amount "in practice, to suicide on the instalment plan."[7]

The allocation of further resources to improving the survivability and endurance of the strategic command-and-control capabilities cannot substantially alter this situation. Command-and-control systems are inherently more vulnerable than the strategic forces themselves, and, while basic retaliatory commands would always get to the forces eventually, the capability to exercise strict control and co-ordination would inevitably be lost relatively early in a nuclear exchange.

Furthermore, the technical and strategic uncertainties are such that, regardless of the care and tight control which they attempt to exercise, decision-makers could never be confident that escalation could be controlled. Uncertainties in weapons effects and the accuracy with which weapons can be delivered mean that collateral casualties can never be calculated precisely and that particular strikes could look much less discriminating to the recipient than to the attack planner. The uncertainties are especially great with respect to the operation of particular C^3 systems in a nuclear environment. The effects of EMP and transient radiation on electrical and electronic equipment have been simulated on many components but rarely on large systems (such as airborne command posts). Moreover much of the simulation of nuclear effects derives from extrapolation of data generated in the period before atmospheric nuclear tests were banned in 1963.

Given the impossibility of developing capabilities for controlling a nuclear exchange through to favorable termination, or of removing the residual uncertainties relating to controlling the large-scale use of nuclear weapons, *it is likely that decision-makers would be deterred from initiating nuclear strikes no matter how limited or selective the options available to them.* The use of nuclear weapons for controlled escalation is therefore no less difficult to envisage than the use of nuclear weapons for massive retaliation.

Of course, national security policies and postures are not designed solely for the prosecution of war. In both the United States and the Soviet Union, deterring war remains a primary national objective. It is an axiom in the strategic literature that the criteria for deterrance are different from those for war-fighting, and capabilities which would be deficient for one purpose could well be satisfactory for the other.[8] The large-scale investment of resources in command-and-control capabilities, together with high-level official declarations that the United States would be prepared to conduct limited, selective and tightly controlled strategic nuclear strikes (perhaps in support of extended deterrence), could therefore be valuable because they suggest U.S. determination to act in limited ways—the demonstrable problems of control notwithstanding. However, viable deterrent postures require both capabilities and credibility, and it would seem that neither can be assumed to the extent that would be necessary for the concept of controlled nuclear war-fighting to act as a deterrent. Rather than devoting further resources to pursuing the chimera of controlled nuclear war, relatively more attention might be accorded to another means of satisfying the objectives that limited nuclear options are intended to meet. This is likely, in practice, to mean greater attention to the conditions of conventional deterrence.

NOTES

1. Testimony of Dr William J. Perry, Under Secretary of Defense for Research and Engineering, in Hearings before the Senate Armed Services Committee, *Department of Defense Authorization for Appropriations for Fiscal Year 1980*, Part 3, March–May 1979, p. 1437.

2. Carl-Friedrich von Weiszacker, "Can A Third World War be Prevented?" *International Security* (vol. 5, no. 1), Summer 1980, p. 205.

3. John Steinbruner, "National Security and the Concept of Strategic Stability," *Journal of Conflict Resolution* (vol. 22, no. 1), September 1978, p. 421.

4. Alain C. Enthoven, "US Forces in Europe: How Many? Doing What?" *Foreign Affairs* (vol. 53, no. 3), April 1975, p. 514; Alain C. Enthoven and K. Wayne Smith, *How Much Is Enough?: Shaping the Defense Program, 1961–1969* (New York: Harper and Row, 1971), p. 128.

5. Harold Brown, *Department of Defense Annual Report Fiscal Year 1981* (29 January 1980), p. 92.

6. Colin S. Gray, "Targeting Problems for Central War," *Naval War College Review* (vol. 33, no. 1), January–February 1980, p. 9.

7. *Ibid.*, p. 7.

8. See André Beaufre, *Deterrence & Strategy*, (London: Faber & Faber, 1965), p. 24; and Glenn H. Snyder, *Deterrence & Defense: Toward a Theory of National Security* (Princeton, N.J.: Princeton University Press, 1961), pp. 3–6.

28 INVITATION TO A NUCLEAR BEHEADING

Barry R. Schneider

Soviet Yankee-class submarines regularly operating 600 nautical miles from the East Coast of the United States can destroy Washington, D.C., within 8 to 10 minutes of launching one of their nuclear missiles.

It might be five minutes or more before the President of the United States could be alerted to the missile launch, too late to board his helicopter for Andrews Air Force Base, too late to escape in his National Emergency Airborne Command Post (NEACP) aircraft.

A ballistic-missile attack by Soviet submarines would likely doom the President, the Vice President, Cabinet members, the Joint Chiefs of Staff, and members of Congress who were in Washington, D.C., at the time. On most days, the American government lives in the shadow of this threat of nuclear decapitation.

The Soviets have repeatedly stressed, in their military training and writings, the importance of using nuclear forces to strike early and often in order to create a favorable outcome to a nuclear war. One of their wartime strategic goals, outlined in the *Soviet Military Encyclopedia*, is "the disorganization of the enemy's system of political and military command and control." In any nuclear war, our political and military leaders and their communications links are likely to be among the Soviets' highest priority targets.

The political and military leaders who are designated members of the chain of command for U.S. forces—they are called National Command Authorities (NCA)—must be able to survive a surprise attack in order to guide the country and carry out retaliatory blows. If the Soviets or other adversaries know the U.S. can survive and respond, they are unlikely to consider an attack worth the risk.

Any nuclear attack on the United States would thus probably be an act of irrational desperation. It is highly probable that even a sudden and annihilating blow against Washington would not prevent a devastating, if uncoordinated, American retaliatory attack. In the event that communications with Washington are totally severed, military officers at command centers outside the capital may have orders to launch a counterstrike.

Nevertheless, if a major weakness exists in deterrence strategy, it is in the vulnerability of the President and his successors to a decapitation attack. If the near complete extermination of U.S. National Command Authorities occurred, and if communication links to the U.S. strategic forces were largely destroyed, a Soviet attack might prevent a coordinated and coherent U.S. retaliation.

To ensure that the U.S. could employ its nuclear forces effectively, we must guarantee the survivability of strategic command, control, and communications—the links between the parts of the system, which are generally labeled C^3 (and sometimes C^3I, to include intelligence activities). C^3 is the nervous system of U.S. military forces. The National Command Authorities are the brain. Kill the brain or paralyze the nervous system and the arms cannot be used effectively. It is clearly in the U.S. interest to convince the Soviets that a nuclear decapitation attack could not work.

In more than 200 years of U.S. history, eight Presidents died in office and another resigned. In each case the Vice President became President and served until the term of office expired. A smooth transition may be impossible, however, under the circumstances of a nuclear attack on Washington.

According to Department of Defense Directive 5100.30, issued December 2, 1971, the National Command Authorities shall consist "only of the President and the Secretary of Defense or their duly deputized alternatives or successors." This system lends itself to confusion because of the twin lines of succession, one for the Presidency (provided for in the Constitution) and the other for the top command of U.S. military forces. In the case of a sitting elected President these top roles are combined in one person, someone who everyone agrees holds the reins of power. However, in the case of a dead, disabled or missing President, the lines of authority are less clear.

For example, who is in charge if the President is dead, the Vice President cannot be located or certified as living, and military decisions have to be made immediately? The answer is (1) [the] Speaker of the House of Representatives, if he is alive and can be found and briefed, or (2) the Secretary of Defense and his successors. Once a Presidential successor like Sen. Thurmond has been "designated" by a central locator system run by the Federal Emergency Management Agency, he becomes the ultimate authority. However, short of finding the next Presidential successor, U.S. military decisions will be made by the Secretary of Defense or his successors.

That this is confusing was demonstrated in the moments following John Hinckley Jr.'s attempted assassination of President Reagan. As many Americans recall, Secretary of State Alexander Haig went on television and declared, "I am in charge." The facts were that Vice President Bush was out of town and President Reagan was unable to make decisions during his operation and the beginning of his recovery at George Washington University Hospital. What Haig overlooked was that Thomas O'Neill, as Speaker of the House of Representatives, was next in line to succeed the President, and the Secretary of State was not. Nor was Haig in charge of U.S. military forces, since the Secretary of State is not one of the designated successors to National Command Authority. That power was held by Secretary of Defense Caspar Weinberger.

Should the President die or be declared incapable of performing his duties, his successors would take power in this order:

1. Vice President . . .
2. Speaker of the House of Representatives . . .
3. President pro tempore of the Senate . . .
4. Secretary of State . . .
5. Secretary of the Treasury . . .
6. Secretary of Defense . . .
7. The Attorney General . . .
8. Secretary of the Interior . . .
9. Secretary of Agriculture . . .
10. Secretary of Commerce . . .
11. Secretary of Labor . . .
12. Secretary of Health and Human Services . . .
13. Secretary of Housing and Urban Development . . .
14. Secretary of Transportation . . .
15. Secretary of Energy . . .
16. Secretary of Education . . .

If U.S. military decisions needed to be made immediately because the U.S. was under attack, and the President and his successors were dead, or could not be located, the Secretary of Defense or his successors have the authority to order military forces into action.

1. Deputy Secretary of Defense . . .
2. Secretary of the Army . . .
3. Secretary of the Navy . . .
4. Secretary of the Air Force . . .
5. Under Secretary of Defense for Policy . . .
6. Under Secretary of Defense for Research and Engineering . . .
7. Eight Assistant Secretaries of Defense and the General Counsel to the Defense Department, in order of their length of service.
8. Under Secretaries of the Army, Navy, and Air Force, in order of their length of service.
9. Ten Assistant Secretaries of the Army, Navy, and Air Forces, in order of their length of service.

Unfortunately, every one of these individuals, whose orders might guide the activities of U.S. military forces in a nuclear war, lives and works in the Washington, D.C., area; and neither the Pentagon nor the White House is designed to survive nuclear attack. Indeed, the Soviet Union could probably destroy any fixed structure in the U.S. above ground, unless some way were found of actively defending it (with planes, missiles, or directed energy beams) or hardening it (that is, insulating it against the effects of blast and heat). Compared with other hardened targets, the White House and the Pentagon are considered soft and easily destroyed.

The chaos that a Soviet nuclear decapitation attack might cause would be difficult to overstate. Perhaps the most difficult question to answer in the hours after an attack would be, "Who is in charge here?" With Washington destroyed and all or nearly all of the Presidential and National Command Authorities dead or dying, and with most C^3 linkages damaged or destroyed, it would be difficult for military commanders to know who the President or top civilian authority was at any given time after an attack began. As one Defense Department C^3I expert wonders, "How does the new President find out that he is President, and how does he convince the National Command Authority that he is the President?"

The job of sorting all this out is delegated to the Federal Emergency Management Agency. [Former] FEMA director Louis Giuffrida has said that "[o]ne of the things we discovered is that there was no authentication system. So that if [someone] got on the horn and said, 'I'm the successor,' and somebody said, 'prove it,' [no one could]. So we're working on that. FEMA will be the authenticating mechanism to say, 'Yeah, this guy is for real. The President's gone, and we don't know where the Vice President is . . . and this is the man.'"

FEMA operates the central locator system that keeps daily tabs on the whereabouts of the President and his 16 successors. FEMA also is responsible for briefing Presidential successors on plans for their dispersal during attack and on procedures for reporting their locations at all times. It is charged by Congress with carrying out drills of the Presidential Successor Dispersal Plans four times a year and for testing the central locator system. Each year it conducts two joint Presidential and Presidential Successor Emergency Support Exercises, in which both the locator systems and plans for evacuation of command authorities go through a trial run. FEMA continues to test and develop the Joint Emergency Evacuation Plan (JEEP) to provide for emergency dispersal of several thousand senior government officials.

One potential problem, however, is that the agency and much of its system of communications may be as vulnerable to nuclear decapitation as the rest of the U.S. government. FEMA headquarters is in downtown Washington, just a dozen blocks from the White House and well within the lethal radius of any thermonuclear weapon exploded over the capital.

Even if the FEMA central locator and authenticator system worked perfectly, however, and even if several Presidential successors survived, they might be ill-suited to take command of an America reeling from a nuclear attack and of military forces engaged in the conflict. How many U.S. Cabinet members know the first thing about national security and military affairs? How many have any notion about the forces at hand, and the means needed to terminate or prosecute the conflict in a manner that would salvage the most for the United States?

At a time when the United States government and the nation's people would require strong and decisive leadership, a successor who might be virtually unknown to the public would be groping for solutions to problems he or she had never been prepared to solve. One can imagine a U.S. government on Day Two of World War III headed by [the] Secretary of Labor (successor No. 11), or by [the] Secretary of Education (successor No. 16). The problems of directing the war could be compounded by the deaths of the Joint Chiefs of Staff, the elimination of the Pentagon and all high Defense Department officials, and the destruction of Strategic Air Command headquarters (SAC) near Omaha and the North American Defense headquarters (NORAD) inside Cheyenne Mountain near Colorado Springs.

The nightmares of those concerned with National Command Authority protection are likely to reach a peak on certain key days of the political calendar: during a Presidential Inauguration, for example, or when the President delivers his State of the Union Message to a joint session of Congress. Not only are virtually all the NCA and their successors present in Washington on those occasions, but they are usually concentrated in the same place or in a single building.

Of course, the Russians have the same problems in defending their top command. Decapitation of the Soviet leadership is theoretically possible every time the Politburo assembles in a meeting or ceremony. May Day in Moscow, when the Kremlin's leaders watch from the same reviewing stand, is a potential decapitation day. Just as Soviet submarines off the Atlantic coastline threaten U.S. leaders in Washington, so too can Poseidon submarines operating in European waters launch missiles that within minutes can destroy Red Square or the Kremlin Palace. In nuclear arms negotiations, both sides should consider agreeing to a mutual redeployment of weapons that would take their two capitals out of range for a decapitation attack.

Fortunately, a bolt-from-the-blue Soviet nuclear attack is unlikely. First, a crisis or escalating conventional conflict in some region of the world is the most likely scenario for such a risky attack. Second, the Soviet rocket forces, ballistic-missile submarines, and strategic bombers could not be brought to full readiness for attack without first giving a warning to the United States. Given their uncertainties about whether they could decapitate the U.S. government, and their inability to know what action U.S. military leaders might take if our top political leaders were killed, the Russians would have to be mad to order a strike on Washington without also trying to destroy our nuclear retaliatory forces. The Soviet action of bringing their forces to full alert could provide strategic warning to U.S. leaders prior to an attack.

To avoid the threat of decapitation, the U.S. government plans to evacuate the National Command Authorities from Washington to National Emergency Airborne Command Post aircraft and to 96 hardened command bunkers in the Federal Relocation Arc, 50 or more miles outside of the city. The 96 hardened command centers are scattered around the countryside and include sites in North Carolina, West Virginia, Virginia, Maryland, Pennsylvania and the District of Columbia.

Survival of our top officials depends upon their ability to rendezvous with the National Emergency Airborne Command Post and to take off by the time

Soviet warheads hit Washington. The NEACP is based at Andrews Air Force Base, about 10 miles east of the White House, although the command authorities could also rendezvous with the aircraft at a number of other designated sites in the Eastern United States.

The President presumably would be transported to the rendezvous point by the Crown helicopter. Timing could be crucial if the crisis is sudden and there has been little advance warning. To fly from the White House to Andrews would take about eight minutes; it might be twice that before the President was safely aloft in the NEACP and away from the D.C. area.

During the "Ivy League" dispersion drill run in March 1982, President Reagan elected to stay in the White House and to send Vice President Bush aloft in NEACP. Earlier, President Carter also decided that in a crisis he would remain in the White House, and his National Security Adviser, Zbigniew Brzezinski, elected to do the same. Instead, Vice President Mondale and the Deputy Assistant for National Security, David Aaron, were designated for travel aloft in NEACP aircraft. In his recent book, *Power and Principle: Memoirs of the National Security Adviser 1977–1981*, Brzezinski related how his career (and life) almost came to an abrupt end on the evening of January 28, 1977, when he decided to test the Presidential emergency evacuation procedures:

> I called in the person responsible for evacuating the President in the event of a crisis. I obtained a detailed account on how long it actually would take to evacuate the President by helicopter. . . . I ordered him to run a simulated evacuation right now, turning on my stopwatch. The poor fellow's eyes . . . practically popped: He looked so surprised. He said, "Right now?" And I said, "Yes, right now." He reached for the phone and could hardly speak coherently when he demanded that the helicopter immediately come for a drill. I took one of the secretaries . . . along to simulate Mrs. Carter, and we proceeded to the South Lawn to wait for the helicopter to arrive. It took roughly two and a half times as long to arrive as it was supposed to. We then flew to a special site from where another evacuation procedure would be followed. To make a long story short, the whole thing took roughly twice as long as it should have. Moreover, on our return we found that the drill somehow did not take into account the protective service and we were almost shot down.

The U.S. government has relocation plans for several thousand top officials who are considered vital to the continuity of government in a national emergency. All will be evacuated to sites in the Federal Relocation Arc or sent aloft in aircraft.

The most important alternative U.S. headquarters is the "underground White House," which is situated inside Raven Rock Mountain in Pennsylvania about 65 miles northwest of Washington and just five miles north of Camp David. This location is the home of the Alternative National Military Command Center and is equipped to house the President and other members of the National Command Authority. In the largest evacuation exercise to date, President Dwight Eisenhower and 1,500 top Federal officials moved the seat of power from Washington to Raven Rock Mountain for three days in 1955. In the same exercise, 13,500 other officials were dispersed to 30 different secret locations in the Arc.

Another important relocation center is a man-made cavern within Mount Weather, situated 50 miles northwest of Washington, just outside Bluemont, Virginia, along the Appalachian Trail. The official name for this command post is the Western Virginia Office of Controlled Conflict Operations.

Inside the mountain is a small city of multistoried buildings, including offices, apartments, dormitories, streets, sidewalks, cafeterias, hospitals, power plants, and a water purifying plant. This subterranean wartime capital is the product of 21 years of demolition, mining, excavation, and building by the U.S. Army Corps of Engineers. The Mount Weather complex contains detailed plans for running and rebuilding the U.S. economy and society, and for reconstituting the U.S. government in wartime conditions.

The sites of Federal Relocation Centers are probably well known to Soviet war planners. Most were built before the Soviet Union had installed its very accurate fourth generation of intercontinental ballistic missiles. Now, Soviet SS-17s, SS-18s and SS-19s are capable of destroying virtually any hardened bunker. With the size and accuracy of these Soviet weapons, the military command posts at Raven Rock Mountain and Mount Weather could be reduced to radioactive ruins within a half hour.

Speaking of the Federal Relocation Centers, Bardyl Tirana, former head of the Defense Civil Preparedness Agency (now part of FEMA), has said, "You know where they are. Presumably if you do, the Soviet Union does. It's the last place I'd want to be."

If dispersion to fixed, hardened sites can no longer protect U.S. leaders from nuclear decapitation, airborne mobility at least provides a solution for the first 72 hours. With aerial refueling, the E4 evacuation aircraft need not land for three days.

But a decapitation attack does not have to kill the U.S. President and his successors to be effective. It must only sever the President's communication lines with the U.S. military and the rest of the government. As General Curtis LeMay, former head of the Strategic Air Command, used to say, "Without communications, the only thing I command is my desk." The same is true of the President or any National Command Authority. A Carnegie Institute for International Peace study recently noted:

> Strategic command, control, communications and intelligence is often characterized as the "weakest link" in America's deterrent against Soviet attack. . . . Most experts say that major portions of the strategic C^3I system have been vulnerable for some time and that survivability of C^3I as a system sufficient to support our declared strategic nuclear policies is far more doubtful than is the survivability of the forces. At the same time that the C^3I system has been recognized as vulnerable to Soviet attack, shifts in American strategic nuclear doctrine have placed greater demands upon it. The challenge is not so much to transmit a single order for all-out attack— though some question even that—as to provide the endurance necessary for a controlled and flexible response.

John Steinbruner, director of foreign policy studies at the Brookings Institution, states the C³I vulnerability problem in stark terms:

> ... The United States does not have a strategic command system that could survive deliberate attack of a sort that the Soviet Union could readily undertake. Fewer than 100 judiciously targeted nuclear weapons could so severely damage U.S. communications facilities and command centers that form the military chain of command that the actions of individual weapons commanders could no longer be controlled or coordinated. Some bomber crews, submarine officers, and ICMB silo launch officers could undertake very damaging retaliation and hence continue to pose a deterrence threat. Nonetheless, even 50 nuclear weapons are probably sufficient to eliminate the ability to direct U.S. strategic forces to coherent purposes.

The C³I network has been neglected, partly because nuclear-weapons effects, notably from radiation, are not completely understood or easily calculated, and partly because protecting the network is both difficult and expensive. The present network was built ad hoc, piece by piece, each part tailored for a specific purpose, but without an authoritative provision for their overall coherent interaction.

The President and the strategic forces might be easier to protect than many of the links in the communications system. Early-warning radars, telephone lines, cables, relay stations, telephone exchanges, transmitters, receivers, and antennae are fixed, soft targets that cannot easily be moved. Some elements of the U.S. C³I system can be dispersed and made mobile, but nearly all are vulnerable to different types of interruption, destruction, and interference. And, as Desmond Ball, an Australian command-control analyst, noted in a recent study published by the London-based International Institute for Strategic Studies: "There will always be some critical nodal points—e.g., where communication links connect to the command posts and, most especially, where the chain of command and control originates at the national command level—which can neither be hardened nor duplicated. It is axiomatic that the chain of command is only as strong as its weakest link."

The C³I network is vulnerable to nuclear blast, heat, and radiation effects, as well as attack by conventional weapons and sabotage. High-altitude nuclear explosions can block out radars, interfere with radio transmission, and short out electrical circuitry. A nuclear explosion emits an electromagnetic pulse (EMP), a large pulse of energy that can create chaos in a C³I system. It can overload power lines, burn out telephone lines, short-circuit microprocessors, and render buried cables ineffective transmitters of messages. The new microchip semiconductors used in all kinds of mechanical, electrical, and communications devices are a million times more vulnerable to electromagnetic pulse than the older vacuum tubes that they have been replacing. EMP could erase computer memories and even change missile flight trajectories by altering internal missile electrical functions. EMP could also create power outages all over the U.S.

According to Daniel L. Stein, professor of physics at Princeton University: "A [one megaton] detonation at 500 kilometers above the central continental

United States will effectively blanket the entire country, as well as parts of Canada and Mexico." Aside from military effects, Stein fears EMP from just a few detonations could cause a coast-to-coast power shutdown in the U.S.

At present, only one of the four National Emergency Airborne Command Post aircraft is hardened against EMP effects, although money [has been] requested and spent to harden the others. Certainly the "Crown Helo" and even the NEACP might not withstand the EMP effects of nuclear detonations. Both types of aircraft are hardened by insulating wiring and sealing cracks that would otherwise permit entry of the EMP voltage. U.S. aircraft and weapons have been tested on an EMP simulator at Kirtland Air Force Base for their ability to withstand an electromagnetic pulse of 50,000 volts per meter. According to one report, even EMP-hardened systems might not survive.

The technical community is divided on this issue. "Some French physicists, among others, envision a pulse of about 100,000 volts per meter," writes science journalist William Broad. "If they are correct, the normal protections the Pentagon has tried to build into communications networks, missiles, aircraft, radars and radios would almost certainly be useless." If overloaded by the EMP pulse, NEACP could be disabled and might fall to the earth like a stone, with the President and his battle staff aboard.

EMP could have other impacts on U.S. C^3 aircraft. The so-called Take Charge and Move Out aircraft (TACAMO) used to relay the go-to-war message to U.S. ballistic-missile submarines are not yet EMP-hardened and just might be silenced in wartime before they could communicate the emergency action message to the submarine fleet.

Looking Glass, an airborne SAC EC-135 aircraft, is another important link between U.S. ICBM forces and the National Command Authority. This airborne post would operate as Strategic Airborne Command headquarters in the likely event that the ground-based SAC headquarters is destroyed in the attack. The importance of *Looking Glass* was illustrated by testimony by the late General John C. Meyers, former SAC Commander, who declared: "If SAC funding is reduced to the level that we can only keep one airplane flying, that plane will be the *Looking Glass*."

Unfortunately, *Looking Glass* could be vulnerable to EMP effects, too. So might other C^3I aircraft, such as planes of the Post-Attack Command and Control System (PACCS), which operate mainly out of Offutt Air Force Base and have maintained a constant airborne patrol over the past 22 years. These aircraft act as alternative command centers for SAC bombers and missile forces.

A U.S. nuclear test in the earth's atmosphere in 1962, code-named Starfish Prime, vividly demonstrated the effects of EMP on electronic circuits. In the test, a missile-borne package was launched from Johnston Atoll in the South Pacific, 820 miles southwest of Hawaii, and exploded 248 miles above the Earth's surface. EMP pulses traveling at the speed of light short-circuited 300 streetlights, disabled numerous power lines, and blew out other electric circuits on Oahu. The EMP pulse disrupted communications throughout Honolulu.

The Limited Test Ban Treaty in 1963 put an end to atmospheric nuclear tests before military physicists could explain the havoc created by EMP in Hawaii. Subsequent underground tests indicated the EMP problem was even worse than originally feared. More recently, the spread of solid-state integrated circuits has served to compound the danger.

The introduction of fiber optics to replace current materials is possibly the most effective means of blocking EMP pulses, since glass fibers do not pick up EMP or conduct electricity. But unless the entire U.S. C³I system could be so revised (at a prohibitive cost), the EMP danger will remain with us.

Ironically, the C³I vulnerability of U.S. and Soviet forces is a great equalizer. Both societies and both command networks are extremely vulnerable to disruption caused by just a few well-placed nuclear weapons.

As John Steinbruner of the Brookings Institution has noted: "The substantial superiority, for example, that the United States believed it possessed in the 1960s was sharply mitigated in reality by command vulnerability, which was particularly acute at the time. The then numerically and technically inferior Soviet forces could have done far more damage with judicious targeting than was ever acknowledged in official U.S. public reviews of the strategic situation.

"U.S. forces have always been seriously vulnerable to an initial attack, and the 1980s will not produce unusual dangers in this regard, as is often alleged."

The danger of decapitation attacks would seem to make a mockery of the idea of fighting limited nuclear wars, or protracted nuclear wars. Even if U.S. leaders somehow survived a first-wave Soviet attack, our command-control network is so perishable in a nuclear environment that a slow, tit-for-tat "walk" up and down the escalation ladder seems unlikely.

Such a conclusion belies . . . official thinking that nuclear war might be kept limited, and that it might be winnable. For a graduated response to nuclear attack implies the survival of a communications-intelligence network to measure the precise response to each escalation. As one observer has concluded: ". . . the number of missiles launched in an attack must be determined immediately, damage assessment must occur within hours, and communications between warring parties must survive the initial strike."

The C³I technology simply is not there, nor will it likely be there even after the United States spends the planned $60 billion on modernizing the network [by the 1990s]. The problems of adequately protecting the network and the leadership simply dwarf the available near-term solutions.

"The kinds of controlled nuclear options to which we're moving presume communication with the Soviet Union," notes Lt. General Brent Scowcroft, former National Security Adviser to President Ford. "And yet, from a military point of view, one of the most effective kinds of attack is against leadership and command and control systems."

Unfortunately, these vulnerabilities undermine our ability to deter war by less than all-out nuclear retaliation in the first minutes of attack.

The vulnerability on both sides after such an exchange of nuclear fusillades might preclude calling off the conflict. Indeed, negotiations to halt the slaughter might be impossible until both sides had expended their nuclear forces in a terrible agony of blow and counterblow. Once begun, a nuclear exchange between the superpowers is likely to be massive and virtually uncontrollable.

29 SOVIET CIVIL DEFENSE: STRATEGIC IMPLICATIONS, PRACTICAL PROBLEMS

John M. Weinstein

The cumulative effect of the massive expansion and modernization of the strategic and conventional forces of the Soviet Union has caused many to reevaluate the strategic balance between the superpowers. Specifically, there has been substantial concern about the Soviet development of a potent first-strike capability. This assessment, arrived at by the last two US administrations, reflects a number of technological improvements in the Soviet Strategic Rocket Forces (SRF) which appear ominous in light of Soviet strategic operational employment plans which stress seizing the strategic initiative through preemptive attacks against American ICBM launch silos, launch control facilities, support and maintenance facilities, strategic bomber bases, submarine berths and loading facilities, and nuclear storage and production facilities.

Within this context, a number of civilian and military analysts take a particular[ly] ominous view of the Soviet Union's long-standing attention to civil defense. In light of America's inattention to civil defense since the aftermath of the Cuban missile crisis, numerous implications have been drawn from alleged Soviet plans and capabilities to undertake crisis relocation of urban populations, to disperse and harden industry, and to achieve rapid postattack recovery. Most serious among these implications is the potential effect of Soviet civil defense capabilities upon the real or perceived stability of deterrence. Specifically, some contend that the Soviet civil defense program threatens deterrence by upsetting the balance of mutual population vulnerability if, under certain conditions, Soviet civil defense measures might limit their fatalities to the low "tens of millions." According to congressional testimony in 1982, significant asymmetries exist in the number of US and Soviet fatalities that would occur in several nuclear warfighting scenarios. In most scenarios, the percentage of American casualties is double that of the Soviet Union and in an all-out Soviet attack upon the US population and its counterforce, military and economic targets, American fatalities might range as high as 88 percent of the population.

Furthermore, it is frequently argued that Soviet civil defense capabilities could threaten deterrence stability to the degree that they protect that country's economic power and recovery prospects relative to those of the United

302

States. Such projected asymmetries are destabilizing because they suggest that under certain circumstances, the Soviet Union might emerge from a nuclear war in a better position than that of the United States. If the Soviet Union were to perceive nuclear war as potentially less costly and, thus, less frightening, they might feel more inclined in a crisis to launch a preemptive strike against the United States.

This essay will examine the effectiveness of the Soviet civil defense program, selected Soviet strategic vulnerabilities, and Soviet views of deterrence. The impact of the Chernobyl nuclear accident in April 1986 will also be discussed.

SOVIET CIVIL DEFENSE: PLANS AND PROBLEMS

Population Protection

Protection of leadership is considered of paramount importance to Soviet civil defense planners. The CIA has noted that sufficient blast-resistant shelter space exists to protect approximately 110,000 Soviet government and Party officials at all levels. More recently, the Department of Defense determined that the few most critical of these facilities were deeply buried and highly survivable.[1] A second priority is the protection of workers at essential industrial installations. By current estimates, the Soviet Union has shelter space for 24–48 percent of the essential work force or 12 to 24 percent of the total work force that would be left behind in the event of crisis evacuation. Those most concerned about the estimated Soviet ability to protect much of their critical political and industrial populace point to several disquieting ramifications. First, while conceding the US ability to destroy shelters which are targeted directly, these shelters must first be identified, hardly an easy or assured task for intelligence. Second, the destruction of these shelters would require continued survival and connectivity of US strategic communications and missile installations as well as the expenditure of a disproportionately large percentage of land-based, hard target-killing warheads on these targets. Third, the survival of the Soviet political and military command and control systems might provide a capability to fight a protracted nuclear war designed to outlast the US adversary. Finally, the survival of key political and industrial cadres would facilitate rapid economic reconstruction vis-à-vis the United States.

Those who question the potential adverse impact of Soviet shelter capabilities counter with several points. Generally, they wonder how a complex society would be able to survive the total devastation of nuclear war—even if one were willing to grant the survival of some proportion of the national leadership *and* an intact command and control system. Does life go on if the "head" survives but the body receives a lethal blow? Beyond this, the actual capabilities of the Soviet civil defense system, such as available shelter space, are open to question. The CIA estimates that the space available for each person in a shelter would be only one-half to one square meter. This space allotment is inadequate according to most analyses of long-term survival requirements. In addition, the Oak Ridge Laboratories maintain that the shelters' ventilation systems are their most vulnerable aspect and that, even if a shelter were not destroyed by a nuclear blast, its inhabitants would risk suffocation and death from asphyxiation or heat exposure. Starvation also would prove to be a severe problem if shelter were required for more than a few days. Chronic Soviet food shortages make it unlikely that the Soviet Union would prestock shelters for more than a few days during peacetime. Furthermore, normal food distribution snarls, and the fact that Soviet citizens buy their food from day to day, are likely to prevent many from bringing additional supplies of food and water to the shelter. Even Deputy Under Secretary of Defense for Strategic and Theater Nuclear Forces, T. K. Jones, an analyst who has written extensively on the dangerous implications of Soviet civil defense capabilities, concedes that inplace urban shelters "could not help much against a US attack designed to destroy populations." Thus, it is argued that the Soviet Union is likely to harbor few illusions about the potential success of its civil defense programs in a nuclear war with the United States. Furthermore, since urban shelters are not in place to protect the average Soviet citizen (assigned the lowest priority in the Soviet civil defense program), such citizens would be forced to build expedient shelters using "handy" materials and tools such as bricks, timber, boards, and shovels. Their plight would be compounded at night, during autumn when the ground is muddy, or winter when the ground is frozen, or during spring and summer when foodstuffs are depleted.

Finally, Leon Goure, author of numerous articles and studies of Soviet civil defense, described elaborate Soviet evacuation plans that are to be carried out by the urban populace within 72 hours after an evacuation order is issued. However, those who question the potential value of such an evacuation point out that the Soviet Union has never practiced full-scale evacuation of a major city; used more than one mode of transportation in their limited practice; conducted a drill without a long period of preparation; or carried out several evacuation exercises simultaneously.

The Soviet road network is one of the country's major strategic vulnerabilities. Because it has been constructed to accommodate travel within that country's cities, it would be hard pressed to support mass exoduses by motor transport or by foot from these cities. One report states that:

> [The Soviet Union] lacks a developed highway system to connect the outlying regions to its industrial hub. Less than 250,000 miles of paved roads exist in the entire nation. No two Soviet cities are connected by a divided highway. . . . In addition, Soviet severe weather conditions hamper what possible road travel exists. During the winter, spring thaw periods, and autumn rainy seasons, Soviet roads are virtually impassable. The Soviets describe their situation as *Rasputitsa* or roadlessness during those months.[2]

In addition to motor transport, Soviet evacuation plans depend heavily on railroads. Most railroads in the Soviet Union, however, are single track. To evacuate large cities by rail transportation, the Soviet Union would have to arrange that the trains were in their assigned evacuation locations and that they were not loaded with freight or allocated to carry troops or supplies to Eastern Europe. That so many logistical problems would be handled by a country whose transportation system is inefficient, at best, during calm and peaceful times is questionable.

Moreover, since most Soviet citizens do not have automobiles, Soviet evacuation plans also call for some 17 million urban residents to walk 30 miles (1.5 mph for 20 hours) and then build expedient protection. How the very young, the very old, and the sick are to make such formidable progress (while carrying two weeks' worth of food, water, and supplies) is not clear. Furthermore, how evacuees in expedient shelters would survive the higher levels of radioactive fallout that would result if the US retaliatory strike included ground bursts is unclear and is seldom addressed by those who assert the effectiveness of Soviet civil defense.

The Soviet urban population, largely an apartment society, is more highly concentrated than the American urban population. This heavy concentration of urban citizens results in certain obstacles to successful evacuation. For instance, Moscow is surrounded on all sides by satellite industrial centers, and Leningrad is similarly bordered on three sides and by water on the fourth. Citizens from these population centers would face major problems evacuating to rural reception centers or areas suitable for the construction of expedient shelters.

Even if one disregards the logistical problems that would attend a decision to evacuate Soviet cities and assumes that such a momentous exodus could be executed, the Soviet Union would still face a major strategic dilemma. The declaratory policy of the United States eschews the targeting of the Soviet population *per se*. Within this context, one may wonder what impact from a Soviet perspective the evacuation of its citizens would have on deterring an American retaliatory strike. Civilian evacuation serves certain humanitarian goals, but it has little effect upon the US ability to destroy critical Soviet military, industrial, and economic targets. The destruction of Soviet civilians would be an unintended effect of US plans to destroy Soviet military and economic infrastructures under certain retaliation scenarios. It could even be argued that the successful evacuation and survival of the Soviet Union's civilian population might prove detrimental to the country's long-term prospects for recovery. In the aftermath of a US retaliatory strike, one may wonder how the Soviet leadership plans to care for two hundred million survivors with the devastation of its economic, agricultural, medical, and transportation infrastructures.

With "strangelovian" logic, one could argue that rapid recovery indeed might be more expeditious and effective with fewer rather than more survivors to drain scarce recovery matériel. The crucial element of civil defense revolves, then, around the ability of the Soviet Union to protect its economy and sustain survivors of a nuclear war.

The Protection of Soviet Industry

Traditionally, Soviet leadership has sought to protect their industry by two means: geographical dispersal and hardening against nuclear attack. Little is debated about the effectiveness of Soviet programs to protect their industry from the primary and collateral effects of a nuclear attack by means of the former. More debate has concerned the effectiveness and implications of Soviet efforts to harden their industrial installations. The Soviet leadership has opted for low-cost means of protecting vital equipment from secondary damage of nuclear explosives. These "engineering-technical" measures include rapid shutdown of equipment for protection against electromagnetic pulse; the use of expedient protective devices (e.g., wooden and metal bracing, covering equipment with sandbags, and the like), acknowledged by the US Arms Control and Disarmament Agency (ACDA) as effective in areas on the periphery of a nuclear blast; contamination protection, and the protection of raw material supplies through underground storage. In a two-year study of the effectiveness of Soviet expedient measures, T. K. Jones concluded: "Russian methods could protect machinery within the three-day warning that would be provided by a Soviet evacuation. A full scale attack could be absorbed and production could renew in four to twelve weeks."[3] Such projections take on chilling importance if one posits that a Soviet preemptive strike knocked out as much as 90 percent of the accurate land-based US missiles, leaving the United States with less accurate SLBMs and a bomber fleet which will confront increasingly sophisticated air defenses to deliver the retaliatory strike. In such a scenario, the relatively limited destructiveness of the US response might seem tolerable to Soviet military planners.

Critics respond that a substantial gap exists between the theoretical and actual abilities to mount a successful first strike. They maintain that the Soviet leaders, who are normally cautious in military operations, would be loathe to gamble the survival of their state on the many unknown parameters relating to the coordination, timing, effects and consequences of so precipitous an action as a nuclear strike against the United States.

These same critics also point to the inability of the Soviet Union to harden many of the critical industries upon which their fragile economy and continued superpower status depend. These vulnerable industries include oil refineries; power plants; chemical storage plants; steel mills; pharmaceutical laboratories; component assembly factories; major truck, tractor, and rolling-stock plants; railheads and marshaling yards; major surface transshipment points and highway intersections; and pipelines. Because these targets cannot be hardened and their destruction does not require the pinpoint accuracy of ICBMs, they remain vulnerable to a US retaliatory strike.

Third, these critics focus upon the observation that after absorbing a first strike, the United States would be able to hit only a "few thousand aim points," precluding the infliction of unacceptable damage on the Soviet Union. Critics committed to an assured destruction philosophy contend that Soviet industry (50 percent of which is contained in 200 complexes) and the transportation and power infrastructure that support it are so concentrated in a narrow crescent stretching from Leningrad through Moscow, Sverdlovsk, Omsk, Novosibirsk and to Irkutsk that the United States would not require many weapons to achieve its Soviet industrial damage requirements. Geoffrey Kemp[4] and Richard Garwin,[5] both prominent students of strategic studies, maintain respectively that as few as seven Poseidon submarines (one-third of the number normally on station at sea) could destroy 61 percent of the Soviet industrial base and that, even if only 10 percent of US ICBMs survived a Soviet preemptive strike, those 100–110 missiles could be retargeted (assuming the survival of American C^3 facilities) to deliver unacceptable damage to the Soviet Union. An ACDA estimate that recognizes the need for no more than 1300 warheads to destroy 70 percent of Soviet industry is consistent with these estimates.

Finally, and most crucial, is that even if the Soviet Union can protect individual pieces of industrial equipment from proximate nuclear detonations, it does not follow that the resumption of industrial production will be a near-term proposition. Industrial reconstitution and recovery will be hampered by a number of factors. For instance, how will production be resumed if the electrical infrastructure and available supplies of and transmission lines for diesel fuel, gasoline and petroleum are destroyed? How will industrial activity and recovery be realized if stocks of raw materials and the six rail transshipment points which load 80 percent of all empty railcars and are critical to the Soviet industrial supply and distribution are destroyed also? How will workers deal with residual radiation in targeted areas, especially in the absence of easy access to medical personnel and supplies? And who will feed, clothe and shelter workers and protect their equipment during the recovery phase?

Postattack Recovery

[In the absence of] effective protection measures, the significant and vulnerable concentration of Soviet industry makes T. K. Jones' prediction that the Soviet Union could recover "within no more than 2 to 4 years from a US nuclear retaliatory attack"[6] appear optimistic at best.

The psychological condition of the survivors is critically important for postattack recovery. Yet those who examine nuclear attack/recovery scenarios say little about this variable, implicitly assuming that as a result of their civil defense training, (1) the survivors of Armageddon would calmly set about postattack reconstruction in a disciplined and effective manner; and (2) that the termination of the nuclear crisis and threat of continued exchanges would be unambiguous and evacuees would willingly return to their homes to aid their fellow citizens and begin reconstruction.

Such discipline and cooperative effort may not occur in the aftermath of nuclear war. The reactions of the survivors of Hiroshima and Nagasaki offer a limited, though imperfect, insight into what might be expected in the aftermath of a Soviet-American nuclear exchange. They expected that they were about to die. As a means of protection from the grotesque scenes around them, they closed their minds to the ubiquitous horror. This psychic numbing, causing profound blandness and insensitivity to the surrounding suffering, was temporary and dissipated as the outside world responded with aid to the victims of the disaster. A nuclear war, however, would result in unprecedented destruction and limit the amount of aid available from the "outside," especially if the war were massive in nature. Robert J. Lifton, a noted psychiatrist who has written extensively on the subject, concludes that the devastation that would attend a nuclear exchange would probably give rise to such extreme psychic numbing as described above that its effects would be irreversible.[7]

According to Lifton, a major consequence of psychic shock could be the inability of the survivors to gather food, to bury their own dead, and perform other basic social rituals. Their behavior could be characterized by extreme suspiciousness and primitive forms of thought. Furthermore, Lifton argues that those from unscathed regions may not be willing to aid the survivors and share their horror. In light of these considerations, the prospects for the assured and disciplined recovery posited by Jones and others appear less certain.

Recovery from a nuclear attack depends heavily on the capability to rescue, feed, and care for the survivors and on the capability to provide repair parts and energy for capital reconstruction. Under certain strategic exchange scenarios Soviet recovery efforts would be hampered severely by numerous obstacles. Massive urban areas could be too "hot"—too radioactive—to enter for several months. Depending upon the profile and scale of a US retaliatory strike, radiation sickness could be widespread, with 80 percent of the Soviet population, including the evacuees, having been exposed to at least 100 roentgens of radioactivity. In light of the coincidence of Soviet major food producing regions and its ICBM fields which would surely be targeted in a counterforce scenario, food would be in short supply. Half of the country's grazing livestock would be dead and, if the attack occurred during the growing season, 30 percent of all crops would be destroyed. Attempts to distribute surviving foodstuffs from farms and emergency storage sites could be delayed for several months, and this estimate is probably optimistic since the Soviet Union's 28 ICBM installations are interspersed throughout the heart of the rail network (see Figure 29-1). The ozone layer might be so depleted that outdoor activity beyond 30 minutes in duration would be hazardous for several years. As much as 80 percent of all medical personnel, supplies, and hospitals are

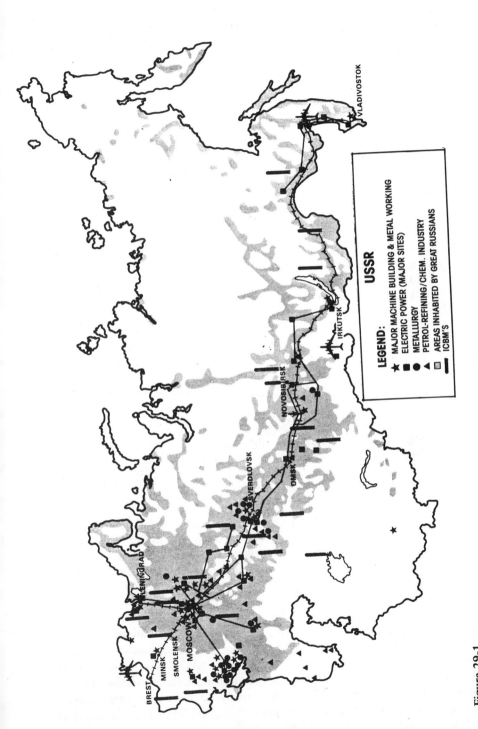

Figure 29-1

Source: Central Intelligence Agency, "USSR Summary Map," Department of Defense, *Soviet Military Power* (Washington, D.C.: U.S. Government Printing Office, 1983).

likely to be destroyed. And, of course, a host of social and psychological problems would ensue.

The most critical obstacle that would hamper Soviet efforts to achieve postwar recovery relates to command and control (C^2). The pace and extent of recovery will depend heavily upon the ability of the national and regional political and party leaders to establish a consensus on national priorities, communicate their directives, and coordinate matériel supply and human effort. These recovery requisites, however, are likely to be affected adversely by the multinational nature of the Soviet society and the potential fragility of the various infrastructures of control. While many analysts have described (1) the polyglot composition of the Soviet Union; (2) the declining percentage of Great Russians and ethnic Slavs in the population relative to the rapidly increasing numbers of Moslems and Central Asians (who traditionally have resisted incorporation into the Russian empire); and (3) the ominous economic and political consequences of these developments for the Soviet policy, relatively few have recognized the Soviet state as multinational when the discussion turns to the matter of strategic deterrence and the requisites of postattack recovery. Indeed this consideration is paramount in Soviet strategic calculations. Recognizing the geographical coincidence of the majority of ICBM fields, key industrial installations and rail lines, and Great Russian population concentrations in a narrow Leningrad to Irkutsk crescent (see Figure III-3), even a limited American counterforce strike against the Soviet Union's missile and C^3 installations would affect most seriously the Great Russians who would perish in numbers disproportionately higher than their rapidly declining percentage of the total population. Whether they would be able to maintain control of the vast governmental, Communist Party, educational, and military hierarchies is questionable. Nuclear war might well usher in the decline of the Soviet empire in light of the current American interest in retaliatory targeting of the Russian dominated infrastructures of political and ethnic control, communication, and transportation in various escalation scenarios.

Even if one assumes that the Soviet infrastructure of political control remained intact in the aftermath of a nuclear strike, it would still have to confront the problem of economic recovery. During this period of incapacitation, could the Soviet leaders be confident that they could maintain the integrity of the Soviet Union? Is it likely that the Soviet-Moslem population might reaffirm religious and territorial ties to a Pan-Moslem movement? Would the nationalists in the Ukraine or the Baltic republics attempt to secede? And would the Russians have the wherewithal to prevent such centrifugal forces? Finally, would the East Europeans be inclined to maintain their political and economic ties to the Soviet Union? Assumptions and the role of uncertainty play heavily on the calculus of deterrence and one cannot be certain of the way leaders in the Kremlin arrive at their strategic estimates.

It is quite possible that, given the priority placed upon leadership survival in Soviet civil defense plans, the Russian leadership may view its own survival as a sufficient objective in its own right. If, however, the Russian leaders entertain uncertainties such as those described above, and in my opinion they do, and if they view civil defense as having a limited mitigating effect upon the problems outlined above, nuclear war necessarily would be viewed as counterproductive to their most basic national interests: the survival and integrity of the Soviet state, its rapid reconstitution and continuation of superpower status.

SOVIET CIVIL DEFENSE: IN SEARCH OF A BOTTOM LINE

The essential debate surrounding the Soviet civil defense program is the extent to which Soviet plans and goals could be translated into damage-limiting benefits in an actual nuclear exchange with the United States. Civil defense, though admittedly imperfect, takes on substantial weight when viewed as a component of a Soviet warfighting strategy that also emphasizes other damage-limiting expedients such as a first strike against US warmaking capabilities and active (e.g., air and antisatellite) defense against actual US retaliatory strikes. If not, why would the Soviet leaders continue to spend increasingly scarce defense rubles on a civil defense program they consider ineffective?

Skeptics of the Soviet civil defense program make several counterarguments. Civil defense spending, they argue, continues due to a number of extraneous factors, such as bureaucratic inertia, legitimizing the continuation of the garrison state, Leninist ideological imperatives, and so forth. Also, to the skeptics, either the devastation of limited war is so great as to render it indistinguishable from unlimited war or there is little chance that a limited war would remain limited. Therefore, they liken Soviet civil defense efforts to the uneasy whistling of a frightened stroller in a cemetery at midnight. Surely, they argue, the normally cautious Soviet leaders recognize (1) the numerous, uncontrollable and uncertain nature of nuclear war, (2) the likelihood that the US deterrent will remain credible into the 1990's, and (3) that nuclear war between the superpowers will be an unprecedented disaster for each combatant—his civil defense preparations notwithstanding.

LESSONS FROM CHERNOBYL: A POSTSCRIPT

The Chernobyl disaster mobilized a large segment of the Soviet civil defense system and provided a rare opportunity to assess its capabilities. While tragic in every regard, Chernobyl was far less demanding or horrific than widespread nuclear war; outside help, such as Kievian transportation assets, was available, and the weather was quite mild.

About a quarter of all military air defense troops were mobilized to deal with the Chernobyl disaster, which obviously would pale to insignificance [compared with] the destruction and carnage of nuclear war. Nonetheless, the Kremlin was appalled at the system's dismal performance. The Red Army newspaper chastised the "lackadaisical" attitudes of civil defense officials and personnel who skipped requisite training; poor civil-military coordination and grossly inadequate medical procedures and supplies were also evident. Eventually, General Altunin, who had directed the Soviet Union's civil defense efforts for more than a decade, was dismissed. The official line that the sixty-five-year-old general was being replaced due to old age was belied by the selection of a successor only four years his junior.

Many of the costs of Chernobyl will not be known for years. The financial and psychological burdens of permanently resettling 135,000 citizens; the massive amounts of concrete, labor, and other construction resources diverted from planned activities; the cordoning off of a 30-kilometer radius of the country's richest farmland around the site and the subsequent massive importation of food; and the long-term medical costs will doubtlessly soar to many billions of rubles.

Unanswered is the question of what the Soviets learned from Chernobyl. The accident clearly demonstrated that Soviet civil defenses, the billions of rubles already spent notwithstanding, would hardly mitigate the effects of hundreds, let alone thousands, of nuclear detonations. In this sense, the performance of the civil defense system seems to support the views of those who ascribe little importance to the existence of Soviet civil defenses in Soviet perceptions of the nuclear balance of terror. More importantly, Chernobyl demonstrated the inability of technology to eradicate human error, the fallibility of technology itself, and the great difficulty of coordinating complex, multidimensional tasks. The lessons are likely to be applied beyond civil defense itself. Indeed, any Soviets who might have entertained thoughts about the efficacy of nuclear warfighting, the feasibility of damage-limitation, or the calculability of a successful preemptive strike will find cause to reconsider.

NOTES

1. Central Intelligence Agency, *Soviet Civil Defense*, NI-78-1000 3, July 1978 (hereinafter referred to as CIA study), pp. 1–3; *Soviet Military Power: An Assessment of the Threat*, Washington, D.C.: Government Printing Office, 1988, pp. 59–62.

2. Keith A. Dunn, *Soviet Military Weaknesses and Vulnerabilities: A Critique of the Short War Advocates*, Strategic Issues Research Memorandum, Strategic Studies Institute, July 31, 1978, p. 12.

3. T. K. Jones and W. Scott Thompson, "Central War and Civil Defense," *Orbis*, Fall 1978, p. 699.

4. See Geoffrey Kemp, *Nuclear Forces for Medium Powers*, Part II, Adelphi Paper No. 107, International Institute for Strategic Studies, 1974, pp. 5, 9.

5. Richard Garwin, Testimony Before Joint Committee on Defense Production, *Civil Preparedness and Limited Nuclear War*, April 28, 1976, p. 55.

6. T. K. Jones, *Defense Industrial Base: Industrial Preparedness and Nuclear War Survival*, testimony before Joint Committee on Defense Production, Part 1, November 17, 1976, p. 84.

7. Robert J. Lifton and Kai Erikson, "Nuclear War's Effect on the Mind," *The New York Times*, March 15, 1982, p. A17.

30 SURVIVING NUCLEAR WAR: U.S. PLANS FOR CRISIS RELOCATION

LOUIS RENÉ BERES

Since 1950 the United States has spent $2.6 billion on civil defense. As part of its comprehensive plan for responding to the threat of a nuclear war, the Reagan administration . . . requested $4.2 billion in budget authority . . . to implement crisis relocation planning (CRP). This "enhanced" form of civil defense calls for the "temporary relocation" of approximately 150 million people from about 400 "high risk" metropolitan and defense-related areas to approximately 2,000 (allegedly) safer "host" areas when nuclear attack appears imminent. By relocating, the Federal Emergency Management Agency, the department charged with crisis response, claims we can double the number of Americans who could survive a nuclear war. FEMA estimates that about 40 percent of the population could survive in the absence of relocation; CRP is designed to raise the survival rate to 80 percent. In short, [Reagan administration] policy suggests that with CRP measures in place, a nuclear war would be survivable for most Americans. . . .

FEMA believes that the population at risk can be protected (1) by high-performance blast shelters in cities; or (2) by relocation (evacuation) to low-risk "host" areas. This assessment flows from the agency's overall plan for Nuclear Civil Protection (NCP), founded upon the two options. Yet, because of the estimated cost of blast shelters (about $70 billion) and also because it believes that "tens of millions can be saved by evacuation," FEMA seeks to achieve a "nationwide capability for crisis relocation," pursuant to policy enunciated in Presidential Directive (PD) 41 (September 1978).

Even under the heaviest possible attack, FEMA expects that "95 percent of our land would escape untouched, except possibly by radioactive fallout." If its assumptions are correct, the FEMA argument minimizes the effects of fallout and disregards long-term ecological effects. In fact, in another recent assessment of evacuation effectiveness, FEMA acknowledges that if the Soviet Union "were to mount an all-out attack on the United States with their present strategic forces, taking into account accuracy, reliability, and other factors, almost the whole population would be located less than 100 miles of at least one nuclear detonation." Indeed, about half of the U.S. population would be in areas experiencing at least "light damage" (overpressure greater than 1 psi).

Note: Some footnotes have been deleted, and others have been renumbered to appear in appropriate order.

Table 30-1. Military-Industrial Attacks*

Distance from Nearest Nuclear Weapons (in miles)	Fraction of Population (in percentages)
10	45
20	65
40	75
100	95
200	99

* According to FEMA calculations.

The significance, as FEMA recognizes, is that (1) virtually every American would be within range of potentially serious fallout radiation exposure, and (2) about half the population would be involved in direct weapons effects (see Table 30-1). . . .

Much of the . . . argument for improved U.S. civil defense . . . flows from the assumption that the Soviets have long been concerned with such defense in their military planning and that they could recover more easily than the United States from a nuclear war. Since Soviet civil defense measures, it is alleged, might limit its fatalities from a U.S. retaliation to the "low tens of millions," this could undermine deterrence by upsetting the balance of mutual population vulnerability. What this argument ignores is that a "rational" Soviet adversary—in deciding whether a first strike would be gainful—would . . . be unimpressed by a possible relative advantage: that it might emerge from a nuclear war in a better position than the United States. This decision would be based only on expectations of whether the result would entail unacceptable damage. Even if the U.S. population were perceived as substantially more vulnerable, a Soviet first strike, to be cost-effective, would always have to assume it would preclude an assuredly destructive U.S. reprisal. . . .

ADMINISTRATION PLANS TO INCREASE NUCLEAR WEAPONS

Our government has yet to admit to us, its citizens, that we are utterly defenseless against the effects of nuclear weapons. Reliable ballistic-missile defense has never existed, nor will it ever. Attempting to institute such defenses may be extraordinarily provocative, since it may encourage the Soviet Union to accelerate its offensive missile capabilities, and even to preempt in the near term. The United States, for its part, lulled into complacence by the delusion of defense, might abandon plans for arms control or even fulfill Soviet fears by preparing for an American first strike.

Our government has also not told us the whole truth about plans to enlarge the inventory of destabilizing nuclear weapons. During the [1990s], the United States plans to build about 17,000 more nuclear weapons. Spending on such weapons is going up much faster than overall military outlays. Under present plans, the United States has allocated $450 billion over the next six years [1986–1992] to prepare for nuclear war. These monies will be used to create threatening counterforce systems that will engender a corresponding Soviet buildup and undermine nuclear deterrence.

The MX

Consider the MX. In spite of an initial rationale of improving survivability of this country's ICBM force, these prompt hard-target kill weapons [have been] placed in existing Minuteman silos. Their only real purpose, therefore, would be in fulfilling counterforce mission objectives: to destroy Soviet nuclear weapons and control systems in the event of a nuclear conflict.

Nuclear war fighting, not survivability, is the true purpose of MX. The decision to deploy the new missiles in existing silos would degrade deterrence by occasioning a U.S. shift to "launch on warning" strategies—firing these weapons upon confirmed assault rather than upon actual attack absorption. With such strategies, this country's major nuclear forces—because of the "use them or lose them" calculation—might be launched before Soviet weapons actually struck. It follows that a predictable result of MX deployment would be a greatly heightened probability of accidental nuclear war or even a Soviet first strike. If the Soviets were to respond to American moves with their own launch-on-warning measures (possibly instigated by the hard-target, counter-silo qualities of the MX, as well as by the U.S. acceptance of launch on warning), this country's MX deployment might even raise the probability of a U.S. first strike. . . .

PLANS FOR CRISIS RELOCATION

A natural complement to the developing U.S. nuclear war-fighting strategy of deterrence, the Reagan plan for crisis relocation [was] founded upon the Carter administration's Presidential Directive 41. Issued 20 September 1978, PD-41 sought to improve deterrence by increasing the number of Americans who could survive a nuclear attack through evacuation. It was also intended to ensure greater continuity of government in the event that deterrence failed, an objective reinforced by PD-58 (August 1980) provisions outlining relocation plans for top federal officials during times of crisis.

There are, however, significant differences between the Carter and Reagan plans. With its National Security Decision Directive 26 in March 1982, the Reagan administration went far beyond PD-41 in terms of the scope and substance of U.S. civil defense. In contrast to PD-41, NSDD-26 represents a clear commitment to making nuclear war more "thinkable"; it calls for "the survival of a substantial portion of the American people in the event of a nuclear attack." In this connection, the Reagan directive [envisioned] survival in a "protracted" nuclear war. According to Louis Giuffrida, [former] FEMA director, "The other thing this administration has categorically rejected is the short-war, mutually assured destruction, it'll all be over in 20 minutes, so why the hell mess around spending dollars on it [sic]. We're trying to inject long-war mentality."

Whether the war will be long or short, FEMA officials assume the United States would have from three to seven days to evacuate its "high risk" areas during a period of rising international tensions. Discounting a surprise attack, this assumption stipulates Soviet conformance to this country's rules in beginning a nuclear war. This, however, is not informed by pertinent evidence. Nor is it consistent with Department of Defense (DoD) assumptions, since the Pentagon continues to base strategic requirements on expectation of a "no warning" attack. It is *this* expectation that provides the rationale for accelerated U.S. improvement and expansion of strategic forces.

Another . . . assumption underlying CRP is that a government-directed civilian evacuation plan in an imminent nuclear conflict would not degenerate into chaos. Analogizing CRP to movement in rush-hour traffic, FEMA says:

It is a difficult and complex problem requiring much planning, but it is possible. After all, we relocate millions of workers from our big cities every evening rush hour. We have moved hundreds of thousands to safety in time of hurricane or flood. And in a case like this, it could save as many as 100 million lives. It would be an orderly, controlled evacuation. Your own local authorities would give detailed instructions through radio, television and the press, telling you what necessities to take along, what arrangements have been made for transportation—by bus, train, or private car—where you will find safety in a small town or rural host area, and what routes to follow to get there.

Ignoring critical differences that exist between natural disasters and a nuclear attack, FEMA offers no factual evidence to back such plans. A report issued several years ago by the secretary-general of the United Nations assessed the relocation option:

Evacuation of population from areas expected to come under attack has to be planned very carefully in advance. Apart from transportation and housing of evacuees, this planning must include at least short-term provisions for the relocated population. Information and instructions to the general public would have to be issued in advance. Even if instructions were available, however, the execution of an evacuation would probably be accompanied by confusion and panic. Large-scale evacuation is, therefore, in most cases, no attractive option.[1]

Key Workers

Further complicating FEMA relocation plans during a crisis, CRP envisions a continuation of critically needed services and essential production in the risk areas. To make such continuation possible, key workers "would be advised to relocate, with their families, to nearby, closer-in host areas—from which [they] would *commute* to their jobs on a two-shift or similar basis [italics in original]." According to Richard Bottoroff, emergency preparedness director of the District of Columbia, members of Congress are not identified as key workers.

When relocated, citizens are told by FEMA to expect the following conditions: "When you arrive, reception centers will be there to welcome you and assign you temporary housing, and special arrangements will be made to upgrade the local level of fallout protection in case the crisis should be followed by attack. In fact, we need fallout protection in place everywhere because there is no telling where it may be needed. But even if you are unable to reach a shelter, you can still improvise some protection."

Shelter Protection

FEMA instructions for shelters in host areas include plans to make basement areas safer and, if no basements are available, to follow instructions for "expedient shelters." As a last resort, relocated populations are advised to seek fallout protection "at the nearest public shelter."

Since people may need to remain in shelters until fallout radiation has decayed to acceptable levels, FEMA has embarked upon a program to construct and distribute "ventilation kits": manually operated devices "to improve both total survival and the ratio of uninjured to injured survivors." FEMA will deploy the kits in "selected counterforce host areas." As of June 1982, of the required 681 plans for counterforce areas (regions which contain strategic offensive forces such as missiles, submarines, or bombers), 344 were in initial stages. These plans, which represent about 50 percent of requirements, cover an estimated risk-area population of more than seven million persons. Such efforts are to be augmented by "radiological defense officers" (RDOs). To support this "keystone of a functioning radiological defense system," FEMA will provide "31 full time RDO's, at the State and State-area level, in the counterforce States."

FEMA recognizes, however, the problematic nature of "fire survival" in residential basements. Even if the agency is correct in assuming that they provide a measure of blast and fallout protection, it notes that "fire survival in residential basements will require active fire defense on the part of the basement occupants. Only above 5-psi blast overpressure, where the residence is expected to be blown clear of the basement, is fire unlikely to pose a significant threat to the survivors." To maximize basement protection, host-area residents are urged to "share your basement."

In the event no basement protection is available, citizens are told to improvise fallout shelters; it is assumed they will have followed prior instructions concerning transport of tools—especially shovels, picks, and hammers—to host areas. According to FEMA, "One fallout-protected space can be developed by moving (on the average) about one cubic yard of earth (about 70 to 100 buckets full of earth)."

The Reagan administration's major objective for CRP [was] "to provide for survival of a substantial portion of the U.S. population in the event of a nuclear attack preceded by strategic warning, and for continuity of government, should deterrence and escalation control fail." As we have already seen, CRP also seeks, inter alia, to "enhance deterrence and stability in conjunction with our strategic offensive and other strategic defensive forces. Civil defense, as an element of the strategic balance, should assist in maintaining perceptions that this balance is favorable to the U.S." This objective stems from the belief that a more survivable U.S. population would reduce the likelihood this country could be coerced in a crisis. Confronted with large-scale civil defense upgrading in the United States, Soviet perceptions of an increasingly invulnerable U.S. population would—in Soviet cost-benefit calculations of alternative courses of action—allegedly reduce projected benefits of "escalation dominance."

In basing crisis relocation planning upon such assumptions, FEMA and the [Reagan] administration [neglected] some important considerations:

- It is by no means clear that CRP would in fact reduce U.S. population vulnerability or that, even if possible, the Soviet Union would see it that way. Leaving aside the hazards of fallout, there is no reason to assume Soviet inability or unwillingness to target relocated populations. It cannot be misunderstood: In order to save lives, evacuation would need to be augmented with effective plans for providing food, water, medical care and supplies, sanitation, security, and filtered air.

- It is clear that CRP would be of no survival benefit in the event of a Soviet "bolt from the blue" surprise attack, which, although one that FEMA regards as the least likely scenario, the Soviets (as recognized by DoD plans) might well view as most rational under certain conditions (e.g., Soviet expectations of an imminent U.S. first strike).

- U.S. resort to CRP would almost certainly be viewed as a provocative act by the Soviet Union, perhaps even "confirming" their oft-stated fears of a U.S. first strike. Such fears have already been heightened by the expanded U.S. plans for fighting a protracted nuclear war and for developing associated counterforce weapons systems (MX, MK-12A RV [nuclear warhead reentry vehicle], Trident II). Still other fear-inducing measures by the United States include . . . rejection of a genuine nuclear "freeze," . . . plans for a space-based defense, and the U.S. refusal to parallel Soviet renunciation of the right to "first use" of nuclear weapons.

- CRP would have no effect on Soviet calculations of expected cost of striking first since it would have no bearing on the survivability and penetration capability of U.S. strategic forces. Even if an enormous "survival asymmetry" were to develop between the United States and the Soviet Union, the latter's inclination to coerce or strike first would be unaffected by its relative invulnerability. The rationality of preemption depends not on anticipating comparative suffering, but only on hoping to avoid or reduce assuredly destructive retaliation.

- All the alleged benefits of CRP hinge on the judgment that a superpower nuclear war would be carefully controlled and cooperative, that there would be a "ladder of escalation" rather than spasm exchanges.

- CRP provides false reassurance to the American people, encouraging the very processes of denial that make nuclear war increasingly likely.

Crisis relocation planning is based upon a number of seriously flawed assumptions. Among these, none is more dangerous than the idea that re-located populations would expect an improved chance to survive. Without normally functioning health-care delivery systems, chronically ill persons would be especially vulnerable; individuals suffering fractures, burns, and lacerations would go without treatment. Coupled with the heightened incidence of both disease and psychological trauma, medical problems would be aggravated by the overwhelming number of rotting corpses. Indeed, according to the distinguished physician Dr. Herbert Abrams: "In order to bury the dead, an area 5.7 times as large as the city of Seattle would be required for the cemetery." . . .

NOTE

1. See Report of UN Secretary-General, *Nuclear Weapons* (Brookline, Mass.: Autumn Press, 1980), p. 102, published with authorization and cooperation of the United Nations.

31 NUCLEAR WAR AND CLIMATIC CATASTROPHE: A NUCLEAR WINTER

Carl Sagan

. . . While it is widely accepted that a full nuclear war might mean the end of civilization at least in the Northern Hemisphere, claims that nuclear war might imply a reversion of the human population to prehistoric levels, or even the extinction of the human species, have, among some policymakers at least, been dismissed as alarmist or, worse, irrelevant. . . . The apocalyptic claims are rejected as unproved and unlikely, and it is judged unwise to frighten the public with doomsday talk when nuclear weapons are needed, we are told, to preserve the peace. . . .

Part of the resistance to serious consideration of such apocalyptic pronouncements is their necessarily theoretical basis. Understanding the long-term consequences of nuclear war is not a problem amenable to experimental verification—at least not more than once. Another part of the resistance is psychological. Most people—recognizing nuclear war as a grave and terrifying prospect, and nuclear policy as immersed in technical complexities, official secrecy and bureaucratic inertia—tend to practice what psychiatrists call denial: putting the agonizing problem out of our heads, since there seems nothing we can do about it. Even policymakers must feel this temptation from time to time. But for policymakers there is another concern: if it turns out that nuclear war could end our civilization or our species, such a finding might be considered a retroactive rebuke to those responsible, actively or passively, in the past or in the present, for the global nuclear arms race. . . .

. . . This article seeks, first, to present a short summary, in lay terms, of the climatic and biological consequences of nuclear war that emerge from extensive scientific studies . . . the essential conclusions of which have now been endorsed by a large number of scientists. . . . They have been reported in summary form in the press, and a detailed statement of the findings and their bases [has been] published in *Science*.[1] . . .

Following this summary, I explore the possible strategic and policy implications of the new findings. They point to one apparently inescapable conclusion: the necessity of moving as rapidly as possible to reduce the global nuclear arsenals below levels that could conceivably cause the kind of climatic catastrophe and cascading biological devastation predicted by the new stud-

Note: Some footnotes have been deleted, and the others have been renumbered to appear in consecutive order.

ies. Such a reduction would have to be a small percentage of the present global strategic arsenals.

II

The central point of the new findings is that the long-term consequences of a nuclear war could constitute a global climatic catastrophe.

The immediate consequences of a single thermonuclear weapon explosion are well known and well documented—fireball radiation, prompt neutrons and gamma rays, blast, and fires. The Hiroshima bomb that killed between 100,000 and 200,000 people was a fission device of about 12 kilotons yield (the explosive equivalent of 12,000 tons of TNT). A modern thermonuclear warhead uses a device something like the Hiroshima bomb as the trigger— the "match" to light the fusion reaction. A typical thermonuclear weapon now has a yield of about 500 kilotons (or 0.5 megaton, a megaton being the explosive equivalent of a million tons of TNT). There are many weapons in the 9 to 20 megaton range in the strategic arsenals of the United States and the Soviet Union today. The highest-yield weapon ever exploded is 58 megatons. . . .

The total number of nuclear weapons (strategic plus theater and tactical) in the arsenals of the two nations is close to 50,000, with an aggregate yield near 15,000 megatons. For convenience, we here collapse the distinction between strategic and theater weapons, and adopt, under the rubric "strategic," an aggregate yield of 13,000 megatons. The nuclear weapons of the rest of the world—mainly Britain, France and China—amount to many hundred warheads and a few hundred megatons of additional aggregate yield.

No one knows, of course, how many warheads with what aggregate yield would be detonated in a nuclear war. Because of attacks on strategic aircraft and missiles, and because of technological failures, it is clear that less than the entire world arsenal would be detonated. On the other hand, it is generally accepted, even among most military planners, that a "small" nuclear war would be almost impossible to contain before it escalated to include much of the world arsenals. . . . For this reason alone, any serious attempt to examine the possible consequences of nuclear war must place major emphasis on large-scale exchanges in the five-to-seven-thousand-megaton range. . . . Many of the effects described below, however, can be triggered by much smaller wars.

The adversary's strategic airfields, missile silos, naval bases, submarines at sea, weapons manufacturing and storage locales, civilian and military command and control centers, attack assessment and early warning facilities, and the like are probable targets ("counterforce attack"). While it is often stated that cities are not targeted "per se," many of the above targets are very near or co-located with cities, especially in Europe. In addition, there is an industrial targeting category ("countervalue attack"). Modern nuclear doctrines require that "war-supporting" facilities be attacked. Many of these facilities are necessarily industrial in nature and engage a work force of considerable size. They are almost always situated near major transportation centers, so that raw materials and finished products can be efficiently transported to other industrial sectors, or to forces in the field. Thus, such facilities are, almost by definition, cities, or near or within cities. Other "war-supporting" targets may include the transportation systems themselves (roads, canals, rivers, railways, civilian airfields, etc.), petroleum refineries, storage sites and pipelines, hydroelectric plants, radio and television transmitters and the like. A major countervalue attack therefore might involve almost all large cities in the United States and the Soviet Union, and possibly most of the large cities in the Northern Hemisphere. There are fewer than 2,500 cities in the world with populations over 100,000 inhabitants, so the devastation of all such cities is well within the means of the world nuclear arsenals.

Recent estimates of the immediate deaths from blast, prompt radiation, and fires in a major exchange in which cities were targeted range from several hundred million to 1.1 billion people—the latter estimate is in a World Health Organization study in which targets were assumed not to be restricted entirely to NATO and Warsaw Pact countries. Serious injuries requiring immediate medical attention (which would be largely unavailable) would be suffered by a comparably large number of people, perhaps an additional 1.1 billion. Thus it is possible that something approaching half the human population on the planet would be killed or seriously injured by the direct effects of the nuclear war. Social disruption; the unavailability of electricity, fuel, transportation, food deliveries, communications and other civil services; the absence of medical care; the decline in sanitation measures; rampant disease and severe psychiatric disorders would doubtless collectively claim a significant number of further victims. But a range of additional effects—some unexpected, some inadequately treated in earlier studies, some uncovered only recently—now make the picture much more somber still.

Because of current limitations on missile accuracy, the destruction of missile silos, command and control facilities, and other hardened sites requires nuclear weapons of fairly high yield exploded as groundbursts or as low airbursts. High-yield groundbursts will vaporize, melt and pulverize the surface at the target area and propel large quantities of condensates and fine dust into the upper troposphere and stratosphere. The particles are chiefly entrained in the rising fireball; some ride up the stem of the mushroom cloud. Most military targets, however, are not very hard. The destruction of cities can be accomplished, as demonstrated at Hiroshima and Nagasaki, by lower-yield explosions less than a kilometer above the surface. Low-yield airbursts over cities or near forests will tend to produce massive fires, some of them over areas of 100,000 square kilometers or more. City fires generate enormous quantities of black oily smoke which rise at least into the upper part of the lower atmosphere, or troposphere. If firestorms occur, the smoke columns rises vigorously, like the draft in a fireplace, and may carry some of the soot into the lower part of the upper atmosphere, or stratosphere. The smoke from forest and grassland fires would initially be restricted to the lower troposphere.

The fission of the (generally plutonium) trigger in every thermonuclear weapon and the reactions in the (generally uranium-238) casing added as a fission yield "booster" produce a witch's brew of radioactive products, which are also entrained in the cloud. Each such product, or radioisotope, has a characteristic "half-life" (defined as the time to decay to half its original level of radioactivity). Most of the radioisotopes have very short half-lives and decay in hours to days. Particles injected into the stratosphere, mainly by high-yield explosions, fall out very slowly—characteristically in about a year, by which time most of the fission products, even when concentrated, will have decayed to much safer levels. Particles injected into the troposphere by low-yield explosions and fires fall out more rapidly—by gravitational settling, rainout, convection, and other processes—before the radioactivity has decayed to moderately safe levels. Thus rapid fallout of tropospheric radioactive debris tends to produce larger doses of ionizing radiation than does the slower fallout of radioactive particles from the stratosphere.

Nuclear explosions of more than one-megaton yield generate a radiant fireball that rises through the troposphere into the stratosphere. The fireballs from weapons with yields between 100 kilotons and one megaton will partially extend into the stratosphere. The high temperatures in the fireball chemically ignite some of the nitrogen in the air, producing oxides of nitrogen, which in turn chemically attack and destroy the gas ozone in the middle stratosphere. But ozone absorbs the biologically dangerous ultraviolet radiation from the Sun. Thus, the partial depletion of the stratospheric ozone layer, or "ozonosphere," by high-yield nuclear explosions will increase the flux of solar ultraviolet radiation at the surface of the Earth (after the soot and dust have settled out). After a nuclear war in which thousands of high-yield weapons are detonated, the increase in biologically dangerous ultraviolet light might be several hundred percent. In the more dangerous shorter wavelengths, larger increases would occur. Nucleic acid and proteins, the fundamental molecules for life on Earth, are especially sensitive to ultraviolet radiation. Thus, an increase of the solar ultraviolet flux at the surface of the Earth is potentially dangerous for life.

These four effects—obscuring smoke in the troposphere, obscuring dust in the stratosphere, the fallout of radioactive debris, and the partial destruction of the ozone layer—constitute the four known principal adverse environmental consequences that occur after a nuclear war is "over." There may be others about which we are still ignorant. The dust and, especially, the dark soot absorb ordinary visible light from the Sun, heating the atmosphere and cooling the Earth's surface.

All four of these effects have been treated in our recent scientific investigation. The study, known from the initials of its authors as TTAPS, for the

Table 31-1. Nuclear Exchange Scenarios

Case	Total Yield (MT)	% Yield Surface Bursts	% Yield Urban or Industrial Targets	Warhead Yield Range (MT)	Total Number of Explosions
1. Baseline Case, countervalue and counterforce[a]	5,000	57	20	0.1–10	10,400
11. 3,000 MT nominal, counterforce only[b]	3,000	50	0	1–10	2,250
14. 100 MT nominal, countervalue only[c]	100	0	100	0.1	1,000
16. 5,000 MT "severe," counterforce only[b,d]	5,000	100	0	5–10	700
17. 10,000 MT "severe," countervalue and counterforce[c,d]	10,000	63	15	0.1–10	16,160

a. In the Baseline Case, 12,000 square kilometers of inner cities are burned; on every square centimeter an average of 10 grams of combustibles are burned, and 1.1% of the burned material rises as smoke. Also, 230,000 square kilometers of suburban areas burn, with 1.5 grams consumed at each square centimeter and 3.6% rising as smoke.
b. In this highly conservative case, it is assumed that no smoke emission occurs, that not a blade of grass is burned. Only 25,000 tons of the fine dust is raised into the upper atmosphere for every megaton exploded.
c. In contrast to the Baseline Case, only inner cities burn, but with 10 grams per square centimeter consumed and 3.3% rising as smoke into the high atmosphere.
d. Here, the fine (submicron) dust raised into the upper atmosphere is 150,000 tons per megaton exploded.

first time demonstrates that severe and prolonged low temperature would follow a nuclear war. . . .

Unlike many previous studies, the effects do not seem to be restricted to northern mid-latitudes, where the nuclear exchange would mainly take place. There is now substantial evidence that the heating by sunlight of atmospheric dust and soot over northern mid-latitude targets would profoundly change the global circulation. Fine particles would be transported across the equator in weeks, bringing the cold and the dark to the Southern Hemisphere. . . . While it would be less cold and less dark at the ground in the Southern Hemisphere than in the Northern, massive climatic and environmental disruptions may be triggered there as well.

In our studies, several dozen different scenarios were chosen, covering a wide range of possible wars, and the range of uncertainty in each key parameter was considered (e.g., to describe how many fine particles are injected into the atmosphere). Five representative cases are shown in Table 31-1 . . . ranging from a small low-yield attack exclusively on cities, utilizing, in yield, only 0.8 percent of the world strategic arsenals, to a massive exchange

Figure 31-1 Temperature Effects of Nuclear War Cases

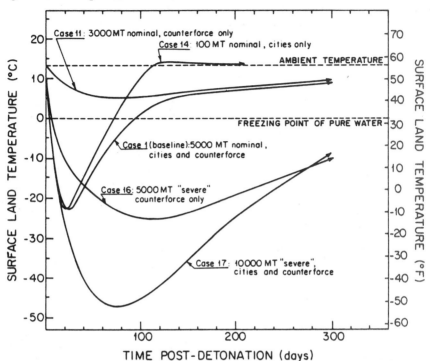

Note: In this figure, the average temperature of Northern Hemisphere land areas (away from coastlines) is shown varying with time after the five Cases of nuclear war defined in Table 31-1. The "ambient" temperature is the average in the Northern Hemisphere over all latitudes and seasons: thus, normal winter temperatures at north temperature latitudes are lower than is shown, and normal tropical temperatures are higher than shown. Cases described as "nominal" assume the most likely values of parameters (such as dust particle size or the frequency of firestorms) that are imperfectly known. Cases marked "severe" represent adverse but not implausible values of these parameters. In Case 14 the curve ends when the temperatures come within a degree of the ambient values. For the four other Cases, the curves are shown ending after 300 days, but this is simply because the calculations were not extended further. In these four Cases the curves will continue to the directions they are headed.

involving 75 percent of the world arsenals. "Nominal" cases assume the most probable parameter choices; "severe" cases assume more adverse parameter choices, but still in the plausible range.

Predicted continental temperatures in the Northern Hemisphere vary after the nuclear war according to the curves shown in Figure 31-1. . . . The high heat-retention capacity of water guarantees that oceanic temperatures will fall at most by a few degrees. Because temperatures are moderated by the adjacent oceans, temperature effects in coastal regions will be less extreme than in continental interiors. The temperatures shown in Figure 31-1 are average values for Northern Hemisphere land areas.

Even much smaller temperature declines are known to have serious consequences. The explosion of the Tambora volcano in Indonesia in 1815 led to an average global temperature decline of only 1°C, due to the obscuration of sunlight by the fine dust propelled into the stratosphere; yet the hard freezes the following year were so severe that 1816 has been known in Europe and America as "the year without a summer." A 1°C cooling would nearly eliminate wheat growing in Canada. In the last thousand years, the maximum global or Northern Hemisphere temperature deviations have been around 1°C. In an Ice Age, a typical long-term temperature decline from preexisting conditions is about 10°C. Even the most modest of the cases illustrated in Figure 31-1 give temporary temperature declines of this order. The Baseline Case is much more adverse. Unlike the situation in an Ice Age, however, the global temperatures after nuclear war plunge rapidly and take only months to a few years to recover, rather than thousands of years. No new Ice Age is likely to be induced by a Nuclear Winter.

Because of the obscuration of the Sun, the daytime light levels can fall to a twilit gloom or worse. For more than a week in the northern mid-latitude target zone, it might be much too dark to see, even at midday. In Cases 1 and 14 (Table 31-1), hemispherically averaged light levels fall to a few percent of normal values, comparable to those at the bottom of a dense overcast. At this illumination, many plants are close to what is called the compensation point, the light level at which photosynthesis can barely keep pace with plant metabolism. In Case 17, illumination, averaged over the entire Northern Hemisphere, falls in daytime to about 0.1 percent of normal, a light level at which plants will not photosynthesize at all. For Cases 1 and especially 17, full recovery to ordinary daylight takes a year or more (Figure 31-1).

As the fine particles fall out of the atmosphere, carrying radioactivity to the ground, the light levels increase and the surface warms. The depleted ozone layer now permits ultraviolet light to reach the Earth's surface in increased proportions. The relative timing of the multitude of adverse consequences of a nuclear war is shown in Table 31-2. . . .

Perhaps the most striking and unexpected consequence of our study is that even a comparatively small nuclear war can have devastating climatic consequences, provided cities are targeted (see Case 14 in Figure 31-1; here, the centers of 100 major NATO and Warsaw Pact cities are burning). There is an indication of a very rough threshold at which severe climatic consequences are triggered—around a few hundred nuclear explosions over cities, for smoke generation, or around 2,000 to 3,000 high-yield surface bursts at, e.g., missile silos, for dust generation and ancillary fires. Fine particles can be injected into the atmosphere at increasing rates with only minor effects until these thresholds are crossed. Thereafter, the effects rapidly increase in severity.[2]

As in all calculations of this complexity, there are uncertainties. Some factors tend to work towards more severe or more prolonged effects; others

Table 31-2. Effects of the Baseline Nuclear War

Effect	Time After Nuclear War	US / S.U. Population at risk	N.H. Population at risk	S.H. Population at risk	Casualty rate for those at risk	Potential global deaths
Blast		H	M	L	H	M-H
Thermal Radiation		H	M	L	M	M-H
Prompt Ionizing Radiation		L	L	L	H	L-M
Fires		M	M	L	M	M
Toxic Gases		M	M	L	L	L
Dark		H	H	M	L	L
Cold		H	H	H	H	M-H
Frozen Water Supplies		H	H	M	M	M
Fallout Ionizing Radiation		H	H	L-M	M	M-H
Food Shortages		H	H	H	H	H
Medical System Collapse		H	H	M	M	M
Contagious Diseases		M	M	L	H	M
Epidemics and Pandemics		H	H	M	M	M
Psychiatric Disorders		H	H	L	L	L-M
Increased Surface Ultraviolet Light		H	H	M	L	L
Synergisms		?	?	?	?	?

(Time scale: 1 hr, 1 day, 1 wk, 1 mo, 3 mo, 6 mo, 1 yr, 2 yr, 5 yr, 10 yr)

Note: This is a schematic representation of the time scale for the effects, which are most severe when the thickness of the horizontal bar is greatest. The columns at the right indicate the degree of risk of the populations of the United States and the Soviet Union, the Northern Hemisphere, and the Southern Hemisphere—with H, M, and L standing for High, Medium, and Low, respectively.

tend to ameliorate the effects. The detailed TTAPS calculations described here are one-dimensional; that is, they assume the fine particles to move vertically by all the appropriate laws of physics, but neglect the spreading in latitude and longitude. . . . It would be helpful to perform an accurate three-dimensional calculation on the general atmospheric circulation following a nuclear war. Preliminary estimates suggest that circulation might moderate the low temperatures in the Northern Hemisphere predicted in our calculations by some 30 percent, lessening somewhat the severity of the effects, but still leaving them at catastrophic levels (e.g., a 30°C rather than a 40°C temperature drop). . . .

Nuclear war scenarios are possible that are much worse than the ones we have presented. For example, if command and control capabilities are lost early in the war—by, say, "decapitation" (an early surprise attack on civilian and military headquarters and communications facilities)—then the war conceivably could be extended for weeks as local commanders make separate and uncoordinated decisions. At least some of the delayed missile launches could be retaliatory strikes against any remaining adversary cities. Generation of an additional smoke pall over a period of weeks or longer following the initiation of the war would extend the magnitude, but especially the duration of the climatic consequences. Or it is possible that more cities and forests would be ignited than we have assumed, or that smoke emissions would be larger, or that a greater fraction of the world arsenals would be committed. Less severe cases are of course possible as well.

These calculations therefore are not, and cannot be, assured prognostications of the full consequences of a nuclear war. Many refinements in them are possible and are being pursued. But there is general agreement on the overall conclusions: in the wake of a nuclear war there is likely to be a period, lasting at least for months, of extreme cold in a radioactive gloom, followed—after the soot and dust fall out—by an extended period of increased ultraviolet light reaching the surface.

We now experience the biological impact of such an assault on the global environment.

III

The immediate human consequences of nuclear explosions range from vaporization of populations near the hypocenter, to blast-generated trauma (from flying glass, falling beams, collapsing skyscrapers and the like), to burns, radiation sickness, shock and severe psychiatric disorders. But our concern here is with longer-term effects.

It is now a commonplace that in the burning of modern tall buildings, more people succumb to toxic gases than to fire. Ignition of many varieties of building materials, insulation and fabrics generates large amounts of such pyrotoxins, including carbon monoxide, cyanides, vinyl chlorides, oxides of nitrogen, ozone, dioxins, and furans. Because of differing practices in the use of such synthetics, the burning of cities in North America and Western Europe will probably generate more pyrotoxins than cities in the Soviet Union, and cities with substantial recent construction more than older, unreconstructed cities. In nuclear war scenarios in which a great many cities are burning, a significant pyrotoxin smog might persist for months. The magnitude of this danger is unknown.

The pyrotoxins, low light levels, radioactive fallout, subsequent ultraviolet light, and especially the cold are together likely to destroy almost all of Northern Hemisphere agriculture, even for the more modest Cases 11 and 14. A 12° to 15°C temperature reduction by itself would eliminate wheat and corn production in the United States, even if all civil systems and agricultural technology were intact. With unavoidable societal disruption, and with the other environmental stresses just mentioned, even a 3,000-megaton "pure" counterforce attack (Case 11) might suffice. Realistically, many fires would be set even in such an attack . . . and a 3,000-megaton war is likely to wipe out U.S. grain production. This would represent by itself an unprecedented global catastrophe: North American grain is the principal reliable source of export food on the planet, as well as an essential component of U.S. prosperity. Wars just before harvesting of grain and other staples would be incrementally worse than wars after harvesting. For many scenarios, the effects will extend . . . into two or more growing seasons. Widespread fires and subsequent runoff of topsoil are among the many additional deleterious consequences extending for years after the war.

Something like three-quarters of the U.S. population lives in or near cities. In the cities themselves there is, on average, only about one week's supply of food. After a nuclear war it is conceivable that enough of present grain storage might survive to maintain, on some level, the present population for more than a year. But with the breakdown of civil order and transportation systems in the cold, the dark and the fallout, these stores would become largely inaccessible. Vast numbers of survivors would soon starve to death.

In addition, the sub-freezing temperatures imply, in many cases, the unavailability of fresh water. The ground will tend to be frozen to a depth of about a meter—incidentally making it unlikely that the hundreds of millions of dead bodies would be buried, even if the civil organization to do so existed. Fuel stores to melt snow and ice would be in short supply, and ice surfaces and freshly fallen snow would tend to be contaminated by radioactivity and pyrotoxins.

In the presence of excellent medical care, the average value of the acute lethal dose of ionizing radiation for healthy adults is about 450 rads. (As with many other effects, children, the infirm and the elderly tend to be more vulnerable.) Combined with the other assaults on survivors in the postwar environment, and in the probable absence of any significant medical care, the mean lethal acute dose is likely to decline to 350 rads or even lower. For many outdoor scenarios, doses within the fallout plumes that drift hundreds of kilometers downwind of targets are greater than the mean lethal dose. (For a 10,000-megaton war, this is true for more than 30 percent of northern mid-latitude land areas.) Far from targets, intermediate-timescale chronic doses from delayed radioactive fallout may be in excess of 100 rads for the baseline case. These calculations assume no detonations on nuclear reactors or fuel-reprocessing plants, which would increase the dose.

Thus, the combination of acute doses from prompt radioactive fallout, chronic doses from the delayed intermediate-timescale fallout, and internal doses from food and drink are together likely to kill many more by radiation sickness. Because of acute damage to bone marrow, survivors would have significantly increased vulnerability to infectious diseases. Most infants exposed to 100 rads as fetuses in the first two trimesters of pregnancy would suffer mental retardation and/or other serious birth defects. Radiation and some pyrotoxins would later produce neoplastic diseases and genetic damage. Livestock and domesticated animals, with fewer resources, vanishing food

330 Carl Sagan

supplies and in many cases with greater sensitivity to the stresses of nuclear war than human beings, would also perish in large numbers.

These devastating consequences for humans and for agriculture would not be restricted to the locales in which the war would principally be "fought," but would extend throughout northern mid-latitudes and, with reduced but still significant severity, probably to the tropics and the Southern Hemisphere. The bulk of the world's grain exports originate in northern mid-latitudes. . . . Thus, even if there were no climatic and radiation stresses on tropical and Southern Hemisphere societies—many of them already at subsistence levels of nutrition—large numbers of people there would die of starvation.

As agriculture breaks down worldwide (possible initial exceptions might include Argentina, Australia and South Africa if the climatic impact on the Southern Hemisphere proved to be minimal), there will be increasing reliance on natural ecosystems—fruits, tubers, roots, nuts, etc. But wild foodstuffs will also have suffered from the effects of the war. At just the moment that surviving humans turn to the natural environment for the basis of life, that environment would be experiencing a devastation unprecedented in recent geological history.

Two-thirds of all species of plants, animals, and microorganisms on the Earth live within 25° of the equator. Because temperatures tend to vary with the seasons only minimally at tropical latitudes, species there are especially vulnerable to rapid temperature declines. In past major extinction events in the paleontological record, there has been a marked tendency for tropical organisms to show greater vulnerability than organisms living at more temperate latitudes.

The darkness alone may cause a collapse in the aquatic food chain in which sunlight is harvested by phytoplankton, phytoplankton by zooplankton, zooplankton by small fish, small fish by large fish, and, occasionally, large fish by humans. In many nuclear war scenarios, this food chain is likely to collapse at its base for at least a year and is significantly more imperiled in tropical waters. The increase in ultraviolet light available at the surface of the earth approximately a year after the war provides an additional major environmental stress that by itself has been described as having "profound consequences" for aquatic, terrestrial and other ecosystems. . . .

Each of these factors, taken separately, may carry serious consequences for the global ecosystem: their interactions may be much more dire still. Extremely worrisome is the possibility of poorly understood or as yet entirely uncontemplated synergisms (where the net consequences of two or more assaults on the environment are much more than the sum of the component parts). For example, more than 100 rads (and possibly more than 200 rads) of external and ingested ionizing radiation is likely to be delivered in a very large nuclear war to all plants, animals and unprotected humans in densely populated regions of northern mid-latitudes. After the soot and dust clear, there can, for such wars, be a 200 to 400 percent increment in the solar ultraviolet flux that reaches the ground, with an increase of many orders of magnitude in the more dangerous shorter-wavelength radiation. Together, these radiation assaults are likely to suppress the immune systems of humans and other species, making them more vulnerable to disease. At the same time, the high ambient-radiation fluxes are likely to produce, through mutation, new varieties of microorganisms, some of which might become pathogenic. The preferential radiation sensitivity of birds and other insect predators would enhance the proliferation of herbivorous and pathogen-carrying insects. Carried by vectors with high radiation tolerance, it seems possible that epidemics and global pandemics would propagate with no hope of effective mitigation by medical care, even with reduced population sizes and greatly restricted human mobility. Plants, weakened by low temperatures and low light levels, and other animals would likewise be vulnerable to preexisting and newly arisen pathogens.

There are many other conceivable synergisms, all of them still poorly understood because of the complexity of the global ecosystem. Every synergism represents an additional assault, of unknown magnitude, on the global ecosystem and its support functions for humans. What the world would look like after a nuclear war depends in part upon the unknown synergistic interaction of these various adverse effects.

We do not and cannot know that the worst would happen after a nuclear war. Perhaps there is some as yet undiscovered compensating effect or saving grace—although in the past, the overlooked effects in studies of nuclear war have almost always tended toward the worst. But in an uncertain matter of such gravity, it is wise to contemplate the worst, especially when its probability is not extremely small. The summary of the findings of the group of 40 distinguished biologists who met in April 1983 to assess the TTAPS conclusions is worthy of careful consideration[3]:

Species extinction could be expected for most tropical plants and animals, and for most terrestrial vertebrates of north temperate regions, a large number of plants, and numerous freshwater and some marine organisms. . . . Whether any people would be able to persist for long in the face of highly modified biological communities; novel climates; high levels of radiation; shattered agricultural, social, and economic systems; extraordinary psychological stresses; and a host of other difficulties is open to question. It is clear that the ecosystem effects *alone* resulting from a large-scale thermonuclear war could be enough to destroy the current civilization in at least the Northern Hemisphere. Coupled with the direct casualties of perhaps two billion people, the combined intermediate and long-term effects of nuclear war suggest that eventually there might be no human survivors in the Northern Hemisphere.

Furthermore, the scenario described here is by no means the most severe that could be imagined with present world nuclear arsenals and those contemplated for the near future. In almost any realistic case involving nuclear exchanges between the superpowers, global environmental changes sufficient to cause an extinction event equal to or more severe than that at the close of the Cretaceous when the dinosaurs and many other species died out are likely. In that event, the possibility of the extinction of *Homo sapiens* cannot be excluded.

IV

The foregoing probable consequences of various nuclear war scenarios have implications for doctrine and policy. Some have argued that the difference between the deaths of several hundred million people in a nuclear war (as has been thought until recently to be a reasonable upper limit) and the death of every person on Earth (as now seems possible) is only a matter of one order of magnitude. For me, the difference is considerably greater. Restricting our attention only to those who die as a consequence of the war conceals its full impact.

If we are required to calibrate extinction in numerical terms, I would be sure to include the number of people in future generations who would not be born. A nuclear war imperils all of our descendants, for as long as there will be humans. Even if the population remains static, with an average lifetime of the order of 100 years, over a typical time period for the biological evolution of a successful species (roughly ten million years), we are talking about some 500 trillion people yet to come. By this criterion, the stakes are one million times greater for extinction than for the more modest nuclear wars that kill "only" hundreds of millions of people.

There are many other possible measures of the potential loss—including culture and science, the evolutionary history of the planet, and the significance of the lives of all of our ancestors who contributed to the future of their descendants. Extinction is the undoing of the human enterprise. . . . [At this point the author examines possible policy responses to avert a nuclear war–induced climatic catastrophe—*eds.*]

V

None of the foregoing possible strategic and policy responses to the prospect of a nuclear war-triggered climatic catastrophe seem adequate even for the security of the nuclear powers, much less for the rest of the world. The prospect reinforces, in the short run, the standard arguments for strategic confidence-building, especially between the United States and the Soviet Union; for tempering puerile rhetoric; for resisting the temptation to demonize the adversary; for reducing the likelihood of strategic confrontations arising from accident or miscalculation; for stabilizing old and new weapons systems—for example, by de-MIRVing missiles; for abandoning nuclear-war-fighting strategies and mistrusting the possibility of "containment" of a tactical or limited nuclear war; for considering safe unilateral steps, such as the retiring of some old weapons systems with very high-yield warheads; for improving communications at all levels, especially among general staffs and between heads of governments; and for public declarations of relevant policy changes. . . .

In the long run, the prospect of climatic catastrophe raises real questions about what is meant by national and international security. To me, it seems clear that the species is in grave danger at least until the world arsenals are reduced below the threshold for climatic catastrophe; the nations and the global civilization would remain vulnerable even at lower inventories. It may even be that . . . the only credible arsenal is below threshold. . . .—a more than 90 percent reduction . . . —adequate for strategic deterrence, if that is considered essential, but unlikely to trigger the nuclear winter. . . .

VI

We have, by slow and imperceptible steps, been constructing a Doomsday machine. Until recently—and then, only by accident—no one even noticed. And we have distributed its triggers all over the Northern Hemisphere. Every American and Soviet leader since 1945 has made critical decisions regarding nuclear war in total ignorance of the climatic catastrophe. Perhaps this knowledge would have moderated the subsequent course of world events and, especially, the nuclear arms race. Today, at least, we have no excuse for failing to factor the catastrophe into long-term decisions on strategic policy.

Since it is the soot produced by urban fires that is the most sensitive trigger of the climatic catastrophe, and since such fires can be ignited even by low-yield strategic weapons, it appears that the most critical ready index of the world nuclear arsenals, in terms of climatic change, may be the total *number* of strategic warheads. . . .

Very roughly, the level of the world strategic arsenals necessary to induce the climatic catastrophe seems to be somewhere around 500 to 2,000 warheads—an estimate that may be somewhat high for airbursts over cities, and somewhat low for high-yield groundbursts. The intrinsic uncertainty in this number is itself of strategic importance, and prudent policy would assume a value below the low end of the plausible range.

National or global inventories above this rough threshold move the world arsenals into a region that might be called the "Doomsday Zone." If the world arsenals were well below this rough threshold, no concatenation or computer malfunction, carelessness, unauthorized acts, communications failure, miscalculation and madness in high office could unleash the nuclear winter. When global arsenals are above the threshold, such a catastrophe is at least possible. The further above threshold we are, the more likely it is that a major exchange would trigger the climatic catastrophe.

Traditional belief and childhood experience teach that more weapons buy more security. But since the advent of nuclear weapons and the acquisition of a capacity for "overkill," the possibility has arisen that, past a certain point, more nuclear weapons do not increase national security. I wish here to suggest that, beyond the climatic threshold, an increase in the number of strategic weapons leads to a pronounced *decline* in national (and global) security. National security is not a zero-sum game. Strategic insecurity of one adversary almost always means strategic insecurity for the other. Conventional pre-1945 wisdom, no matter how deeply felt, is not an adequate guide in an age of apocalyptic weapons.

If we are content with world inventories above the threshold, we are saying that it is safe to trust the fate of our global civilization and perhaps our species to all leaders, civilian and military, of all present and future major nuclear powers; and to the command and control efficiency and technical reliability in those nations now and in the indefinite future. For myself, I would far rather have a world in which the climatic catastrophe cannot happen, independent of the vicissitudes of leaders, institutions and machines. This seems to me elementary planetary hygiene, as well as elementary patriotism. . . . [At this point the author examines the growth of American and Soviet strategic inventories since World War II and discusses ways they might be reduced to a level below the threshold at which climatic catastrophe might be set in motion—*eds.*]

VII

In summary, cold, dark, radioactivity, pyrotoxins and ultraviolet light following a nuclear war—including some scenarios involving only a small fraction of the world strategic arsenals—would imperil every survivor on the planet. There is a real danger of the extinction of humanity. A threshold exists at which the climatic catastrophe could be triggered, very roughly around 500–2,000 strategic warheads. A major first strike may be an act of national suicide, even if no retaliation occurs. Given the magnitude of the potential loss, no policy declarations and no mechanical safeguards can adequately guarantee the safety of the human species. No national rivalry or ideological confrontation justifies putting the species at risk. . . .

National security policies that seem prudent or even successful during a term of office or a tour of duty may work to endanger national—and global—security over longer periods of time. In many respects it is just such short-term thinking that is responsible for the present world crisis. The looming prospect of the climatic catastrophe makes short-term thinking even more dangerous. The past has been the enemy of the present, and the present the enemy of the future.

The problem cries out for an ecumenical perspective that rises above cant, doctrine and mutual recrimination, however apparently justified, and that at least partly transcends parochial fealties in time and space. What is urgently required is a coherent, mutually agreed upon, long-term policy for dramatic reductions in nuclear armaments, and a deep commitment, embracing decades, to carry it out.

Our talent, while imperfect, to foresee the future consequences of our present actions and to change our course appropriately is a hallmark of the human species, and one of the chief reasons for our success over the past million years. Our future depends entirely on how quickly and how broadly we can refine this talent. We should plan for and cherish our fragile world as we do our children and our grandchildren: there will be no other place for them to live. It is nowhere ordained that we must remain in bondage to nuclear weapons.

NOTES

1. R. P. Turco, O. B. Toon, T. P. Ackerman, J. B. Pollack and Carl Sagan [TTAPS], "Global Atmospheric Consequences of Nuclear War," *Science* [222 (December 23, 1983): 1283–1292]; P. R. Ehrlich, M. A. Harwell, Peter H. Raven, Carl Sagan, G. M. Woodwell, et al., "The Long-Term Biological Consequences of Nuclear War," *Science* [222 (December 23, 1983): 1293–1300].

2. The climatic threshold for smoke in the troposphere is about 100 million metric tons, injected essentially all at once; for sub-micron fine dust in the stratosphere, about the same.

3. P. Ehrlich, et al., loc. cit. footnote 1.

32 NUCLEAR WINTER REAPPRAISED

Starley L. Thompson
Stephen H. Schneider

... The discovery of "nuclear winter"[1] ... has been ... compelling scientifically. ... It has even been referred to as an inadvertent manifestation of Herman Kahn's "doomsday machine."

The nuclear winter hypothesis, stated simply, contended that the smoke and dust placed in the atmosphere by a large nuclear war would prevent most sunlight from reaching the earth's surface and produce a widespread cooling of land areas. The first two climatic conclusions of the theory were the most important: effects would be severe (weeks of sub-freezing temperatures), and effects would be widespread (at least hemispheric in scale). These grim scientific conclusions gave rise to two unique implications: the possibility of human extinction, and the potential suicide of an attacker even without retaliation by the attacked party. These implications, if confirmed, would indeed approach the definition of the traditional doomsday machine.

Another assertion was added to the hypothesis in the form of a scientific judgment: namely, that a "threshold" existed above which the climatic effects of a nuclear attack would become catastrophic. Thus, this doomsday machine did not possess a hair trigger, and would allow nuclear wars to be fought at some level substantially below the destructive potential of the current nuclear arsenals without global climatic catastrophe.

An additional major scientific conclusion closely followed the announcements of severe and widespread effects, but it initially received much less attention. Despite early suggestions that a nuclear winter was quite probable as long as a substantial number of large cities were attacked, many scientists concluded that the magnitude of effects would indeed be strongly dependent on uncertain, or even unknowable, factors.

The severe conclusions about nuclear winter provoked a broad spectrum of suggested responses for strategic policy. For many who took nuclear winter seriously, a perceived solution was a drastic reduction of nuclear arms to a level no greater than that necessary to constitute a minimal deterrent. On the other hand, the U.S. Department of Defense—which accepted the possibility of nuclear winter—argued that strengthening deterrence, combined with more research into nuclear winter, would be the best response.[2] ...

... On scientific grounds the global apocalyptic conclusions of the initial

Note: Some footnotes have been deleted, and others have been renumbered to appear in consecutive order.

nuclear winter hypothesis can now be relegated to a vanishingly low level of probability. . . . But, at the same time, there is little that is thoroughly understood about the environmental effects of a nuclear war. In particular, we do not think that all environmental effects should once again be considered as "secondary." . . . Our current understanding of environmental effects will be reviewed and then used to bolster arguments for strengthened strategic stability, not necessarily excluding newer strategic systems, but at significantly reduced levels of arsenals.   *

II

It is reasonable to ask why the scientific basis of the theory of nuclear winter still provokes such divergent scientific opinions. The answer involves both the complexity of the problems and the severity of predicted effects. It is important to remember that the widespread radioactive fallout and ozone effects, although substantial, were never really thought by knowledgeable researchers to have a doomsday potential. In contrast, the original nuclear winter results showed truly catastrophic consequences arising from general war scenarios in the best available calculations. Thus, this new hypothesis could not be readily dismissed. Moreover, the problem of nuclear winter involves more scientific disciplines and more crucial areas of uncertainty than the earlier environmental problems. In particular, estimates of smoke production cannot be made from old nuclear test data and cannot be well bounded theoretically.

Initially, the scientific basis of nuclear winter rested exclusively with the TTAPS group and their first calculations. After the original discovery that smoke could pose the most serious environmental threat of nuclear war, the TTAPS group began to use a computer model to study the effects of war-generated smoke and dust on the earth's climate. The model was one-dimensional; that is, it did not take into account north-south and east-west directions, but instead treated the earth as a homogeneous all-land sphere having a temperature that depended only on the up-down direction (atmospheric altitude). Thus, the model had no geography, no winds, no seasons, instantaneous spread of smoke to the hemispheric scale, and no feedback of atmospheric circulation changes on the rate of smoke washout by rainfall. Despite these limitations, the TTAPS calculations did offer state-of-the-art estimates of the sunlight and infrared radiation absorption of a *given* amount of smoke and dust in a vertical column of the atmosphere. . . .

III

. . . One of the most controversial concepts to emerge from nuclear winter research was the notion that a threshold amount of smoke could trigger catastrophic climatic effects. This notion was based on a number of simulations in the TTAPS study, but was primarily founded on a hypothetical "100-megaton war" in which 100 major cities were targeted exclusively. The smoke so generated was sufficient to cause northern hemispheric land surface temperatures to drop well below the freezing point in the one-dimensional model. . . .

If one accepts the idea of a threshold for nuclear winter for the sake of strategic argument, then the question of how to quantify it becomes important. Given the substantial uncertainties in defining a threshold, and the potentially grave consequences of exceeding it, the argument was made for deriving a threshold based on a worst-case smoke-producing assumption of targeting. Taken in this light, the strategically dubious "100-megaton war" can be seen as a worst-case assumption serving to delineate a prudent threshold. The 100-megaton scenario used 1,000 warheads, but it was never suggested that the threshold would be very well defined. For example, in his *Foreign Affairs* article, Sagan set a crude threshold of around 500 to 2,000 warheads, primarily attributing the uncertainty to assumptions of targeting and weapon yields.

Ironically, just when the strategic implications of the threshold concept were starting to be debated in the strategic policy community, the strongest scientific arguments against the concept emerged. To understand why the threshold concept is not scientifically persuasive, one must be aware of the limitations inherent in the models that do not take account of geography.

It is tempting to interpret a calculation in which surface temperature is represented as a single global number in terms of a dramatic physical threshold, e.g., the freezing point. But such calculations cannot capture the true geographical and seasonal heterogeneity of climate. A global model developed at the National Center for Atmospheric Research studied the inclusion of north-south and east-west dimensions and how such improvements would modify the results of one-dimensional models.[3]

We found that the oceans, with their vast storage of heat, would reduce the magnitude of average continental cooling by a factor of two in the summer, compared to the cooling calculated by assuming a land-covered planet. The estimated cooling effect in winter was smaller by a factor of ten than the TTAPS annual estimate, because northern hemisphere mid-latitude land areas are already cold in winter. Even when we assumed a uniform smoke cloud to exist over the middle part of the northern hemisphere, the surface temperature reduction was unevenly distributed—much less along western coasts and even more than one-dimensional model results in some mid-continental cold-weather fluctuations in summertime.

In short, simulations using geographically realistic models produced such a wide range of consequences for any given war scenario that it became clear that the elegant and strategically compelling idea of a threshold was an artifact of a simplified model. . . . Hence, it is questionable to predict any strategic policy options on the existence of a nuclear winter threshold, even a "fuzzy" one.

IV

Although the bulk of the news media coverage of the nuclear winter debate in late 1983 concentrated on the more dramatic conclusions and criticisms of the theory, there was some press attention to the increasingly complex scientific research efforts that were under way. As these scientific efforts intensified in 1984 and 1985, however, popular interest in nuclear winter appeared to have decreased. On the other hand, interest in the scientific community picked up momentum as the issues became more complex and thus more scientifically exciting.

In 1982, after the discovery of the smoke problem, an international group of scientists began to plan a major study of the environmental consequences of nuclear war under the auspices of the Scientific Committee for Problems of the Environment (SCOPE)—a subgroup of the well-respected International Council of Scientific Unions. The SCOPE findings were released in two volumes in September 1985, the first covering physical effects and the second biological and other environmental effects.[4] Also in 1982, a group of U.S. scientists at the National Academy of Sciences (NAS) realized that a reassessment of the atmospheric effects of nuclear war was needed . . . This new NAS study, co-chaired by Harvard's George Carrier and retired Vice Admiral William Moran, was released in December 1984.[5]

Both studies of physical effects stressed the same two themes. First, that there remained great uncertainties—some that could never be resolved—over every link in the chain of phenomena leading to the two roughly defined phases of environmental effects: "acute" (one to 30 days) and "chronic" (months to years). Second, despite the cascading uncertainties, both reports concluded in strong language that very large climatic effects were possible and should not be ignored. . . .

It is noteworthy that both studies examined war scenarios that were not based on either worst-case assumptions or most likely scenarios.[6] Instead, "baseline" cases were considered that were believed at the time to be plausible examples of a large general nuclear war. . . . In a sense, these reports . . . helped to legitimize nuclear winter as a scientific research topic in general, and the use of mathematical climate models as appropriate tools for prediction in particular.

The SCOPE effort went further than the NAS report because it included a study of biological effects. . . . Consideration of the biological consequences was appropriate for two basic reasons. First, if a global "deep freeze" scenario is considered, then it is rather obvious that the biological consequences would be catastrophic to both natural and agricultural systems worldwide. But by late 1984 it was becoming increasingly apparent that such global freeze scenarios were of exceedingly small probability, and that the response of vegetation to coolings of less intensity and shorter duration needed to be assessed. This, of course, is a more challenging scientific problem than simply observing that everything would freeze. . . .

The second reason to consider biological consequences before all the physical facts were confirmed is simply that it is important for physical scientists to know what variables are of greatest importance to estimating biological damages from low temperatures, radioactivity or other factors. Therefore, having some idea of what was important to the biologists could help the physical scientists choose their approaches to atmospheric research questions.

Finally, the SCOPE biological report was important for what it did—and did not—say. It did not discuss the plausibility of human extinction as a result of nuclear war, thus implicitly rejecting the notion that extinction was a "real possibility." It did, on the other hand, follow up on the indirect global societal effects of nuclear war that had been known for decades but never treated in a very quantitative manner. For example, the SCOPE biologists calculated that at least hundreds of millions of people could die of starvation in noncombatant nations from disruption of food trade alone, even if no smoke, dust or radioactivity entered their territories. Any comprehensive assessment of the indirect consequences of nuclear war clearly needs to consider not only environmental effects, such as atmospheric changes and radioactive fallout, but disruptions of basic social functions as well (e.g., trade in basic commodities such as food, fertilizer, medicine, spare parts and fuel). . . .

Let us sum up: despite the continued potential for serious nuclear winter effects, there does not seem to be a real potential for human extinction; nor is there a plausible threshold for severe environmental effects. Thus, the two unique conclusions of the original nuclear winter idea with the most important implications for policy have been removed. . . .

[At this point the authors examine state-of-the-art research on nuclear winter to determine the extent to which the indirect environmental effects will be significant compared to the direct effects of nuclear war. Much of the attention focuses on the use of models and simulations of global weather patterns using realistic geographic features. An important finding is that the average temperature changes are considerably less than the estimates made in the original TTAPS study. As the authors put it, "These temperature changes more closely describe a nuclear 'fall' than a nuclear winter." Continuous removal of damaging amounts of smoke from the atmosphere bear significantly on this finding and conclusion—eds.]

V

Our current understanding of the climatic effects of nuclear war has changed the way that many previously proposed policy implications of nuclear winter should be viewed. Indeed, several of the strategic implications of nuclear winter, as it was originally conceived, are no longer justified: for example, the anxieties about a "threshold" for severe effects and the notion that climatic effects alone would serve as an in-kind retaliation against the major preemptive strike. The idea of automatic suicide is now unsupportable given that a scenario of weeks of continuous subfreezing temperatures on a continental scale is no longer plausible. However, the substantial amounts of smoke, dust and radioactivity that would necessarily be injected into the atmosphere in any large-scale preemptive strike should still add some measure of deterrent value, even if short of assured national suicide.

Apart from biologically oriented environmental effects, atmospheric smoke and dust could affect strategic surveillance, early warning, missile defense, communications, and attack assessment during a nuclear war. The primary effect would be obscuration of visible and infrared light that could, for example, degrade the information available from satellites or hinder the atmospheric propagation of laser beams used for communications or defense. . . . The present informed judgment is that strategic C^3 [command, control, and communications systems] could be maintained for only a short time if a massive attack were directed at the C^3 facilities themselves[7]—probably a shorter time than it would take obscuration to become a serious problem.

In summary, obscuration effects would not likely be as important in a *small* protracted war (if such a thing is possible) as in a large general war, and they may simply be irrelevant in a conflict in which C^3 and missile defense systems were attacked early. But since the effect of obscuration depends on the uncertain details of how a nuclear war would be fought, obscuration itself adds yet another uncertainty that may add some measure of additional deterrent.

There are policy changes that could minimize all potential effects related to nuclear winter, but we believe that these should also be judged by other criteria. For example, drastic cuts (by 90 to 99 percent) in the world's strategic arsenals would likely reduce the threat of environmental effects, but such a policy also has serious drawbacks. For example, verification of small numbers of weapons would be difficult, and "break-out" growth to larger arsenals would be a perceived threat. A small deterrent force might also be misread as a "weak" deterrent, thus reducing the inhibitions against a preemptive strike in times of crisis. In addition, horizontal nuclear arms proliferation could be encouraged, as some countries could achieve nuclear superpower status with a much smaller effort; one result of this could be even more difficulty in reaching arms control agreements. Lastly, it is possible that given a relatively limited number of weapons, one would choose to announce publicly a primarily countervalue (and thus smoke-producing) targeting policy to maximize the deterrent threat of one's strategic force. Nuclear winter, clearly, is not valid as a *sole basis* for embracing drastic cuts in nuclear arsenals. . . .

Wide-area non-nuclear strategic defense, if it were possible, could reduce many effects of a nuclear war, but it is the subject of intense controversy in its own right. It seems likely that the antimissile systems that would be deployed first would be to protect point targets (e.g., missile silos) since that defense task is much easier than defending something as large and "soft" as a city. In this case, as in the case of drastic cuts in the arsenals, an adversary may choose to shift targeting toward cities in an attempt to maintain a credible deterrent, which in turn increases the risks of nuclear winter. Alternatively, an adversary might seek to overwhelm the defense by increasing offensive deployments, which also raises those risks. But in the absence of such changes in offensive strategy—and given our current understanding of environmental effects—concerns about nuclear winter add only a small component to the overall SDI debate. . . .

Reducing the total explosive megatonnage of the world's strategic arsenals would also lessen the chances of global environmental effects should a nuclear war be fought. It is true that the trend of the past two decades has shown a reduction in the total yield of the U.S. arsenal, but future plans, such as the deployment of the next generation of D-5 missiles on Trident submarines (nearly 2,000 megatons of explosive equivalent on about 20 submarines), and to a lesser extent the deployment of MX missiles, do not bode well for the continuation of this trend. In any case, a more fundamental consideration of strategic arms deployment should be the need to stabilize and strengthen deterrence by avoiding systems that are tempting targets for a preemptive strike by virtue of their poor survivability and obvious utility for a disarming counterforce attack.

VI

Official U.S. responses to the nuclear winter theory went through early phases of disarray and cynicism, to settle eventually on qualified acceptance and a low-level interagency research program overseen by the Office of Science and Technology Policy, with highly focused research efforts sponsored by the Defense Nuclear Agency, Department of Energy and the National Science Foundation. Relative to official U.S. reticence, the Soviet Union has, to many Western observers, appeared steadfast in its ostensible acceptance of the absolute horrors implied by the earliest nuclear winter scenario. Remarks by Soviet spokesmen have especially emphasized the idea that nuclear winter "retaliation" would be automatic following a nuclear strike by either side. . . .

The Soviet position, however, is frequently believed to have been adopted for its propaganda value, presumably in the hope that U.S. and West European public opinion could be used to pressure the United States into arms control negotiating positions more favorable to the Soviets. . . . Nuclear winter [research], at least that which has been made available to the West, has not up to now been as helpful and forthcoming as we would have hoped. Some limited fire data have been received, and some Soviet scientists did participate in the international SCOPE assessment. For climate estimates, Soviet scientists have typically used war scenarios and other parameters taken from U.S. research and applied them to rather less capable computer models.

It is well known that differing perceptions of technical and political problems often contribute to the difficulties the superpowers have in coming to agreements on strategic issues. If environmental effects were perceived to be extreme enough for some sort of policy action other than research, then a response to nuclear winter could face the problem of asymmetric superpower perceptions. For example, if neither side believed in nuclear winter, despite any scientific evidence to the contrary, then the problem of mismatched responses would be moot. Similarly, if both sides believed comparably, then they would have some common ground for working out mutually satisfactory responses to the perceived threat. Problems arise, however, if one side perceives nuclear winter to be a genuine threat, but the other side does not. . . .

Apart from . . . hypothetical asymmetric perceptions of the nuclear winter problem, there are real, physical asymmetries between the superpowers regarding potential climatic effects. It is rather ironic, given the Soviet Union's greater capacity to produce smoke by attacking NATO countries, that advanced simulations show that the more poleward position of the U.S.S.R. and the greater landmass of the Eurasian continent put the U.S.S.R. at a disadvantage vis-à-vis the United States in terms of climatic effects. This is true for the same reason that the U.S.S.R., on the whole, experiences more severe normal winters than does the United States. . . .

We cannot pretend to know what the legacy of the nuclear winter hypothesis will be. Perhaps it will be a scientific reconfirmation that the effects of a large nuclear war would not merely be scaled-up versions of effects from a war fought with conventional weapons. In the final analysis, though, we must recognize that whatever our level of understanding of the effects of nuclear weapons, and whatever our ability to apply technical fixes to weapons, defenses or doctrines, the problem of avoiding nuclear war is not amenable to scientific solution. This problem arises more from political differences than from the latest technical capabilities. If nuclear winter has made us more aware of the urgent need to find political solutions to the arms race and the threat of nuclear war, that alone will have made the entire exercise worthwhile regardless of the scientific disposition of the remaining uncertainties.

NOTES

1. The theory was made public at the "World After Nuclear War" conference held Oct. 31 to Nov. 1, 1983, in Washington, D.C. The principal scientifiic results were first published several weeks later (Richard Turco, O. Brian Toon, Thomas Ackerman, James Pollack, and Carl Sagan, "Nuclear Winter: Global Consequences of Multiple Nuclear Explosions," *Science*, Dec. 23, 1983, pp. 1283–92). [TTAPS (pronounced "taps") is the acronym made up from the initials of the researchers in this group and is often used to identify the study—*eds.*]

2. Caspar W. Weinberger, *The Potential Effects of Nuclear War on the Climate*, a report to the U.S. Congress, Department of Defense, March 1985.

3. Curt Covey, Stephen Schneider and Starley Thompson, "Global Atmospheric Effects of Massive Smoke and Dust Injections From a Nuclear War: Results From General Circulation Model Simulations," *Nature*, Mar. 1, 1984, pp. 21–25. These results were publicly presented by Schneider on Nov. 1 at the "World After Nuclear War" conference (see footnote 1).

4. A. B. Pittock et al., *Environmental Consequences of Nuclear War, Volume I: Physical and Atmospheric Effects*. New York: John Wiley and Sons, 1986, 359 pp. M. A. Harwell and T.

344 Starley Thompson and Stephen Schneider

C. Hutchinson, *Environmental Consequences of Nuclear War, Volume II: Ecological and Agricultural Effects.* New York: John Wiley and Sons, 1985, 523 pp.

5. National Research Council, *The Effects on the Atmosphere of a Major Nuclear Exchange.* Washington, D.C.: National Academy Press, 1985.

6. There are two philosophies regarding the choice of scenarios in scientific studies of the nuclear winter problem. One, represented by Carl Sagan, considers the use of clearly stated near-worst-case scenarios to be essential to elucidating risks as apocalyptic as those associated with the original nuclear winter findings. The opposing philosophy has been expressed by George Rathjens and Ronald Siegal: "Individual and public policy views should be based . . . on a best estimate of the probability and severity of nuclear winter effects, taking into account all the attendant uncertainties. . . . [Difficult trade-offs] should *not* be made on the basis of the possibility that nuclear winter cannot be excluded." G. W. Rathjens and R. H. Siegel, "Nuclear Winter: Strategic Significance," *Issues in Science and Technology,* Winter 1985, pp. 124, 127. The relative acceptability of either of these views should depend on the perceived probability and severity of effects; e.g., if the probability of climatic catastrophe were shown to be one-in-ten, then even costly policy responses to the threat could be defended much more cogently than if the same consequences had chances of one-in-a-hundred.

7. Charles A. Zraket, "Strategic Command, Control, Communications, and Intelligence," *Science,* June 22, 1984, pp. 1306–11. Paul Bracken, *The Command and Control of Nuclear Forces.* New Haven: Yale University Press, 1983.

NUCLEAR NOMENCLATURE: A SELECTIVE DICTIONARY OF ACRONYMS AND TERMS

ACRONYMS

ABM	Antiballistic missile
ACDA	Arms Control and Disarmament Agency, U.S.
ADM	Atomic demolition munition
ALCM	Air-launched cruise missile
ASBM	Air-to-surface ballistic missile
ASAT	Antisatellite system
ATB	Advanced technology bomber
BMD	Ballistic missile defense
CBD	Civilian-based defense
CEP	Circular error probable
C³I	Command/control/communication and intelligence
CTB	Comprehensive Test Ban treaty
CM	Cruise missile
DEW	Direct energy weapons
DSAT	Defensive satellite weapon
EMP	Electromagnetic pulse
ERW	Enhanced radiation weapon
FEMA	Federal Emergency Management Agency, U.S.
FOFA	Follow-On Forces Attack
GLCM	Ground-launched cruise missile
ICBM	Intercontinental ballistic missile
INF	Intermediate-range nuclear forces
IAEA	International Atomic Energy Agency
MARV	Maneuvering reentry vehicle
MRBM	Medium-range ballistic missile
MIRV	Multiple independently targetable reentry vehicle
MAD	Mutual assured destruction
NCA	National command authority
NTM	National technical means of verification
NATO	North Atlantic Treaty Organization
NPT	Nuclear Non-Proliferation Treaty
NUT	Nuclear utilization theory
NWFZ	Nuclear weapon-free zone
PGM	Precision guided munition
PTB	Partial Test Ban Treaty
PAL	Permissive action link
PAR	Phased-array radar

RV	Reentry vehicle
SIOP	Single Integrated Operational Plan
SLCM	Sea-launched cruise missile
SALT	Strategic Arms Limitations Talks
START	Strategic Arms Reduction Talks
SDI	Strategic Defense Initiative
TTBT	Threshold Test Ban Treaty
WTO	Warsaw Treaty Organization

TERMS

Afterwinds. Wind currents set up in the vicinity of a nuclear explosion directed toward the burst center, resulting from the updraft accompanying the rise of the fireball.

Aggression. The first use of armed forces against another to realize political, economic, social, military, or other objectives.

Air-breathing. A flying weapon that travels through the atmosphere and uses air in its propulsion system. Examples are jet aircraft and cruise missiles. Air breathing weapons are typically slower than ballistic missiles, which are not air-breathing weapons.

Air burst. The explosion of a nuclear weapon at such a height that the expanding fireball does not touch the earth's surface when the luminosity is at a maximum.

Air-launched cruise missile (ALCM). A cruise missile designed to be launched from an aircraft.

Air-to-surface ballistic missile (ASBM). A ballistic missile launched from an airplane against a target on the earth's surface.

Antiballistic missile (ABM). Any ballistic missile used to intercept and destroy an incoming hostile missile. An antiballistic missile system would include such technology (weapons, targeting devices, guidance and tracking radar, and so on) as needed to provide adequate defense.

ABM Treaty. Formally entitled the "Treaty between the United States of America and the Union of Soviet Socialist Republics on the Limitation of Anti-Ballistic Missile Systems," this treaty is one of the two agreements signed at Moscow in 1972, known collectively as the SALT I agreements. The ABM Treaty entered into force on October 3, 1972, and is of unlimited duration. The treaty prohibits development of many types of antiballistic missile systems and limits deployments on each side to a specified number of land-based units, which use only rocket interceptors and ground-based radar.

Antisatellite system (ASAT). A weapon system designed to destroy enemy surveillance and hunter-killer satellites.

Area defense. An ABM defense covering a large area. Usually implies the capability to protect "soft" (i.e., not "hardened" missile silos or bunkers) targets.

Arms control. Any measure limiting or reducing forces, regulating armaments, and/ or restricting the deployment of troops or weapons that is intended to induce restrained behavior or is taken pursuant to an understanding with another state or states.

Arms race stability. The objective of minimizing the risk of war by slowing the pace of technological development and deployment of weapons while seeking simultaneously various confidence-building and arms-control measures.

Assured destruction. The theoretical capability to inflict an unacceptable level of damage on an attacker in response to its aggression.

Atomic demolition munition (ADM). A nuclear device, sometimes also called a nuclear land mine, emplaced and detonated on or beneath the ground or under water.

Atomic weapon (or bomb). A weapon based on the rapid fissioning of combinations of selected materials, thereby incuding an explosion (along with the emission of radiation) caused by the energy released by reactions involving atomic nuclei.

Ballistic missile. Any missile designed to follow the trajectory that results when it is acted upon predominantly by gravity and aerodynamic drag after thrust is terminated. Ballistic missiles typically operate outside the atmosphere for a substantial portion of their flight path and are unpowered during most of the flight.

Ballistic missile defense (BMD) system. A weapon system designed to destroy offensive strategic ballistic missiles or their warheads before they reach their targets.

Blast wave. A pulse of air in which the pressure increases sharply at the front, accompanied by winds, as a result of an explosion.

Boost phase. The phase of a missile trajectory from launch to burnout of the final stage. For ICBMs, this phase typically lasts from 3 to 5 minutes.

Battlefield nuclear weapon. Short-range tactical nuclear systems such as nuclear artillery shells designed for use against enemy forces in the field.

Bus. The post-boost phase vehicle that contains and eventually dispenses warheads in space.

Catalytic war. An unwanted nuclear war between the United States and the Soviet Union provoked by a calculating third party.

Circular error probable (CEP). A measure of the delivery accuracy of a weapon system. It is the radius of a circle around a target of such size that a weapon aimed at the target has a 50 percent probability of falling within the circle.

Civil defense. Passive measures designed to minimize the effects of enemy action on all aspects of civilian life, particularly to protect the population and production base. Civil defense includes emergency steps to repair or restore vital utilities and facilities.

Civilian-based defense (CBD). A policy in which a whole population and society's institutions become the fighting forces using a variety of forms of psychological, economic, social, and political resistance and counterattack.

Clean weapon. One in which measures have been taken to reduce the amount of residual radioactivity relative to a "normal" weapon of the same energy yield.

Collateral damage. The damage inflicted on the non-targeted surrounding human and nonhuman resources as a result of military strikes on enemy forces or military resources.

Command/Control/Communication and Intelligence (C^3I). The arrangement of facilities, equipment, human personnel, and standardized operating procedures aimed at facilitating the acquisition, processing, and dissemination of information needed by decisionmakers in planning and executing operations.

Comprehensive Test Ban (CTB) treaty. A proposed treaty between the United States, the Soviet Union, and Great Britain that would seek to end all nuclear weapons tests.

Counterforce strategy. A strategy designed to use nuclear weapons to destroy an opponent's nuclear and general military resources. To be credible, a counterforce strategy requires the possession of large numbers of highly accurate nuclear weapons.

Countervailing strategy. U.S. strategic policy announced by the Carter administration in 1980 designed to convince the Soviets that "no course of aggression by them that led to use of nuclear weapons, on any scale of attack and at any stage of conflict, could lead to victory, however they may define victory."

Countervalue strategy. A strategy designed to use nuclear weapons to destroy an opponent's population and industrial centers. A countervalue strategy (compared to a counterforce strategy) is more compatible with less accurate and more powerful nuclear weapons.

Crisis stability. The objective of minimizing the risk of war by reducing the incentives for and probability of a preemptive nuclear attack.

Cruise missile (CM). A pilotless, subsonic non-ballistic missile capable of carrying a nuclear or non-nuclear warhead through the atmosphere along a pre-programmed course to its target. A cruise missile's flight path remains within the earth's atmosphere and is usually ground-hugging so as to avoid detection.

Damage limitation. The objective of trying to limit as much as possible the destruction caused by a nuclear exchange should deterrence fail.

Decapitation. Destruction of an adversary's leadership and command structure in order to prevent it from ordering a retaliatory response.

Declaratory policy/doctrine. Public pronouncements regarding military policy, whether factual or deliberately misleading, designed to influence foreign and/or domestic audiences.

Decoupling. The fear that the United States would fight on behalf of Europe in the event of a Soviet attack but would not risk its own homeland by using strategic nuclear weapons against the Soviet Union, even if the Soviets were to use nuclear weapons against Western Europe. In this way the U.S. nuclear deterrent would become separated or "decoupled" from European defense.

Defensive satellite weapon (DSAT). A device that is intended to defend satellites in space by destroying attacking ASAT weapons.

Deterrence. The prevention from action by fear of the consequence. Deterrence is a condition resulting from creation of a state of mind brought about by the existence of a credible threat of unacceptable counteraction in response to a contemplated attack on an adversary, thereby inhibiting the temptation to initiate such an attack.

Deterrence by denial. Deterring an adversary not by the threat of punishment but by denying him the realization of his goals. Deterrence by denial is closely associated with nonprovocative defense concepts. It is also associated with war-fighting capabilities, which seek to deter by the threat of being able to fight and win a nuclear war.

Direct energy weapons (DEW). Intense energy beam weapons currently being explored as advanced weapons technologies for possible BMD use. Included are various chemical and free electron lasers, nuclear-powered x-rays, particle beams, and microwave weapons.

Direct radiation. Exposure to radioactive contamination occurring during a nuclear explosion, which, while intense, is limited in range.

Disarmament. Reduction of military forces or armaments, especially to levels resulting from international agreements.

Dual-capable system. Aircraft and cruise missiles able to deliver either conventional or nuclear warheads.

Electromagnetic pulse (EMP). A sharp pulse of radio frequency (long wavelength) electromagnetic radiation produced by a nuclear explosion. The intense electronic and magnetic fields can damage unprotected electrical and electronic equipment over a large area.

Enhanced radiation weapon (ERW). A weapon designed to produce minimum blast effects and maximum prompt radiation; produces lethal doses of radiation without causing excessive collateral damage. Popularly known as a neutron bomb.

Equivalent megatonnage. The effective destructive power of a nuclear weapon, defined in terms of the size of the area it would destroy.

Escalation. The deliberate or unpremeditated expansion of the scope of violence of a war to a higher level of threat or destruction.

Euromissiles. Missiles with less-than-intercontinental capability but which are capable of striking the Soviet Union if launched from Western Europe, and vice versa.

Extended deterrence. The goal, usually by a superpower, to prevent not only an attack on itself but also an attack on others, such as allies or clients, usually but not necessarily exclusively through the threat of nuclear retaliation.

Fallout. The process or phenomenon of the descent to the earth's surface of particles contaminated with radioactive material from a radioactive cloud, produced by detonation of a nuclear device above the earth's surface. **Early** or **local fallout** refers to those particles that reach the earth within 24 hours after a nuclear explosion. **Delayed** or **worldwide fallout** consists of the smaller particles that ascend into the upper troposphere and into the stratosphere and are carried by winds to remote parts of the earth. Delayed fallout ultimately returns to nearly all areas of the earth's surface, mainly by rain and snow, over a period of months or years.

Federal Emergency Management Agency (FEMA). U.S. government agency responsible for developing plans for federal disaster assistance, including plans and capabilities to be put into operation in case of a nuclear attack.

Fire ball. The luminous sphere of hot gases which forms a few millionths of a second after a nuclear explosion as the result of the absorption by the surrounding medium of the thermal X rays emitted by the extremely hot (several tens of million degrees) weapon residues.

Firebreak. The psychological barrier separating conventional from nuclear war; an obstacle to the onset of the latter as a result of the existence of the former.

Fire storm. Stationary mass fire, generally in developed urban areas, causing strong, inrushing winds from all sides which prevent such fires from spreading while providing fresh oxygen that increase their intensity.

First strike capability. The capacity to launch a preemptive nuclear strike against an adversary, thereby eliminating its ability to retaliate with an effective second strike.

Fission. The process whereby the nucleus of a particular heavy element splits into (generally) two nuclei of lighter elements, with the release of substantial amounts of energy. The most important fissionable materials are Uranium 235 and Plutonium 239.

Flash burn. A burn caused by excessive exposure of bare skin to thermal radiation.

Flexible response. A shorthand description of NATO's strategy for dealing with a Soviet or Warsaw Pact thrust against Western Europe. Flexible response is a policy referring to the capability to react to a broad spectrum of threats, ranging from infiltration and conventional threats to response to a nuclear initiative by the adversary.

Follow-On Forces Attack (FOFA). NATO doctrine to repel an attack by striking enemy forces and installations deep inside Warsaw Pact territories at the onset of conflict.

Fratricide. The destructive effect of the earlier-detonating weapons in a barrage on those weapons that arrive later.

Fusion. The process whereby the nuclei of light elements, especially those of the isotopes of hydrogen (deuterium and tritium), combine to form the nucleus of a heavier element with the release of substantial amounts of energy.

Galosh ABM System. Soviet antiballistic missile system deployed around Moscow.

Geosynchronous orbit. An orbit about 35,800 kilometers above the equator. A satellite placed in such an orbit revolves around the earth once per day, maintaining the same position relative to the surface of the earth. It then appears to be stationary and is useful as a communications relay or as a surveillance post.

Ground-launched cruise missile (GLCM). A cruise missile launched from ground installations.

Hard-point defense. Defense of specific military facilities, such as missile silos, bomber bases, and command and control facilities. Defense of hard targets is compared to "soft" target defense, such as cities and transportation systems.

Hard-target-kill capacity. The ability to destroy a missile protected by a reinforced or "hardened" container, such as an ICBM missile silo, otherwise designed to withstand the blast and radiation effects of a nuclear explosion.

Horizontal escalation. The expansion of the scope of armed conflict to other regions or participants beyond the original parties to the war.

Horizontal proliferation. The spread of nuclear capabilities from nuclear to non-nuclear states and/or nongovernmental political entities.

Intercontinental ballistic missile (ICBM). A rocket-propelled vehicle capable of delivering a nuclear warhead across intercontinental ranges. An ICBM may have single or multiple warheads, may be fixed or mobile, and may be land- or sea-based. An ICBM consists of a booster, one or more re-entry vehicles, possibly penetration aids, and, in the case of a MIRVed missile, a post-boost vehicle.

International Atomic Energy Agency (IAEA). The UN-affiliated international organization charged, among other objectives, with monitoring the production and use of special fissionable materials.

Intermediate-range nuclear forces (INF). A term coined by the U.S. to refer to all theater nuclear forces except battlefield nuclear weapons. In 1987 the United States and the Soviet Union agreed to eliminate all long-range (LRINF) and short-range (SRINF) forces, were mostly located (prior to the 1988 INF U.S.-U.S.S.R agreement) in Western Europe and the European area of the Soviet Union.

Kiloton. The amount of energy that would be released by the explosion of 1,000 tons of TNT equivalent.

Kinetic-energy weapon. A weapon that uses kinetic energy, or energy of motion, to kill an object. Examples of weapons that use kinetic energy are rocks, bullets, nonexplosively armed rockets, and electromagnetic railguns.

Launcher. The equipment that launches a missile. ICBM launchers are land-based launchers and can be either fixed or mobile. SLBM launchers are the missile tubes on a ballistic missile submarine. An ASBM launcher is the carrier aircraft with associated equipment. Launchers for cruise missiles can be installed on aircraft, ships, or land-based vehicles or installations.

Launch-on-warning. Retaliatory strikes triggered upon notification that an enemy attack is in progress, but before hostile forces or ordnance reach their targets (see also launch-under-attack).

Launch-under-attack. A policy advocated by some military strategists as a solution to the perceived problem of ICBM vulnerability that calls for launching ICBMs against an adversary upon acquiring evidence that an attack was underway but before its actual effects were felt. This policy is sometimes labelled "launch-on-warning."

Launch-weight. The weight of a fully loaded missile at the time of launch. It includes the aggregate weight of all booster stages, the post-boost vehicle, and the payload.

Layered defenses. The use of several layers of BMD at different phases of the missile trajectory. Each layer is designed to be as independent as possible of the others, and each would probably use its own, distinctive set of missile defense technologies.

Limited war. An armed conflict fought for limited political objectives and often with other restrictions, as on the number of participants and geographic area of conflict.

Maneuvering reentry vehicle (MARV). A nuclear warhead capable of changing course while it streaks through the atmosphere.

Massive retaliation. U.S. strategic policy during the 1950s which threatened China and the Soviet Union with massive nuclear strikes against their homelands for reasons and under circumstances that the United States would determine.

Medium-range ballistic missile (MRBM). A ballistic missile with a strike range of 600 to 1,500 nautical miles (1,100–2,800 km).

Megaton. The amount of energy that would be released by the explosion of 1,000 kilotons (1,000,000 tons) of TNT equivalent.

Midcourse phase. The phase of a ballistic missile trajectory in which the RVs travel through space on a ballistic course toward their targets. The phase lasts up to 20 minutes.

Midgetman. A small, single-warhead mobile missile under development by the United States with a view toward deployment in the 1990s.

Minimum deterrence. A policy relying on the retention of only enough nuclear weapons to provide an assured destruction capability.

Minuteman III. Principal U.S. intercontinental ballistic missile, introduced in 1970, with a potential range of 7,020 nautical miles and a payload consisting of three 160-kiloton independently targetable warheads.

Multiple independently targetable reentry vehicle (MIRV). A ballistic missile payload consisting of two or more nuclear warheads, each of which can be separately assigned different targets.

Mutual assured destruction (MAD). The condition or situation describing the ability of both the United States and the Soviet Union to inflict massive countervalue damage after absorbing a full-scale nuclear strike from the adversary.

Mutual deterrence. The situation that obtains between two powers when each is deterred from attacking the other because the damage expected to result from the victim's retaliation is perceived to be unacceptably high.

National Command Authority (NCA). U.S. political and military leaders designated as members of the chain of command for U.S. military forces.

National technical means (NTM) of verification. National assets for monitoring compliance with an arms control or other agreement. NTM include photographic reconnaissance satellites, aircraft-based systems such as radars and optical systems, and sea- and ground-based systems, such as radars and antennas for collecting telemetry.

No first use. A pledge by a nation that it will not be the first to introduce nuclear weapons into a conflict.

Nonprovocative defense. A mode of defense popular among various political groups in Europe that generally emphasizes defensive rather than offensive weapons and concepts. Types of nonprovocative defense concepts include area defense; wide area covering defense; the fire barrier; and integrated and interactive forward defense, all of which seek to deter aggression by denial.

North Atlantic Treaty Organization (NATO). The military alliance between the United States, Canada, and Western European countries designed to forestall a Soviet invasion of the West.

Nuclear club. Consists of the states known to possess nuclear weapons: the United States, the Soviet Union, the United Kingdom, France, China, and India.

Nuclear deterrence. A strategic doctrine based on the assumption that a potential aggressor can be dissuaded from provocative action or war by (a) the possession of nuclear forces sufficient to deny the enemy its political-military objectives at any level of conflict (counterforce deterrence), or (b) the possession of nuclear forces sufficient to launch a massive urban-industrial retaliatory strike (countervalue deterrence).

Nuclear freeze. A proposal to halt the testing, production, and deployment of all nuclear weapons and nuclear delivery systems.

Nuclear non-proliferation. The set of institutions and procedures for the transnational management of nuclear activities and restriction of the number of states possessing deployed nuclear weapons capabilities.

Nuclear Non-Proliferation Treaty (NPT). The multilateral agreement officially known as the Treaty on the Non-Proliferation of Nuclear Weapons signed in 1968 that prohibits: (a) the transfer by nuclear weapon states to any recipient whatsoever of nuclear weapons or other nuclear explosive devices or control over them; (b) the assistance, encouragement, or inducement of any non-nuclear weapon state to manufacture or otherwise acquire such weapons or devices; and (c) the receipt, manufacture, or other acquisition by non-nuclear weapon states of nuclear weapons or other nuclear explosive devices.

Nuclear radiation. Particulate and electromagnetic radiation emitted from atomic nuclei through various processes. In terms of nuclear weapons, the most important radiations are alpha and beta particles, gamma rays, and neutrons.

Nuclear terrorism. Terrorism is the systemic use of terror as a means of coercion. Nuclear terrorism involves the use or threatened use of nuclear weapons or radioactive materials by an actor, either state or nonstate, for coercive purposes.

Nuclear utilization theory (NUT). A body of strategic doctrine that imbues nuclear weapons with a war-fighting role. The acronym NUTs is sometimes used to refer to those theorists who advocate preparing to utilize nuclear weapons in war should deterrence fail. NUTS is also sometimes used to refer to nuclear utilization target selection.

Nuclear weapon (or bomb). A general name given to any weapon in which the explosion results from the energy released by reactions involving atomic nuclei, either fission or fusion or both. Thus, the atomic and the hydrogen bombs are both nuclear weapons.

Nuclear weapon-free zone (NWFZ). An area in which the production and deployment of nuclear weapons are prohibited.

Nuclear winter. The climatic aftermath of a nuclear war in which vast areas of the earth could be subjected to prolonged darkness, abnormally low temperatures, violent windstorms, toxic smog, and persistent radioactive fallout.

Overkill. A destructive capacity in excess of that required to achieve identified objectives.

Overpressure. The shock or blast caused by a nuclear explosion, usually measured in pounds per square inch.

Partial Test Ban Treaty (PTB). The multilateral agreement officially known as the Treaty Banning Nuclear Weapons Tests in the Atmosphere, in Outer Space and Under Water, signed in 1963. The treaty prohibits "any nuclear weapon test explosion, or any other nuclear explosion" in the atmosphere, in outer space, or under water.

Payload. Weapons and penetration aids carried by a delivery vehicle. In the case of a ballistic missile, the reentry vehicle or vehicles and anti-ballistic missile penetration aids placed on ballistic trajectories by the main propulsion stages or the post-boost vehicles; in the case of a bomber, the bombs, missiles, or penetration aids carried internally or attached to the wings or fuselage.

Permissive action link (PAL). A device designed to preclude arming or launching a nuclear weapon until the insertion of a prescribed discrete code or combination so as to prevent unauthorized use.

Phased-array radar (PAR). A radar with elements that are physically stationary, but with a beam that is electronically steerable and can switch rapidly from one target to another. Used for tracking many objects, often at great distances.

Plutonium fuel cycle. A fuel cycle in which separated (reprocessed) plutonium is routinely recycled as fresh fuel for a nuclear power reactor. The reprocessed fuel can either be recycled to light-water reactors or used as fuel for breeder reactors, which produce more plutonium than they consume. Plutonium is readily used in making nuclear weapons.

Point defense. The use of ballistic missile defenses to defend a limited geographic area, such as a missile silo, against attacking missiles.

Post-boost phase. The phase of a missile trajectory, after the booster's stages have finished firing, in which the various RVs are independently placed on ballistic trajectories toward their targets. In addition, penetration aids are dispensed from the post-boost vehicle. The length of this phase is typically 3 to 5 minutes.

Preemptive strike. An attack launched by one party in the expectation that an attack from its adversary is imminent. A preemptive strike is designed to forestall or lessen the destructive impact of the expected attack. A preemptive nuclear strike is usually expected to entail a counterforce strategy.

Precision guided munition (PGM). A highly accurate conventional weapon capable of being directed toward its target after firing.

Preventive strike. Conflict initiated in the belief that armed combat, while not imminent, is inevitable, and that delay would involve greater risk.

Reentry vehicle (RV). A small container containing nuclear warheads. Reentry vehicles are released from the last stage of a booster rocket or from a post-boost vehicle early in the ballistic trajectory. They are thermally insulated to survive rapid heating during the high velocities of reentry into the atmosphere and are designed to protect their contents until detonation at their targets.

Robust. As used in connection with discussions of SDI and BMD, robust describes a system, indicating its ability to endure and perform its mission against a reactive adversary. It is also used to indicate ability to survive under direct attack.

Sea-launched cruise missile (SLCM). A cruise missile launched from a submarine or surface ship.

Second strike capability. The capacity to execute a nuclear attack against an adversary after having already absorbed a first strike. For a deterrent strategy to be credible, any potential adversary must be convinced that its opponent will retain and be willing to utilize a second strike capability, even after absorbing a first strike.

Security dilemma. The condition wherein the decision of one state to arm for defensive purposes causes a second state to also arm, thereby breeding insecurity in the first, and the perceived need to arm even further, out of fear that the second state is arming for offensive purposes. In a world characterized by anarchy and the absence of central institutions for conflict management and resolution, security is prized by all but realized by few.

Sensors. Electronic instruments that can detect radiation from objects at great distances. The information can be used for tracking, aiming, discrimination, attacking, and kill assessment. Sensors may detect any type of electromagnetic radiation or several types of nuclear particles.

Single Integrated Operational Plan (SIOP). Highly classified plan designed to coordinate use of U.S. strategic nuclear weapons in the event of war.

Shock wave. A continuously propagated pressure pulse (or wave) in the air, water, or earth initiated by the expansion of the hot gases produced in an explosion. A shock wave in air is generally referred to as a blast wave, because it resembles and is accompanied by strong, but transient, winds.

SS-18. The largest ICBM in current Soviet inventory able to carry 10 RVs but capable of holding many more.

Stable deterrence. A situation between two nuclear adversaries in which neither has the capacity or incentive to launch a first-strike against the other.

Strategic Arms Limitations Talks (SALT). A series of negotiations between the U.S. and the U.S.S.R. begun in 1969 in an effort to limit and reduce both offensive and defensive strategic arms. The first round of negotiations, known as SALT I, concluded in 1972 with two agreements, the ABM Treaty and the Interim Agreement on Certain Measures with Respect to the Limitations of Strategic Offensive Arms. SALT II, begun in November 1972, resulted in a treaty signed by the U.S. and the U.S.S.R. in 1979, which was never ratified by the United States.

Strategic Arms Reduction Talks (START). A series of Soviet-American negotiations begun in 1982 in an effort to reduce offensive strategic weapon arsenals.

Strategic Defense Initiative (SDI). The U.S. research and development program designed to produce a space-based ballistic missile defense. Sometimes popularly referred to as "Star Wars," particularly by opponents of SDI.

Strategic stability. A situation in the overall relation of forces between potential adversaries which leads them to conclude that any attempt to settle their conflict by military means would clearly constitute a risk of calculably unacceptable proportions.

Stealth. Advanced technology bomber (ATB) designed to be virtually invisible to enemy radar, thereby enabling it to elude Soviet air defenses.

Surface burst. The explosion of a nuclear weapon at the surface of land or water at a height above the surface less than the radius of the fireball at maximum luminosity.

Tactical weapons. Weapons intended for battlefield operations as opposed to those intended for targeting against an adversary's homeland.

Terminal phase. The final phase of a ballistic missile trajectory, lasting about a minute or less, in which the RVs reenter the atmosphere and detonate at their targets.

Theater nuclear forces. U.S. forward-based systems, primarily in Europe but also in Asia, which provide a tactical nuclear-weapons link between American conventional and strategic nuclear forces, thus coupling American nuclear capabilities to the defense of its allies. Theater nuclear forces are designed for use in specific regional settings. During the 1980s theater nuclear forces generally came to be called intermediate-range nuclear forces (INF).

Thermal radiation. Electromagnetic radiation emitted from a fireball as a consequence of its very high temperature. Essentially, thermal radiation consists of ultraviolet, visible, and infrared radiation.

Thermonuclear weapon. A weapon in which part of the explosive energy results from thermonuclear fusion reactions. The high temperatures required are obtained by means of a fission explosion.

Threshold Test Ban Treaty (TTBT). A treaty between the United States and the Soviet Union on the Limitation of Underground Nuclear Weapon Tests signed in 1974 but not yet ratified. The treaty establishes a nuclear "threshold" by prohibiting nuclear tests having a yield exceeding 150 kilotons of TNT equivalent.

Transarmament. The process of changing over from a military- to a civilian-based defense system.

Transition. As used in connection with discussions of SDI and BMD, transition refers to the period in which the world strategic balance would shift from offense-dominance to defense-dominance.

Triad. The term used to refer to the three components of the U.S. strategic deterrent capability consisting of ICBMs, SLBMs, and intercontinental bombers.

Throw-weight. The useful weight placed on a trajectory toward the target by the boost stages of a ballistic missile.

Uranium fuel cycle. A "once-through" fuel cycle in which natural uranium containing mostly non-fissile U-238 and less than 1 percent fissile U-235 is enriched for use in generating electrical power. Most nuclear power reactors now in use, known as light-water reactors, depend on the uranium fuel cycle. Unless chemically reprocessed, spent fuel cannot be used directly to make nuclear weapons.

Verification. The process of determining, to the extent necessary to adequately safeguard national security, that a party to an agreement acts in conformity with its stipulations.

Vertical proliferation. The development and enlargement of a state's nuclear capacity in terms of further refinement, accumulation, and deployment of nuclear weapons.

War-fighting strategy. Combat actions, as opposed to deterrence (which theoretically is designed to prevent rather than prosecute wars).

Warhead. That part of a missile, projectile, torpedo, rocket, or other munition which contains either the nuclear or thermonuclear system, the high explosive system, the chemical or biological agents, or the inert materials intended to inflict damage.

Warsaw Treaty Organization (WTO). The military alliance between the Soviet Union and its Eastern European allies. Often called the Warsaw Pact.

Yield. The energy released in an explosion. The energy released in the detonation of a nuclear weapon is generally measured in terms of the kilotons (KT) or megatons (MT) of TNT required to produce the same energy release. The total energy yield is manifested as nuclear radiation, thermal radiation, and shock and blast energy.

ACKNOWLEDGMENTS (continued from p. iv)

"The Long-Term Future of Deterrence," by Joseph S. Nye, Jr. From Joseph S. Nye, Jr., "The Long-Term Future of Deterrence," in Roman Kolkowicz, ed., *The Logic of Nuclear Terror* (Boston: Unwin Hyman, 1987), pp. 233–249. © 1987 by Unwin Hyman, Inc. Reprinted by permission.

"Soviet Nuclear Strategy and Arms Control Under Gorbachev: New Thinking, New Policy," by Peter Zwick. Adapted especially for *The Nuclear Reader*, Second Edition, from Peter Zwick, *Soviet Foreign Relations: Process and Policy* (Englewood Cliffs, NJ: Prentice Hall, 1989).

"U.S. Nuclear Strategy: Characteristics and Common Criticisms," by the U.S. Office of Technology Assessment. From US Congress, Office of Technology Assessment, *Ballistic Missile Defense Technologies*, OTA-ISC-254 (Washington, DC: U.S. Government Printing Office, September 1985).

"The Objectives of Ballistic Missile Defense: A Strategic Issue," by Robert M. Bowman. From testimony by Robert Bowman in Committee on Appropriations, Subcommittee on the Department of Defense, *Army Research, Development, Test, and Evaluation*, Hearings on Department of Defense Appropriations for 1985.

"Offense and Defense in the Postnuclear System," by Andrew C. Goldberg. Abridged with consent of the author from *The Washington Quarterly*, Vol. 11, Number 2 (Spring 1988), Andrew C. Goldberg, "Offense and Defense in the Postnuclear System," by permission of The MIT Press. © 1988 by the Center for Strategic and International Studies and the Massachusetts Institute of Technology.

Part II: Weapons

"First Phase of Pentagon's Ballistic Missile Defense," *Washington Post National Weekly Edition*, April 4–10, 1988. Reprinted with permission.

"Beancounting and Wargaming: How to Analyze the Strategic Balance," by Marie Hoguet. Reprinted by permission of *Arms Control Today*, June 1984, pp. 8–9, 12. Copyright 1984 The Arms Control Association.

"First Strike Weapons at Sea: The Trident II and the Sea-Launched Cruise Missile," by the Center for Defense Information. From *The Defense Monitor*, Vol. 16, No. 6, 1987, pp. 1–7. Reprinted with permission of the Center for Defense Information.

"National Security Policy and Arms Control," by Robert L. Pfaltzgraff, Jr. Reprinted from *National Security: Ethics, Strategy, and Politics* by permission of the author and publisher, Pergamon-Brassey's International Defense Publishers, Inc., McLean, Va. 22102. Copyright 1986 © Pergamon-Brassey's International Defense Publishers, Inc.

"Lessons of the INF Treaty," by Lynn E. Davis. From *Foreign Affairs*, Vol. 66, No. 4 (Spring 1988): pp. 720–734. © 1988 by the Council on Foreign Relations, Inc.

"Defending Post–INF Europe," by Jeffrey Record and David B. Rivkin, Jr. From *Foreign Affairs*, Vol. 66, No. 4 (Spring 1988): pp. 735–754. © 1988 by the Council on Foreign Relations, Inc.

"The Military Role of Nuclear Weapons: Perceptions and Misperceptions," by Robert S. McNamara. Reprinted with permission of the author from *Foreign Affairs*, Vol. 62 (Fall 1983), pp. 59–80.

"Breaching the Firebreak," by Michael T. Klare. Reprinted from *World Policy Journal* Vol. II, No. 2 (Spring 1985).

"Deep Cuts and the Risks of Nuclear War," by Joseph S. Nye. Reprinted from "How Does Arms Control Affect Risks of Nuclear War? by Joseph S. Nye, *Harvard International Review* (May/June 1987), pp. 4–5.

"The Effect of Strategic Force Reductions on Nuclear Strategy," by John D. Steinbruner. Reprinted by permission of *Arms Control Today*, May 1988, pp. 3–5. Copyright 1988 The Arms Control Association.

"Pinioning the Genie: International Checks on the Spread of Nuclear Weapons," by Ian Smart. From *The World Today*, Vol. 42, No. 1 (January 1988), published by the Royal Institute of International Affairs, London.

"The Star Wars Defense System: A Technical Note," by Robert S. McNamara. Reprinted with permission of the author from *Blundering Into Disaster: Surviving the First Century of the Nuclear Age*, by Robert S. McNamara, published by Pantheon Books. Copyright 1986, 1987 by Robert S. McNamara.

"Managing the Transition from Offense to Defense," by Charles L. Glaser. From Wells and Litwak's *Strategic Defenses and Soviet-American Relations*, Copyright 1987 by the Wilson Center. Reprinted by permission of Ballinger Publishing Company.

"Nonprovocative and Civilian-Based Defenses," by Stephen J. Flanagan. Condensed from Stephen J. Flanagan's "Nonprovocative and Civilian-Based Defenses" In Nye, Allison, and Carnesale's *Fateful Visions: Avoiding Nuclear Catastrophe*, Copyright 1988 by Center for Science and International Affairs. Reprinted by permission of the Ballinger Publishing Company.

Part III: War

"How Might a Nuclear War Begin?" by the Harvard Nuclear Study Group. Reprinted by permission of the publishers from *Living With Nuclear Weapons*, by the Harvard Nuclear Study Group, Cambridge, Mass.: Harvard University Press, Copyright © 1983 by the Harvard Nuclear Study Group.

"Nuclear Holocaust," by Jonathan Schell. From *The Fate of the Earth*, by Jonathan Schell. Copyright © 1982 by Jonathan Schell. Reprinted by permission of Alfred A. Knopf, Inc. Originally appeared in *The New Yorker*.

"Civilian Casualties from 'Limited' Nuclear Attacks on the U.S. and USSR," by Barbara G. Levi, Frank N. von Hippel, and William H. Daugherty. Reprinted from "Civilian Casualties from 'Limited' Nuclear Attacks on the USSR," *International Security*, Vol. 12, No. 3 (Winter 1987/88) by permission of the authors and MIT Press, Cambridge, Massachusetts. Copyright © 1987 by the President and Fellows of Harvard College and of the Massachusetts Institute of Technology. The editors also acknowledge the authors' "The Consequences of 'Limited' Nuclear Attacks on the United States," which appeared in *International Security*, Vol. 10, No. 4 (Spring 1986).

"Can Nuclear War Be Controlled?" by Desmond Ball. Reprinted by permission from *Adelphi Papers* No. 161. London: International Institute for Strategic Studies, 1981.

"Invitation to a Nuclear Beheading," by Barry R. Schneider. Reprinted by permission of the author and The Conference Board from *Across the Board*, Vol. 20 (July/August 1983), pp. 9–16.

"Soviet Civil Defense: Strategic Implications, Practical Problems," by John M. Weinstein. Adapted especially for this book by the author. An earlier version appeared in Strategic Issues Research Memorandum, May 5, 1983, Strategic Studies Institute, U.S. Army War College.

"Surviving Nuclear War: U.S. Plans for Crisis Relocation," by Louis René Beres. From *Armed Forces and Society* 12 (Fall 1985), pp. 75–93. Reprinted with permission of the Publisher, Seven Locks Press, Cabin John, MD 20818.

"Nuclear War and Climatic Catastrophe: A Nuclear Winter," by Carl Sagan. Reprinted by permission of the author. Article appeared originally in *Foreign Affairs* 62 (Winter 1983/84): 257–292, as "Nuclear War and Climatic Catastrophe: Some Policy Implications."

"Nuclear Winter Reappraised," by Starley L. Thompson and Stephen H. Schneider. Reprinted by permission of *Foreign Affairs*, Summer 1986. Copyright 1986 by the Council on Foreign Relations, Inc.